The Deindustrialization
of America

The
Deindustrialization
of America

Plant Closings, Community Abandonment,
and the Dismantling of
Basic Industry

BARRY BLUESTONE

BENNETT HARRISON

Basic Books, Inc., Publishers

NEW YORK

Library of Congress Cataloging in Publication Data

Bluestone, Barry.
    The deindustrialization of America.

    Includes bibliographical references and
index.
    1. Plant shutdowns—United States. 2.   United
States—Industries.   3.   Capital movements—
United States.   I.   Harrison, Bennett.   II.   Title.
HD5708.55.U6B58   1982   338.6′042   82–70844
ISBN 0–465–01590–5 (cloth)
ISBN 0–465–01591–3 (paper)

Contents

PART III

Why and How the American Economy
Is Undergoing Deindustrialization

Contents

PART IV

The Great Reindustrialization Debate

Acknowledgments

THIS BOOK originated in a research project commissioned in 1979 by a coalition of trade unions and community organizations concerned with the causes and consequences of plant closings all across the United States. The reports that emerged from that project, entitled *Capital and Communities* and *Corporate Flight*, owed their completion and dissemination to a number of friends and co-workers including: Larry Baker, Joyce Beck, Andrew Bornstein, Rob Bracken, Rademase Cabrera, Deborah Davis, Bill Dodds, Carol Fitzgerald, Fay and Lesli Gentile, Barbara Griffith, Jon Guillory, Ed James, Sheila Knodle, Nancy Kragh, Ruth Kremen, Nora Lapin, Carol Ridner, Carrie West, and—from the very beginning—Virginia Richardson.

The person who, more than any other, saw the possibilities for expanding the original study of plant closings into a book on the whole problem of private industrial investment and disinvestment was our editor and publisher at Basic Books, Martin Kessler. Early opportunities to try out some of these ideas in print were afforded by Robert Kuttner, editor of *Working Papers* magazine, who encouraged us at every step. Other friends who discussed the basic themes of the book with us, who read and criticized one chapter or another, who suggested ideas of their own, and who generally sustained us during long periods of too much writing and too little sleep include Irving Bluestone, Gordon Clark, John Friedmann, Maryellen Kelley, Elliot Liebow, Ann Markusen, Doreen Massey, S. M. Miller, Andrew Reamer, Paul Schervish, Donald Shakow, Derek Shearer, and Diane Zaar.

The book was written and last minute research conducted at the Social Welfare Research Institute of Boston College. The entire staff participated in some way at one time or another, from chasing down statistics to designing tables, suffering with a perpetually recalcitrant word-processing system, and proofreading. We are forever indebted to Beth Cataldo, Martha Connor, Tom Entwistle, Alan Matthews, Chris

McHugh, Maura Meagher, Mary Regan, Mary Ellen Schriver, and Julie Zappia. Above all, Marilyn Dorgan, Carol Pepin, Virginia Richardson, and Nancy Small made sure that the production of the final manuscript went smoothly.

Finally, we want to dedicate our work to the movement of individuals and organizations who have been struggling for several years to resist the economic destruction of their communities and to create new forms of local economic development that promise to offer a greater degree of stability to workers and their families and more democratic forms of control over the economic destiny of their communities. It would be impossible to name everyone who has helped or inspired us during these four years of collective work. Therefore the following should think of themselves as representatives of a much larger group: Ira Arlook, Jeff Blum, Eileen and Ron Carver, Steve Dawson, Jeff Faux, Sheldon Friedman, Dick Gillette, Amy Glasmeir, Georgia Herbert, Carol Katz, Ed Kelly, Mel King, Staughton Lynd, Pat McGuigan, Kari Moe, Rebecca Morales, Jeanne Myerson, Tim Nulty, Bob Ross, Bill Schweke, Harley Shaiken, Phil Shapira, Dave Smith, Janet Soglio, Lee Webb, and Goetz Wolfe.

PART I

Introduction

Chapter 1

Capital vs. Community

ON JUNE 30, 1980, *Business Week* finally sounded the alarm. The decline of the American economy had become so serious that the nation's leading business journal decided to devote an entire special issue to detailing a comprehensive plan for revitalizing the U. S. economy. In a tone of uncharacteristic dismay, the editors concluded:

> The U. S. economy must undergo a fundamental change if it is to retain a measure of economic viability let alone leadership in the remaining 20 years of this century. The goal must be nothing less than the reindustrialization of America. A conscious effort to rebuild America's productive capacity is the only real alternative to the precipitous loss of competitiveness of the last 15 years, of which this year's wave of plant closings across the continent is only the most vivid manifestation.[1]

The average person did not have to read *Business Week* to know that America was in trouble. Since the early 1970s every day had brought yet another sign of how bad things were becoming.

In Detroit, Polish factory workers, who had been among the hardest hit by wave after wave of automobile plant shutdowns for three straight years, were told that the world's largest car company was willing to build a new factory and to give them jobs that they desperately needed —only if the city was willing to tear down their neighborhood to create space for the new facility.

In Pittsburgh, the U. S. Steel Corporation called a press conference to announce that it would permanently close down fourteen mills in eight states (principally in Pennsylvania and Ohio) within the year, thus laying off over 13,000 workers. Its reward was an $850 million tax break from the federal government, which it later put toward the down payment on the purchase of Marathon Oil.

In southern California, the conglomerate that acquired a nationally known cosmetics firm decided to shut down its entire Los Angeles operation and move it to Tennessee. Although the new acquisition was profitable in Los Angeles, it was not profitable *enough*, according to the standards established by the new owners.

By the beginning of the 1980s, every newscast seemed to contain a story about a plant shutting down, another thousand jobs disappearing from a community, or the frustrations of workers unable to find full-time jobs utilizing their skills and providing enough income to support their families. Despite the ballyhoo surrounding the opening of new high-tech firms in the North and the West, and the expansion of boomtowns in the South, nearly everyone was coming to recognize that something was dangerously amiss. The system that seemed so capable of providing a steadily growing standard of living during the turbulent 1960s had become totally incapable of providing people with a simple home mortgage, a stable job, or a secure pension.

One thing is certain. The economy has, for all practical purposes, ceased to grow. During the 1960s, overall real U. S. economic growth averaged 4.1 percent per year. As a result, the nation's gross national product (GNP) expanded by a hefty 50 percent over the decade. This permitted the average family to enjoy one third more real, spendable income at the end of the decade than at the beginning. People complained about the war and persistent inequality, but—with the notable exception of millions of black, brown, and teenaged workers—few among the great middle class could grumble about the rate at which we were becoming, in Galbraith's words, "the affluent society."

The 1970s were different altogether. GNP grew by only 2.9 percent per year. By 1979 the typical family with a $20,000 annual income had only 7 percent more real purchasing power than it had a full decade earlier. Ten years had brought a mere $25 more per week in purchasing power for the average family. Moreover, every bit of this growth came between 1970 and 1973, before the first OPEC price shock. Since 1973 there has been virtually *no* real income gain. Thus even before the 1980s began, the American standard of living no longer placed us first among the developed nations of the world. In fact, the best we could do was tenth, not counting the Middle Eastern oil sheikdoms of Kuwait and Abu Dhabi. By 1980 Switzerland, Sweden, Denmark, West Germany, Luxembourg, Iceland, France, the Netherlands, and Belgium had all surpassed the United States in per capita GNP.[2]

That the average Swiss or Danish family enjoys a higher standard of living than that of the average American is disturbing to a generation raised on the unchallenged perception of America as Number One. But the U. S. standard of living does not need to be compared to that of the Swiss or the Danish to recognize the depth of the economic crisis. When he was campaigning for the presidency in 1976, Jimmy Carter suggested the use of a "misery index" to judge just how badly the economy was performing. To compute the misery index, you simply add the inflation and unemployment rates. In 1980 it reached nearly 20 percent, nearly three times its average level during the 1960s.[3] Today the mortgage rate might be included in the misery index. If so, the index of misery now common in communities all over the country would be closer to 40 percent—a quantum leap in this measure of distress.

Adding to the economic despair is America's apparent inability to compete in the global marketplace. Our share of the world's manufactured exports has fallen from more than 25 percent to less than 17 percent in the last twenty years, and relative to our strongest competitors, it could easily be argued that we are being rapidly pushed to the sidelines. It is disturbing to learn, for example, that the 1980 trade deficit with Japan reached over $10 billion. Even more shocking is a listing of the two countries' major exports. In terms of dollar value, the number one Japanese product sold to America was passenger motor vehicles, followed by iron and steel plates, truck and tractor chassis, radios, motorbikes, and audio and video tape recorders. In contrast, America's top seven exports to Japan, in order of dollar value, were soybeans, corn, fir logs, hemlock logs, coal, wheat, and cotton.[4] The trade deficit hides the disconcerting fact that, at least with respect to our most important competitor, the United States has been reduced to an agricultural nation trying desperately to compete with the manufacturer of the world's most sophisticated capital and consumer goods.

Deindustrializing America

Underlying the high rates of unemployment, the sluggish growth in the domestic economy, and the failure to successfully compete in the international market is the deindustrialization of America. By *deindustrialization* is meant a widespread, systematic disinvestment in the nation's basic productive capacity. Controversial as it may be, the essential problem with the U. S. economy can be traced to the way capital—in the forms of financial resources and of real plant and equipment—has been diverted from productive investment in our basic national industries into unproductive speculation, mergers and acquisitions, and foreign investment. Left behind are shuttered factories, displaced workers, and a newly emerging group of ghost towns.

The traces of widespread disinvestment show up in an aging capital stock at home and in the diversion of investment resources to American corporate subsidiaries operating abroad. In 1979 the average age of the capital stock, from sprawling factories to intricate machine tools, was 7.1 years.[5] Hence, much of our productive equipment was put in place when oil prices were much lower. As a consequence, much of the capital stock is energy-inefficient and, for this reason, outmoded. In the steel industry, the capital situation is particularly serious. According to industry experts, the steel companies are modernizing their equipment at less than half the rate needed to keep plants up to date on a twenty-five-year cycle.[6] Across all sectors in the economy, the average rate of new investment has not even kept pace with the growth in the labor force.[7]

This does *not* mean that corporate managers are refusing to invest, but only that they are refusing to invest in the basic industries of the country. U. S. Steel has billions to spend, but instead of rebuilding steel capacity, it paid $6 billion to acquire Marathon Oil of Ohio. General Electric is expanding its capital stock, but not in the United States. During the 1970s, GE expanded its worldwide payroll by 5,000, but it did so by adding 30,000 foreign jobs and reducing its U. S. employment by 25,000. RCA Corporation followed the same strategy, cutting its U. S. employment by 14,000 and increasing its foreign work force by 19,000.[8] It is the same in the depressed automobile industry. Ford Motor Company reports that more than 40 percent of its capital budget will be spent outside the United States, while General Motors has given up its plans to build a new multibillion-dollar plant in Kansas City, Missouri, and instead has shifted its capital spending to one of its facilities in Spain.[9]

The movement of capital can take many forms that progress from the virtually invisible to the drastic and dramatic. The most subtle policy consists of the redirection of profits generated from a particular plant's operations without management tampering with the establishment itself. For example, the managers of a multibranch corporation may decide to reallocate profits earned from a particular plant's operations to new facilities or for new product development. Such "milking" of a profitable plant turns out to be especially common among conglomerates, whose managers are trained to treat certain of their acquired subsidiaries as "cash cows" (a term they themselves use). The older plant is not run down or dismantled in the short run. However, the loss of control over retained earnings increases the subsidiary's chances of encountering trouble in the future. A step beyond the milking operation is the conscious decision to reallocate capital by running down a plant simply by failing to replace worn out or obsolete machinery. In this case, management not only uses the profits from an existing operation, but its depreciation reserves as well, for investment elsewhere. Of course, this type of capital reallocation produces a self-fulfilling prophesy. A plant that is not quite productive enough to meet the profit targets set by management will very soon be unable to make any profit at all.

Another method for shifting capital involves physically relocating some of the equipment from one facility to another, or selling off some of the old establishment's capital stock to specialized jobbers. The plant remains in operation for the time being, but often at a much lower level of production. Indeed, the equipment may not even be moved or sold, but simply turned off when the managers decide to subcontract (or "outsource") to another firm part of the work that used to be done in the plant. The physical capital is still there, but from the point of view of production this is also a case of disinvestment.

Finally, management can move capital by completely shutting down a plant. It can sell as many of the old facility's assets as possible. In a few cases it may even load some of the machinery onto flatcars or moving vans and set up essentially the same operation elsewhere. This

7

last option earned the epithet "runaway shop" in the 1930s, and again in the 1950s, when industries such as shoes, textiles, and apparel left New England for the lower-wage, non-unionized South.

A Trivial Problem?

Because so much disinvestment is invisible to all but those who work on the shop floor or to the managers who actually plan it, there has been a tendency by academic researchers and journalists to recognize deindustrialization only when the plywood goes up over the windows and the "Out of Business" sign is posted, or when a plant is actually relocated physically to another community elsewhere in the country or abroad.

As a consequence of this narrow definition of the problem, there has been a tendency to depict the widespread concern over capital flight and disinvestment as essentially groundless.[10] And, indeed, if only plants that are physically moved from one place to another are counted, the problem does appear trivial. Using data from the Dun and Bradstreet Company (D & B), a well-known private business credit-rating service, David Birch of M.I.T. has shown that between 1969 and 1976 only about 2 percent of all annual employment change in the private sector in the United States was the result of runaway shops.[11]

Perhaps because of such statistics on capital "flight," some analysts believe that the pace of capital transfer (particularly out of the older "sunset" industries) has not been rapid *enough*. M.I.T. economist Lester Thurow is probably the most highly respected advocate of this position:

> To have the labor and capital to move into new areas we must be able to withdraw labor and capital from old, low-productivity areas. But . . . disinvestment is what our economy does worst. Instead of adopting public policies to speed up the process of disinvestment, we act to slow it down with protection and subsidies for the inefficient.[12]

Thurow believes that unless we learn to disinvest more rapidly, America will never again be able to compete effectively in the international marketplace.

Capital vs. Community

This idea is certainly not a new one. Forty years ago Joseph Schumpeter wrote that capitalist economies can only evolve to higher levels of prosperity through a "process of Creative Destruction."[13] According to Schumpeter, a healthy economy requires perpetual reincarnation. The old industrial order, like a forest with its cycle of decay and renewal, must undergo constant transformation to provide the material sustenance for fresh enterprise. If this fails to occur, the economy and the entire society surrounding it will stagnate and eventually crumble. In essence, burgeoning modern industries, such as those that produce sophisticated mini-computers or fast-food chains that annually spew out billions of identical cheeseburgers, arise from the remains of presumably obsolete textile, steel, and automobile plants. Disinvestment, and lots of it, provides the only engine for reinvestment somewhere else.

Is it possible that America's real problem is not *enough* disinvestment? Certainly, looking no further than Birch's famous 2 percent figure, one would probably have to agree with Thurow. But looking just below the surface and taking into account *all* the ways that capital moves, a very different conclusion is in order.

Using the same data base that Birch uses, one finds the amount of job loss due to disinvestment is anything but trivial. In fact, once all the ways that a plant (or store or office) can be closed down (or made obsolete) are accounted for, it is evident that somewhere between 32 and 38 *million* jobs were lost during the 1970s as the direct result of private disinvestment in American business. The chances of even a large, established manufacturing plant closing down within a given seven-year period during the last decade exceeded 30 percent. The life of smaller firms has become so precarious that only two out of five establishments that existed in 1969 were still in business under the same owners in 1976. As a result of plant closings in New England industries such as shoes and apparel, anywhere from two to four jobs were eliminated for every single new job created by new capital invested elsewhere in the region. And this disinvestment phenomenon was hardly limited to the old mill-based industries. In the New England aircraft industry, 3.6 jobs were destroyed for every new one created; in the metalworking machine industry the ratio was 1.6 to 1.0.

Moreover, contrary to popular belief, the deindustrialization process has not been limited to the "Frostbelt." Almost *half* the jobs lost to plant closings (and relocations) during the 1970s occurred in the Sunbelt states of the South and the West. In fact, the odds of a southern manufacturing plant shutting down were actually a little *higher* than for establishments in the North. Bankruptcies were responsible for some of the job losses, but a great many of the shutdowns occurred in establishments owned and operated by profitable companies. Traditional business failure may explain a substantial proportion of the closings of very small, independently owned businesses, but in an era of huge conglomerates and multinational, multiunit enterprises, the major reason for disinvestment lies elsewhere.

The Personal and Social Costs of Deindustrialization

It would be convenient if there were some simple way to define, let alone measure, the optimal amount of disinvestment. Then there would be a standard against which to test the actual amounts of "creation" and "destruction" associated with the capital investment decisions of corporate managers. A possible estimate could be made as to how the victims of deindustrialization should be compensated for their losses. Unfortunately no such simple balancing of costs and benefits is even remotely possible. At best what the process of creative destruction is *supposed* to do for the economy can be compared with its actual consequences.

Doing this reveals an enormous amount of evidence that the economic reincarnation process is not working according to the book. Disinvestment is supposed to free labor and capital from relatively unproductive uses in order to put them to work in more productive ones. But very often this is not the case. Virtually all studies of workers who lose their jobs as the result of a plant closing show that a large proportion of the unemployed take years to recover their lost earnings and many never find comparable work at all. For example, automobile workers who lose their jobs in this high productivity industry are found two years later to be in jobs that pay on the average 43 percent less. Even six years after losing their jobs, these workers have recovered only about five sixths of the salaries they would have been earning had they not been laid off. Similar long-term earnings losses are recorded for steel workers, meat packers, aircraft employees, and those who refine petroleum, produce flat glass, and make men's clothing.[14] These are not merely personal losses, for when a worker is forced out of a high productivity job into a low productivity job, all of society suffers. Real productivity goes down when the experienced, skilled autoworker in Flint, Michigan, ends up buffing cars in the local car wash.

The same is true for investment capital. Moving resources out of an obsolete textile mill into a new high-tech factory may increase the productivity of those working with the new equipment, while society may benefit from the products of the new industry. But this will almost definitely not be the case when the resources that are released are used merely to acquire another existing business, to speculate in real estate or pork bellies, or to shift investment abroad.

The costs of disinvestment go well beyond lost wages and foregone productivity. Workers and their families suffer serious physical and emotional health problems when their employers suddenly shut down operations, and the community as a whole experiences a loss of revenue needed for supporting police and fire protection, schools, and parks. Entire cities and towns can be brought to the brink of bankruptcy, as has happened in Detroit, Cleveland, and a host of smaller municipalities throughout the industrial Midwest. The creative destruction process breaks down in an obvious way when deindustrialization produces permanently elevated levels of unemployment. The U. S. Bureau of Economic Analysis has estimated that each one-point increase in the unemployment rate, sustained over an entire year, costs the American economy more than $68 billion in foregone gross national product, $20 billion in federal tax revenues, and $3.3 billion in added expenditures for unemployment benefits, food stamps, and other forms of public aid.[15]

What about the bright side of the Schumpeterian process—the newly developing sectors and regions that benefit from the vast influx of fresh capital? Do these "sunrise" sectors make up for the losses elsewhere and make the whole process worthwhile? The evidence from the growth areas is not auspicious.

Boomtowns like Houston, Texas, that have doubled in population since 1960 have had their highway, water, sewer, and school systems stretched to the limit, as capital has rushed in to take advantage of the "good business climate." The lopsided development that goes along with such frenzied capital investment almost invariably leaves its mark: abject poverty counterposed to extravagant wealth, a despoiled environment, and crime rates that eclipse even those in the deindustrialized regions from which capital is fleeing.

Moreover, with industry moving so rapidly, those who lose their jobs in the older sectors of the economy rarely have a chance at employment in the new ones—even within the same region. As a result, the creative destruction process has become synonymous with our conception of the "throwaway" culture. Instead of recycling people and communities through the development process, the pace of capital mobility has become so fast that people and communities are carelessly discarded to make room for new ones.

Supply-Side Metaphysics and Other Explanations for the Crisis

The laid-off steelworker in Ohio and the young couple in California in search of an affordable mortgage experience the current economic crisis in the United States in different ways. But they all share the feeling that something has gone badly awry. Whenever things do go wrong with the economy, even temporarily, there is no limit to the number of explanations that suddenly appear. This certainly was the case during the Great Depression, which in its own time was attributed to nearly everything from prohibition to sunspots. Astrologers and numerologists were then as prominent as economists (and on the average their explanations may have been no more unreasonable!). We are in such a time again.

For a tiny, but influential, clique of self-described neo-conservatives, the root of the current crisis is to be found, not in some technical maladustment in the economic machinery, but deep in the moral fiber of society. Sociologists like Amitai Etzioni and writers like George Gilder and Irving Kristol warn of an insidious moral decadence that has invaded our affluent society.[16] Gilder, whose book *Wealth and Poverty* became an overnight best-seller when it was rumored that President Reagan kept it at his bedside, sums up this perspective well.

> The problem of contemporary capitalism lies not chiefly in a deterioration of physical capital, but in a persistent subversion of the psychological means of production—the morale and inspiration of economic man.[17]

Essentially, these "spiritual decay" theorists believe that Americans have lost what Gilder calls the "psychological means of production"— the commitment to innovation, entrepreneurship, and old-fashioned hard work. We have simply become too extravagant, Etzioni warns. In contrast, for example, to the earnest Japanese, the average American has "turned away from hard work, saving, entrepreneurship, self-discipline and deferred gratification—the values and behavior traits that historically underlie our progress."[18] Simply put, we have no one to blame but ourselves. The crisis of American capitalism is fundamentally a crisis of spirit, requiring a moral solution rather than a purely economic one.

While secular theologians like Gilder, Etzioni, and Kristol have made much of the moral corruption of modern society, a larger band of economists has generated more than a little controversy by blaming the entire demise of the U. S. economy on "big government." Supply-siders like Arthur Laffer, Jude Wanniski, and (the unreconstructed) David Stockman, the director of President Reagan's Office of Management and Budget, believe that high taxes, generous welfare programs, and business regulation stand as barriers to economic recovery because they allegedly all but eliminate the reward for hard work and provide a strong disincentive to savings and new productive investment.[19] Workers would love to work more, but after they pay the IRS, they are left with so little that it is not worth the effort. Similarly, investors would be willing to sink more into productive capital, but the after-tax rates of return are so meager that it makes more sense to consume their savings in luxurious living or to speculate in tax-sheltered, often unproductive investments. Shrinking the size of government is practically all that is necessary to get the economic engine running again, if these supply-siders are right.

Those who do not blame the average worker or the government for the crisis often blame the Japanese. The entrance to the parking lot at Solidarity House, the United Auto Workers' international headquarters in Detroit, bears the sign: "Park Your Import in Tokyo!" With 250,000 members of their union on indefinite lay-off, the union's frustration at seeing the Japanese share of auto sales reach 2.3 million units, or 22 percent of the total domestic market, is understandable. In 1960 the Japanese sold a total of 38,809 cars worldwide![20] By 1979 the Japanese were exporting nearly $26 billion worth of cars, stereos, video records, televisions, machine tools, and other goods to the United States, $450 worth for every American family. The United States, however, exported only $17.5 billion back to Japan.

It is easy to make scapegoats of the American worker, the federal government, and the Japanese. But it turns out to be very hard to make the argument stick. Looking at the number of workers who hold down two jobs to make a decent living, observing the growing incidence of "workaholism," and taking note that in the last decade overall labor force participation increased from 60 to 64 percent, it is hard to argue that people are working less. In surveys, corporate managers rarely describe their own employees as lazy or unproductive. In fact, one such survey, appearing in *Productivity*, a well-regarded monthly business magazine, reports that top managers at 221 major firms cited poor management, weak capital spending, and poor training programs as the major causes of depressed productivity—not workers themselves.[21]

Blaming the crisis on people's declining willingness to save for a rainy day requires somehow explaining a great deal of evidence that personal savings rates have not changed appreciably at any time since the late nineteenth century.[22] If the blame is put on high taxes, welfare spending, and business regulation, an explanation somehow has to be found for how fifteen other countries (including Germany, Sweden, and Italy) collected a higher proportion of GNP in taxes and spent more on social welfare, but managed throughout most of the 1970s to record greater economic growth than the United States.[23] And blaming our troubles on the Japanese hardly takes away from the fact that we buy Japanese products not because they cost less—in most cases they no longer do —but because they have learned how to build more attractive and better quality products. Clearly, the blame for deindustrialization rests elsewhere.

Managerial Strategy and Class Struggle in the Postwar Era

Deindustrialization does not just happen. Conscious decisions have to be made by corporate managers to move a factory from one location to another, to buy up a going concern or to dispose of one, or to shut down a facility altogether. These things never happen automatically nor are they simply a passive response to mysterious market forces. The planning behind such decisions is usually intricate, often costly, and extensive.

Deindustrialization is the outcome of a worldwide crisis in the economic system. The very successes of the long postwar expansion generated conditions that ultimately turned the normal, and often healthy, disinvestment process into a torrent of capital flight and wholesale deindustrialization. During the boom years, U. S. economic expansion abroad generated enormous short-run profits, but in the course of doing this it helped to establish excess (unused) productive capacity in one basic industry after another. Through their multinational subsidiaries and the profitable sale of patents and licenses to foreign enterprises, the leading American firms even helped to generate their own future competition. In the 1970s this competition came back to haunt them in virtually every major industry: steel, automobiles, shipbuilding, and electronics, to name a few.

With no rational way to divide up the international market, U. S. firms found themselves subject to intense world competition and as a consequence, shrinking profits. One possible reaction to this situation would have been to try to meet the new competition in the old-fashioned way—an active search for new markets, increased research and development, and investments in more efficient technology. Some American firms took this route, but many more decided instead to abandon the competition altogether (as in electronics), to reduce their investments (as in steel), or to focus all their energies on reducing labor costs and circumventing public sector taxes and regulations. In a desperate attempt to restore, or preserve, the rates of profit to which they had become accustomed in the halcyon days of the 1950s and 1960s, American corporate managers in the 1970s went to extraordinary lengths to shift capital as rapidly as possible, from one activity, one region, and one nation to another. In the process, the industrial base of the American economy began to come apart at the seams.

To be sure, capital flight has always been a tactic that management wished to have at its disposal in order to "discipline" labor and to assure itself of a favorable business climate wherever it set up operations. But only in the last two decades has systematic disinvestment become, from management's perspective, a *necessary* strategy, and from a technological perspective, a *feasible* one.

It is crucial to view this development in the light of post–World War II economic history. It was not only international competition that was threatening corporate profits. The postwar series of labor victories that successfully constrained the flexibility of management by regulating the workplace and forcing the corporate sector to underwrite part of the costs of the "social safety net" also contributed to the profit squeeze.

From the middle of the 1930s to the 1970s, organized labor in the United States won major concessions on a broad set of issues that ultimately limited capital's flexibility in its use of labor. One indicator of this loss in flexibility and of the subversion of unquestioned managerial discretion can be found in the sheer size of the contract documents negotiated between unions and employers. The initial agreement between the United Automobile Workers (UAW) and General Motors (GM), signed in 1937, covered less than one-and-a-half pages and contained only one provision: union recognition. By 1979 the UAW-GM contract, with its extensive array of provisions covering each of the company's 140 production units, contained literally thousands of pages printed in proverbial small type. In exacting detail the contract specifies hundreds of items from wage scales and a cornucopia of fringe benefits to limits on subcontracting and the pacing of each machine and assembly line; it even goes so far as to establish some rules governing the introduction of new technology.

Each of these rules and regulations was forced into place by labor for the explicit purpose of increasing job security and limiting the discretionary power of management. With the important—indeed absolutely critical—exception of limiting the right of management to reduce the aggregate size of its labor force, these incursions by organized labor were highly successful. As long as management *had* to deal with labor where workers were well organized, it was constrained to operate within the set of rules that unions had long struggled to secure.

Moreover, using the power of the State, labor won important concessions from industry through the regulatory process. Minimum wages,
fair labor standards, occupational health and safety provisions, equal
employment opportunity, extended unemployment benefits, and improvements in workers' compensation constitute only a partial list of
the gains made by labor during this period. Taken together, these
victories limited management's ability to extract the last ounce of
productivity from labor and thus the last ounce of profit.

During the heyday of American economic power, from 1945 to
about 1971, industrialists were able to reap healthy profits while afford-
ing these concessions to organized labor. The so-called social contract
between labor and management even proved advantageous to the corporate sector, for it assured some semblance of labor peace needed for
continued economic expansion. Corporations did not complain as bit-
terly in the early 1960s when they were earning an average annual real
rate of return of 15.5 percent on their investments. Their attitudes
changed dramatically, however, when profits began to slip near the end
of the decade. By the late 1960s, the profit rate for non-financial
corporations had declined to 12.7 percent. It fell further as the result
of increased international competition. By the early 1970s, the average
rate had declined to 10.1 percent, and after 1975, it never rose above
10 percent again.[24]

Management found that it could no longer afford the social contract
and maintain its accustomed level of profit. Instead of accepting the
new realities of the world marketplace, one firm after another began
to contemplate fresh ways to circumvent union rules and to hold the
line on wages. Of course, labor was not initially ready to concede its
hard-won victories; therefore to accomplish its goal of reasserting its
authority, management had to find some mechanism for disarming
organized labor of its standard weapons: the grievance process, various
job actions, and work stoppages. The solution was capital mobility. If
labor was unwilling to moderate its demands, the prescription became
"move"—or at least threaten to do so. For one enterprise, this entailed
disinvestment. When entire industries adopted this strategy, the result
was deindustrialization.

The capital mobility option had always been available to some extent. The early American canal systems and the coming of the steam
locomotive allowed the transfer of production to new communities

along the new transportation routes. What is different today is the distance and speed over which that transfer can take place. Satellite-linked telex communication and wide-bodied cargo jets provide a technical environment that has allowed production to become far more spatially "footloose" than ever before. The linking of communications systems to computers permits central management to coordinate worldwide operations at lightning speed, while jet aircraft permit the movement of physical commodities at near the velocity of sound—a far cry from the 3.2 mile per hour of barge traffic on the Erie Canal in the 1840s.

The capital mobility option provided by the new technology has shifted the fulcrum of bargaining power in favor of capital to an unprecedented degree. It gives employers the ability to effectively insist upon smaller wage improvements or, as has been seen in an increasing number of core industries, actual wage rollbacks. In essence, the capital mobility option provides industry with the power to make "take it or leave it" propositions stick. There are some signs in the auto, steel, and rubber industries that the strategy is actually beginning to work. But the cost to workers and communities in the form of plant closings and labor displacement has been enormous.

The capital mobility strategy is not merely aimed at organized labor. The newly enhanced ability to move capital between regions within the same country provides corporate management with the necessary economic and political clout to insist upon reductions in local taxation, and therefore cuts in community services and the social safety net. The competition between local governments to retain existing capital or to attract new private investment is leading to an extraordinary retrenchment in social programs as we have known them. The most noteworthy victories of the corporate sector in this regard are found in Proposition 13 in California and Proposition 2½ in Massachusetts. These substantial tax cuts were actively supported by the banking and business communities of each state, which suggested that failure of passage would seriously undermine the "business climate" in their regions. The interregional rivalry to attract capital, in light of the high degree of threatened or real capital mobility, has led the business press to write that the nation is in the midst of a new civil war—a new "war between the states."[25] Without the heightened ability to move capital, this could not have happened.

The election of Ronald Reagan elevated the "civil war" to a new level. To reindustrialize America, the federal government is insisting on creating a "good business climate" in the United States through extreme cuts in corporate taxes, drastic reductions in the government's guarantee of the social safety net, and the virtual deregulation of the private sector. Washington has joined the corporate sector in declaring a class war on workers and their communities.

Ironically, there were those in the business community who foresaw this a long time ago. In a special commentary in October 1974, *Business Week* predicted a slower growing economy in which

> some people will obviously have to do with less, or with substitutes, so that the economy as a whole can get the most mileage out of available capital . . . . Indeed, cities and states, the home mortgage market, small business, and the consumer, will all get less than they want because the basic health of the U. S. is based on the basic health of its corporations and banks: the biggest borrowers and the biggest lenders. Compromises, in terms of who gets and who does without, that would have been unthinkable only a few years ago, will be made in the coming years because the economic future not only of the U. S. but also of the whole world is on the line today.[26]

The editors went on to observe that the idea that income and resources would have to be redistributed to big business would be a hard pill to swallow. To get the American people to swallow it, they predicted, was going to require a "selling job" beyond anything that any country had attempted in modern times.

The Contradiction Between Capital and Community

At the root of all of this is a fundamental struggle between capital and community. In a brilliant paper, planning theorist John Friedmann of UCLA, has developed a particularly dramatic formulation of the contradiction between the imperatives of capital and people's need for community and economic security. It is so beautifully formulated that it is worth quoting at length:

Two geographies together constitute a "unity of opposites." I shall call them *life space* and *economic space*. Although both are necessary for the sustenance of modern societies, they are inherently in conflict with each other. Over the last two centuries, economic space has been subverting, invading, and fragmenting the life spaces of individuals and communities.

Life space is at once the theater of life, understood as a convivial life, and an expression of it . . . . Life spaces exist at different scales [and] are typically bounded, territorial spaces . . . . Places have names. They constitute political communities.

In contrast, economic space is abstract and discontinuous, consisting primarily of locations (nodes) and linkages (flows of commodities, capital, labor, and information). As an abstract space, it undergoes continuous change and transformation.

Economic space is open and unlimited; it can expand in all directions. Indeed, its continuous expansion is vital to the reproduction of capitalist relations as a whole. Expansion occurs ruthlessly . . . .

We can see the result in the dissolution of life spaces and their progressive assimilation to economic space. The capitalist city has no reverence for life. It bulldozes over neighborhoods to make way for business. It abandons entire regions, because profits are greater somewhere else. Deprived of their life spaces, people's lives are reduced to a purely economic dimension as workers and consumers—so long, at least, as there is work.[27]

What deindustrialization ignores is that "people want to improve their community, not abdicate from it."[28] An unfettered investment policy destroys communities and personal assets while it creates an industrial "refugee" crisis of serious proportion—whole subcommunities without life space *or* work. Ultimately the process of creative destruction is unsustainable, as Joseph Schumpeter himself reluctantly admitted in sections of his classic work seldom cited by his more recent admirers:

Can capitalism survive? No, I do not think it can . . . its very success undermines the social institutions which protect it, and inevitably creates conditions in which it will not be able to live and which strongly point to socialism as the heir apparent.[29]

In the long run, people simply will not accept the degree of instability, insecurity, and other expressions of "pure rationality" that the process requires. As Schumpeter implied, capitalism and democracy are ultimately incompatible.

Capital vs. Community

The Great Reindustrialization Debate is over precisely these issues. How do we build a stable, humane, equitable community and still have economic growth? And how can we go about the business of constructing a productive economy which produces livelihoods without destroying lives?

PART II

The Extent and Consequences of Deindustrialization

Chapter 2

Closed Plants; Lost Jobs

JUST AFTER the Second World War, in one fell swoop the Chance-Vought Division of United Aircraft moved an entire industrial complex from Bridgeport, Connecticut, to Dallas, Texas. This particular relocation, which had financial assistance from the federal government, has been described as one of the most spectacular migrations in industrial history—fifteen hundred people, two thousand machines, and fifty million pounds of equipment were involved.[1]

The relocation of Chance-Vought was an especially dramatic example of the "runaway shop." Even today, when companies literally pick up and move, the wholesale disruption of people's lives garners newspaper and TV headlines. Especially when the move is from the "Frostbelt"—the states of the old industrial Northeast and upper Midwest —to the "Sunbelt" or overseas, it reinforces the popular impression that "capital flight" is a matter of manufacturing firms literally relocating their plant and equipment into areas where wages are lower, unions are weaker, and local government provides the good business climate that corporate managers dream about. And there is no question that such dramatic relocations *do* occur; during the decade of the 1970s, we estimate that between 450,000 and 650,000 jobs in the private sector, in both manufacturing and non-manufacturing, were wiped out somewhere in the United States by the movement of both large and small runaway shops. But it turns out that such physical relocations are only the tip of a huge iceberg. When the employment lost as a direct result of plant, store, and office *shutdowns* during the 1970s is added to the job loss associated with runaway shops, it appears that more than 32 million jobs were destroyed. Together, runaways, shutdowns, and permanent physical cutbacks short of complete closure may have cost the country as many as 38 million jobs.

The process of capital disinvestment in older plants, industries, or regions, and reinvestment in other activities or places, can take many forms. For example, when General Electric builds a new steam iron factory in Singapore and subsequently sells an older one outside of Los Angeles, thus eliminating nearly a thousand jobs in the process, that is capital shift. Or when Pratt & Whitney Aircraft or the Ford Motor Company transfers subcontracts for machine-tooled parts from local suppliers to shops located in other countries, causing widespread layoffs in Connecticut and outright plant shutdowns in Michigan, that, too, is capital flight. Private disinvestment in a particular locale occurs when a conglomerate buys a business that was operating profitably in one place and moves it to another, as Norton Simon has done with the Max Factor cosmetics firm, shifting production from California to Tennessee. The loss in social productivity is even greater—going beyond the mere shifting of existing facilities around the map—when a conglomerate acquires a profitable company, milks it of its cash, runs it into the ground, and then closes it down altogether. By all accounts this is what happened to the Youngstown Sheet and Tube Company, a steel mill in Ohio's Mahoning Valley, after it was acquired by the Lykes Corporation (now itself part of the giant Ling-Temco-Vought (LTV) conglomerate).

Remarkable as it may seem, in a country whose national census bureau regularly pokes into the minutest details of people's private lives, measuring how many children they have or why their mothers did not go to work last week, the government makes only the most minimal demands on private companies to report their investment transactions. Data on the investment decisions by managers in the service sector are almost completely nonexistent, even though hospitals, supermarkets, and television stations obviously buy and sell buildings and machinery, too. Because companies are virtually allowed to select depreciation schedules from a menu offered by the Internal Revenue Service to fit their cash flow requirements, official published statistics on the extent to which an industry's capital stock is being run down by its managers have become artifacts of the political process, almost useless for measuring actual disinvestment.

Few people have the necessary time, access, or money to pierce the veil of secrecy that firms have thrown up around their investment transactions. With the federal government unwilling to require companies to disclose the details of their investment activities, direct measurement of all of the many different forms of capital movement is virtually impossible. What we *can* measure now—thanks not to any government program, but to the availability of information generated by the private sector itself, for its own internal use—are plant (as well as office, store, shop, and warehouse) relocations and shutdowns.*

Over the decade of the 1970s, in twelve states, plant closings shut down more jobs than were added through new start-ups. Elsewhere, jobs created by the opening of new business establishments barely offset the losses connected with the closings of older ones (except in those states containing the mining and energy industries, where the net growth was considerable). But even where more new plants were opened than shut down, millions of workers, their families, and their communities experienced severe economic and emotional dislocation. Typically, the businesses that started up were located in different places and were in different industries (usually services rather than manufacturing); they required different skills, paid lower wages, provided less job security, or simply would not hire the people who had been laid off.

Private Business Investment and Disinvestment in the U. S., 1969–76

Dun and Bradstreet Incorporated (D & B) keeps detailed records on various aspects of the economic activity of American businesses. The 1969–76 Dun's Identifiers File covers nearly 5.6 million business estab-

*Most of this chapter is devoted to a presentation of our findings on closings, relocations, and the "export" of jobs through foreign investment in the 1970s. Toward the end, however, we will look briefly at new estimates of some indirect forms of industrial disinvestment: namely, the extent to which the largest manufacturing corporations have been putting their capital into buying up *existing* facilities rather than constructing new ones, and whether these corporations physically expanded the plants they already had on line at the beginning of the decade. Other measures of deindustrialization will appear in chapter 6, in the context of case studies of particular industries and companies.

lishments. About 88 percent of these are independently owned and operated; the rest are the branches, subsidiaries, and headquarters of corporations. The data are especially valuable in that they refer to the activity of each of a company's workplaces or *establishments,* rather than reporting only on the aggregate behavior of the company or *firm* as a whole.

Yet even this detailed data source does not permit the measurement of investment and disinvestment per se. Rather, the D & B file breaks down net job change over time in a given industry in a particular location into the sum of:

- employment created as a result of new plant, store, or office openings in the original location, plus
- employment generated through the relocation of an existing plant, store, or office into this location, plus
- jobs created through the expansion of establishments that were already operating in this location at the beginning of the period of analysis

minus those elements of employment change that make up job loss:

- employment destroyed through establishment closures
- jobs lost as the result of the physical "outmigration" of establishments that used to do business in this location
- jobs destroyed through the contraction of existing plants, stores, and shops

Employment gains and losses associated with the opening, closing, and relocation of a business establishment are unambiguously the result of private investment and disinvestment activity. This is not so with the expansion and contraction data. Employment change associated with expansion over some period of time usually includes some jobs that have been added to an existing plant or store, with little or no new physical investment having taken place—economists call this "increased utilization of existing productive capacity." The remaining job growth *is* the result of the addition of new physical capacity, for example, a new wing on a building, three new machines, or the rehabilitation of an existing conveyer belt. But there is no way to separate these two sources of job change out of the D & B data labeled "expansions." The same holds for the information on "contractions." (Later in this chapter we will show how one researcher has made some headway in connection with this by conducting his own extensive interviews with a sample of the companies monitored by D & B.)

Thus, when a company opens, closes, or physically relocates one of its individual establishments, private investment or disinvestment occurs and can be measured in terms of the number of jobs that are created or destroyed at that location. When employment expands in a particular industry in a particular place, there may be some new investment, but that is not certain. Conversely, when employment contracts within existing establishments, it can only be inferred that some disinvestment *might* have occurred. Like so many other researchers who have worked with these data, we have relied on the help of David Birch in his role as director of the Program on Neighborhood and Regional Change in the M.I.T. Department of Urban Studies and Planning, where he has been doing pioneering work with the D & B data for several years.[2] In addition to making the details of his own work available, Birch prepared for us an extract of the D & B data covering the New England region, in connection with our own ongoing research on economic development in that part of the country.[3] This extract provides greater detail than Birch himself has published so far. What follows draws upon both Birch's national tabulations and an analysis of our own New England extract.

Table 2.1 presents our findings on employment creation and destruction in the private sector from the end of 1969 through the end of 1976. Included besides factories are other "for profit" facilities in the private economy such as stores, shops, bus companies, and insurance brokerage houses. (For convenience, however, we will henceforth refer to all business establishments as *plants.*) Because of the ambiguity of the method by which D & B records relocations or migrations of plants, we have chosen to lump them together with the openings and closings.[4] Detailed data on each state are presented in table A.1 in the Appendix at the end of the book.

In the United States, between 1969 and 1976, private investment in new plants created about 25 million jobs. This amounts to an average of 3.6 million jobs created each year as the direct result of plant openings. On the other hand, by 1976 shutdowns had wiped out 39 percent of the jobs that had existed in 1969—a total of 22 million jobs over seven years, or on average, about 3.2 million jobs destroyed each

TABLE 2.1

Jobs Created and Destroyed As a Result of Openings, Closings, Relocations, Expansions, and Contractions of Private Business Establishments in the United States: 1969–76 (in thousands of jobs)

Region	Number of Jobs in 1969	Employment Change: 1969–76				Net Job Change[d]
		Jobs Created		Jobs Destroyed		
		By Openings and Inmigrations[a]	Expansions[b]	By Closures and Outmigrations[c]	Contractions[b]	
U. S. as a whole	57936.1	25281.3	19056.1	22302.3	13183.2	8851.9
Frostbelt	32701.2	11321.5	9470.4	11351.7	7212.1	2228.1
Northeast	15824.6	4940.4	4347.5	5881.5	3589.0	−182.6
New England	3905.3	1251.2	1131.0	1437.2	952.1	−7.1
Mid-Atlantic	11919.3	3689.2	3216.5	4444.3	2636.9	−175.5
Midwest	16876.6	6381.1	5123.0	5470.2	3623.2	2410.7
East North Central	12563.6	4670.6	3581.8	3962.6	2651.7	1638.1
West North Central	4313.0	1710.6	1541.2	1507.6	971.5	772.7
Sunbelt	25234.9	13959.8	9585.7	10950.5	5971.0	6624.0
South	16044.5	8934.2	5964.6	6824.3	3803.3	4271.2
South Atlantic	8204.1	4651.2	2913.0	3547.9	2014.2	2002.1
East South Central	3065.2	1518.2	1089.9	1211.0	631.9	765.2
West South Central	4775.2	2764.8	1961.7	2065.4	1157.2	1503.9
West	9190.4	5025.6	3621.1	4126.2	2167.8	2352.7
Mountain	1941.9	1226.1	953.6	977.9	481.0	720.8
Pacific	7248.5	3799.6	2667.6	3148.3	1686.8	1632.1

SOURCE: David L. Birch, The Job Generation Process (Cambridge, Mass.: M.I.T. Program on Neighborhood and Regional Change, 1979), Appendix A.

NOTES: The regional data shown here are sums of the figures for each state, taken from table A.1 in the Appendix. The basic unit of observation is the "establishment" (plant, store, or shop). These estimates are based on Dun and Bradstreet's Dun's Identifiers File. We inflated the D & B counts of private sector closings and so forth by the ratio of U.S. Department of Labor estimates of state-by-state employment in the years 1969, 1972, and 1974 to the D & B counts for those same years. Sample sizes vary from a low of 44 percent in Wyoming in 1969 to a high of 85 percent in South Carolina in 1974. See note (a) to table A.1 for details on our estimation procedure.

[a]We aggregate openings (or start-ups, or what Birch calls "births") and "inmigrations" (plants that are new to the area but that are known to have previously existed elsewhere) into a single category. See note (b) to table A.1 for an explanation.

[b]These columns refer to employment change in establishments that neither relocate nor shut down during the period of analysis.

[c]We aggregate "closures" (or shutdowns, or what Birch calls "deaths") and "outmigrations" (plants that previously operated in the area, closed there, and then reopened elsewhere) into a single category. See note (b) to table A.1 for an explanation.

[d]Because employment change associated with recorded relocations (inmigrations and outmigrations) is so small— between 0.2 percent and 2.0 percent of net employment change over any particular period of time in any state—there is some, but probably little, double-counting in these regional and national totals.

year. Therefore, about 110 jobs were created by new plant openings for every 100 jobs destroyed by plants shutting down.[5]

This relationship between the openings and closings of plants varied substantially among the various regions of the country (and even within regions, as is shown in table A.1). Jobs created through new business start-ups generally exceeded job losses resulting from shutdowns in the Midwest and the Sunbelt, although more jobs were terminated than created even in some of the Sunbelt states, such as Delaware, Idaho, and Utah.* On the other hand, in every state in the Northeast, private industry destroyed more jobs through plant closings than it created through new openings. Whether 22 million jobs destroyed through shutdowns represents socially unacceptable or (as Thurow would have it) insufficiently rapid capital shift is the subject of the next two chapters. But one thing ought to be immediately clear: plant closings are not confined to the old industrial "Frostbelt;" they occur in large numbers in every region of the country and as such they are a *national* phenomenon.

Indeed the greatest surprise is in the South. We know that the overall pace of economic growth has been greater in the sixteen states making up this region than anywhere else. But even in spite of its legendary "good business climate," between 1969 and 1976 industry apparently saw fit to withdraw enough of its capital there to destroy almost 7 million jobs as a direct result of shutdowns, with another 3.8 million lost through cutbacks in existing operations.

Up to this point, the behavior of establishments of all sizes has been taken into account. But considering the political furor over shutdowns and their impacts on people and communities, it is surely the large manufacturing plants that have caused the greatest concern. What can be said about this category of private industry? Birch has begun to address this question by estimating what the chances are that an establishment that is in business on a particular date will still be there at some future time, or will have closed during the period. His detailed findings are reproduced in table A.2 in the Appendix. Not surprisingly, the larger the facility, the less likely it is to be shut down, even during

---

*Of course, social problems can arise even where there is a net gain in employment. It is often difficult for those who are shut out of jobs in one sector to obtain jobs in the industries that are growing elsewhere in the region. It is also true that the jobs in the expanding industries often do not pay wages commensurate with what those who have been laid off used to earn. These questions will be investigated in chapters 3 and 4.

recessions. Of all "small" establishments (those with between one and twenty employees) existing in 1969, between one half and three fifths were out of business by 1976, depending upon industry and region. The chances of survival were a little better for small manufacturing plants than for non-manufacturing establishments, and generally worse in the Midwest than elsewhere.

Knowing the fragile economic markets within which small companies operate, none of this should be particularly surprising. But the rate for large enterprises certainly is. The proportion of establishments with 500 or more employees that closed their doors sometime between 1969 and 1976 ranged from 15 percent to more than 35 percent, again depending on region and industrial sector. This is a rate of shutdown —a key element in the overall rate of capital disinvestment—far beyond anything that anyone ever expected to find. It should be emphasized once again that these data refer to individual establishments, that is, stores, plants, and shops, and not to whole companies. The failure rate of companies has, of course, been much lower.

Focusing now on the largest manufacturing plants (those with 100 or more employees), table 2.2 shows that by far the largest absolute number of closings of large, established (pre–1970) manufacturing plants occurred in the Northeast. With only 24 percent of the nation's population in 1970, the Northeast suffered 39 percent of the shutdowns of this type of establishment.

Still, what is perhaps even more dramatic is the large absolute num-

TABLE 2.2

Closings Occurring by December 31, 1976 in a Sample of Manufacturing Plants That Had Already Been Operating on December 31, 1969 With More Than 100 Employees at That Time

Region	Number of States	Percentage of U.S. Population	Number of Plants in the Sample in 1969	Number in the Sample Closed by 1976	Proportion of 1969 Plants That Closed by 1976	Interregional Percentage Distribution of Closings
Northeast	9	24.1	4,576	1,437	.31	38.6
North Central	12	27.8	3,617	904	.25	24.2
South	16	31.0	3,101	1,042	.34	28.0
West	13	17.1	1,155	344	.30	9.2
TOTAL	50	100.0	12,449	3,727	.30	100.0

Source: Birch, *The Job Generation Process*, appendix D; and *1970 Census of Population*.

ber of closings of this scale that took place in the South. During this seven-year period, one out of every three existing plants shut down operations. In fact, the *proportion* of pre–1970 large manufacturing plants that closed by the end of 1976 was *actually higher* in the South than in any other part of the country!

There is a widespread tendency to view an entire region as though it were homogeneous. This is reflected in the media's (and Congress's) obsession with the "Sunbelt-Frostbelt" imagery. However, evidence has been uncovered of extraordinarily *uneven* development within regions, including the Sunbelt. During the late 1960s and early 1970s, Massachusetts was considered a terminal case. Yet just over its border, the southern towns of New Hampshire were experiencing an unprecedented boom. The same holds true in the South. While Houston, Dallas, and Oklahoma City were brimming with new migrants who were lured to these areas by oil, chemicals, and new manufacturing opportunities, older areas of the South were crumbling. Some of this loss was no doubt due to rural to urban relocation. But a new wave of U. S. reinvestment abroad—in textiles, apparel, electronics assembly, and other labor-intensive industries—was probably an even larger factor. These were the industrial sectors on which the (especially the rural) "New South" of post-World War II America was established, and which were being seriously eroded by shutdowns in the years during and after the Vietnam War. For example, during the 1970s, almost 60 percent of all the textile mill closings in the United States occurred in the South.[6]

So far, these results pool the corner grocer, the multinational corporation's branch plant, and the successful family business that is acquired by a diversified conglomerate. For several reasons, the data should be broken down according to *who owns the business*. Small, independently owned, and often family-run, firms might be expected to have high failure rates because they are generally more vulnerable to the business cycle, suffer more restricted access to debt finance (and/or must pay more for it), and have no "parent" or home office to bail them out of trouble. Corporate branch plants presumably have all of these advantages—along with access to the corporation's own internally retained earnings—as, in theory, do the subsidiaries of conglomerates.

Unquestionably, most plant shutdowns are the unplanned outcome of intensified domestic and international corporate rivalry. But, as chapter 6 will show, there are often real profits to be made when a cash-conscious corporate management deliberately writes off a still viable plant, or when the central managers of a diversified conglomerate deliberately milk a subsidiary of its cash flow and then shut it down (if they cannot find another buyer). In these cases, plant shutdowns are likely to be the result of a planned strategy to increase companywide profits. On the other hand, the closing of an independently owned business is more likely to be the result of a truly involuntary failure.[7]

Our estimates of start-ups and closings by type of ownership are unfortunately limited at the moment to New England. Similar counts could indeed be constructed for other states and regions, but Birch has not done so, and the extract used here from the D & B file is limited to this area.

Between 1969 and 1976 plant closings in Massachusetts cost the state about 730,000 jobs (about 40 percent of the stock of jobs at the beginning of the period). For New England as a whole, the closings eliminated slightly more than 1.4 million jobs. Corporations and conglomerates together were responsible for a disproportionate amount of job destruction—about 15 percent of the establishment "deaths," but *half* of all the jobs lost. Moreover, our own fieldwork on subcontracting and procurement networks in this region convinces us that a great many of those closings of independently owned businesses were the *indirect* result of losses of orders and other spillovers generated by the corporate shutdowns. This important issue will be discussed in chapter 3.

The ways in which ownership affects the likelihood of an establishment shutdown (and indeed whether new openings exceed closings) vary among industries. Take two industries that are highly important to, and quite typical of the old and new economic bases of, the region: metalworking machinery and department stores. For every new job created in these industries in New England by an independently owned business, 1.6 jobs were destroyed in metalworking and 1.0 in department stores. But in establishments controlled by conglomerates, for every job created, 4.6 jobs were destroyed in metalworking, while 4.0 were eliminated in department stores. The same pattern of disproportionate closing activity by conglomerates took place in women's apparel, shoes, computers, aircraft engines, supermarkets, hotels, and motels (see table A.3 in the appendix).

The Deindustrialization Wave of the Late 1970s

The D & B data with which to update a systematic, region-by-region analysis of shutdowns and contractions beyond the end of 1976 have not been made available. But even if just a projection were made from the previous finding of about 3.2 million jobs lost per year in the country as a result of plant closures alone (not counting redundancies created by private disinvestment short of total shutdown), it would be concluded that, over the whole decade of the 1970s, a minimum of 32 million jobs were probably eliminated in the United States as a direct result of private disinvestment in plant and equipment. Making the (very conservative) assumption that one third of the job loss associated with establishment contractions was attributable to disinvestment short of complete shutdown (with another two thirds connected to personnel layoffs not accompanied by reductions in physical productive capacity), then from table 2.1 it may be inferred that, all together, over 38 million jobs were lost through private disinvestment during the 1970s. That would seem to be deindustrialization with a vengeance. It certainly creates skepticism about the claim that not enough "creative destruction" is taking place in America.

In fact, there is good reason to believe that these estimates may actually *undercount* the total job loss for the decade. The reason is that a truly major wave of closings and retrenchments in some of the country's most basic industries—autos, steel, and tires—struck American workers during the last several years of the period. Corporate managers in these and many other industries found themselves confronting an unprecedented profit squeeze associated with intensified international competition and chronic stagflation. Especially in their older product lines, these managers were forced to become more cost conscious than at probably any time since World War II. To cut costs, firms focused their attention on cutting jobs.

Faced with the challenge of old plant and equipment that had been inadequately maintained or upgraded, and confronted by workers whose costs of living (and therefore wage requirements) were also being driven up by inflation, American industrial managers in the closing years of the 1970s resorted to truly draconian measures. Wholesale rationalization and industrial restructuring were undertaken. Sometimes, capital was removed from domestic facilities and reinvested outside the country. There was a growing tendency for managers to use profits that had been made, for example, in steel and oil to diversify into totally unrelated activities—that is, to follow the conglomerate model. Some companies moved plants from highly unionized areas in the North and the Far West into the South. And most dramatically of all, there was an unprecedented wave of total plant shutdowns in some of the most well known companies in the United States. As had been true even before 1976, these shutdowns occurred throughout the country, even in the Sunbelt.

Between January 1979 and December 1980, domestic automobile manufacturers closed or announced the imminent shutdown of twenty facilities employing over 50,000 workers. As a consequence of these closings and of the output reductions in other auto plants, suppliers of materials, parts, and components to the automotive industry closed nearly 100 plants, eliminating the jobs of about 80,000 additional workers. Altogether, the downturn in the industry in just these two years may have boosted unemployment in the supplier network by anywhere from 350,000 to 650,000 jobs—depending on whether the Congressional Budget Office or the AFL-CIO is making the estimate.[8]

Among the major permanent closings in the last years of the decade were thirteen Chrysler plants employing nearly 31,000 workers, five Ford plants including the huge facility at Mahwah, New Jersey, and seven plants in the General Motors system.[9] Of these twenty-five shutdowns, eleven were located in Michigan and six more were in other midwestern states. But even the Sunbelt lost some of its automobile capacity. Ford shut down its large Los Angeles assembly plant in 1980, while Chrysler closed a small facility in Florida. In 1981–82, the wave became a flood, affecting every region of the country.

In the steel industry, almost all of the major companies cut back operations during the late 1970s. On Thanksgiving Day, 1979, in a message that certainly could not have brought much holiday cheer to steelworkers throughout the country, the U. S. Steel Corporation made a dramatic announcement in the *New York Times:*

The United States Steel Corporation announced yesterday that it was closing 14 plants and mills in eight states. About 13,000 production and white-collar workers will lose their jobs. The cutback represents about 8 percent of the company's work force. The retrenchment was one of the most sweeping in the industry's history . . . in spite of high demand for steel in the last two years. [28 November 1979]

The fourteenth shutdown was U. S. Steel's mill in Youngstown, Ohio, which single-handedly wiped out 3,500 jobs and provoked an occupation of the corporate headquarters by an angry group of steelworkers. The anger and frustration were perhaps understandable since, barely two years earlier, the closing of the Campbell Works of the Youngstown Sheet and Tube Company had destroyed 4,100 jobs in the same city. Between 1977 and early 1981, American steel manufacturers shut down enough plants to reduce the nation's steel-making capacity by 11 percent.[10]

As we now know, the invasion of the domestic auto market by Japanese manufacturers and the spurt in oil prices after 1973 combined to force huge cutbacks in domestic car production. It was inevitable that American tire manufacturers would feel the brunt as well. Moreover, while these companies had held out as long as they could from replacing the old bias-ply technology with the far longer-lasting radial tires, competition from foreign radial manufacturers such as France's Michelin and Japan's Bridgestone finally forced the Americans into their own major restructuring program. According to the Research Department of the United Rubber Workers of America, between mid-1975 and early 1981, there were twenty-four domestic plant shutdowns, eleven of them in Sunbelt cities, accompanied by nearly 20,000 permanent layoffs. (The *New York Times* reported on April 19, 1980, that some of these shutdowns involved radial tire plants, as well as the "obsolete" bias-ply factories.)

Eleven of the closed facilities had been part of the Firestone Tire and Rubber Company. Others had been operated by Goodyear, B. F. Goodrich, Uniroyal, and several smaller firms. Even while they were shutting down their older plants, rather than upgrading them or building new facilities in the same cities, Goodyear and Uniroyal were simultaneously expanding into other parts of the Sunbelt as well as overseas. Uniroyal now produces tires in Brazil, Turkey, Spain, and Australia. The company with the fewest actual closings during this period, General Tire, had already completed its own restructuring process earlier by successfully diverting profits from its tire business into television, radio, cable television, rocket-propulsion equipment, plastics, soft drink bottling, and a commercial airline.[11]

In one industry after another, the late 1970s was a time for unprecedented retrenchment. Combined with the continued trend toward the differential branching of operations based in older industrial areas into places with cheaper or less well organized labor, these restructuring schemes produced a spate of newspaper articles, like this in the *Boston Globe,* on high-technology in the far Northeast:

> A major Massachusetts computer company has put even more of its money where its mouth has been for years and announced plans for continued expansion outside the state. Data General Corporation of Westboro said yesterday it plans to purchase a 125-acre site in Wake County, North Carolina, on which it will construct a 300,000 square-foot facility next year for final assembly, testing and shipping of computers . . . . Data General's new manufacturing complex will augment two other facilities already in North Carolina. One, a research laboratory opened in 1977, is located in Raleigh and the other, a manufacturing plant in Johnson County, is situated nearby. This plant opened in 1978 and this year was expanded to 280,000 square feet. The two facilities employ more than 1,000 people. [18 September 1979]

to the far Northwest, where the timber industry is undergoing major disinvestment, as reported in the *Wall Street Journal:*

> Tacoma, Washington—Weyerhaeuser Co. may trim about 1,000 salaried employees from its 11,000 member work force over the next year, George Weyerhaeuser, president of the forest products concern, told employees in a letter . . . . Mr. Weyerhaeuser noted that "after tax net income in 1977 was $42 million higher than that of the second most profitable competitor. However, this income was generated from a much larger investment base in timberlands and plants. Our current concern is with the return we are generating from our ongoing activities." Mr. Weyerhaeuser said the company retains its goal of achieving a growth rate of 15% a year. [16 February 1978]

Some of the older cities of the "Frostbelt" were especially hard hit. In a single issue, the *Newark Record* (Newark, N. J.) announced three major shutdowns:

> 500 workers [are] scheduled to be laid off from Westinghouse's 85-year-old, fortress-like factory . . . the Pittsburgh-based company announced that it

would close its [Newark, N. J.] relay instruments division by late 1979 and move the operation to Coral Springs, Florida . . . . This year, in addition to the Westinghouse move, Stauffer Chemical Company announced it would shut its 250-employee Passaic [N. J.] plant and reopen the operation in South Carolina. The Wiss Company, a Newark-based hand-tool manufacturer owned by [a Texas conglomerate], soon will lay off 725 workers as it moves its operation to Georgia. [5 July 1978]

The *Wall Street Journal* reported that in the mid-Atlantic states, consumers were treated to an extraordinary series of escalated shutdowns by one of the region's largest retail food chains:

Philadelphia: Food Fair Inc. said it filed for protection under Chapter 11 of the Federal Bankruptcy Act [but that] its 440 supermarkets and 70 discount department stores will remain open with normal operations. [3 October 1978]

Philadelphia: Food Fair Inc. plans to close 89 supermarkets in New York and Connecticut. [27 October 1978]

Food Fair Inc. [owes] $15 million . . . to . . . employees . . . who lost their jobs when the company closed 212 supermarkets and 79 J. M. Field department stores [including *all* its stores in Philadelphia]. [18 September 1979]

But if the most widely publicized shutdowns in the closing years of the 1970s were in the North, southern workers had their own deindustrialization with which to contend. Once thriving towns, Fayetteville, Tennessee; Tupelo, Mississippi; Guntersville and Muscle Shoals, Alabama; and Kennett, Missouri, which had experienced seemingly unlimited industrial growth in the years after World War II, were losing one plant after another by the late 1970s. While the typical closure was the small, family business unable to survive in the face of chronic inflation and rising labor costs, the branches of major corporations such as Scoville Industries and Monsanto Chemical were also shut down. In fact, observed the chief economist of the Tennessee Valley Authority, "many of these towns had been in trouble for much of the decade." By 1980–81, unemployment rates in many of the more industrialized southern areas stood above 10 percent. Of the 170 acres in Fayetteville's new industrial park on the east side of the city, 150 were vacant in early 1981. These are the kinds of conditions normally associated with the old mill towns of New England.[12]

Other Sunbelt states experienced unexpected waves of plant closings during the late 1970s and into the early 1980s. None was more unprepared for such a shock than the state of California.[13]

- In Los Angeles since 1978, eight companies alone (including Uniroyal, U. S. Steel, Ford, Pabst Brewing, and now Max Factor) shut down the jobs of almost 18,000 workers. General Electric announced it would close its neighboring Ontario flatiron plant in early 1982, and Bethlehem Steel is widely rumored to follow suit within the next twelve to eighteen months.
- By the spring of 1982 in Salinas, four plants—Firestone, Peter Paul-Cadbury, Walsh, and Spreckles Sugar—will have accounted for the elimination of 2,400 jobs since the summer of 1980.
- Up on the North Coast, of the 500 lumber mills that were in operation in 1960, a mere twenty were still doing business in 1981.
- The permanent layoffs affected the whole spectrum of skilled and semi-skilled occupations. In Santa Maria, for example, the shutdown of Piper Aircraft dislocated engineers, R & D specialists, machinists, sheet metal workers, assemblers, mechanics, and clerk-typists.

From South Gate to Hayward to Sacramento, across the state as a whole, in the single year 1980, at least 150 major plants closed their doors permanently, displacing more than 37,000 workers. The problem has taken on epidemic proportions, affecting industries as varied as automobiles and trucks, rubber, steel, textiles, lumber, food processing, and housewares.

The Diversion of Corporate Investment into the Acquisition of Existing Businesses

While conglomerates controlled a small percentage of all businesses before 1976 (although they were responsible for a much larger proportion of all jobs), conglomerate *behavior*—the acquisition of existing facilities in diverse product and service lines bearing little or no relation to the acquirer's original industry—seems to have increased during the closing years of the decade. Thus, for example, during the three years following 1976, the U. S. Steel Corporation reduced its capital expenditures in steel making by a fifth. Profits were redirected into the acquisition of chemical firms, shopping malls, and other activities; so much so that, by 1979, forty-six cents of every new dollar of U. S. Steel capital investment was going into the corporation's non-steel ventures. Moreover, in 1979 while each dollar of depreciated *non*-steel plant and equipment was being replaced by $2.90 of new capital investment, in the steel operations the replacement rate was only $1.40.[14]

In other industries, General Electric makes everything from toaster ovens to jet engines. And Mobil Oil acquired the Montgomery Ward department store chain and the Container Corporation of America. In 1979 alone, according to *Business Week*, U. S. corporations made acquisitions totalling $40 billion—more than the total spent on research and development by all private firms in the nation.[15]

A recent study conducted by a Duke University professor of Management, Roger Schmenner, sheds additional light on this aspect of the deindustrialization process. Using yet another information source from Dun and Bradstreet, supplemented by extremely detailed and careful follow-up interviews, Schmenner was able to measure the extent to which 410 of the country's largest manufacturing corporations (most of the *Fortune* 500) acquired *existing* production facilities during the 1970s as an alternative to physically constructing new ones.[16]

In the United States during the 1970s, two out of every three new *Fortune* 500 manufacturing plants were actually not "new" at all, but rather acquired from other owners. In every region, the majority of factories added to these corporations' holdings were acquired rather than built anew. This fraction was greater in the Frostbelt than in the Sunbelt, attaining its highest level in the mid-Atlantic states of New York, New Jersey, and Pennsylvania. There, more than three out of every four manufacturing plants that were added to the ownership rolls of the *Fortune* 500 during the last decade resulted from acquisitions of already existing facilities rather than from investment in new plant and equipment.

Moreover, during the 1970s these 410 corporations physically expanded only *one in seven* of the plants they owned at the start of the decade. Even in the West South Central region, where the oil industry is centered, only one out of every five manufacturing or processing plants was physically expanded. Table A.4 in the appendix presents some of Schmenner's results in greater detail.

The "Exporting" of Jobs Through Foreign Investment by American Corporations

Even as they have been disinvesting in domestic industry, U. S. corporations have continued to shift capital beyond the country's borders, into Canada, Western Europe, and the Third World. As a result, since the end of World War II, the growth of American corporate investment in other countries has been enormous. Between 1950 and 1980, direct foreign investment by U. S. businesses increased *sixteen times,* from about $12 billion to $192 billion. Over the same period, gross private domestic investment grew less than half as rapidly, from $54 billion to about $400 billion.[17] The total overseas output of American multinational corporations is now larger than the gross domestic product of every country in the world except the United States and the Soviet Union.

During the decade of 1957–67 alone, a third of all U. S. transportation equipment plants were located abroad. For chemicals, the ratio was 25 percent; for machinery, it was 20 percent.[18] By the end of the 1970s, overseas profits accounted for a third or more of the overall profits of the hundred largest multinational producers and banks in the United States. In some corporations, the fraction was much higher. In 1979, for example, 94 percent of the profits of the Ford Motor Company came from overseas operations; for Coca Cola, it was 63 percent. In 1977, Citicorp derived 83 percent of its banking profits from its overseas operations.[19]

During the early 1970s, a great ideological struggle was waged around the question of whether and to what extent American workers were hurt or helped by the multinationals' overseas investment activities. The Research Department of the AFL-CIO insisted that domestic jobs were being destroyed. The multinationals' chief Washington lobbyist, the Emergency Committee for American Trade, with help from Harvard Business School and Commerce Department studies, tried to make the opposite case.[20]

The central question in what Richard Barnet and Ronald Müller call "the great statistical battle" is: What would or could the multinationals have done had they not been allowed to invest overseas? Assuming that they would have tried to export an equivalent volume of goods and services from their domestic home base, could they have succeeded? Or would foreign competitors have stolen their overseas markets? Might some of those markets never have been brought into existence without the presence of the multinationals "on the scene" to advertise, elicit, and otherwise "develop" customers? And if the multinationals had not been able to produce abroad for sale back into the United States, would they have tried to meet that *domestic* demand by expanding production and employment at home?

Believing that American firms would *not* have attempted an equivalent level of production inside the United States (for domestic sale and for export), or that, having tried, they would have failed to penetrate or hold onto their foreign markets, the conclusion can be reached that foreign investment does, on balance, *create* jobs at home. Conversely, the assumption that at least some of those foreign markets could be supplied by ordinary exports rather than through the creation of overseas branches or subsidiaries, and that American companies *would* expand production at home if they had no other way to meet the domestic demand for T-shirts, toys, and electronic components, leads to the conclusion that foreign investment does indeed on balance *destroy* domestic jobs.

On this question, the protagonists, each in his own way, have tended to make the most extremely favorable assumptions for their respective positions. In *Global Reach,* Barnet and Müller set forth both sides of the matter:

The favorable studies of the companies assume that if a worker now employed by a global corporation were not working for the corporation, he would be unemployed. The labor studies assume, on the other hand, that he is infinitely employable in the United States if only the corporations will keep their capital in the country. Both assumptions are too simple. [Moreover] the company computers all operate on the assumption that foreign investment is "defensive"—i.e. that if the company did not locate a factory in a cheap labor market abroad, a Japanese or European firm would take over the market . . . (Union computers, on the other hand, act as if comparatively high labor costs in the United State make little difference in the competition with foreign corporations.) But even assuming that all foreign investment is "defensive," there are ways to protect a market position other than building a factory in Taiwan. Companies could have put more money into research and development [and into new, more productive, plant and equipment] in the United States . . . . We could also ask what would have happened to the U. S. employment picture if U. S. firms had not been so ready to sell off their comparative advantage to their competitors by licensing technology to them for quick profits.[21]

The corporate formulation is also incomplete to the extent that it ignores access to cheap foreign labor used in producing commodities overseas for *sale in the United States* as a motive for their foreign investment. Twenty-nine percent of all U. S. imports in 1976 came from the output of overseas plants and majority-owned subsidiaries of American multinational corporations.[22] As Pogo once said: "We have met the enemy and he is us!"

Whether government-imposed restrictions on foreign investment would have forced U. S. multinational corporations to make alternative investments at home instead, is really impossible to say. A slightly different (and answerable) question is this: Had they gone ahead and invested domestically, and had that additional capital gone into a mix of activities similar to what American industry was in fact already putting its capital into at home, how many new jobs might have been created, and for whom? Most important, would this have been a *larger* number than the jobs lost as a result of the enforced inability of American multinationals to invest abroad?

Using data on individual industries, two Cornell economists, Robert H. Frank and Richard T. Freeman, have attempted to answer this question. Their study explicitly embodies the crucial premise that large corporations exercise market power that enables them to outlast or defeat competitors by absorbing or passing along to customers at least some unfavorable production cost differentials, or by deploying various price-cutting strategies. Thus, Frank and Freeman's equations incorporate the degree of market—oligopoly—power in an industry, along with comparative data on overseas and domestic production costs (especially labor) taken from corporate income statements filed with the U. S. Department of Commerce.

In 1970 U. S. corporations undertook $10 billion in direct foreign investment. Frank and Freeman find that "even though sales in foreign markets would [have shrunk] by more than half in the event of a ban on foreign investment, such a ban would nevertheless be likely to produce [a net] increase in domestic employment demand."[23] Workers in the nonelectrical machinery sector were by far the most severely affected by this foreign investment. Among a series of calculations based on different assumptions about international competitiveness and relative production costs, the average domestic job loss resulting from that $10 billion of foreign investment was determined to be about 160,000 for 1970, with about 44,000 of these displaced jobs in *non-manufacturing* (in 1970, direct U. S. foreign investment in services, mining, and construction was $5.3 billion, over half of the $10 billion total). Using a 1970 input-output table, indirect manufacturing job loss —the elimination of work in (mostly domestic) companies supplying producers' goods to the multinationals—was estimated to average another 105,000. Moreover, had the $10 billion stayed at home, the duration of joblessness in American labor markets in 1970 would have decreased on the average from 6.4 to 5.3 weeks, with an attendant decrease in unemployment insurance and welfare payments.

Frank and Freeman conclude from their number crunching that "even allowing for considerable deficiencies in the data, the net impact of foreign investment by U. S. multinationals is a substantial domestic employment demand reduction."[24] Specifically, every $1 billion of direct private U. S. foreign investment seems to eliminate (on balance) about 26,500 domestic jobs.

Raymond Vernon of the Harvard Business School has argued that even if American multinationals' overseas activities *do* displace domestic production jobs, they nevertheless create new jobs in the home offices of these corporations—in finance, management, information systems, and clerical work.[25] To this position, Barnet and Müller have a strongly worded response. In the mind of the theorist, perhaps

> jobs may be interchangeable. In the real world, they are not. A total of 250,000 new jobs gained in corporate headquarters does not, in any political or human sense, offset 250,000 old jobs lost on the production line. When Lynn, Massachusetts becomes a ghost of its former self, its jobless citizens find little satisfaction in reading about the new headquarters building on Park Avenue and all the secretaries it will employ.[26]

This issue of who loses the most from the domestic employment impacts of overseas investment by American corporations is addressed in the second half of the Frank-Freeman study. When the job losses estimated earlier are translated into an occupational forecast for the United States, it is found that machinists, machine operators, craftspersons, and clerical workers suffer the greatest degree of economic dislocation from foreign investment. Note that office workers are not immune.

Finally, the authors report on the estimated impacts on U. S. government revenues, wages, and labor's share of the national income. The foreign investment obviously drives domestic government revenues below what they would have been had the $10 billion been invested domestically. The simple reason for this is that the profits made on overseas investments generate an anemic tax return to the U. S. Treasury, due to the way our Internal Revenue Code subsidizes foreign investment through special tax credits[27] (see chapter 5).

As for the impacts of foreign investments on labor income, wages at home are estimated to be lower by between 3 percent and 13 percent, depending on one's assumption about the differential premium on profits demanded by American multinationals as a condition for investing overseas. The lower the premium, the more jobs created outside the United States, and the greater the consequent domestic wage loss. Finally, labor's share of national income is estimated to have been between 2 percent and 6 percent lower than it would have been had the foreign investment been redirected to the domestic economy.[28]

Chapter 6 will argue that the competition among the world's largest multinational corporations became more intense during the 1970s than at any time since World War II. Because of this, U. S. companies may well now be in a position where to not invest abroad is indeed to risk losing markets altogether. In other words, changes in global economic conditions since 1970 may have reduced the extent to which foreign investment by American firms destroys domestic jobs.

But this is speculation. So far, the available evidence indicates that, while foreign investment may be good for corporate profits, a number of policy simulations certainly call into question how good it is for jobs and income.

Conclusion

What is to be made of all this? What people seem to be feeling (and what most analysts in universities and in the media seem to be studiously misunderstanding) is a deepening sense of *insecurity*, growing out of the collapse all around them of the traditional economic base of their communities. Their very jobs are being pulled out from under them. And instead of providing new employment opportunities, a higher standard of living, and enhanced security, the decisions of corporate managers are doing just the opposite.

Working people's feelings about this are not without foundation. Deindustrialization is occurring—on a surprisingly massive scale. It can be seen from North to South and East to West. It is happening as the largest, most powerful corporations in the nation shut down older plants in the industrial heartland (*and* in the Old South) to move to new industrial zones in the New South and overseas; as small businesses confront bankruptcy, close down themselves, or are bought up, milked dry, and then shut down later by larger firms; and as more and more corporations become multinational and conglomerate in nature, shifting finance capital (and even capital goods) all over the map (often at lightning speed) in an effort to maximize their own profits and increase their span of control over the global economic system.

It may well be, as David Birch has found, that only about 2 percent of all private sector annual employment change in the United States now results from actual physical relocations of businesses—the classic runaway shop.[29] But as has been seen, such a limited image of the nature and magnitude of capital shift hardly scratches the surface. Counting only those effects that are presently "countable"—plant closings, relocations, and estimated physical contractions—a sizeable fraction of all the private sector jobs that existed at the beginning of the decade of the 1970s had been destroyed by the end of the decade through private disinvestment in the productive capacity of the American economy. How social disorganization of this magnitude can be considered "insufficient" for the achievement of some abstract notion of a "healthy economy" is, to be frank, beyond understanding.

Nevertheless, the question remains: How much economic dislocation is *too much* dislocation? Or, in Lester Thurow's words, has the pace of private disinvestment in (mainly) older industries been too *slow?* To deal with that question requires a look at what has been happening to the people and the communities that have experienced job loss as a result of the deindustrialization of America during the 1970s and early 1980s. To the extent that the economic, social, and psychological dislocation that they have experienced has largely been transitory, it would be difficult to conclude that the pace of deindustrialization has been too great. But if large numbers of workers, families, and communities are found to have been seriously injured by these economic processes, then there are stronger grounds for supporting the hunch that the pace of private capital mobility in the modern era has become unacceptably rapid; indeed, perhaps even out of control.

Chapter 3

The Impact of Private

Disinvestment on Workers

and Their Communities

TWO YEARS after the Lykes Corporation shut down the Campbell Works of the Youngstown Sheet and Tube Company, *Fortune* magazine decided to investigate the subsequent employment experiences of the 4,100 displaced Ohio steelworkers. In an article entitled, "Youngstown Bounces Back," the magazine concluded that after only two years the workers and community were back on their feet.[1] How *Fortune* could come to this cheery conclusion must have seemed quite mystifying to those in Youngstown, for even the story's own data appear to contradict it.

Fortune found that 35 percent of those displaced were forced into early retirement—at less than half of their previous salary. Another 15 percent were still looking for work and 10 percent were forced to move. Many of these workers returned after they failed to find adequate jobs elsewhere. Of the remaining 40 percent, some took huge wage cuts. For example, Ric Ayres, a former rigger at the mill, ended up taking a job selling women's shoes for $2.37 an hour. One photograph in the article, showing a young man seated at a piano, was captioned: "Crane operator Ozie Williams, thirty-two, has a lot of time to practice his music. He is one of the 600 steelworkers still unemployed."

The "Youngstown Bounces Back" story turned out to be embarrassingly ill-timed. Only days before the article appeared on the newstands, U. S. Steel announced the closing of its own massive Youngstown works as well as thirteen other plants, prompting outraged workers to occupy the mill. In one day, 13,000 additional workers had lost their jobs. U. S. Steel chairman David Broderick saw the closings as one more step in the company's strategy to regain its competitive position and boost its profitability. The workers saw the closings in very different terms—the loss of their economic security and the potential destruction of their community. The closings were described by company officials as inevitable, by workers and their supporters as unconscionable.

Assessing the overall impact of plant closings like those in Youngstown is a difficult enough task. Any assessment is always colored by a person's own particular perspective. It matters whether one is the ship's passenger or the iceberg in Carl Sandburg's, "The People, Yes."

"Isn't that an iceberg on the horizon, Captain?"
"Yes, Madam."
"What if we get in a collision with it?"
"The iceberg, Madam, will move right along as though nothing had happened."[2]

For U. S. Steel, consolidating its operations conceivably will lead to increased profits. Its jettisoning of the Youngstown plant along with its other facilities in Ohio and Pennsylvania may allow the corporation to move right along as though nothing had happened in Youngstown. It may even permit new investment elsewhere, creating new employment opportunities for other workers and their families. But for those who comprise the industry's current work force, who own or work in supplier plants, who provide the retail trade and services purchased by steelworkers when they are employed, and who provide the fire and police protection and teach in the schools that steelworkers' children attend, the costs of the closings, like those at Youngstown Sheet and Tube, are real.

The problem, not unlike that encountered in simply adding up the number of plant closings or the number of workers affected by them, is that almost no hard data exist with which to measure these social costs. Gains or losses in corporate profits are easily measured and regularly appear in stockholder reports and on the pages of the *Wall Street Journal*. But the evidence on the social impact of capital mobility tends to be submerged in Gross National Product accounts and disguised by poorly measured and impersonal unemployment figures. The only way to measure these effects—given that we have no set of systematic "social accounts" in the United States—is to appeal to the few surveys run by social scientists and medical researchers to assess the degree of long-term unemployment, income loss, and deterioration in physical and emotional well-being caused by particular plant closings. In only a few cases is there broader-based statistical research on the impact of capital mobility and economic dislocation on workers and their families. Likewise, there is only a smattering of research on the wider community impacts that accompany deindustrialization.

Nevertheless this is what there is to work with; as it turns out, it tells quite a story in itself.

The Loss of Jobs

At a minimum, almost any kind of capital mobility produces some short-term, or "frictional," unemployment. A new machine is brought into a plant, an old one is shipped out, and two workers are subsequently let go. If the two readily find comparable jobs, or better ones, the income loss to them and their families, and the productivity loss to society, are inconsequential. At the other extreme, as usually occurs when a plant like the Campbell Works in Youngstown closes down, the displacement can be devastating for some workers. The consequences are especially severe if the shutdown occurs during a recession when the competition for other jobs is fierce, or if it occurs in a small or remote community where no other jobs exist. The serious problems begin with unemployment, but they seldom stop there.

Evidence from a broad array of case studies suggests that long-term unemployment is the result of plant closings for at least one third of those directly affected. The family income loss that accompanies it is nearly universal and often substantial. In a report prepared for the Federal Trade Commission, C & R Associates reviewed twelve case studies of factory shutdowns and reported that "in all the studies reviewed the impact on the employees was severe."[3] This is not exactly a new story. In 1961, ten months after Mack Truck abandoned its 2,700-employee assembly plant in Plainfield, New Jersey, 23 percent of its work force were still without jobs, well after unemployment benefits were exhausted.[4] A similar proportion remained unemployed *two years* after the 1956 Packard plant shutdown involving 4,000 workers. Another third of the Packard work force found jobs after the closing but lost these within the first twenty-four months of the original plant shutdown. Having lost all their seniority, often amounting to ten years or more, these workers were vulnerable to layoffs on their new jobs.[5]

More recent research corroborates the evidence from these earlier studies. Writing at Cornell University, Professors Robert Aronson and Robert McKersie surveyed workers who lost their jobs in upstate New York when Westinghouse, Brockway Motors, and then GAF shut down operations in their communities between November 1976 and July 1977.[6] The researchers found that nearly 40 percent of the work force experienced unemployment of forty or more weeks while one quarter of the 2,800 affected workers spent a year or more without work. Their vulnerability to unemployment continued even beyond this point. Two years after the closings, 10 percent of the original sample group were still unemployed.[7]

A plant closing during a recession is likely to be even more devastating in terms of re-employment possibilities because of the absence of jobs in other sectors. Thus when Armour and Company closed its Oklahoma City meat-packing plant during the 1960–61 economic downturn and laid off four hundred of its work force, 50 percent remained unemployed for at least six months.[8] More recently, the closing of a chemical company branch plant in Fall River, Massachusetts during the 1975 recession resulted in unemployment that lasted on the average nearly sixty weeks, with some workers idled as long as three years. Thirty-nine percent of the workers in the sample found jobs only after their unemployment compensation had long been exhausted.[9] Ironically, despite the obvious economic distress following the closing of Youngstown Sheet and Tube, conditions would have been much worse if employment in the automobile industry had not expanded to partially fill the void in steel. A temporary boom in output at the Lordstown complex of the General Motors Corporation cushioned the immediate blow to the Youngstown community.[10]

These particular findings are necessarily based on a handful of plant closings, since only a tiny fraction of all shutdowns have been surveyed by social scientists. Such sobering evidence might therefore be ignored or at least criticized as unrepresentative. However, there is evidence from a nationwide sample of approximately 4,000 men, all over the age of forty-five, that confirms these findings as anything but atypical.[11]

Herbert Parnes and Randy King followed this group over a seven-year period from 1966 to 1973. They found that almost one in twenty of this national sample, who had worked for the same employer for at least five years, experienced permanent involuntary separation during the survey period. Even among this experienced group, 20 percent remained unemployed for at least six months before finding another job.[12] Moreover, the subsequent employment record of those separated from their jobs never regained its previous stability. At the time of the 1973 survey, at least two years after initial separation, 6 percent of the total group of displaced workers were unemployed, as compared with only 1 percent of a control group with the same demographic characteristics, but with no record of permanent job termination. Seventy-six percent of the control group, but only 66 percent of the displaced group, worked all fifty-two weeks in 1973.[13] These results are remarkably consistent with the findings of the individual plant closing studies.

The Parnes and King analysis reveals some surprises. For example, no one appears to be immune to job loss, no matter how well placed. Popular conceptions notwithstanding, displacement respects neither educational attainment nor occupational status. There is virtually no difference in educational background between those displaced and the total population at risk. Similarly, there were no substantial differences among professionals, clerical workers, operatives, and service workers in the chances of being displaced. In the words of these Ohio State researchers: "Apparently the risk of displacement from a job after reasonably long tenure is insensitive to conventional measures of human capital and to the particular occupations in which men are employed."[14] When a plant shuts down, or operations are permanently curtailed so that some workers receive layoffs without recall, engineers lose their jobs along with janitors.

This does not imply that all groups are equally vulnerable to dislocation related to capital mobility. In the Cornell study mentioned earlier, women were found to be twice as likely as men to be unemployed for longer than a year.[15] As secondary earners, it is possible that some married women had the "luxury" of an extended job search, but for most, the problem was finding comparable employment. The latter is certainly true for nonwhite minorities, as Gregory Squires of the U. S. Civil Rights Commission notes.[16]

Blacks are especially hard-hit because they are increasingly concentrated within central cities and in those regions of the country where plant closings and economic dislocation have been most pronounced. While blacks constituted 16 percent of all central city residents in 1960 —before the recent spate of primarily northern-based shutdowns— they accounted for 22 percent of the urban population in 1975. Similarly, blacks and other people of color did not share in the suburban housing and business boom of this period. In spite of fifteen years of civil rights legislation, they were at best able to increase their share of the suburban population from 4.8 percent to 5.0 percent by 1978.[17] Moreover, as the number of jobs grew more rapidly in the South, whites moved in to take the overwhelming majority of them.[18]

To add to the inequity of burden, nonwhite minorities also tend to be concentrated in industries that have borne the brunt of recent closings. This is particularly true in the automobile, steel, and rubber industries. One Washington bureaucrat remarked during the hearings on the Chrysler loan guarantee that it should have been named the Coleman Young bail-out bill and filed under one of the titles of the Civil Rights Act (Young is the black mayor of Detroit). In August 1979 virtually 30 percent of Chrysler's national employment was made up of black, Hispanic, and other minorities, while over half of its Detroit work force was nonwhite.[19] These groups are also at greater risk because they are more dependent than whites on wages and salaries as sources of family income. Eighty percent of minority earnings are derived from wages and salaries, compared to only 75 percent for whites.[20]

How capital mobility can have a discriminatory impact, either intentionally or not, is shown clearly in two examples provided in Squires's work.[21] When a laundry located in St. Louis began to decentralize in 1964, its work force was 75 percent black. By 1975 after it had opened up thirteen suburban facilities and reduced its downtown operations, its black work force was down to 5 percent. In 1976 a Detroit manufacturer relocated production to its facility in a rural county just over the state line in Ohio. Salaried employees, most of whom were white, were offered assistance in finding new jobs. Hourly employees, most of whom were black, received no such aid. As a result, minorities, who had constituted 40 percent of the work force at the Detroit facility, comprised barely 2 percent at the Ohio plant.[22]

The nearly immutable code of "last hired, first fired," combined with entrenched patterns of housing segregation, have left minorities at a real disadvantage when manufacturing plants close down, retail shops move out, and economic activity spreads to the suburbs and beyond. The dream of jobs with high wages and decent fringe benefits that once lured blacks to the North has turned into a nightmare for those who now face termination in the once bustling factories of the industrial Midwest.

Income Loss and Underemployment

The incidence of job loss and the duration of unemployment are, of course, only two measures of the personal costs associated with economic dislocation. Not only do workers lose jobs, but the new jobs they eventually get do not provide as much income or status.

Again, the Parnes and King national sample confirms what had been found in the case studies. Almost *three fifths* of the displaced workers experienced a decline in occupational status, in contrast to only one fifth of the control group. What is most revealing about this result is that the downward occupational mobility was most acute among professional and managerial workers. In the initial 1966 survey, 27 percent of the workers eventually displaced, and an identical proportion of the control group, were in these top occupational categories. Seven years later, the proportion of displaced workers in these categories had fallen to 18 percent, while the proportion among the control group had actually increased to more than one third.[23]

In essence, the data indicate that permanently laid-off workers do not suffer merely a temporary loss. Many appear to make no complete occupational recovery even after a number of years, and some victims *never* recover. One example, provided by Parnes and King, is the forty-eight-year-old accountant who in 1966 had served with his employer for twenty-seven years. His annual earnings were $18,500 at the time of his layoff. After being unemployed for over a year, he finally found a job as a salesman. By 1973 he had worked for only eighteen weeks at that job, earning $4,000—implying an annual salary of somewhat under $12,000. In another example, in 1966 a fifty-seven-year-old metal roller with an eighth grade education and forty years of service in his job earned $9,000 per year. After his separation from this job, he was unemployed for thirteen weeks before finding a job as a gardener at an annual salary of $3,000.[24]

Thanks to the efforts of researchers at the Public Research Institute of the Center for Naval Analyses in Virginia, there now are some statistical estimates of income loss that apply to entire industries.[25] Using Social Security data, Louis Jacobson and his colleagues have been able to calculate the earnings losses of permanently displaced, prime-age male workers in a number of key industries.[26] To do this, Jacobson calculates the actual earnings of workers in a given industry who remain continuously employed in that sector. This earnings trajectory is then compared with the earnings records of workers who experience permanent layoffs from the same industry.[27] For most cases there is an immediate drop in income subsequent to termination followed by a rise in earnings as those displaced find new employment in other firms. Of course, some job losers are affected quite adversely, with their earnings falling to zero, while others find comparable work almost immediately. The "actual earnings profile" reflects the *average* earnings of the full cohort of displaced workers.

Jacobson's estimates listed in table 3.1 indicate that in the first two years following involuntary termination, the average annual earnings loss ranges from less than 1 percent for workers formerly employed in the production of TV receivers to more than 46 percent in steel. Even after *six years,* workers in some industries continued to suffer as much as an 18 percent shortfall. Those displaced from the better-paying, unionized industries like meat-packing, flat glass, automobile, aerospace, steel, and petroleum refining experienced the greatest reduction in income. But even in the low-wage sector including women's apparel, shoes, toys, and rubber footwear, six or more years elapsed before displaced workers caught up with those who had the good fortune to hold on to their jobs.

Presumably, many, if not most, of these workers received unemployment insurance benefits (UIB) when they first lost their jobs. However, during this period, as is true of the present, UIB had a 26-week maximum. Clearly this could only compensate for a small portion of the earnings loss in the first two years and only a minuscule fraction during the full six. Furthermore, workers who found another job immediately following a layoff—even one that paid well below their previous wage —were not eligible for unemployment benefits at all. On the other hand, workers in a small number of industries such as auto manufacturing may have been employed by firms that paid supplemental unemployment benefits (SUB). A few displaced workers might also have qualified for trade readjustment assistance (TRA), but these "better off" workers are by far the exception, not the rule.

TABLE 3.1

Long-Term Earnings Losses of Permanently Displaced Prime-Age Male Workers

	Average Annual Percentage Loss	
Industry	First 2 Years	Subsequent 4 Years
Automobiles	43.4	15.8
Steel	46.6	12.6
Meat-Packing	23.9	18.1
Acrospace	23.6	14.8
Petroleum Refining	12.4	12.5
Women's Clothes	13.3	2.1
Electronic Components	8.3	4.1
Shoes	11.3	1.5
Toys	16.1	−2.7
TV Receivers	0.7	−7.2
Cotton Weaving	7.4	−11.4
Flat Glass	16.3	16.2
Men's Clothing	21.3	8.7
Rubber Footwear	32.2	−.9

SOURCE: Louis S. Jacobson, "Earnings Losses of Workers Displaced from Manufacturing Industries," in William G. Dewald, ed., *The Impact of International Trade and Investment on Employment*, A Conference of the U. S. Department of Labor, (U. S. Government Printing Office, 1978), and Louis S. Jacobson, "Earnings Loss Due to Displacement," (Working Paper CRC-385, The Public Research Institute of the Center for Naval Analyses, April 1979).

This is clearly evident in a recent study of job loss among blue-collar women in the apparel and electrical goods industries conducted by Ellen Rosen.[28] Here it was found that even after including UIB and TRA on top of any reemployment income, 92 percent of the affected workers suffered an annual income loss, with over 20 percent losing more than $3,000. On average, these women ended up losing over one fifth of their normal yearly income following termination. This figure is nearly identical to the 18 percent cut in median family income found by Aronson and McKersie in their upstate New York study.[29]

Other research reveals similar degrees of economic loss. When the Mathematica Policy Research Center interviewed approximately 1,500 displaced workers, over 900 of whom received TRA in addition to regular unemployment compensation, it was found that in the first year after layoff, total household income for those in the Mathematica TRA sample dropped by about $1,700 in real terms.[30] Three-and-a-half years after layoff, those who were never recalled by their initial employers still had, on average, lower real weekly earnings than before. Moreover, about 38 percent of the original sample lost their health insurance coverage sometime during the initial unemployment stint.

Workers stand to lose all or part of their pension rights as well. Many Packard workers were left without a penny after paying into their retirement fund for years. A study commissioned by the Federal Reserve Bank of Boston showed that, during the early 1970s of all the Massachusetts shoe workers displaced by shutdowns, 62 percent lost the pension benefits that they otherwise would have enjoyed had their plants remained in business.[31] Enactment of the Employee Retirement Income Security Act (ERISA) in 1974 curbed many of the earlier abuses of pension rights, but corporate termination of a particular plant or division—or what the U. S. Department of Labor, Labor-Management Services Administration calls a "partial termination"—still can result in some benefits not being paid.[32]

When the Diamond-Reo Corporation went out of business in 1975, 2,300 UAW members, including 500 retirees and 750 vested active employees, were affected. Vested active employees are those who are presently working and have sufficient seniority to qualify for company pensions when they retire. Since the pension plan was seriously underfunded, before ERISA all 750 vested actives would have lost their pension rights and the retirees would have suffered severe cutbacks averaging nearly 80 percent of their monthly pension benefits. Because of ERISA, about four out of five of the retirees suffered only relatively minor cutbacks in their expected pensions. But, for the one in five who chose non-guaranteed early retirement supplements, there were drastic cutbacks. An even more serious loss was borne by the 750 vested employees who had not yet retired.[33]

How workers fare after a permanent layoff, if they do not drop out of the labor market altogether, depends on the types of jobs they find when they go to look for new work. Our own research, based on the Social Security Longitudinal Employer-Employee Data file (LEED)—the same one used by Jacobson—reveals that post-separation earnings are largely determined by which market segment a displaced worker eventually enters. By way of example, consider what happened to prime-age workers in the New England aircraft industry when that sector went into a tailspin as a result of slackened procurement for the Vietnam war. Those who ended up in "secondary" jobs did considerably worse than those who remained in the aircraft industry or were able to transfer to other companies in the "primary" segment of the labor market.*

Aircraft workers who were able to retain their jobs earned 21.1 percent more in 1972 than they did in 1967 (see table 3.2). Those who left the region following the severe layoffs that began in 1968, to search out aircraft industry jobs elsewhere, did not fare quite as well, averaging only a 16.5 percent earnings gain. Those who left the industry altogether but found work in other parts of the primary labor market, had higher earnings in the later year, but their wage gain was only one third as large as that achieved by those who were able to keep their aircraft jobs.

By contrast, those forced to take menial jobs in restaurants, hospitals, and various other sectors where they could not use their aircraft industry skills lost, on average, 26 percent of their former income levels (even before accounting for inflation). An additional 6 percent of the original sample had no "covered" earnings in 1972, despite the fact that they neither retired nor became disabled. Those in this category either had no wage income at all during the year or worked in jobs not covered

---

*The "primary" segment includes most industries in the construction, durable manufacturing, wholesale trade, public utility, and higher-skill service sectors. Generally these are industries that have a more stable employment pattern and normally pay higher than average wages. The "secondary" segment includes most nondurable manufacturing, retail trade, and lower-skill personal service industries, ones usually characterized by higher turnover, greater seasonality, and lower average wages.[34]

TABLE 3.2

What Happens to the Earnings of Workers Who Leave the Aircraft Industry
(in current dollars)

1972 Industry/Region	Number of Workers	Percentage in Category	1967 Average Earnings	1972 Average Earnings	Percentage change in Average Earnings
Aircraft/inside New England	37,700	64.7	$9,575	$11,595	+21.1
Aircraft/outside New England	600	1.0	9,829	11,455	+16.5
Other "Primary"[a] Industries	11,900	20.4	8,733	9,345	+7.0
Other "Secondary"[b] Industries	2,100	3.6	6,054	4,468	−26.2
Not in Jobs Covered by Social Security	3,700	6.3	6,175	0	—
Disabled, Deceased, Unknown	2,300	3.9	—	—	—
Total	58,300	100.0			

SOURCE: Special tabulations of Social Security LEED File prepared by Alan Matthews and Barry Bluestone, Social Welfare Research Institute, Boston College, September 1979.
[a]"Primary" Industries include most durable manufacturing, wholesale trade, public utilities, and some services.
[b]"Secondary" Industries include most nondurable manufacturing, retail trade, and lower-skill requirement, higher-turnover personal services.

by social security, mainly in the federal government. Similar results to those obtained in aircraft were found for the metalworking machinery industry, although those who ended up in secondary jobs were not affected quite so adversely.

To the extent that the relative earnings losses represent real losses in productivity, table 3.2 suggests that one third of the entire New England aircraft labor force experienced a productivity loss ranging from 4.6 percent for those who left the region for aircraft jobs elsewhere to 47.3 percent among those who ended up taking secondary jobs. For those who found no job at all after leaving the industry, the social efficiency loss was, mathematically speaking, infinite.

Leaving the aircraft industry has even worse consequences for women than for their male counterparts. Men who ended up in secondary jobs experienced a 14 percent earnings loss on average, while women lost a whopping 40 percent. Adding to this disparity is the difference in the probability that a woman would end up in the secondary segment. Only one out of fifty men employed in aircraft in 1967 was located in a secondary job in 1972. In sharp contrast, nearly one in eight women experienced such an industrial "demotion." For women, getting into a high productivity, high-wage manufacturing job is a real victory; being forced out involves a real defeat.

Even these numbers present too sanguine a picture of income loss. Unlike other studies, these particular tabulations do not distinguish between voluntarily leaving and involuntary layoffs. Consequently we cannot tell whether the workers who left aircraft or metalworking did so voluntarily, were the subjects of layoff, or experienced a plant closing. Since people who quit often leave because they have found better jobs, the earnings statistics in table 3.2 almost certainly underestimate the losses of those who left involuntarily.

Loss of Family Wealth

Families who fall victim to brief periods of lost earnings are frequently able to sustain their standards of living through unemployment insurance and savings. Unfortunately for the victims of plant closings, the consequences are often much more severe, ranging from a total depletion of savings to mortgage foreclosures and reliance on public welfare. Families sometimes lose not only their current incomes, but their total accumulated assets as well.

During the Great Depression, the waves of plant closings that spread across the country drove millions of families into poverty. A study completed in 1934 of Connecticut River Valley textile workers showed that two years after the mills closed down, 75 percent of the families affected were living in poverty, compared with 11 percent before the shutdown.[35] More than one in four families was forced to move in order to find lower rents. Some families lost their houses when they fell behind on mortgages. Thirty-five percent reported no new purchases of clothing, and the consumption of other items was reduced significantly.

This experience did not die out with the end of the Depression. A similar fate is faced by workers and their families who suffer permanent layoff today. When the Plainfield, New Jersey, Mack Truck facility shut down in 1960, workers had to reduce their food and clothing consumption substantially, and they turned to borrowing and installment credit for other necessities.[36] Aircraft workers in Hartford County, Connecticut—the jet engine capital of the world—responded to the loss of their jobs in the mid-1970s by sharply reducing their expenditures on food, clothing, and medical care in addition to a long list of "luxury" items such as recreation and house repair. Out of the eighty-one workers interviewed in a study by Rayman and Bluestone, three of these displaced jet engine workers lost their houses to foreclosure.[37] Among participants in the upstate New York study conducted by Aronson and McKersie, 11 percent reported cutting back on housing expenses, 16 percent reduced their food consumption, 31 percent bought less clothing, and 43 percent spent less on recreation. In what could lead to a mortgaging of their families' health, one in seven reduced their expenditures for medical care.[38] These figures are remarkably close to those found in the Hartford County research.

Such grave consequences are found in other case studies as well. In his study of the Wickwire shutdown (Colorado Fuel and Iron Corporation), Felician Foltman found that workers were often forced to sell their automobiles and personal possessions in order to qualify for relief payments.[39] Even more recently, the closing of a chemical company in Massachusetts forced families to rely on food stamps and housing assistance after their savings were used up.[40] In the wake of permanent layoffs in the mid-1970s at the RCA Mountaintop semi-conductor complex near Wilkes-Barre, Pennsylvania, researchers reported a major increase in young males on state welfare—a condition only permitted by law once someone virtually exhausts all of his savings and cashes in all of his assets.[41]

Somewhat of an embarassment to the research community is the fact that so little is known about the loss in assets suffered by workers when they lose their jobs. Saving for a rainy day is a normal part of a family's security umbrella, but for many it is never enough to cover the damage caused by the downpour from a plant closing.

Impacts on Physical and Mental Health

The loss of personal assets places families in an extraordinarily vulnerable position; for when savings run out, people lose the ability to respond to short-run crises. The first unanticipated financial burden that comes along—an unexpected health problem, a casualty or fire loss, or even a minor automobile accident—can easily hurl the family over the brink of economic solvency. The trauma associated with this type of loss extends well beyond the bounds of household money matters.

Medical researchers have found that acute economic distress associated with job loss causes a range of physical and mental health problems, the magnitudes of which are only now being assessed. Simply measuring the direct employment and earnings losses of plant closings therefore tends to seriously underestimate the total drain on families caught in the midst of capital shift.

Dr. Harvey Brenner of Johns Hopkins University, along with Sidney Cobb at Brown University and Stanislav Kasl at Yale University, have done careful studies in this area. Writing in *Psychometric Medicine*, Kasl and Cobb report high or increased blood pressure (hypertension) and abnormally high cholesterol and blood-sugar levels in blue-collar workers who lost their jobs due to factory closure.[42] These factors are associated with the development of heart disease. Other disorders related to the stress of job loss are ulcers, respiratory diseases, and hyper-allergic reactions. Higher levels of serum glucose, serum pepsinogen, and serum uric acid found in those experiencing job termination relative to levels in a control group of continuously employed workers suggest unduly high propensities to diabetes and gout.[43] Compounding these problems is the fact that economically deprived workers are often forced to curtail normal health care and suffer from poorer nutrition and housing.

The Kasl and Cobb findings are by no means unique. Aronson and McKersie write that two fifths of their sample reported deterioration in their physical and emotional well-being since their termination. Headaches, upset stomachs, and feelings of depression were the most widely-reported health problems.[44] Aggressive feelings, anxiety, and alcohol abuse were the observed psychological consequences of the Youngstown steel closings. Similar conditions were widely reported among the aircraft workers in the Hartford County study. In most of these cases, the factor of time seems to be essential. Those who need much of it to find another job suffer the most.

Workers generally lose health benefits when they lose their jobs. According to Don Stillman of the United Auto Workers, fewer than 30 percent of the unemployed have any health insurance at all.[45] Those who do have to spend 20 to 25 percent of their unemployment benefits merely to continue their former coverage—if continuation is available at all. Premiums for non-group coverage average twice those for group plans, yet the benefits are lower. There are so many deductibles that non-group health insurance covers an average of only 31 percent of a family's incurred medical costs.

Brenner's work gives evidence of yet a much broader and deeper problem. Making use of correlation and regression analysis, he has been investigating the statistical linkages between so-called economic stress indicators and seven indices of pathology. The economic stress indicators include per capita income, the rate of inflation, and the unemployment rate. The indices of pathology are:[46]

- age and sex specific mortality rates
- cardiovascular-renal disease mortality rates
- suicide mortality rates
- homicide mortality rates

- mental hospital admission rates
- imprisonment rates
- cirrhosis of the liver mortality rates

Using national data for the period 1940–73, Brenner found that unemployment plays a statistically significant role in affecting several forms of "social trauma." In particular, he concludes that a 1 percent increase in the aggregate unemployment rate sustained over a period of six years has been associated with approximately:[47]

- 37,000 total deaths (including 20,000 cardiovascular deaths)
- 920 suicides
- 650 homicides
- 500 deaths from cirrhosis of the liver
- 4,000 state mental hospital admissions
- 3,300 state prison admissions

These results, of course, do not directly address the question of unemployment caused by deindustrialization *per se*. But it is likely that permanent layoffs cause even more "social trauma" than unemployment arising from other causes. For example, in the aftermath of the Federal Mogul Corporation closing of its roller-bearing plant in Detroit, eight of the nearly 2,000 affected workers took their own lives.[48] This macabre statistic is unfortunately not unusual. In their study of displaced workers, Cobb and Kasl found a suicide rate "thirty times the expected number."[49]

Of course, suicide is only the most extreme manifestation of the severe emotional strain caused by job loss. Family and social relationships are nearly always strained by protracted unemployment. Richard Wilcock and W. H. Franke, in their now famous work on permanent layoffs and long-term unemployment, suggest that social, medical, and psychological costs may even outweigh direct economic costs in severity. They note:

Perhaps the most serious impact of shutdowns, particularly for many of the long-term unemployed, was a loss of confidence and a feeling of uselessness. . . . The unemployed worker loses his daily association with fellow workers. This loss means not only disappearance of human relationships built up over a period of years, but also the end of a meaningful institutional relationship. When he is severed from his job, he discovers that he has lost, in addition to the income and activity, his institutional base in the economic and social system.[50]

Loss of a work network removes an important source of human support. As a result, psychosomatic illnesses, anxiety, worry, tension, impaired interpersonal relations, and an increased sense of powerlessness arise. As self-esteem decreases, problems of alcoholism, child and spouse abuse, and aggression increase. Unfortunately these tragic consequences are often overlooked when the costs and benefits of capital mobility are evaluated.

Special psychological problems arise when a plant closing occurs in a small community, especially when the establishment was the locality's major employer. Writing about the closing of a plant in southern Appalachia, Walter Strange notes that the people

> lost the central focus which had held the community together—its reason for existence—a focus which was held in common as community property, one which provided not only for economic needs but . . . a structural framework which gave coherence and cohesion to their lives.[51]

These effects typically lessen or disappear following successful re-employment. Yet, "stressful situations" caused by a plant closing can linger long after the final shutdown has occurred. Moreover, feelings of lost self-esteem, grief, depression, and ill health can lessen the chances of finding reemployment; this failure, in turn, can exacerbate the emotional distress, generating a cycle of destruction.[52] Ultimately a debilitating type of "blaming the victim" syndrome can evolve, causing dislocated workers to feel that the plant closing was their own fault. Strange argues "that those feelings of self-doubt can create fear of establishing a new employment relationship or complicate the adjustment process to a new job."[53] As the sociologist Alfred Slote put it, in his seminal work on job termination:

> The most awful consequence of long-term unemployment is the development of the attitude, "I couldn't hold a job even if I found one," which transforms a man from unemployed to unemployable.[54]

The "Ripple Effects" in the Community

While the impact of disinvestment on individual workers and their families, is probably the correct place to begin any inquiry into the social costs of unregulated deindustrialization, it cannot be the end of such an inquiry. For when mills or department stores or supermarket chains shut down, many other things can happen to a community. These can be extraordinarily costly as they ripple through the economy.

The primary effects are, of course, visited on those closest to the production unit that ceases operations. The unit's own employees lose salaries and wages, pensions, and other fringe benefits; supplier firms lose contracts; and the various levels of government lose corporate income and commercial property tax revenue. These in turn result in a series of secondary shocks including decreased retail purchases in the community, a reduction in earnings at supplier plants, and increased unemployment in other sectors. Finally, these events produce tertiary effects in the form of increased demand for public assistance and social services, reduced personal tax receipts, and eventually layoffs in other industries, including the public sector. What begins as a behind-closed-doors company decision to shut down a particular production facility ends up affecting literally everyone in town, including the butcher, the baker, and the candlestick maker. By the time all of these "ripple effects" spread throughout the economy, workers and families far removed from the original plant closing can be affected, often with dramatic consequences.

Some of these ripple (or multiplier) effects are felt immediately, while others take time to work through the economy. Some will dissipate quickly (especially if the local economy is expanding), while others may become a permanent part of the local economic environment. The extent of the impact of any particular closing will depend also on whether the plant or store was a major employer in the area, or an important purchaser of goods and services produced by other area businesses. All of these indirect impacts will be multiplied if a number of closings or cutbacks occur in the area simultaneously.

Systematic research that statistically accounts for all of these crucial ecological factors is, like the data on plant closings themselves, almost totally nonexistent. Nevertheless, it is possible to assemble bits and pieces of evidence that provide at least some sense of what can be involved at the wider community level when a major employer shuts down or leaves town. Here the experiences of just a few places— Newark, New Jersey; Youngstown, Ohio; Detroit, Michigan; Johnstown, Pennsylvania; Cortland County, New York; and Anaconda, Montana—must suffice. This is not because there are only a few isolated instances of economic disaster associated with capital mobility, but because social scientists have not had the foresight or the resources to produce more than a handful of studies. In fact, literally hundreds of communities have gone through the trials faced by the towns and cities considered here.

J. Wiss & Son, a large cutlery manufacturer, had been in business in Newark, New Jersey since 1848. When it was acquired by a Texas conglomerate and relocated to North Carolina in 1978, the state AFL-CIO decided to undertake a community-impact assessment, using methods and data suggested by the U. S. Chamber of Commerce. The direct loss of 760 manufacturing jobs, according to this study, cost the city an additional 468 jobs "in stores, banks, bus service, luncheonettes, taverns, gas stations, and other local businesses." More than $14 million in purchasing power was removed from the local economy, half of which had resided in local bank deposits used for loans to finance mortgages, home improvements, purchases of automobiles, televisions, refrigerators, and other major appliances.

Even charities suffered. No longer available were the annual contributions of $22,000 by the Wiss employees or the $11,000 corporate gift. Among the losers were the community's retarded children who were aided by these funds, the Associated Catholic Charities, the Jewish Community Federation, the Red Cross, the Salvation Army, the Presbyterian Boys Club and Hospital, and the Cerebral Palsy Foundation—all of which were associated with the Essex and West Hudson County United Way.[55]

The planned restructuring of the Bethlehem Steel plant in Johnstown, Pennsylvania, in 1973 would have directly eliminated 4,500 jobs as a result of conversion to electric furnaces from what were justifiably considered archaic coke ovens, blast furnaces, and open hearths. While the demand for steel increased unexpectedly in 1974 and kept the Johnstown facility booming through the end of 1976, the projected loss of those 4,500 jobs would have induced a $40 million decline in annual payroll from Bethlehem and more than $4 million in canceled orders to area suppliers. Retail sales would have been cut by $20 million. All together, another 3,000 jobs would have been lost as a result of these ripple effects.[56] This estimate turns out to be fully consistent with a U. S. Chamber of Commerce claim that a community loses, on the average, two service sector jobs every time three manufacturing jobs disappear.[57]

Moreover, the steel cutback that eventually did occur in Johnstown in 1979 apparently made the city "an unattractive place to do business, no matter what kind."[58] In the wake of the downsizing of the firm, other companies pulled up stakes altogether.

> In 1980 the Pennsylvania Electric Company (Penclec) announced it would move its administrative headquarters from Johnstown to Reading, dislocating some 120 administrative personnel and eliminating 85 [other] jobs. Then, a local bakery that had been in business for decades in Johnstown closed, throwing 100 people out of work, and a Chevrolet dealership folded after more than sixty years in business, eliminating another 77 jobs.[59]

The employment climate became so bad that the local Bureau of Employment Security estimated that more than 10,000 people had left the area by the end of 1979, most of them under age forty. Even then, the March 1980 official unemployment rate was more than 12 percent.

In Youngstown, the projected community costs were every bit as high. A Policy Management Associates (PMA) study of the Youngstown Sheet and Tube closing concluded that the overall job loss from the 4,100 steel plant layoffs would ultimately reach 12,000 to 13,000 other workers and in turn would cause retail sales to drop by $12–23 million each year.[60]

When the company in the classic "company town" closes down, all of these effects are magnified tremendously. The case of Anaconda, Montana provides a perfect example.[61] Anaconda Copper & Mining Co. had operated a huge copper smelter there for over seventy-five years when the Los Angeles-based Atlantic Richfield Co. (ARCO) acquired it. Two years later, on September 29, 1980, ARCO announced that it was abandoning the smelter, thus eliminating 80 percent of the entire annual payroll in this community of 12,000 people. Needless to say, the announcement sent a Richter scale shock wave through the town.

The action erased 1,000 jobs in Anaconda and 500 more in neighboring Great Falls. The fallout was immediate. In two weeks, new unemployment claims added 691 recipients to the rolls and before long, one in six in the work force was out of work. The food-stamp rolls grew by 190, to 434 families. About 170 workers chose early retirement rather than the $3,500 in severance pay.

> But those were just the clackings of the first dominoes to fall here . . . . All told, the state estimates, the smelter closing will result in the loss of $42 million in annual payroll in a county with only $51 million in income to begin with. Other dominoes were not long in falling.
>
> First Federal Savings & Loan of Great Falls closed its branch here, eliminating three jobs with a $35,000 annual payroll and a $100,000 operating budget.
>
> Joe Maciag and 70 others lost their jobs at the Butte, Anaconda & Pacific Railway, an ARCO subsidiary that hauled copper for processing.
>
> True Value Hardware cut its two full-time employees to 20 hours each— and reduced their pay from $4 an hour to $3.10, a $98 weekly pay loss.
>
> And Dee, the Chevrolet dealer, kept vacant a $4.50-an-hour apprentice mechanic job after the 20-year-old worker who had held it decided there was no future here and moved to Cut Bank, Mont.[62]

In all these ways, the ARCO smelter closing "echoed through the city." By December, the Chamber of Commerce found that thirty-six businesses it surveyed (excluding the railroad) had laid off, on the average, 20 percent of their employees. One fourth of the businesses said they anticipated further layoffs, and one third had canceled expansion plans. Most reported their business had dropped 10–50 percent, despite both the severance payments made by ARCO to its recently "pink-slipped" workers and the various forms of unemployment insurance and public aid supplied to those directly and indirectly affected.

The secondary victims of the smelter closing often had recourse to fewer public and private benefits than the smelter workers themselves. "The businessmen are getting the brunt of it right now," the town's Chevrolet dealer told a *Los Angeles Times* reporter. "They gave [the smelter workers] $3,500 in severance pay—I got caught with $500,000 in cars."[63]

The physical and emotional trauma associated with this particular closing was also striking. Workers sold their $55,000 houses for $35,000 in order to take jobs elsewhere. Businesses that normally would have provided a comfortable retirement for their owners went bankrupt, leaving them with nothing more than Social Security for their old age. Visits to the Alcohol Service Center increased by 52 percent, and there was a 150-percent increase in the number of persons seeking drug counseling. The patient load at the Mental Health Center jumped 62 percent.[64] To add injury to insult, on the day the smelter closing was announced, the local water company raised its rates. No one in town overlooked the fact that the water company was also owned by ARCO.

With the immense size of some industries like automobile and steel, entire regions behave as though they were company towns. The key losses flowing from the recent automobile layoffs are felt in steel, ferrous castings, aluminum, synthetic rubber, glass, plastics, textiles, and machine tools. The U. S. Department of Labor (DOL) has estimated that for every 100 jobs in the motor vehicle industry, 105 jobs are wiped out in the direct supplier network.[65]

Economists talk about these indirect losses in terms of "employment multipliers." In this case, the DOL study reveals a multiplier of 2.05, since an initial loss of 100 jobs leads to an eventual total loss of 205. In studies of the automobile industry that were performed by the Transportation Systems Center of the U. S. Department of Transportation, the value of the multiplier was estimated to be even higher—in the range of 2.4 to 3.0.[66]

Our own estimates using the M.I.T. Multiregional Input-Output Model (MRIO) suggest a multiplier in the same range.[67] Beginning with a potential loss of 5,000 jobs in automobile assembly in Michigan, the MRIO permits a measurement of the effect of such a cut on all other industries in the United States on a state-by-state basis. According to this analysis, the original displacement of the assembly workers would eventually affect over 8,000 auto workers in all, as parts suppliers in Michigan and elsewhere eliminate jobs due to reduced orders. Along with Michigan, the midwestern states share the heaviest burden, with Ohio losing over 1,000 auto industry jobs, Indiana another 630, and Illinois and Wisconsin each losing at least 200.[68]

In all, the 8,000 jobs potentially lost nationwide in the automobile industry would ultimately cause a decline in employment among *all industries* of more than 20,600. In other words, more than 12,000 non-auto industry jobs would be affected. For example, iron-ore miners in Minnesota—probably working in that state's northern "iron range" —will lose their jobs because, with fewer domestic cars produced, there is less need for sheet steel and consequently less demand for iron ore. Indeed, because of the staggering complexity and interrelatedness of the economy, nearly *every* industry will be touched sooner or later by the layoffs in the Michigan plants. Somewhere in the production chain —either in the direct manufacture of automobiles or, for that matter, in the weaving of the cloth that goes into the upholstery—workers will suffer short work weeks or temporary layoffs. Some will lose their jobs permanently. The biggest losers in this instance are those who work in closely allied industries such as steel, rubber, metalworking machinery, and metal stampings.

Of course, non-manufacturing workers are deeply affected as well. Over 1,000 jobs throughout the nation in transportation and warehousing would potentially disappear as a consequence of the original cutback in automobile assembly operations in Michigan. Nearly 1,800 wholesale and retail trade jobs and over 500 jobs in related business services will be affected. Presumably auto dealers, advertisers, truckers, and accountants will feel the pinch when some Detroit assembly lines close down for good. The same is obviously true when a steel or tire factory shuts down or even a major chain of supermarkets or discount department stores. The employment multipliers will differ from industry to industry depending on how well an industry is integrated into the entire production chain. But no instance of a plant, store, or office shutdown is an island unto itself.

Public Revenues and Social Expenditures

The public sector suffers, too. Until recently, Draper Looms was the most important employer in the small town of Hopedale, Massachusetts. In the late 1960s, the 150-year-old mill was acquired by Rockwell International, which closed it down in October 1978 laying off some 3,000 workers. Draper owned 45 percent of Hopedale's land and paid 30 percent of the town's property taxes. When the final shutdown occurred, the town's finances were thrown into disarray, almost to the point of bankruptcy. In testimony before the U. S. House Committee on Small Business, the town's attorney, Robert Phillips, explained the state of Hopedale's finances in the wake of the closing:

> In summary, in two years, starting with January 1, 1978, and ending in January 1, 1980—because January 1 is our assessing date—the value of those [Draper] properties dropped from $13.7 million to $8.3 million, which is a loss of $5 million in tax valuation and over $300,000 in tax revenue. That means that $300,000 in tax [burden] has now been shifted over to the residential homeowner and to the small storeowner.
>
> This poses a significant problem in our town finances since practically 70 percent of our local revenues are raised by real estate taxation. That means that, unless we can take this enormous plant and complex and get new businesses in there and keep the thing viable and operative, we are going to suffer a very severe economic loss. The town would almost be eligible for a Chapter 13 bankruptcy reorganization or something like that. We've got to keep the thing going.[69]

The Massachusetts Executive Office of Economic Affairs has developed a rule of thumb according to which every $10,000 salary-level job lost to the state costs it about $1,336 in foregone state and local taxes.[70] Just in direct property taxes, the closing of the Uniroyal tire plant in Chicopee, Massachusetts, which employed 1,600 people, deprived the city of over half a million dollars in annual revenue. To compensate for this deficit, the city needed to add $5 in taxes per $1,000 assessed valuation to every other property in town.[71]

The same type of losses are suffered by larger towns and cities as well. In the wake of the Youngstown Sheet and Tube closing, Policy Management Associates concluded that in the first thirty-nine months following the shutdown, the communities around Youngstown would lose up to $8 million in taxes, the county government another $1 million, the state $8 million, and the federal treasury as much as $15 million—for a total tax loss that would approach $32 million. The managers of the Campbell Works themselves projected that the town of Campbell (situated on the edge of Youngstown) would suffer an annual loss of over half a million dollars in personal income taxes, and an additional $130,000 in yearly property taxes. They forecast that the school budget deficit would rise by $1 million.[72]

The steel firm's managers were not altogether wrong, but they sorely underestimated the financial shock to the community. As a result of the Campbell closing, the townspeople were forced to increase their own property taxes by more than $11 million in one year—from $39.8 to $51 million. More than half the increase came when voters approved a $5.8 million increase in September 1979. A total of $3.5 million was added to the existing $10.8 million school levy so that the same number of dollars would be produced when valuations dropped. Even then, the Campbell schools had to obtain a $750,000 loan from the state to keep classrooms open, and became the first in Ohio to apply for a second emergency loan from the state to avoid complete bankruptcy.

Moreover, these tax losses can have a hidden cost, to the extent that they impair a municipality's ability to float its bonds. Campbell itself had negotiated the sale of a bond issue just before the shutdown but was unable to complete it when—immediately after Sheet and Tube's demise—the buyer backed out.[73]

The Chrysler Federal Loan Guarantee very likely saved the city of Detroit, the sixth largest city in the country, from immediate bankruptcy. If Chrysler had gone under, 15 percent of Detroit's manufacturing work force would have found themselves on the streets at once. By itself this one automobile company employs over one in twenty of the entire city's labor force. Between the local income tax foregone by those who work in Detroit-based Chrysler plants, and the foregone property tax now paid by the company, a huge chunk of the city's revenue would be lost. Chrysler workers in Detroit pay over $280 million annually in federal income taxes.[74] Assuming that what Detroit gets in taxes is approximately equal to one seventh of this amount, based on what was then its 2.5 percent income tax levy, Detroit would immediately have lost $40 million in revenues. Add to this the $34 million that Chrysler pays to the city in its own annual tax payments, and the total comes to $75 million. Still, this figure does not come close to representing the total loss, for it ignores the multiplier effect altogether. As a postscript it should be noted that even though Chrysler was saved (at least for the time being), drastic cutbacks in the company, combined with other automobile industry losses, forced the city to raise the income tax levy to 3.5 percent in July 1981. If the city referendum on the matter had failed, Detroit would have been bankrupt in less than a week's time.

Of course the Chrysler bankruptcy would have had its own ripple effects well beyond the boundaries of the Motor City. So enormous is the national, and international, payroll of Chrysler that a total shutdown would have cut off perhaps half a *billion* dollars in annual federal, state, and local income taxes normally paid by workers in both Chrysler and the businesses linked to it.[75] Such is the public cost of widespread deindustrialization.

Disinvestment on a large scale draws on the government treasury in two ways. First, it immediately reduces tax revenues. Then, gradually, it increases the need for additional public expenditures. In some instances, particularly in smaller towns and cities, or when an entire industry lays off a large portion of its work force, both occur simultaneously. Tax receipts fall precisely when the need for public expenditures rise.

Thus, when the Youngstown Sheet and Tube closing was removing $32 million from the public treasury, various relief programs—mainly Trade Readjustment Assistance (TRA)—were costing another $34 to $38 million.[76] By this accounting, the public loss from the shutdown could have reached nearly $70 million in slightly over three years. This amounts to more than $17,000 per displaced worker, very little of which was paid for by Lykes, the conglomerate owners who closed the mill.

A potential loss of the same magnitude, per worker, was calculated by the U.S. Department of Transportation (DOT) as part of the background material for the Chrysler Loan Guarantee Congressional debate. According to DOT estimates, the average federal cost for one displaced Chrysler worker adds up to $14,100 while the cost to the state government adds another $600.[77] Of this total, the average federal tax loss is judged to be $5,000 per worker, extended unemployment compensation $4,400, and TRA $4,700. The state's loss is credited exclusively to foregone state income and sales tax receipts.

These numbers may still underestimate the real net cost to the treasury, for they exclude other public transfers. For example, while the DOT assumes in its 1980 Auto Report that Chrysler workers will receive no food stamps, Medicaid, or welfare assistance, the same report suggests that the cost of these items may reach an average of $3,800 for workers displaced from related supplier plants. These workers are presumed to be lower-paid and therefore more likely to qualify for these benefits.

Yet there is ample evidence that these programs *are* used by auto workers and other higher-wage workers and their families when their incomes drop to the point where they are eligible for them. Despite eligibility for TRA and other income supplements, Aronson and McKersie found in the Westinghouse, GAF, and Brockway Motors cases in upstate New York that there was "a large rise in the monthly caseload of food stamps in Cortland County in the three months preceding the shutdown, and the demand remained high for the rest of 1977. . . . The increase in the monthly caseload for food stamps, from 275 in October 1976 to 590 in April 1977, is best viewed as a conjunction of factors, the most important of which was the Brockway termination."[78] The reason food-stamp demand remained high was that many Brockway workers were forced to take jobs that paid substantially below their previous rates and then needed to rely on food stamps to make up part of the difference.

Food-stamp benefits became a major source of income supplementation for the unemployed beginning with the 1975 recession, when the average number of persons participating in the program rose from about 12 million to more than 18 million in two years. By 1979 the average monthly benefit per person was over $30 and total program benefit costs reached $6.5 billion annually.[79]

Even the nation's basic welfare program for the impoverished, Aid to Families with Dependent Children (AFDC), appears to be used when workers lose their jobs. Detailed statistical analysis of the AFDC program has demonstrated a significant link between the level of unemployment in a community and the size of AFDC case loads. Using a "counterfactual" technique that asks what the AFDC case load would be if the unemployment rate were to reach a recession level (8 to 10 percent), researchers at the Social Welfare Research Institute at Boston College (SWRI) found that the number of recipients would be higher by 12 to 29 percent. In Georgia, for example, the case load would have increased from 109,300 to 129,600—or by 18.6 percent—in fiscal year 1974 under the recession level unemployment scenario. This would have cost the state of Georgia and the federal treasury that shares the AFDC costs almost $35 million in that one year. Similarly in New York City the case load would have been nearly 15.3 percent higher under these depressed conditions. Simulated annual expenditures for AFDC would have risen to over $1 billion in 1974, compared to the actual $880 million paid out.[80]

Sensitivity to employment conditions varied between the states, depending on the extent to which AFDC is used as a substitute for unemployment benefits. But in *every* jurisdiction studied, it was a statistically significant factor and usually a more powerful explanator of case-load levels than changes in the benefit level. To the extent that private disinvestment is a significant factor contributing to the elevation of local unemployment levels, AFDC costs are another community impact associated with deindustrialization.

This is apparently true even when the unemployment is concentrated among relatively high-skilled, well-paid workers. A corresponding SWRI study of the AFDC-UP program—the small public assistance program for *intact* families—showed that the depression that hit the aerospace industry in Seattle, Washington, in the early 1970s led to a boost in case-load and expenditure levels.[81] Employment plummeted by 60,000 in a matter of less than two years. Despite the fact that someone can receive AFDC-UP benefits only after exhausting every other income source and practically all family savings, 462 additional applications directly attributed to the layoffs were made to the UP program. Given the average annual AFDC-UP benefit at the time, these applicants cost over $1.2 million in aid. This is a small amount by comparison with unemployment insurance payments, but clearly not trivial for one city. Today, food stamps and Medicaid benefits would have been added to the total for these displaced workers.

It is not easy to calculate the total costs to society of the widespread unemployment caused by deindustrialization, but there are some estimates of the toll that unemployment takes on the federal government and hence on the taxpayer. Research by the U. S. Bureau of Economic Analysis suggests that in 1980 every percentage point increase in the unemployment rate reduced the nation's Gross National Product by $68 billion and cut federal tax receipts by $20.2 billion. At the same time that tax revenue was sharply lower, federal outlays automatically increased because of the added cost of unemployment benefits and other forms of assistance. Altogether, this cost taxpayers $4.1 billion including $2.4 billion in regular unemployment insurance benefits, nearly $500 million in extra food stamps, and almost $100 million in added AFDC benefits.[82] If the deindustrialization process has been responsible for boosting the average unemployment rate by three percentage points—from somewhere around 6 percent to something closer to 9 percent—then plant closings and other forms of disinvestment may be robbing the nation of $200 billion annually in foregone output, $60 billion in federal tax receipts, and forcing Americans to spend over $12 billion more each year in income assistance. This is obviously no small price to pay, and these figures do *not* include foregone taxes and added expenses for state and local governments.

The revenue and social expenditure costs to local, state, and federal treasuries constitute only the secondary effects of capital flight. In those communities where plant closings take with them a good portion of total local revenues, the entire public sector can suffer. Layoffs among police, fire, school, and sanitation workers are not uncommon in communities hard hit by such closings. This occurred in the Mahoning Valley following the rash of steel shutdowns in that area.[83]

It also happened in Detroit as a consequence of the auto crisis. There, hundreds of police officers were furloughed in September 1980 when the city faced imminent bankruptcy.[84] This was in addition to the more than 700 teachers dismissed by the city after the defeat of a property tax measure in August that was placed on the ballot by the City Council in a desperate move to find revenues to compensate for lost income taxes.[85] These cuts forced the city's school superintendent to reduce the school day at elementary schools by 25 minutes and by nearly an hour at all of the middle schools. Poor schools and inadequate police protection are the key factors behind middle-class flight to the suburbs. The fact that, today, Detroit has fewer city employees than it did thirty years ago cannot portend well for its ability to attract higher-income families—those families who can choose to go where there are quality services and a safe and secure community environment —back to the urban center.[86]

Community Anomie and "Anti-Union Animus"

Thus far, the quantifiable social impacts of business closings have been stressed. But other, and in some respects more profound, impacts are not so easily expressed in numbers—let alone in numbers of dollars.

In terms of a variety of standard indicators, the Brockway closing in upstate New York had a relatively minor impact on the Cortland County community. Nevertheless,

> The situation in Cortland appears to have had very adverse effects on the social cohesiveness of the community. A repeated assertion by members of the community was that: "the psychological effects outweighed the real effects" of the shutdown. Soon after the Brockway termination, a bumper sticker began to circulate that reflected this anomie—"The last person to leave Cortland please shut out the lights." The shutdown was coincident with the departure of the Montgomery Ward store from downtown Cortland, compounding the "depression psychology" prevalent in the community. The gas shortage, retrenchment in the [State University] system affecting Cortland State in 1977, the short work week of many municipal workers—all resulted in a poor job market for Cortland and impeded efforts to help the Brockway dischargees as a group with special needs.[87]

The state of "anomie" described for Cortland County—evident in community disorientation, anxiety, and isolation—is found almost universally in case studies of plant closings. Those who observed Hopedale, Youngstown, Anaconda, Detroit, Johnstown, Hartford County, and other communities hit by deindustrialization all come to the conclusion that the social "psyche" is damaged by the sudden loss of economic security. The damage, in many cases, has far-ranging consequences beyond the apparent emotional response of anger, frustration, or victimization. Victims lose faith in the "system," leading to a kind of dependency that precludes redevelopment of their communities. Although some struggle heroically to salvage what is left after a major shutdown, there is often the widespread attitude embodied in the statement of one victim: "We put thirty years into building this mill and this community, and it has all come to naught. I can't see that I've the energy to start all over again."

There is a strange silver lining behind all of this—for management. Compelling evidence exists that the layoffs created by plant closings can actually improve the business climate. The swelling of the ranks of the unemployed creates a reserve of malleable workers and even potential strikebreakers. The memory of such drastic dislocation can have what labor relations experts call a "chilling effect" on future labor-management negotiations. Surviving firms in the area gain the advantage of being able to hire the most highly skilled of the dischargees without having to bid them away from their former jobs. This obviously creates the conditions for the previously cited finding that workers experiencing sudden unemployment almost always suffer a significant drop in earnings, at least on their next job.

The strength of the labor relations impact of the three New York state plant closings studied by Aronson and McKersie seems to have especially impressed these researchers. With respect to the GAF closing in Binghamton, they note that "local union leadership felt that the uncertainty regarding GAF's future, and a pool of 1,100 potential strikebreakers in the displacees, severely constrained its ability to strike successfully."[88] In the wake of the Cortland shutdown, the researchers reported that they repeatedly encountered an "anti-union animus" related to the widespread belief in the community that it was "the local union's 'exhorbitant' demands and 'intransigent' position in the negotiations" before the shutdown that caused the closing.

> Further, it was rumored that the pall cast over other negotiations by this anti-union sentiment and the fear of job loss had induced other unions bargaining with local firms to settle negotiations quickly.[89]

Finally, perhaps the most "socially disconcerting" finding of all was the

> "blacklisting" of Brockway workers. . . . Employers were hesitant to hire persons accustomed to high wages and union benefits, while the community at large felt that the militant stance and strike by the union had caused the closing. In short "they got what they deserved."[90]

Conclusion

Whether it is "what they deserve," when deindustrialization occurs, the overwhelming weight of the evidence suggests that workers receive a heavy blow, only a part of which can be systematically quantified. A large majority of those directly affected endure at least temporary income loss, while a significant minority suffer long-term damage to their standards of living and to their physical and emotional well-being. Through the employment and income multiplier effects, a slew of innocent bystanders are victimized as well.

The Impact of Private Disinvestment on Workers

Deindustrialization affects each community and each individual in a different way. For communities that are experiencing growth in other sectors of their economy, the costs of plant closings are a lot less than for those already mired in a recession. Workers who possess skills that are in great demand are more readily re-employed than those whose skills are made obsolete by disinvestment. Minorities fare worse than whites; in general women fare worse than men. But no one is completely immune. Young workers who are just reaching the point where they have a toehold in the economy can be permanently set back by a plant closing. Middle-aged workers who have reached their peak earning years face giant reductions in income if they are forced out of the jobs where they have experience and still many potential years of productive employment. Older workers face the prospect of being "too old to find new work, but too young to die." Rural boomtowns gone "bust," like Anaconda, Montana, surrounded by mountains and sagebrush, face many of the same problems of older central cities that have lost their industrial base.

Finally, it should be noted that despite the high (personal) costs of disinvestment pictured here, the price paid by workers, their families, and their communities is likely to be much higher in the future. The precedent shattering reductions in social safety net programs passed by Congress in 1981—including restrictions on extended UIB, the virtual elimination of TRA, the reticence toward any further corporate bailouts, and state government initiatives to cut back on unemployment benefits—all suggest that from now on, deindustrialization will entail much more suffering for those who have the misfortune to experience it.

Chapter 4

Boomtown and Bust-town:
How the Market
Produces Reindustrialization

FEW PEOPLE, and certainly not those who have spent any time in cities like Youngstown and Detroit, or in towns like Anaconda, Montana, would deny that deindustrialization is an agonizing experience for the families and communities that must contend with it. Yet the belief lingers that disinvestment is somehow a necessary precondition for the constant renewal and reinvigoration of the economy. It is part of the grand scheme of creative destruction—a reminder that omelettes can be made only by cracking eggs.

The omelettes, in this case, are presumably cities like Houston, the southern metropolis that *U. S. News & World Report* claims is "bursting out all over." Houston is not a city, it declared,

> It's a phenomenon—an explosive, roaring urban juggernaut that's shattering traditions as it expands outward and upward with an energy that surprises even its residents . . . . Absorbing capital, people and new corporations like a sponge, Houston is constantly being reshaped—physically by the wrecking ball and new construction and culturally by newcomers with fresh ideas and philosophies.[1]

In a twenty-page special advertisement in *Fortune*, Houston recently paid tribute to itself as the new international city of America. The statistics are indeed impressive. By the end of 1980, Houston led the nation in "almost every economic indicator," including growth in population, employment, retail sales, and per capita income. It was first among the nation's cities in residential construction, and in the latter part of the 1970s, in overall construction. Office space tripled during the decade; bank deposits quadrupled. Office towers went up by the dozen, while millionaires were turned out as though on an assembly line. The spirit of prosperity lost elsewhere in the country seems to be incarnate in Houston. As one leading Texas architect put it, "People still think big and act big here. They have the confidence that the rest of the country seems to lack."[2]

The Quintessential Boomtown

In part, Houston is what *re*industrialization is all about. This exploding metropolis and cities like it have been able to attract billions of dollars of investment in practically no time at all. Between 1971 and 1978 alone, ninety-nine large firms moved into the city followed by thousands of smaller supplier establishments.[3] This created so many jobs that despite population growth of more than half a million residents during the 1970s, unemployment rates have generally remained below 4 percent. In 1979 the area's economy generated 79,000 new jobs, driving the jobless rate down to an extraordinary 2.6 percent. The nationwide unemployment rate was nearly three times larger.

By the middle of this decade, Houston will surpass Philadelphia in population, making it the nation's fourth largest city. Only New York, Los Angeles, and Chicago will be bigger; this will give each of the four census regions of the country its own natural "capitol city." Houston's 45 percent population boom during the last ten years contrasts with Frostbelt declines of 27 percent in St. Louis, 24 percent in Cleveland, and 23 percent in Buffalo. More than 1,000 new residents arrive every week, many making the same cross-country trek as Houston's founders —the Allen brothers from New York who bought the land site for $10,000 in 1836.[4]

Houston is perhaps not exactly typical of all the new boomtowns in America, but its evolution illustrates how reindustrialization is supposed to work. What has attracted capital and people to the city is its energy industry. It is a city built on oil. Thirty-four of the thirty-five largest U. S. petroleum companies have their headquarters there, or have major divisions for exploration, production, research, and marketing. Four hundred other oil companies and more than 1,600 suppliers and manufacturers of oil-related equipment have settled in the surrounding area, as have hundreds of marine service enterprises, drilling contractors, seismic companies, and pipeline installers. About 40 percent of the nation's oil is refined in Houston and the nearby Texas Gulf Coast. Altogether the area manufactures about 60 percent of the country's basic petrochemicals.[5] Based on this incredible wealth, the financial community has attracted foreign bankers from Germany, England, France, Saudi Arabia, Switzerland, Brazil, and Hong Kong. More than forty-five foreign banks are represented in the city.

Unabashedly the city boasts that "it is not just lukewarm towards business, it is *pro-business*" (emphasis theirs). Its advertisements placed in business journals to attract even more capital remind potential investors that "Texas is virtually a tax haven."[6] It is one of only four states in the nation without an income tax on corporate earnings and is one of just six states with no personal income tax. As a result, according to the U. S. Census Bureau, Houston's per capita tax burden is a mere $175 compared with New York City's $841 and Boston's $695. To add to its attractiveness, its workers' compensation costs are among the lowest in the nation, and it is one of the so-called right-to-work states that have outlawed the union shop.

With a pro-business climate to attract investment, the city's public relations office has only the job of convincing corporate executives— those who manage these investment dollars—that, despite the heat and humidity, Houston is a charming place to live. One advertisement, aimed particularly at those in the North, claims "everything is dehumidified and air conditioned" with a housing selection to meet every need. With ballet, opera, concerts, and theater, seven four-year colleges, and the largest medical complex in the world, the city's backers believe they have rounded up everything necessary to create "the good life" and to continue to attract capital and labor.

Houston is not alone in the burgeoning Sunbelt. Rapid economic growth has meant that family incomes in the South are quickly catching up with those in the rest of the country. Between 1953 and 1978 median family income, adjusted for inflation, rose by two thirds in the Northeast, the North Central states, and the West. But in the South, family incomes nearly doubled.[7] Whereas southern incomes averaged only 73 percent of those elsewhere in the country in 1953, by the dawn of the 1980s, they approached 90 percent. Moreover, between 1973 and 1978 while real incomes were actually falling outside the South, they were rising in the Sunbelt. The median family in the Northeast received 3.5 percent *less* real income in 1978, while the average southern family—despite double digit inflation—was able to enjoy a modest (2.3 percent) improvement over its 1973 income.

The standard of living in the South is actually better than these numbers indicate because living costs are so much lower. The Bureau of Labor Statistics estimates that in 1979 a family of four needed $19,025 to maintain an "intermediate" standard of living in Houston. To maintain the same standard in Boston cost $24,381 and in New York, $23,856.[8] The median family income in the South is 14.6 percent lower than that in the Northeast, but the budget requirement is 22 percent less in Houston. As a result, the typical family in this Sunbelt metropolis—despite its lower *money* income—enjoys 7.4 percent more real purchasing power than the median family in Beantown and 5.6 percent more than the same family in the Big Apple. For the wealthy in cities like Houston, the cost of living differential is even greater, proving what many boomtown residents already know—that it is cheaper to live high off the hog in Texas than in New York, Boston, or other northern cities. Excluding Anchorage and Honolulu, the cities of New York, Boston, and Washington, D. C. are the most expensive to live in (if you can afford an intermediate- or higher-budget standard of living) while three of the leading Sunbelt cities, Dallas, Atlanta, and Houston, are the cheapest. At an intermediate budget level, food costs in Houston are 8 percent lower, transportation costs are 13 percent lower, and housing costs and personal income taxes are less than half what they are in Boston. Boomtown growth seems to be the yellow brick road in the nation's otherwise gloomy economic landscape.

The "Downside" of the Boomtown Story

Indeed the economic juices of the nation seem to be flowing swiftly to areas like Houston, and millions of transient families are following the flow. Youngstown's loss seems to be Houston's gain, so that on average the nation prospers.

But does it? A closer look at America's new boomtowns suggests that not all is well there either. The movement of capital imposes enormous social costs on the "winners" just as it does on the "losers." Like the boomtowns of the nineteenth-century Wild West, much of the glitter is true gold, but not everyone in town is overjoyed with the social conditions that accompany its discovery.

No one can deny the fact that explosive economic growth in the Sunbelt has brought "the good life" to many of the region's residents and to those who have migrated to the area. Yet this is only one side of the Sunbelt story. To leave off here would be to totally ignore the other side of the "boomtown syndrome"—the often destructive consequences of unplanned rapid development.

With a deliberate policy of enacting no zoning laws and doing practically no planning, Houston and other boomtown cities have been virtually overrun by the influx of capital. Growth has occurred so rapidly and haphazardly that boomtown metropolises now paradoxically exhibit many of the same urban woes that plague northern central cities.[9] To most city planners, "Houston's sprawling growth represents how not to do it. In Houston, developers can build what they want, when they want, where they want. While such laissez faire certainly engenders boom-town vitality, it also creates boom-town problems."[10]

Among these are highway congestion, air pollution, water shortages, overcrowded schools, and a housing crisis marked by some real estate prices that have tripled in a matter of a few years. Twenty-five percent of the city's streets remained unlighted, 400 miles were unpaved, and 29 percent of the poor lived in substandard housing—even as recently as 1978.[11] Every day nearly 200 newly registered cars join the armada that clog Houston's freeways.[12] As a result, a commute that took thirty minutes five years ago takes an hour today. And there is no alternative way to get to work. What passes for the bus system, according to *Newsweek*, is "a joke"; the more charitable *Wall Street Journal* calls

it merely "decrepit."[13] Only eighty-two buses—four fifths of them paid
for by the federal government—serve Houston's 400,000 residents.[14]
This situation is typical of many Sunbelt cities built during the age of
the internal-combustion engine. In neighboring Albuquerque, New
Mexico, 95 percent of all trips in and around the metropolitan area are
done by car.

Other city services suffer as well. Annexation of suburban communities, combined with successful attempts at limiting property-tax levies
to lure yet more industry, leave many a boomtown with inadequate
revenues for even the most basic social services. This is certainly true
in Houston where there is only one policeman for every 600 people and
the average police response time to an emergency call is twenty-six
minutes.[15] (This amounts to one third of the police protection of
Philadelphia and less than half of that found in other big cities.)[16] The
frighteningly slow emergency response time in Houston is almost surely
due to the fact that a total of only seven police stations service the city's
556 square miles![17]

Yet perhaps the worst legacy of uncontrollable boomtown expansion is not in poor social services but in the violence done to a community's social fabric. As a consequence of the hyper-investment
boom, the disparity between rich and poor is becoming increasingly
evident throughout the Sunbelt, creating a dualism reminiscent of
the pre–Civil War South. In 1978 the richest 5 percent of the Sunbelt population enjoyed a far larger share (16.4 percent) of income
than the top 5 percent in any other region, and the bottom 20 percent have less (only 4.8 percent) than anywhere else.[18] The wealthiest one fifth of the southern population has nearly nine times the
aggregate income of the poorest fifth. Outside the South, that differential is 7.4 to 1.

Reflecting on these data, Georgia State Senator Julian Bond fears
"the creation of a permanent underclass in the new South."[19] *Fortune*
magazine, a champion of Sunbelt development, admits that the black
population (16 percent of the Sunbelt) has "scarcely shared in the
economic upsurge."[20] Again the statistics tell a gloomy story. In spite
of boom conditions all around them, over *one third* (35.1 percent) of
all blacks in the South—more than 4.8 million—were still below the
official poverty line in 1980. More than a quarter (27.3 percent) of what
the Census Bureau calls the "Spanish-origin" population shared the

same fate.[21] In Houston the poverty has been described in particularly graphic terms:

> Left behind in Houston's headlong flight toward growth and economic success are an estimated 400,000 people who live in a 73-square-mile slum that, says a college professor, has an infant mortality rate "that would have embarrassed the Belgian Congo."[22]

As a partial consequence of extreme income inequality, acutely visible in the juxtaposition of new industrial wealth and old rural squalor, the new boomtowns are experiencing a crime wave. In 1979, reports the FBI, Houston distinguished itself with one of the highest murder rates in the country: 40.4 killings per 100,000 residents, two thirds higher than New York City's homicide record.[23] It is at least partly for this reason that the Commission on the Future of the South—made up of bankers, a judge, college presidents, and regional politicians—concluded that the South is a "time bomb" ready to go off.[24] The unmet need for services for new residents is so staggering that the whole urban system may be on the brink of an explosion. The Fantus Company, which helps businesses select new plant locations, has even gone so far as to lower its official assessment of Houston's business climate, precisely because of poor public services.[25] The city's own residents agree. In a recent University of Houston survey, only 26 percent of those who live in the city now think the impact of rapid growth has been "good."[26]

Houston's problems are not unique. In many ways, they can be found in all of the boomtowns that have become the victims of too much unplanned development too fast. Atlanta has even sorrier stories to tell.[27] And so do many of the cities in Florida.[28] Every six minutes, the equivalent of a family of four moves to the Sunshine State seeking jobs or a retirement home. The new residents require housing, roads, schools, sewers, and water. Given the extremely fragile ecology of Florida, fresh water is a real problem—as it is in the booming Southwest. The Florida aquifer, the water table underlying the state, is down to its lowest level in recorded history. Fresh-water wells are being destroyed by salt-water seepage and some lakes are down by as much as 12 feet. Air pollution is killing Dade County's palm trees, while the state's rivers are dying of chemicals, sewer waste, and algae. The water and sewage system is simply overloaded and many experts fear a real environmental calamity. A leading Florida newspaper editor summed up his assessment of the situation to a group of state planners saying, "[Florida] is going to die of thirst or choke to death on a glut of people, exhaust fumes, concrete, and sewage unless the public wakes up."[29]

Silicon Valley, California, the bustling home of the computer "chip" in Santa Clara County, suffers from the same boomtown syndrome. At the end of World War II, Santa Clara County was known for its fruit orchards and Stanford University. Today, it is blanketed with 500 electronics firms that make components for everything from the cruise missile to Space Invader computer games. Between 1960 and 1975, employment in the valley grew by 156 percent—three times the national rate and twice that of California.[30] High-tech workers flocked into the area the way that retirees headed for Florida. And with the influx came the same problems.

By 1980 there were over 670,000 jobs, but only 480,000 housing units in the county. As a result the *average* price for a house soared to well over $100,000.[31] Cheaper houses were bid up in price so rapidly that low-income families were displaced in the process. With no viable mass transit, the freeways became jammed and the average commuting time reached three hours or more for workers living in the southern parts of the county. Federal air-quality standards are now violated at least 10 percent of the time. With land prices out of control and the air spoiled, the fruit orchards have entirely disappeared.[32]

This drama of industrialization that has gone haywire seems quite ubiquitous across the Sunbelt. University of California regional economist Ann Markusen estimates that between 5 and 15 million Americans are now involved in rapid-growth boomtowns in the Southwest and Mountain states alone.[33] In many of the thousands of smaller communities, particularly where new capital-intensive energy investment is leading to exaggerated boom-bust cycles, long-time residents are finding themselves evicted from their homes, and the competition for land is resulting in the direct displacement of agricultural and tourist related jobs. The newly introduced production techniques and skill requirements often mean that the higher-wage jobs created in the capital-intensive sector are not available to those who lose their jobs in more traditional lines of work.[34] Indeed, as will be discussed later in this chapter, much of this high-tech development often leads to job creation for technicians and managers brought into the area by the companies, *not* for local residents. This population influx places added stress on a city or town's existing school, water, and sanitation services —usually at the expense of those same local citizens who could not obtain the jobs.

There has never been a comprehensive or systematic cost-benefit analysis of the boomtown syndrome. But economists and sociologists have at least devoted some attention to particular case studies of economic expansion. From these we can hazard some generalizations about the costs of rapid economic development. One group of sociologists, led by Gene Summers of the University of Wisconsin, has recently compiled evidence from 186 case studies of what they term the "industrial invasion of nonmetropolitan America." They found that the net gains from boomtown development are not anywhere near as great as most people imagine. In the majority of cases only a small proportion of the new jobs created are filled by previously unemployed persons. In thirteen studies that examined this specific question (excluding one special case in which the Area Redevelopment Administration stipulated the hiring of unemployed workers as a *quid pro quo* for federal grant support), the proportion of jobs filled by the previously unemployed was less than 11 percent.[35] What employment opportunities are created by the establishment of a new plant are often taken by workers from outside the immediate area, both commuters and inmigrants. "Possessing more education, better skills, or the 'right' racial heritage, these newcomers intervene between the jobs and the local residents, especially the disadvantaged."[36]

Of course, other jobs are created in the process of new plant location through the ripple effect described in the previous chapter. These are mostly in wholesale and retail trade and in services. But even there the net gain is not as great as normally imagined, for in half of all the case studies of new industrial development, the estimated employment multiplier is below 1.2. That is, ten new jobs in a new manufacturing firm generate, in the majority of cases, less than two new *local* jobs in other sectors. Part of the reason for the low local multiplier effect is that new establishments that are part of a larger firm or conglomerate tend to use the services of suppliers that are already doing business with the home office rather than ones from the local community. Another reason is that commuters tend to patronize retail establishments in their home towns rather than where they work. Moreover, in many communities where the process of industrialization is just beginning, there is surplus capacity in the retail trade and service sector that can absorb some of the new growth.

One surprising finding is how often new industrial development fails to reduce measured unemployment at all. To be sure, in two thirds of the case studies unemployment rates declined after new industry came to town. But in most cases the impact on unemployment was less than 1 percentage point.[37] Regional experts believe this is due to the fact that the perceived promise of new jobs slows the rate of outmigration, causes local labor-force participation to increase, and attracts inmigrants who take a disproportionate share of the new opportunities.

In light of these private sector impacts, it is useful to consider the net gain to the public sector. Here the sociologists are in near agreement. New industry clearly is associated with an increase in the public sector costs of delivering basic services to residents. Utilities, especially water and sewage, appear to be the primary source of increased local cost. The need for new roads, schools, and police and fire protection is also important. What makes matters worse is that since industry is often attracted through the provision of tax holidays and other incentives, the revenue generated by new establishments is often not sufficient to pay for the increased service needs. As a result, the overall net gain of boomtown growth is often small, and sometimes even negative.

The unrealized burden of boomtown expansion goes beyond that which is easily measured. Paradoxically, both the physical and emotional health consequences of boomtown developments turn out to be similar to those found in communities like Youngstown and Akron that experience acute capital loss. El Dean V. Kohrs, for example, finds that unplanned expansions

> always seem to leave in their wake the grim statistics of mental depression, family disorganization, emotional damage, alcoholism, delinquency, and dissipation. These boomtown crises are not new to rural America, but the social consequences are becoming clearer today, and they are being felt in more parts of the country . . .[38]

A growing segment of the population in the Sunbelt now recognizes the immense social costs that accompany unplanned and anarchic hyper-investment. They are being forced to pay for some of these costs through rapidly rising tax rates, although until recently they were getting the federal government to pick up a large share.[39] With the new Reagan "federalism" forcing local communities to shoulder more of the fiscal burden, the contradictions of boomtown growth are becoming more evident. "Deep inside," notes Juan de Torres, an economist for the Conference Board, "the people of the South simply don't want their areas to grow any larger."[40] The boomtown expansion has simply been too rapid for the city's public services, the environment, and the people themselves.

The Costs of Reindustrializing the North

The Sunbelt does not hold claim to being the only region of the country undergoing economic change with its accompanying social benefits and social costs of boomtown development. Just in the last half decade, led by New England, older Frostbelt areas of the nation have begun to bounce back to life after decades of industrial decline. Given up as permanently comatose, these "mature" economies have begun to rebound on the strength of industries that did not even exist before World War II. The region's reindustrialization effort appears to be confirmed by both a dramatic decline in the official unemployment rate and—until very recently—daily newspaper reports of record sales and profits in the region's new high-tech industries that manufacture and service computers, jet engines, medical instruments, and a broad range of equally sophisticated products.[41]

For those caught up in the euphoric revitalization in New England, there are indeed some encouraging trends. Unemployment rates that reached over 15 percent as late as 1975—nearly two thirds above the U. S. average—are now among the lowest of the industrialized states. By 1981 the economy had improved enough for Massachusetts to boast about its unemployment rate, the second lowest among the leading manufacturing states and only slightly higher than that in booming Texas. Even the central cities were experiencing a renaissance, according to most press accounts. New York City, only hours away from total bankruptcy in 1975 with $13 billion in outstanding accumulated debt, reported a budget surplus in 1980. While the city lost 500,000 jobs between 1969 and 1976, its jobless rate fell to 7.3 percent in mid-1980, only slightly above the national average. In other northeastern cities there are also signs of rebirth. For example, no fewer than seven brand-new hotels were going up in downtown Boston during the summer of 1981.

This resurgence of economic activity follows a period that saw the leading industries of New England—apparel, textiles, and shoes—all but disappear. In 1940 more than one in five workers in the region were employed in such mill-based industries as textiles, apparel, and shoe manufacture. By 1977 this proportion was down to one in ten. With the bankruptcy of one mill after another, and the relocation of the survivors to the South, there was little around to re-employ those who had toiled in semiskilled blue-collar occupations in once thriving cities such as Fall River, Lowell, and Lawrence, Massachusetts. Block after block of enormous factory buildings lay empty. Employment in women's apparel plants plummeted from over 80,000 in 1959 to less than 36,000 in 1975; one third of all shoe industry jobs disappeared in the same period, as did one third of those in paper mills.[42] Because of industry declines like this, New England's unemployment rate remained almost continuously above the national average through the end of 1977.[43]

The coming of age of the computer, and particularly the development of the "mini-computer," appears on the surface to have changed all of this. Based on its high concentration of university research centers surrounding Harvard, M.I.T., and Northeastern (to name the most prominent in the engineering field), the area around Boston became an incubator for new high-tech firms that spun off from the research laboratories into production. Led by Digital Equipment, Prime Computer, Data General, and Wang, employment in this sector expanded rapidly.[44] In Massachusetts, employment in office machines and computers exploded by 43 percent in a twenty-four month period between the end of 1976 and 1978. Computer-programming services grew by nearly 65 percent while employment in engineering and scientific-instrument firms expanded by more than 70 percent.[45] Overall, in just two year's time more than 47,000 jobs in Massachusetts' high-tech firms were generated, an increase of 22.4 percent. High tech became to New England what oil is to Houston.

Based at least partly on this new growth node, other industries in New England blossomed. Employment in department stores doubled between 1959 and 1976, while the number of hospital jobs rose to more than 171,000 from less than 81,000. There was also associated expansion in business services, from hotels and motels (to house visiting businessmen and conventioneers) to banking services and insurance. By the end of the decade, it seemed that reindustrialization through the private market was really working. But was it?

Compared to the 15-percent unemployment rates in the mid-1970s, all of this economic activity was naturally welcomed by New Englanders and applauded by its political leaders (who in fact frequently claimed credit for it!). Yet, the type of reindustrialization that is occurring in this region leaves much to be desired—in very much the way that boomtown growth leaves Sunbelt cities and towns often reeling under the influence of a too rapid capital influx. Here the problem is less a matter of too much capital, as it is the types of jobs that the capital creates. The jobs in the new high-tech industries and in the retail trade and personal service sectors do not come close to making up for the jobs lost through deindustrialization of the mill-based economy.

There are at least five problems with the reindustrialization now occurring in New England. The first is that despite massive job creation, wage levels have actually fallen relative to other regions (including the South), especially in terms of purchasing power. The second is that the type of economic development occurring in the region is producing an increasingly unequal distribution of income, both between and within (most) industries. Third, employment is becoming more unstable in several respects: there is a growing incidence of part-time and part-year jobs in many cases where full-time jobs are desired; the degree of employee turnover is extremely high; and some of the growing industries (for example, aircraft engines) are subject to sharp boom-bust swings in output and employment that produce grave insecurity among those who do find jobs. Fourth, there appear to be significant barriers to upward mobility for many of the region's workers—especially those who once worked in the mill industries. Finally, there is a tendency for the fastest growing industries to continue to undergo geographical restructuring, subjecting the region to the same dispersal of production and employment it suffered earlier in apparel, textiles, and shoes. Of course, as was seen in chapter 2, the process has become more complex than in the days of the old runaways, but the bottom line is ultimately the same: jobs, income, and taxes are shifted to some other region.

Examining this in more detail helps to explain why even under the best circumstances, this type of reindustrialization does not compensate for the losses suffered as a result of prolonged disinvestment. Take the proliferation of low-wage jobs. While some of the new high-tech companies pay at least as much as the old mill-based jobs, the majority of all new employment is in the service sector of the economy, where the pay is extremely low. By 1977 over half of all New England jobs were in the service sector, while only one eighth were to be found in the high technology field. Even during the computer boom of the late 1970s, three new jobs were created in other sectors of the Massachusetts' economy for every one job created in the high-tech area.[46] Many of the former were in retail trade and personal services where wage rates are pegged to the statutory minimum. As a result, the majority of the jobs created in the course of New England's economic renaissance are hardly sufficient to provide an adequate standard of living for the normal-sized family. Most pay significantly less than the jobs they replaced in the mill industries. A family is required to take two full-time jobs at a McDonald's fast food outlet or in a discount department store to make up for the loss of one job in a unionized woolen mill.

What is being generated in New England is a "dual economy." On the one hand, high-tech developments are creating some relatively high-wage jobs (many of which are taken by well-educated inmigrants to the area). On the other, a large number of low-wage jobs are being generated in the retail trade and service sectors of the economy. Moreover, the impact of technological and organizational changes in both manufacturing and services seems to have tended to eliminate (or downgrade) those jobs that fall in the middle of the skill (and wage) spectrum.

Because of this job pattern, reindustrialization relying exclusively on the private sector has brought with it an increasing inequality in the distribution of earnings. This can be seen both within and across industries in New England. The same Social Security file used in chapter 3 to examine the destinations of those who lost their jobs in the aircraft industry, can be used to measure the change in the earnings distribution between 1957 and 1975. Table 4.1 presents median earnings and a standard measure of inequality, the Gini index,* for all workers covered by Social Security in New England and for workers in selected industries in the region.[47]

Earnings inequality grew substantially in nine of the thirteen industries shown, and only declined in two. But what is perhaps most important is that inequality increased *most* both in those industries at the heart of the reindustrialization boom—office machines and computers and electronic components—and in the most rapidly growing trade

TABLE 4.1

The Growth in Earnings Inequality in the New England Economy Among Year-Round Workers: 1957–75

	Year and Earnings			
	1957–58		1975	
Industry	Median	Gini	Median	Gini
All covered employment	$3,640	.332	$8,270	.381
Manufacturing				
Women's outerwear	2,170	.325	5,135	.352
Paper mills	4,425	.187	11,430	.188
Commercial printing	4,135	.315	9,830	.279
Shoes	2,720	.286	5,600	.315
Metalworking machinery	4,980	.270	11,290	.294
Office machines and computers	4,010	.184	10,840	.287
Electronic components	3,740	.293	7,040	.328
Aircraft engines	5,000	.197	13,150	.217
Non-manufacturing				
Department stores	2,305	.386	4,616	.443
Supermarkets	2,860	.367	4,680	.430
Commercial banks	3,080	.296	7,375	.302
Hotels and motels	1,880	.364	4,010	.398
Hospitals	2,365	.323	7,440	.310

SOURCE: Computations by Alan Matthews, Social Welfare Research Institute, Boston College, using Social Security Administration's *Longitudinal Employer-Employee Data File*, containing a 1 percent sample of the Social Security records of all covered employees who ever worked inside New England between 1957 and 1975. Table includes only wages and salaries actually earned in New England for workers who were employed in all four accounting quarters of the year.

* The Gini index, a measure of distribution commonly used by social scientists, is constructed so that increases in its value signify growing inequality while decreases indicate a more equal distribution. The range in Gini values is bounded by 0 and 1. When the index is 0, there is perfect equality—each individual receives an equal amount of resources. When the index equals 1, there is "perfect inequality" where one individual receives everything and all others get nothing.

sectors—department stores, supermarkets, and hotels and motels. This is what is producing the dual economy characterized by a large low-wage sector for the lesser skilled and a high-wage sector for those with substantial training. For anyone caught in between, there is unfortunately little middle ground—the types of jobs that once were provided by the mill-based economy. The Gini index for "all covered employment" sums up the situation quite well. It increased from .332 in 1957–58 to .381 in 1975, a 15 percent increase in relative earnings inequality of year-round workers in less than a generation.

For those displaced from the old mill-based industries, reindustrialization has created a serious problem. With a "missing middle" in the economy, the loss of a mill job has meant that the newly unemployed worker either had to make the leap up to the higher-skill jobs in the top end of the labor market or settle for work that is lower-skill, lower-wage, and more unstable. Making the transition to the new jobs in computer programming, systems installation, and technical consulting has not proven easy for many of them.

Again the Social Security file is helpful, supplying answers to some pertinent questions about mobility. What has happened to those workers who eventually left (or were displaced from) the old mill industries? How many were able to find jobs in the new high-tech companies or in the highly unionized, high-paying engineering industries? How many were forced to accept jobs in the predominantly low-wage and more unstable services, where they probably had to take wage cuts? And finally, from what industries and from where do the new high-tech industries recruit their new work forces?

Consider the 833,200 people in the New England LEED sample whose principal activity in 1958 was to work in the mill industries. In the period after 1958, as continuing deindustrialization swept through the sector, 674,000 of them left the mills. By 1975 only 18,000 of this group—fewer than 3 percent—were employed in the high-tech industries of the region. (Another 2,000 had migrated to high-tech jobs outside New England.) More than five times as many ended up in trade and service jobs, either inside or outside of the region. A huge number dropped out of the labor force (or went into jobs not covered by Social Security). In essence, as chapter 3 revealed, losing one's job as a result of deindustrialization tends to propel one downward in the industry hierarchy toward lower productivity jobs—not upward.[48]

By contrast, the high-tech companies in New England tend to recruit young, inexperienced people out of school or out of the home, especially women. They also typically recruit their most experienced workers from each other, or from outside the region. Of the roughly 353,000 high-tech employees in New England in 1975, over 200,000 entered the civilian labor force after 1958. Another 56,000 came to their current high-tech employer from other high-tech firms and 34,000—nearly one tenth of the work force—migrated into New England to take jobs there. A scant 19,000 made their way up from the service sector in New England into high tech.

Thus despite the favorable unemployment rate statistics, reindustrialization like that occurring in New England leaves most former mill workers *outside* the mainstream of the new economic base. The transfer from the deindustrialized sector to the newly invigorated parts of the economy affects only a minuscule number of those bumped from what had been the very core of the traditional economy. At best, reindustrialization of that region seems to have created jobs for the sons and daughters of those displaced, but not for the generation that actually worked in the mills. In this sense, reindustrialization may work out as in the textbooks, but it takes a generation to succeed. Moreover, the vast majority of jobs created—those responsible for lowering the official unemployment rate—are found in the lower-wage, more unstable sectors of the economy. This explains the continuing erosion of relative incomes in the ostensibly reinvigorated New England region, the growing disparity in worker earnings and family incomes, and the continued need for high levels of public assistance and other forms of social safety net programs.

This side of reindustrialization is often hidden from view. It suggests that whatever the merits of industrial reinvigoration, the process itself does not come close to compensating the victims of disinvestment. The group of winners in this game appears to be very different from the group of losers. From neither the perspective of social justice nor, for that matter, of social efficiency can this type of reindustrialization be judged adequate for coping with the trauma of large-scale regional disinvestment.

Is Migration the Solution?

For those who can no longer make a living in the deindustrialized regions (or sectors) of the economy, the standard prescription in free enterprise economies has always been: move. One is supposed to pick up stakes and set out for newer and greener pastures. The massive wave of migration to the Sunbelt, despite its impact on Sunbelt communities themselves, is presumably just what the economy needs.

Indeed the migration to the Sunbelt has been astounding. Between 1970 and 1979 almost 7 million people moved to the South from other regions of the country. Another 4.7 million moved to the West.[49] This stream of migrants is so vast that if they all had come from the six New England states, this entire region would have been left without a single man, woman, or child. Of course there was outmigration from the Sunbelt states and return migration to areas like New England. Still, from population movements alone, the South and West had a *net* gain of nearly 3.7 million during the 1970s (see table 4.2).

TABLE 4.2
Regional Migration Patterns: 1970–74 and 1975–79
(in thousands)

	Northeast	North Central	South	West
1970–74:				
Immigration	1,035	1,800	3,377	2,141
Outmigration	1,993	2,512	2,312	1,536
Net Migration	−958	−712	+1,065	+605
1975–79:				
Immigration	1,035	1,830	3,585	2,552
Outmigration	2,138	2,737	2,513	1,615
Net migration	−1,103	−907	+1,072	+937

SOURCE: U. S. Department of Commerce, Bureau of the Census, "Geographical Mobility: March 1975 to March 1979," in *Current Population Reports*, (Washington D.C.: U.S. Government Printing Office, 1973), Series P-20, no. 353, table A, p. 1.

The rapid pace of migration during the first half of the decade was actually eclipsed by the number of movers in the second half (reinforcing the conjecture that the annual job losses in the 1969–76 period reported in chapter 2, large as they were, were still not as great as the number at the end of the decade). Eight percent, or almost one in every twelve Americans sixteen years of age and older, in 1979 were living in a different state in 1979 from where they had lived just five years earlier.

The Frostbelt states of the Northeast and the North Central regions were the big losers to the South and the West. Over 1.2 million people left the Northeast for the South between 1975 and 1979, while nearly 1.5 million left the Midwest for the same southern destinations. Another 1.6 million northerners left for the West during this restless period.

Presumably a good number of these migrants were fleeing the towns and cities where automobile, steel, and tire plants were closing. In search of jobs, they sought the Sunbelt's opportunities in the very places mentioned at the beginning of this chapter: Houston, Albuquerque, Phoenix, Silicon Valley, and Dade County. Yet despite the extraordinary levels of unemployment in states such as Michigan and Ohio, nearly a million people moved (or returned) from the South to the North Central region and another 620,000 came to the Northeast. Something about the North was certainly attractive, or something about the Sunbelt was overrated.

Interstate mobility is by no means equal across age groups or income classes. Generally lower-income families tend to migrate more than those at the higher end of the income spectrum. Likewise younger families tend to be the most mobile. In 1979 very young, predominantly newly-formed, families with incomes under $5,000 were nearly five times as likely to move between states as were families whose head was between 45 and 54 years of age and whose income was in excess of $25,000.[50] This trend is perhaps natural, for younger families often try out various labor markets. Older adults are more likely to be established in their careers and settled in a neighborhood with a house they own. They are less inclined to move because they have more invested there, both emotionally and financially.

Geographical mobility is nothing new to Americans. After all, America is a nation of immigrants. Between 1820 and 1978 nearly 49 million people emigrated to the United States.[51] The number of immigrants peaked during the first decade of this century when 8.8 million people arrived at Ellis Island in New York, the Port of Galveston in Texas, and through the Golden Gate in San Francisco. During that single decade, America's population swelled by over 11 percent simply as a consequence of this influx.

There are many reasons for this, as well as other, waves of migration. The Pilgrims emigrated to escape religious persecution. Africans were forced to emigrate here as slaves. The Irish fled their homeland to avoid starvation. The Chinese were often impressed into the merchant marine. Later groups would come to flee what they saw as government persecution—Russians in the last days of the czar, the Hungarians in 1956, wealthy Cubans after the 1959 revolution, and now the Haitians escaping the tyrannical rule of their native island and the Vietnamese their war-torn country.

To be sure, other groups emigrated not for religious or political reasons, but to improve their standards of living. The Italians, for example, came in the early twentieth century to seek jobs in America's booming industrial sector. More recently, Mexicans, Puerto Ricans, and Jamaicans came hoping to emulate the experience of groups such as the Italians, only to find that their arrival fifty years later coincided with the demise of the industrial base and the rise of the low-wage service economy. As a result they generally failed to obtain the upward mobility experienced by many earlier immigrant groups.

"Push" and "Pull" Factors in Domestic Migration

Each of these examples illustrates the two leading theories used to explain geographical mobility. One theory suggests that population movements can be understood best in terms of "push" factors at the place of emigration—religious, political, or economic pressures. Where people emigrate is of less consequence as long as the level of "persecution" there is less. The other theory suggests that "pull" factors are what really count. People actively search for "greener pastures" and when they find them, they move. From this obviously simplistic view of mobility, it would probably seem that the Pilgrims, the Irish, the Russians, the Hungarians, the Cubans, the Haitians, and the Vietnamese were pushed out of their homelands, while the Italians, Jamaicans, Mexicans, and Puerto Ricans could not resist the pull of American wage levels.

An analysis of migration *within* the United States finds some of the same forces at work. Blacks, as freed slaves, moved north during Reconstruction to escape the political violence of the Ku Klux Klan even when job opportunities above the Mason-Dixon line were not particularly good. Yet, in general, Americans in the work force move for economic, not political reasons, and with the possible exceptions of the allure of Hollywood and retirement places in the sun, most movement appears to be a reaction to bad economic conditions at home rather than potentially good conditions elsewhere. John Steinbeck commented on this in *The Grapes of Wrath*: the Joad family, Okies of the Great Depression, moved West not because California was paved with gold, but because Oklahoma was paved with dust.

The newest and most sophisticated economic studies of why families move seem to corroborate this. For example, based on data covering the years 1968 to 1972, Julie DaVanzo finds that "unemployment or dissatisfaction with a job does 'push' a family to move . . . [and] recent arrivals to an area who cannot find acceptable employment are especially prone to move again."[52] In contrast, workers with jobs will seldom sacrifice them in order to move even when other locations offer higher wage rates or lower unemployment. In economic terms, staying rather than moving is a "normal good"; unless there are extraordinarily compelling economic reasons for moving, people generally prefer to remain where they are. Migration is an "inferior good," meaning that most migration is, at least partly, coerced by economic conditions. The 32 to 38 million jobs lost when plants closed during the 1970s would obviously qualify as supplying these conditions.[53]

There are a sufficient number of reasons why migration, for the most part, is an inferior good. Following DaVanzo, and the earlier research of John Lansing and Eva Mueller and of Michael Greenwood, seven reasons can be listed: (1) direct costs (actual outlays for transportation and moving of belongings); (2) information costs; (3) emotional costs; (4) opportunity costs (earnings foregone) while moving or looking for a new job; (5) loss of friendships and community ties; (6) costs of disposing of assets (selling a house); and (7) financing costs.[54]

Most of these are obvious. Moving, particularly when a person is settled—and especially when he or she owns a house (with an 8 percent mortgage!)—involves at least short-run moving and possibly long-run financing costs. The time and effort of packing up belongings and moving each time a better job offer comes along is clearly expensive. Just finding out about possible job offers, particularly if they are clear across the country, can be costly. So can lost earnings if search for a new job requires forfeiting the old one.

Psychological costs and the loss of friendships and community ties cannot be easily measured, but clearly they also are critical. The longer a person has been in the same place, the more costly these are to bear. Lansing and Mueller found from their own interviews that 12 percent of all moves were made "to be closer to other family members" and not necessarily for any economic reason.[55] Studies by Ruth Fabricant and by Philip Nelson suggest the importance of emotional costs in deterring migration.[56] And the high return migration rates noted in most studies reflect this phenomenon.

The personal costs of migration that induce workers to remain where they are suggest something quite important about capital mobility and labor's attempts to keep up with it: migration is by far a "second best" solution to the problem of disinvestment. According to proponents of rapid capital transfer, deindustrialization in a particular region provides an *opportunity* for workers to move into more productive roles in the economy. What the actual data on migration tend to show is that the costs of taking advantage of that opportunity—if it exists at all—are by no means small. When workers are allowed to retain their jobs and remain in their communities, even in the presence of higher-wage job opportunities elsewhere, they generally opt to do so. This appears to be a perfectly rational choice, given the fact that the sum total of measurable plus unmeasurable psychological costs can easily outweigh the value of better paid jobs.

This all boils down to the strong inference that an immense number of workers are being *forced* to move each year, not because of the positive pull of Sunbelt opportunities, but because of the push of economic dislocation at home—notably including plant closings. This can hardly qualify most migration as "voluntary," except in a most disingenuous sense. The glorious image of workers moving freely along the golden road to new jobs and higher standards of living is certainly tarnished by the fact that many of those who respond to economic incentives to move often respond out of desperation rather than hope.

The Social Costs of Migration

Besides the personal costs of migration, there exists a host of social costs that can hardly be overlooked. One is that migration is concentrated among younger, better educated, and often more highly productive workers. These will be the first workers attracted away from areas where labor demand is growing slowly to areas where it is increasing most rapidly. The selective character of migration results in growing interregional wage differentials. This can lead, as the eminent Swedish economist Gunnar Myrdal has suggested, to uneven development rather than a closing of the gap between rich and poor.[57]

This has already occurred in areas hard hit by fiscal crisis or by extensive plant closings. Those who are young and can find jobs in new communities will tend to migrate, while older workers, the elderly, and those only peripherally attached to the labor force tend to remain. This makes it extremely difficult for affected communities to bounce back, for they no longer command the labor resources that make a particular location attractive to potential business. Certainly this is part of the explanation for the continued deterioration of central cities in many parts of the country, and in some cases for entire industrial regions.

There are other social costs as well. Regions that lose people whose education has been financed by local taxation forfeit the ability to tax the resulting higher income and are therefore unable to recoup the costs of their educational investment.[58] This is part of the so-called brain drain that has plagued Third World countries in the past and now threatens the educational systems in many Frostbelt communities.

Finally, there are the consequences for social services and the environment discussed at length earlier both in this chapter and in the previous one. Whenever there is rapid migration into an area, congestion is likely to increase, and more public services must be provided. Excess capacity, and hence, waste, will develop in the production of social services (schools, health, sanitation) in areas from which people are moving, and new investment in social services will be needed in areas to which they go.

Thus the creation of an "industrial refugee class" of millions of displaced workers seeking jobs in new locations and new communities has both personal and social costs well beyond what the proponents of rapid deindustrialization often suggest. The costs of migration must now be added to the personal and social costs incurred by communities undergoing deindustrialization and to the same costs incurred by the boomtowns of the Sunbelt and other areas undergoing rapid industrialization. Taken as a whole, these costs surely suggest that the magnitude and speed of capital mobility in America now far exceed what might be called a socially-manageable level.

The "Socially-Manageable Velocity" of Capital

Whether economic growth is good or bad for a community obviously rests in part on a question of "capital velocity"—the missing element in the investment/disinvestment debate. The relative value of social benefit to social cost depends to a great extent on whether there is sufficient time allowed for the effects of capital disinvestment to dissipate or for the effects of new investment to be absorbed. None of the economists who are enthusiastic proponents of unrestricted capital mobility seem to have taken this into account.

In the case of communities losing capital, the social problems attending disinvestment occur in their most drastic form when the loss is precipitous and unexpected. People have no chance to prepare for the deindustrialization process or to obtain the training and skills necessary to be reabsorbed successfully into the dynamic sectors of the economy. At the same time, the public sector loses an immediate source of revenue, making it difficult to provide public services when they are needed the most. Obviously, societies must struggle to identify a sensible, socially-manageable *speed* of disinvestment: certainly something less than the velocity of a telex message from central headquarters to a local unit, ordering it to shut down operations.

In a country like Sweden where an active employment and training policy exists, where as many as 2 to 3 percent of the work force at any single time are in training for new occupations in new industries, the investment/disinvestment process can proceed more swiftly without generating the same social costs likely to exist in a country where retraining has a lower priority. Similarly, with its commitment to continual full employment, Japan is (so far) better able to absorb rapid economic change than is the United States, where high levels of unemployment have become a fact of life.

The same issue of socially-manageable velocity applies to boomtown growth. How much expansion can be absorbed, and how quickly, depends on the dynamics of the people and the environment of the community involved. Clearly there is a problem of growth in Florida where the water table is perpetually under attack. The same is true of the dry Southwest. With suitable planning and reasonable forecasts, new schools can be built, teachers hired, roadways, water, and sewage systems constructed, and job training designed to meet the needs of both industry and the work force. But when the capital influx is totally unrestrained, the absorptive capacity of the social system can be quickly overwhelmed.

The two poles of the development cycle—investment and disinvestment—obviously are related to each other. While it might seem that there is no need to think of the two in strict zero-sum terms, or to suggest that investment in one place absolutely requires disinvestment elsewhere, there is in fact a historical tendency for this phenomenon to occur under capitalism (this will be examined in detail in the next two chapters). Growth in the Sunbelt, for example, *is* surely happening at the expense of the Frostbelt, just as growth in the new cities *within* the South tends to take place at the expense of the rural areas there.

If the velocity of capital mobility were to fall within the absorptive capacity of both the losing and gaining communities, then a rearrangement of investment might lead to some sort of "balanced" development. However, when the pace of capital mobility exceeds a socially-manageable level, the result simply reproduces a pattern of uneven and unequal development as serious as the initial pattern that set that capital in motion in the first place. In the losing area incomes plummet and existing social (not to mention physical) structures decay and crumble from lack of use. In the gaining area incomes rise, but very unequally, and social structures are taxed beyond their capacity. Once the boom begins, it may go even beyond the point where exorbitant costs cause a reassessment of private investment decisions. Likewise, deindustrialization may spiral downward well beyond the point where new investment is warranted, before there is any correction by the private market. This sort of overshooting—analogous to a faulty thermostat that reacts too slowly to changes in the temperature of the room —has been shown to characterize a wide variety of interregional growth situations, from the United States to southern Europe, Latin America, and Southeast Asia.[59]

Conclusion

The private market may eventually provide the "right" investment signals, as true believers in the "invisible hand" have always maintained. But the sticky point lies in the word "eventually." The massive social costs of deindustrialization and boomtown growth suggest that "eventually" may be too far in the future to be of much comfort to the residents of Youngstown or, for that matter, Houston. The unprecedented rapidity with which American corporate managers have been shifting capital from one place or sector to another is certainly to blame for the social violence that we see in ghost towns and boomtowns alike. It is precisely in this sense that capital mobility is now occurring too fast.

PART III

Why and How the
American Economy
Is Undergoing
Deindustrialization

Chapter 5

Corporate Strategy
and Government Policy
During the *Pax Americana*:
1946–71

WHY ARE entire industries undergoing systematic dismantling in all parts of the country? Why are so many leading U. S. corporations refusing to reinvest in the upgrading of their older facilities in the nation's basic sectors? Why do they prefer instead to acquire already existing plants, to diversify into unrelated activities, or to go abroad *instead* of building at home? It is clear that the deindustrialization of America is having severe repercussions on working people and their communities. But why is it occurring at all? And why *now*?

In one way or another, most of the existing explanations of deindustrialization—by authors like George Gilder, Jude Wanniski, Arthur Laffer, Amitai Etzioni, David Stockman, Jack Kemp, and even to some extent Lester Thurow—revert to the time-honored practice of blaming the victim. The stagnation of American productivity and the erosion of corporate profits, which have led companies to shift their capital out of older sectors and locations, all too often are at-

tributed to the selfishness, impecunity, or just plain lack of motivation of American workers (or to the incompetence of their elected
governments).[1]

We have a different notion of "the way the world works." To
understand deindustrialization requires a careful analysis of modern
corporate managerial strategies in the context of an increasingly interdependent and competitive global economic system. We need to examine three interrelated phenomena: the struggles between firms for
shares of the market, the conflicts between employers and workers over
wages and profits, and the role that government plays in mediating
these crucial contests.

To make sense out of the current developments, it is necessary to
reinterpret American economic history since the end of World War
II and to comprehend the transformation from the heyday of modern
American capitalist growth—the *Pax Americana,* during which
U.S.-based companies dominated the international economy—into the
crisis atmosphere of the 1980s. The growth between 1945 and roughly
1971 in overall production and especially in corporate profits is the
subject of this chapter. In the next, the onset of the international
economic crisis in the 1970s experienced by business, workers, and
governments inside the United States will be examined. It is necessary
to find out what kinds of strategies were developed by American corporate managers to maintain profits in the face of the crisis, how deindustrialization has been part of that corporate response, and how the 1980
election of the most conservative national government in half a century
has promoted the long-run interests of capital, at the expense of personal security and community economic stability.

A Quarter-Century of American Economic Growth

The United States emerged from the Second World War with the only
major functioning army, with more than half of all the usable productive capacity in the world, and as the banker and creditor to both
former allies *and* former enemies.[2] Such overwhelming economic and
military superiority had not been seen in the world since the turn of

the century when British pre-eminence had begun to wither under the challenge from newer industrial countries.

America's domination of the global economy was cemented by the establishment of the dollar as the capitalist world's principal reserve currency at the 1944 Bretton Woods Conference. Daniel R. Fusfeld, a professor of Economics at the University of Michigan, has shown how the Bretton Woods agreement on fixed exchange rates pegged to the dollar contributed to the takeover of foreign industries by U. S. corporations.[3] Under the system of international payments that prevailed until 1971, each nation was responsible for keeping the value of its currency within 1 percent of its par value. To keep it within that range, the central bank of each country was required to sell or buy its own currency on foreign-exchange markets. By running persistent and large capital-account deficits in its balance of international payments, the United States effectively forced foreign central banks to buy excess dollars with their own currencies in order to decrease the supply of dollars in circulation. This provided American investors with the francs, marks, and other European currencies necessary to buy assets in France, Germany, and elsewhere. Thus, as the price for international stability, foreign central banks were put in the awkward position of financing the takeovers of their own countries' industry.

In this environment, American corporations were able to make massive investments abroad in new plant and equipment, producing commodities for foreign markets and, later on, for re-importing back into the United States itself. These direct shifts of private American capital became truly enormous during the 1960s. One corporation alone, General Electric, increased its overseas capacity fourfold, from twenty-one foreign plants in 1949 to eighty-two in 1969.[4] The proportion of total plant and equipment investment located outside the United States doubled in the metal and machinery industries, from an annual average of 14 percent during 1957–61 to 28 percent during 1967–70. By the early 1970s, nearly one third of annual U. S. automobile company investment was being placed abroad.[5]

The widespread plants, mines, distribution centers and offices of the multinational corporations made up entire production systems linked on a global scale. Their creation changed the very meaning of the oldest and most sacred concept in economics: *competition*. By 1970, "close to three-quarters of total U. S. exports and upwards of one-half of all imports [were] transactions between the domestic and foreign subsidiaries of the same [U. S. and foreign] multinational conglomerate corporations."[6] Bulova Watch provides a clear example. Bulova now manufactures watch movements in Switzerland and ships them to Pago Pago, in American Samoa, where they are assembled and then shipped to the United States to be sold. Corporation President Harry B. Henshel said about this arrangement: "We are able to beat the foreign competition because we *are* the foreign competition."[7]

As a result of this unprecedented global expansion, the proportion of total after-tax profits of U. S. corporations earned abroad rose steadily from about 10 percent at the beginning of the 1950s to over 20 percent at the beginning of the 1970s. (By 1978 as a result of the kinds of overseas co-production, licensing, and subcontracting arrangements that will be examined in the next chapter, *one third* of the overall profits of the hundred largest American corporations and banks were extracted from operations located in other countries.)[8]

During the 1960s, the productive capacity of the American economy nearly tripled, even after accounting for inflation. This meant uninterrupted, unparalleled, and unprecedented economic expansion from the end of the 1961 (Eisenhower) recession to the 1969–70 (Nixon) crash. It was a period in which economists declared the business cycle obsolete and families saw their real incomes grow by a third.

Exports to overseas markets and production abroad were more than matched by an enormous burst of growth in the home market, abetted after the early 1960s by explicit government deployment of expansionary fiscal policies. Growth of the federally debt-financed, discretionary incomes of working families provided an opportunity for business to develop and market a wide range of new consumer goods and services. The postwar suburbanization of middle-class households, itself in part an aspect of this explosive consumerism, set the scene for the proliferation of shopping centers, tract-housing projects, and a seemingly endless array of services related to the automobile, from drive-in restaurants to drive-in movies.

And of course there was the private automobile itself. No single product—with its extensive linkages to other economic sectors, including highway construction and petroleum refining—has ever so dominated the imagination of the population, or the base of a national economy, as did the car. At its peak in 1965, the domestic automobile industry turned out 11.1 million cars, trucks, and buses in a single year.[9] Nearly 10 percent of the value of all U. S. manufacturing shipments in that year consisted of motor vehicles and motor vehicle parts.[10] When all of the employment indirectly created by the automobile is taken into account, from used-car salesmen to typists in the automobile insurance industry, it has been "guesstimated" that perhaps one out of every six Americans owed his or her job to the existence of the private car. No wonder, then, that the postwar boom is identified with the automobile, or that the decline of the domestic automobile industry has played such a central role in our own time in bringing the problem of deindustrialization to the attention of so many people.

The Revolution in "Permissive" Technology

At the root of the American expansion in the 1950s and 1960s are two enormously important phenomena: one is the development of a new "permissive" technological environment that provided the technical means for the expansion. The other was the continued centralization of capital that provided the financial and administrative means to take advantage of it.

The period under discussion is characterized by almost breath-taking changes in technologies that *permit* managers to shift capital (and products) across long distances, and to operate far-reaching networks of production facilities. Of course, it is hardly a new development for business to *want* to be able to move as far as possible at the cheapest cost. But until comparatively recently, the prevailing technologies of transportation, communication, and production sharply constrained such free-wheeling mobility.

Consider, for example, the prevailing mode of freight transport in the years before the Civil War. The Erie Canal ran 363 miles from Albany to Buffalo. In 1830 it took four to six days to make the complete journey at a speed that ranged all the way up to 3.8 miles per hour. Those attempting to reach Buffalo from Schenectady in less than fifty hours often found themselves facing a $10 speeding fine levied by the overseers of the canal.[11] Even then the canal opened up the possibility for runaway shops. It enabled producers to move away from Albany to seek cheap land on which to place their plant, a better supply of water power, or cheaper labor.

The introduction of the railroad and later the interstate highway system further reduced the time, and therefore the cost, of moving things between places. As a result the technical environment became more permissive for capital migration. In this way, the South could be opened up to textile production directly, or indirectly linked to northern capitalists.

The Wright Brothers and Alexander Graham Bell revolutionized this environment still further. The introduction of air travel and the telephone allowed production to take place at ever greater distances from consumer and supplier markets. In an emergency, products with a high dollar value relative to their weight could be airlifted for quick delivery, and a central office manager in New York could be in close communication with a factory manager in Los Angeles—coordination of production could be accomplished almost instantly by telephone. By the end of the 1950s, a transportation and communications technology was available that permitted firms to think of themselves in national and international terms rather than as tied to a single region or nation.

The development of these "forces of production" had taken a quantum leap during World War II. Government-financed research and development, cost-plus military procurement contracts, and—immediately after the war—the tremendous pent-up industrial demand for every sort of producers' equipment all helped to revolutionize the technologies of transportation and communication. The progeny of this revolution came with the birth of the jet age—its jumbo transports, telex, and the computer with its satellite communication links. These developments allowed production and coordination to be carried on in a truly worldwide market. The textile conglomerate that moved to North Carolina could now also operate in South Korea and South America, its managers able to control the looms in all these locations by buttons on a computer console at its central headquarters in New York. At their beck and call, banks of computers could keep worldwide, instantaneous track of every spindle, every loom, every worker. From its world headquarters in Dearborn, Michigan, a manager at Ford could adjust the speed of an assembly line in Australia or change the shape of a hood ornament in Germany.[12] (How the workers in these different locations might *respond* to such attempts at "remote control" is, of course, another story.)

The jumbo jet and the computer were only the beginning. Multinational corporations are now operating their own global communications systems, thus entirely bypassing individual countries' local government services—and regulations. One example is the creation of a new business service, Satellite Business Systems (SBS). This partnership of IBM, Comsat, and the Aetna Life Insurance Company is designed explicitly to help multinational corporations facilitate communication among their local factories, regional sales offices, and division and corporate headquarters. According to one study of these developments

> when SBS begins operations overseas . . . no longer will transnational enterprises be reliant on national postal, telegraph and telephone authorities for *any* of their information needs, removing the last link in their activities susceptible to governmental scrutiny and action.[13]

The new technology has also permitted a substantial amount of "deskilling." In the years following World War II, inside the factory and later the office, managers were introducing new machinery and radically reorganizing work tasks in ways that reduced their dependence on high-priced skilled labor. For example, the principle of the assembly line was applied to everything from food processing to the assembly of television sets and the packaging of cosmetics. So-called numerically-controlled machine tools, based at first on mechanical principles but then becoming increasingly computerized, were developed in industries such as automobile, aircraft, and electric products. These tools greatly reduced the range of machining skills needed in any one employee. In later years, in an even older trade, microcomputerized sewing systems were invented that effectively removed the stitchers' control of the pace of piecework production and reduced their work to a set of simple machine-tending tasks, able to be done by unskilled, low-paid workers.[14]

The creation of these new technologies, and the work reorganizations to implement them, made it easier for managers to take advantage of new sources of cheap and—at least, initially—tractable labor in peripheral locations, both within the country and beyond its borders. Together with the new developments in transportation and communications, these new production techniques thus made it both possible and attractive for firms to shift certain fragments of the production process out of the "home" region, altogether. This sort of spatial reorganization of production, bound up in industrial-organization literature with theories of the "product cycle" or "innovation cycle"[15], consists in part of actual physical relocations and (more commonly) of the branching policies of multiplant or multistore corporations.

New techniques are not invented at random, only to become commercially successful once an entrepreneur happens to stumble up against one. At least in the modern age, technology is simply too expensive to produce without an explicit purpose. In this sense, necessity truly is the mother of invention. It is the logic of the competitive market that creates the need for these technological advances—that makes them *profitable*. Wide-bodied cargo jets were not built because it was technologically possible to do so. They were built because there was a demand for rapid and capacious transportation that could be used to connect global production. Computer networks were explicitly designed to permit coordination of production between widespread territories. The most advanced machine tools, computerized numerical control (C/NC) equipment, were developed at the expense of the U.S. Air Force in large part to alleviate dependence on skilled machinists. So it goes.

But despite our fascination with new gadgets and space-age technologies, the mere existence of a permissive environment for capital mobility does not assure that industrialists in the era of the *Pax Americana* would have been able to take advantage of it. There had also to be a transformation in the organizational form of ownership and management of capital itself, capable of exploiting the new opportunities afforded by the technologies facilitating decentralized production. No other development has had more influence on the deindustrialization of America than has the emergence of these forms.

The Growing Centralization and Concentration of Control Over Production

Whatever their theoretical and ideological persuasions, all social analysts agree that the organizational structure of American business has undergone a radical change since the nineteenth century. A greater and greater share of the productive capacity of the economy—financial assets, physical assets, and labor power—has come under the control of those increasingly complex, hierarchically-structured, private bureaucracies called corporations.

To be sure, more traditional, less complex, "competitive" business enterprises still exist. In fact, in terms of sheer numbers, most firms in the United States are still describable in this way, although the share of small, and especially independently-owned, businesses in the total private economy is on the decline (see chapter 7). But power has passed overwhelmingly to the corporate sector and to the public bureaucracies that regulate, procure goods and services from, and trade executives with the corporations. And the largest of these are getting bigger and more powerful over time.[16]

This process, the *centralization of control* over production by relatively fewer and fewer, ever more powerful organizations, is closely related to the growing *concentration of economic power.* Orthodox economists prefer to reserve the term "concentration" for describing the extent to which a small number of corporations control most of the sales in their particular industry. Centralization and sales concentration normally, but not always, occur simultaneously (as in the automobile companies). But there are many exceptions, notably the big oil companies, which control a large number of relatively small subsidiary businesses, no one of which dominates its own particular industry. This is centralization of economic power without apparent concentration.

Table 5.1 shows the growing industrial concentration in the United States from the end of World War II to the early 1970s. These indices, called "concentration ratios," measure the proportion of total industry sales attributable to the four largest firms in each industry. For example, 90 percent of all breakfast cereal foods sold in 1972 were manufactured by just four firms—Kellogg's, Post, General Mills, and Quaker Oats. Ninety-three percent of all the sales of domestic motor vehicles in the early 1970s belonged to General Motors, Ford, Chrysler, and the American Motors Corporation.

These numbers are watched closely by economists who specialize in industrial organization, and by Federal Trade Commission (FTC) officials, because they suggest which companies may have the greatest opportunity for directly controlling their own prices and output. A firm that can both dictate price, free of market pressure, and restrict output

TABLE 5.1

Percentage of Sales Accounted for by the Four Largest Producers in Selected Manufacturing Industries: 1947–72

SIC	Industry	Percentage of Sales	
		1947	1972
2043	Cereal breakfast foods	79	90
2065	Confectionery products	17	32
2067	Chewing gum	70	87
2092	Malt beverages	21	52
2211	Weaving mills, cotton	18[1]	31
2254	Knit underwear mills	21	46
2279	Carpets and rugs	32[2]	78
2311	Men's and boys' suits and coats	9	19
2337	Women's and Misses' suits and coats	3[1]	13
2421	Sawmills and planing mills	11[1]	18
2771	Greeting card publishing	39	70
2829	Synthetic rubber	53[1]	62
3211	Flat glass	90[1]	93
3312	Blast furnaces and steel mills	50	45
3421	Cutlery	41	55
3511	Turbines and turbine generators	90[2]	93
3555	Printing trades machinery	31	42
3585	Refrigeration and heating equipment	25	40
3624	Carbon and graphite products	87	80
3633	Household laundry equipment	40	83
3636	Sewing machines	77	84
3641	Electric lamps	92	90
3661	Telephone and telegraph apparatus	90	94[3]
3674	Semiconductors and related devices	46[2]	57
3679	Electronic components	13	36
3692	Primary batteries, dry and wet	76	92
3711	Motor vehicles and car bodies	92[4]	93
3724	Aircraft engines and engine parts	72	77
3743	Locomotives and parts	91	97[4]
3861	Photographic equipment and supplies	61	74
3996	Hard surface floor covering	80	91

Source: U. S. Department of Commerce, Bureau of the Census, *Census of Manufactures, 1972*, Table 5, pp. SR2-6—SR2-49.
[1.]1954 data [2.]1963 data [3.]1970 data [4.]1967 data.

by barring the entry of new firms, is in a position to earn monopoly profits, to control the pace of technological progress, to more closely determine the rate of capital expansion, and to more easily ignore product quality or safety.

Others are concerned about concentrated industries for political reasons. The firms that control the output of a vital commodity, such as oil, gain tremendous political power simply by their ability to with-hold supply at critical times. A private concentrated industry can do this in very much the same way as a public cartel such as the Organiza-tion of Petroleum Exporting Countries (OPEC) in the Middle East.

But concentration also has implications for capital mobility, which is the main concern here. In highly concentrated industries the control over capital location and therefore jobs is wielded by a small set of decision makers. If one or even several firms in an unconcentrated industry decides to move, that decision will usually have minimal conse-quences for the industry's total labor force. Yet a single decision by one corporate board in a concentrated industry can—as discussed in chap-ter 3—affect the livelihood of tens of thousands of workers and the stability of entire communities.

The numbers in table 5.1 reveal that in many industries, concentra-tion is actually growing—and in a few, quite rapidly. For example, the concentration ratio in the malt beverage industry grew by two and one-half times between 1947 and 1972. National brewers such as Bud-weiser, Miller, and Pabst squeezed local breweries out of existence. A similar trend exists in carpets and rugs, greeting cards, refrigeration equipment, and laundry equipment. Even among such historically highly competitive industries as knit underwear, men's and boy's suits, and women's and misses' dresses, the degree of concentration more than doubled between 1947 and 1972.

Higher concentration has by no means been limited to the manufac-turing sector. It is possible to construct analogous indicators for a select group of non-manufacturing industries.[17] Our research reveals a high, and rising, incidence of concentration within metal mining, petroleum and gas extraction, and even general merchandising (retail trade). The growth of large department store chains such as Sears and K-Mart, and of retail holding companies such as Federated, Allied, and Dayton-Hudson, is responsible for the tremendous increase in concentration in the retail sector. As in the case of concentrated manufacturing owner-ship, narrowing control over key non-manufacturing sectors of the economy brings an increasing tendency toward monopoly pricing, re-stricted output, political influence, and centralized control over capital location.

Of course, by excluding imports, all of these statistical measures of concentration exaggerate to some extent the decline of inter-firm competition. As has become painfully clear to American companies—and to their workers—Toyotas and Datsuns certainly compete in price with Chevrolets and Fords. Moreover, in a number of industries, even the official domestic concentration ratio has declined since the end of World War II.

But part of this apparent decline in concentration is an illusion. Whether, and to what extent, concentration ratios change over time depends partly on the kind of merger activity taking place. *Horizontal* mergers of firms producing essentially the same product clearly increase measured concentration ratios. In contrast, *vertical* mergers in which, for example, a steel company purchases its iron-ore suppliers or fabrication firms that were once its own customers, may not noticeably affect concentration at all within these industries.

Moreover, *conglomerate* mergers, where a single firm acquires companies with totally different products or services, can actually lead to decreased measured concentration. For example, if a conglomerate buys a relatively small firm in a concentrated industry and then expands this division, the four-firm concentration ratio may fall (unless, of course, the top four firms expand at the same rate). More important, conglomerate penetration into even the most competitive industry can lead to oligopolistic pricing behavior at lower concentration ratios than before.

It is precisely these impacts of conglomeration that are conveniently ignored by groups such as the U. S. Chamber of Commerce, when they claim that evidence of stable four-firm concentration ratios in some industries implies a high degree of "free market competition" in the American economy.[18] These criticisms only show that *sales*-based industry ratios do not adequately measure the concentration of economic power, especially in the case of vertical and conglomerate mergers. Other statistics do, however. For example, between 1955 and 1970, the *Fortune* 500 increased their share of *employment, profits,* and *assets* in all U. S. manufacturing and mining by between 40 and 70 percent.[19]

The increasing centralization of capital, through which relatively fewer companies came to control relatively more assets, jobs, and decisions about economic life, occurred in several stages. The scene was set during the forty years following the Civil War. Then, a number of financially powerful, politically well connected companies came to control sizeable shares of the markets and natural resources in their own industries. This head start, together with their considerable financial power, allowed these firms to grow large enough to take advantage of "economies of scale": the lower unit costs of production that result from managers' being able to greatly elaborate the division of labor within the workplace and to spread fixed costs over many units of output.

Around the turn of the century, increases in centralized control over capital began to be achieved through the acquisition of smaller companies in particular fields by larger ones, or, less frequently, by the merger of two giants. Either way, between 1890 and 1905 these horizontal combinations produced the first great wave of births of the major product-identified corporations whose names have become household words: U. S. Steel, American Tobacco, International Harvester, and General Electric. According to the leading expert on the subject, John Blair, "The driving force behind the formation of many of these consolidations was the desire to eliminate competition".[20]

The second wave of corporate mergers and acquisitions took place from the mid-1920s through the early years of the Great Depression. The characteristic feature of this phase of centralization was the absorption into the largest firms of companies that either supplied their resources or unfinished goods, or distributed their final products. This kind of vertical combination was accomplished mainly by giant corporations acquiring the assets of businesses such as mining, metalworking, and food distribution, rather than by stock transfers as earlier. The financial backing for this activity came, to a great extent, from the leading investment-banking houses. Among the corporate giants emerging from this era of vertical combination were Kennecott Copper, B. F. Goodrich, General Foods, and especially the major petroleum companies. Through networks of wholly-owned or franchised gasoline stations, they gained control over the entire process from drilling and refining to the selling of gas. The new giants also spawned a veritable menagerie of trade-marks, from Borden's Elsie the Cow to the RCA Victor dog concentrating intently on "his master's voice."

Even before World War II, some of the more cash-rich companies had begun to move beyond horizontal and vertical acquisition strategies to consolidate their control over products and markets in totally unrelated businesses. But the first giant corporation to devote itself exclusively to the buying and selling of other companies came into existence during the war. Based in Rhode Island, Textron Incorporated was founded by Royal Little in 1943, to provide blankets and other textile products to the U. S. army. Textron went on to set an international standard as the first fully integrated conglomerate, buying and selling between 1943 and 1980 over one hundred different companies in industries as diverse as textiles, aerospace, machinery, watch bracelets, and pens. It was diversification with a vengeance. The tendencies that characterize corporate development had led to the emergence of an organizational entity to which whole businesses were nothing more than commodities to be bought and sold. No longer would the survival of the parent firm depend on its successes or failures in any one—or even several—product markets. (For a listing of Textron's divisions and subsidiaries, see table A.5 in the appendix).

In the years immediately before the Great Depression, substantially unrelated or conglomerate mergers accounted for fewer than one fifth of all corporate mergers in the country. By the late 1960s, according to the Federal Trade Commission's data displayed in table 5.2, more than four fifths of all mergers were conglomerate in nature.

There have been three distinct merger waves since the end of World War II (figure 5.1). The first occurred during 1949–55; the second took place from 1964–68. One way to appreciate the enormity of the merger boom of 1968 is to realize that, in that year alone, if the capital that went into acquiring existing companies had been spent instead on new plants and equipment, national investment in 1968 would have been 46 percent higher than it was.[21]

TABLE 5.2

Distribution of Corporate Mergers by Type and Period: 1926–68
(in percentages)

Type of Merger	1926–30	1940–47	1951–55	1956–60	1961–65	1966–68
Horizontal and related	75.9	62.0	39.2	30.1	22.5	8.6
Vertical	4.8	17.0	12.2	14.9	17.5	9.8
Conglomerate	19.3	21.0	48.6	55.0	60.0	81.6
Total	100.0	100.0	100.0	100.0	100.0	100.0

SOURCE: Subcommittee on Antitrust and Monopoly of the Committee on the Judiciary, U. S. Senate, *Hearings on Economic Concentration,* 91st Cong., 1st sess., 1969, pt. 8A, appendix, p. 63.

There was a sharp decline in the asset value of major industrial mergers after 1968; but by 1973 the rate had begun to pick up again and, as figure 5.1 clearly shows, rose throughout the remainder of the decade and into the 1980s. What is more, much larger companies are now being bought.

The explanation for this postwar "urge to merge" is straightforward

FIGURE 5.1

Real Assets of All Large Manufacturing and Mining Companies Acquired: 1948–79 (1967 = 100)

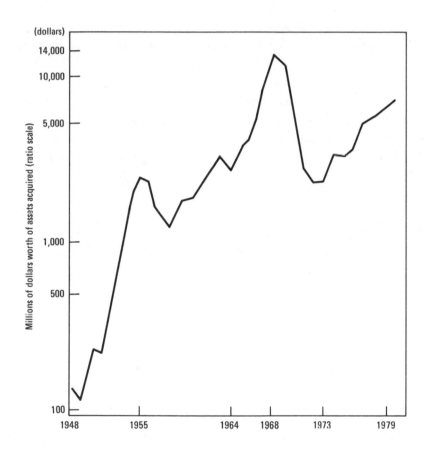

SOURCES: Federal Trade Commission, *Statistical Report on Mergers and Acquisitions* (Washington, D.C.: Bureau of Economics, July 1981) p. 115; deflator (producers price index for all industrial commodities) is taken from Council of Economic Advisors, *1980 Economic Report of the President* (Washington, D.C.: United States Government Printing Office, 1980), table B-56, p. 268. This series only counts assets in acquired firms that had at least $10 million in assets in the year in which they were acquired.

enough. From the perspective of the firm, the pressures of competition had simply become too great to allow managers and their financial advisors in the key banks to forego opportunities for increasing their companies' "flexibility": the capacity to move in whatever new directions the rapidly changing world situation might present, or to protect themselves from being caught in potentially damaging situations (like the overthrow of a government in Central America or the loss of a war in Southeast Asia). The key to corporate/conglomerate flexibility is *cash*. The ability to grow, diversify, shift gears, and purchase protection from nationalization by foreign governments, all require sufficient liquidity to be able to pay the bills. This constant need for cash explains why conglomerate managers are often quite prepared to sell even profitable subsidaries. (This behavior will be documented in detail in the following chapter).

There is also a personal motivation to promote merger activity. In contrast to middle management, individual top corporate and conglomerate managers may stand to gain personally from following the urge to merge. The editors of a prominent business journal, writing about the Xerox Corporation's takeover of C.I.T. Financial Corporation in 1968, observed that:

> Among the biggest gainers will be C.I.T.'s top management . . . if the merger goes through, they could end up with a combined stock market gain on their own personal stock options of approximately $10 million, a gain which C.I.T. on its own probably couldn't have achieved for many, many years.[22]

How National Tax Laws and Regulations Promoted Centralization and Concentration

In the years following World War II, a host of public policies promoted and facilitated the centralization and concentration of control over private capital. Especially in the form of tax breaks to business, these political and legal "incentives" were often publicly justified as potential "job-creation" devices. But whatever the official rationale, the *de facto* outcome of government policy was to promote and protect concentrated economic power both in the United States and throughout the world.

Consider the U. S. Tax Code. This system of laws and regulations contains a long list of provisions ostensibly designed to encourage capital investment by providing tax benefits that reduce the net cost of buying productive assets.

As a consultant to the FTC, Boston University law professor, Alan Feld, conducted a detailed study of the impacts of the Tax Code on industrial concentration. Three elements in the code are particularly important in this regard. *Accelerated depreciation allowances* in effect grant the companies with the largest tax liabilities interest-free loans by reducing their taxable income in the earlier years. *Investment tax credits* allow deferral of a portion of the tax indefinitely; for the largest firms, they can approach total tax forgiveness. And mineral resource—notably oil—depletion allowances grant a tax deduction to cover "the cost of making the hole in the ground."

In one recent year alone (1978), the cost to the U. S. Treasury in foregone revenues from these three "incentives" was about $10.9 billion. And all three benefits, according to Feld, went disproportionately to the largest corporations.[23] In 1978, for example, U. S. Steel paid only $8 million in taxes on net profits of $250 million, an effective rate of 3.2 percent. The year before, with net profits of $135 million, U. S. Steel paid *no* taxes, and in fact received $36 million in federal tax credits.[24]

All corporations in theory can take advantage of these provisions in the tax code, but as with the personal income tax, those who most avail themselves of tax incentives are the wealthiest. This helps to induce the uneven development of the corporate sector. Those firms that are already large and concentrated can boost their after-tax profits, while the firm that is struggling to grow usually has little net profit against which it can charge, for example, accelerated depreciation. Thus the law is heavily biased in favor of the most profitable and most capital-intensive firms.

The U. S. Tax Code includes many other pro-concentration provisions as well, including deductions for advertising and political lobbying expenses, special treatment of capital gains, and the "loss carryback" provision according to which a corporation with a history of profits incurring a loss in the current year may carry it back to offset those earlier profits and obtain an immediate refund of the earlier taxes paid. Such an arrangement clearly favors established corporations over new ones.

Another spur to concentration is the federal tax-deductibility of the interest that corporations (and especially banks and insurance companies) receive when they purchase the industrial development bonds issued by state and local governments. Several researchers have shown that the largest and most powerful firms that already have the highest credit ratings enjoy the greatest benefits from this highly inequitable (and also, as it turns out, quite inefficient) approach to financing local economic development.[25]

With respect to the fostering of mergers, which clearly promote concentration, Feld concludes that:

> The Federal income tax provides a generally benign climate for acquisitions. The acquiror ordinarily incurs no tax on purchase of an asset. The acquiror pays tax determined by the gain on a stock investment only when the gain is realized. . . . Generally, shareholders of the target corporation can defer tax when they exchange their stock for stock of an acquiring corporation in a reorganization . . . a sale for cash incurs capital gains tax, while an exchange in a reorganization often can net the shareholder something close to cash but without tax.[26]

Furthermore, if the acquiring firm were to distribute the stock of its new subsidiary to a group of shareholders, it would be required to pay taxes immediately on the capital gains. Thus the code has a powerful built-in disincentive to deconcentration by retarding the distribution of stock in the operating subsidiaries of large corporations.

Because all of these tax loopholes confer their greatest benefits on the largest corporations—or, alternatively, because it is the largest and most profitable firms that are in the best position to make use of these benefits—their net effect is to promote concentration. By the end of the era of the *Pax Americana,* the combined effect of this complement of tax loopholes was to reduce the effective 1973 tax rate of the hundred largest manufacturing companies to about 25 percent. The rate for all other companies was something closer to 44 percent.[27]

The Tax Code is only the most prominent aspect of a regulatory environment whose net effect has been to promote the centralization of control over capital. Other laws allow conglomerates in particular to engage in a wide variety of accounting practices that can often, under the right macroeconomic conditions, help them to project an image of continued growth in the net earnings of the firm as a whole, thereby keeping upward pressure on the price of their stock. The tricks involve the use of varying methods of depreciation and inventory valuation. Managements' objective is to enable the conglomerate

> to report substantial increases in earnings per share without improving operating efficiency. As earnings per share of conglomerates increased year after year, stock prices increased even more rapidly. Since most mergers were based on exchanges of stock . . . the ever-increasing stock prices of the conglomerates enable them to acquire more and larger companies.[28]

For the most part, mergers and acquisitions have never been seriously challenged by the Justice Department or strongly penalized by the courts. Litigation is expensive and can take literally years and years; few officials have had the stamina to stay with it. During the heyday of American capitalism, of all the 14,000 mergers that took place between 1950 and 1967, fewer than 200 were challenged—and half of these involved small firms. The government won 90 of these challenges, yet in only 48 "were the companies required to divest themselves of anything."[29]

Taxes, Tariffs, and Other Government Regulations Supporting the International Expansion of Capital

So far, in this reconstruction of the role of the State in promoting the centralization of American capital following World War II, the emphasis has been on the domestic scene. But the international expansion of U. S. capital was perhaps even more crucial to the process of American economic growth in this period.

U. S. military policy and American foreign aid were vitally important in extending the global reach of American industry. Whatever their manifest military purposes, American troops, military advisors, offshore cruising naval vessels, strategic long-range bombers, and, eventually, long-range ballistic missiles all helped at least indirectly to protect and extend American business interests abroad. During these years, the U. S. government made commitments to a whole network of antidemocratic dictatorships, whose leaders seemed dedicated, along with keeping themselves in power locally, to promoting the entry of American business enterprise into their economies. In this context, many of America's new Third World allies—South Korea, Taiwan, Brazil, and Argentina—courted U. S. firms by offering terms that were unbelievably tempting, especially low wages and prohibitions on free union activity. The modern equivalent of U. S. gunboats—much more subtle covert intelligence operations and secret funding of military and paramilitary operations—protected these regimes from internal dissent and external attack, while U. S. diplomats averted their eyes from the official government terrorist campaigns to crush free trade unions and, for that matter, free democratic popular elections of any kind.

While unquestionably less important in promoting the global expansion of American business than military and foreign policy, favorable foreign tax and tariff regulations also played a role. As with the new technologies in production, transportation, and communications, it is not the case that the preferential tax and tariff treatment of foreign investment *caused* U. S. corporate managers to shift their capital abroad. Rather, these public policies *reinforced* corporate decisions that were based on more important factors: markets, labor costs, and political security. But this is no trivial point. It implies that managers who invested abroad were rewarded with windfall profits from the IRS.

For example, the U. S. Tax Code was rewritten to permit American corporations to credit all of their foreign income taxes against their domestic tax liabilities on a dollar for dollar basis. This constitutes a far greater saving than is normally available on other business expenses, which are usually deducted from revenue to arrive at the taxable "bottom line."

Consider this example. Suppose Corporation X, based in the United States, has a fully owned subsidary operating abroad, Corporation Y. This firm makes $1 million profit one year and pays $250,000 in income taxes to its host country, repatriating the remaining $750,000 to its parent firm, Corporation X. In 1967 at the maximum statutory U. S. corporate income tax rate of 46 percent, the U. S. Treasury might have expected to receive

.46 × net profits of Corporation X =

.46 × ($1,000,000 − $250,000) = $345,000

Under the terms of the Foreign Tax Credit, however, the revenue received by the Treasury would be only:

(.46 × $1,000,000) − $250,000 = $210,000

The owners of Corporation X are therefore richer by $135,000, and the federal treasury is poorer by this amount.

An even larger and more controversial tax incentive for foreign investment has been the provision allowing U. S. firms to defer the payment of taxes to this country until the profits are actually repatriated. Multinationals have become adept at postponing repatriation by using profits earned on existing overseas operations to finance further foreign investments. In some cases repatriation is put off almost indefinitely so that, for all intents and purposes, *no* U. S. taxes are ever paid.

Multinationals also dodge the U. S. tax collector by engaging in the practice of "transfer pricing." The U. S. parent firm—Corporation X—might set an arbitrarily high price for an item or service that it sells to the overseas subsidiary, Corporation Y. As a result, the latter will show a smaller profit to be repatriated to the United States. Alternatively, if tax rates in the subsidiary's host country are very low, the American parent may do exactly the opposite: overprice its imports or underprice its exports with the subsidiary, so that the larger amount of profit is exposed to the tax collector of the low-tax foreign country. In some instances, this transfer pricing strategy is pursued simply to present a trade union that is challenging the multinational in one of its product lines with an artificially deflated profit picture during wage negotiations.[30]

The very quality of multinationality gives these giant corporations the opportunity to play off one country against the other. Thus, it has become quite common for

U.S. based international companies to create a headquarters and a two-tier legal structure. On top, the U.S. parent. In the first tier, a holding company, incorporated in a low-tax nation which levies no taxes on dividends from abroad. And in the second tier, all the national subsidiaries, legally owned by the first tier holding company. The holding company is used as a low [tax] cost reservoir and conduit for sending funds between national subsidiaries.[31]

As a result of all of these various tax breaks, by the end of the *Pax Americana*, U. S. corporations in 1972 paid to the U. S. government only $1.2 billion in taxes on foreign earnings of over $24 billion—an effective tax rate of just 5 percent.[32] Think of how overjoyed the typical factory or office worker would be if the federal government taxed her or his personal income at such a rate.

Subsidies for foreign investment have also been available to industry through certain provisions of the U. S. Tariff Code. For example, during the 1960s American corporations created a number of so-called "export platforms" abroad. Components would be made in domestic plants, shipped to low-wage European and Third World countries for assembly, and then re-imported back into the United States for sale to the home market. Under tariff item 806.30, which was actually created in 1930 to promote the assembly of automobiles and other metal products in Canada, but not utilized extensively until the 1960s, duty is paid only on the value added in the foreign assembly process, not on the entire market value of the assembled product. Item 806.30 is now used by the manufacturers of aircraft parts, steel mill products, and, of course, "chips"—the semiconductors (integrated circuits imprinted on silicon chips) that drive computers and miniature memory units for everything from calculators to microwave ovens. Passed in 1963, tariff item 807.00 extended the same provisions to the textile, apparel, television, and radio industries. In the five years following creation of tariff item 807.00 (over the strenuous objection of the International Ladies' Garment Workers' Union), the duty-free value of imports brought into the country under this and item 806.30 jumped by 400 percent, twice the rate of all dutiable imports during the same period.[33] (The export platform strategy will be studied more closely in the next chapter.)

Over the years a host of other federal programs were created to subsidize foreign investment. These include: the Overseas Private Investment Corporation, the Commodity Credit Corporation, and the U. S. Export-Import Bank. Among its other activities, the latter has used $310 million of taxpayer money to finance the transfer by Dow Chemical, Ford, Alcoa, Goodyear, B. F. Goodrich, Armco Steel, Kaiser, Reynolds, and Union Carbide of $410 million worth of equipment from their American plants to various subsidiaries in the Third World.[34]

The Postwar "Social Contract" Between Capital and Labor

American corporate leaders realized almost immediately after World War II that their new national and international opportunities for profit could more easily be pursued if their domestic relations with labor could be stabilized. The trade union movement had been growing since the late 1930s. Labor militancy ebbed somewhat during the war but revived explosively immediately afterwards. In 1946 more Americans went out on strike than in any other year in the nation's history. If labor peace could be secured—by either breaking the unions or coming to an accommodation with them on matters of wages and fringe benefits —it could give corporations the breathing space needed to undertake the major investments and work reorganizations necessary for launching their global reach. If they were successful, the wealth accumulated in the process could even be shared with the American working class, at least to the extent necessary to nullify the further organizing capabilities of the unions.

In this way, postwar economic growth both required industrial peace and, at the same time, promised to generate the material basis for sustaining it by raising workers' standard of living. Moreover, the new economic doctrines of Keynesianism taught that such a burst of new consumption by working families would itself contribute to the process of economic expansion. This wealth in turn made it possible for government to legitimate the new order (based on corporate expansion and international Cold War military policy) by greatly expanding the "social wage": that amalgam of benefits, worker protections, and legal rights that acts to generally increase the social security of the working class.

Achieving labor peace through sharing a greater part of the benefits of economic growth was a new strategy for employers, and one that they only grudgingly accepted. The history of American class relations, between the end of the Civil War and the end of World War II, is filled with confrontation in the workplace between organized labor unions and associations, and increasingly defensive managers who at times resorted to the active police power of local—and even, on occasion, the federal—government to quell labor unrest. It is also a history of labor participation in grass-roots politics, both within the Democratic party and to some extent in third party movements. This direct political activity produced a number of explicitly pro-labor and socialist electoral victories in state and local jurisdictions across the country.[35]

Out of these local electoral victories and influence over national party platforms came a series of public programs to underwrite the social security of workers, whether or not they belonged to unions. The objective was to reduce workers' absolute, immediate dependence on their employers. Nearly all of the legislation that makes up the social wage (widely referred to in this country as the "social safety net") was first written and implemented at the state and municipal level, especially in the populist Midwest and in patrician-paternalistic Massachusetts, and only subsequently rationalized by the national government under Presidents Wilson and Franklin Roosevelt.

For example, the first workmen's compensation law to pay workers for job-related injuries and disability was passed in 1909 in the state of Montana.[36] The principle of unemployment insurance was pioneered in Massachusetts in 1916, although the first bill to actually pass a state legislature was not drafted until the early 1930s in Wisconsin, and a national program was not instituted until 1935 as a provision of the Social Security Act. The first state welfare boards preceded both workmen's compensation and unemployment insurance. Massachusetts appointed the first state board to oversee local relief charities in 1853, but it was not until 1917 that a modern department of public welfare was created in the state of Illinois—followed by Massachusetts in 1919. By 1926 five states had aid programs for widowed mothers and another six had general programs of support for mothers with children, nine years before the federal government created a national minimum in what later became the program of Aid to Families with Dependent Children (AFDC).

In the 1930s a prairie fire of social legislation spread throughout the nation. The utter desperation of the Great Depression, combined with continued labor victories in the workplace and the election booth, instilled not altogether unrealistic fears of an imminent popular uprising in the United States. Within this climate, the national government produced a wave of national laws designed to legitimate, but also to circumscribe, union activity. The Norris-LaGuardia Act of 1932 put a stop to the use of court-ordered injunctions forbidding workers to strike or picket. The Wagner Act of 1935—often called "Labor's Magna Carta"—created the National Labor Relations Board and gave workers in the private sector the right to organize unions and to collectively bargain with management over wages and work rules. To protect this right, the act prohibited companies from committing a variety of "unfair labor practices," including the blacklisting of prospective employees who were union members or organizers. Finally the Fair Labor Standards Act of 1938 abolished child labor, established the first minimum wages, and institutionalized the eight-hour day.[37]

Under the umbrella of these hard-won legal provisions, labor union activity in the United States blossomed. The movement was bolstered by the tight labor markets created by World War II and by the national priority assigned to the defense industries to push out military production with practically no regard to cost. So greatly was organized labor's power reinforced by these market conditions that by 1946 it could stage strikes over postwar wage and fringe-benefit demands that involved one out of every ten American workers. These actions took place in all parts of the country, in a wide variety of industries, and were often of long duration. The United Automobile Workers struck GM for 113 days. For a major employer like General Electric, the 1946 national strike by the United Electrical Workers was the largest and longest that corporation had ever faced.[38]

An extreme reaction by business was inevitable. The Cold War with the Soviet Union had begun, and fears of Russian expansion abroad and subversion at home were easily fanned under the pretense of fighting communism. The militant wings of the largest industrial unions were purged, under the pressure of a nationwide anticommunist movement whose most visible spokespersons were Senator Joseph McCarthy and then Congressman Richard Nixon. Beginning in the key defense plants, strikes were soon broken throughout the country. Loyalty oaths were introduced to screen out supposed radicals. In short, management was willing to share the proceeds from economic growth to some extent, but it was absolutely unwilling to concede any control over the process of production to what it viewed as "radical elements."

In this context, the almost continuous attempt since 1937 by the National Association of Manufacturers and the Chamber of Commerce to amend the Wagner Act was finally successful. In 1947 over President Truman's veto, Congress compromised the Wagner Act's guarantee of the right to organize, to strike, and to secure a union shop by passing the Taft-Hartley Act.[39] Section 8(b) established a number of unfair labor practices for which *unions* could be held legally accountable, including sympathy strikes and "secondary boycotts." Section 301 made labor contracts legally enforceable, which gave employers the opportunity to sue any union that called a strike in violation of a no-strike clause in the labor-management agreement.

Most important of all, section 14(b) of the new law allowed individual states to override federal statutes and to enact so-called "right-to-work" laws, which outlawed compulsory union membership whether or not a majority of the workers in a unit voted for it. In the years to come, section 14(b) would seriously set back union organizing in the South (whose congressional delegation had worked the hardest for it) and would lead to the decertification of many unions that had previously won representation elections. By making dues-paying voluntary, 14(b) undermined the financial strength of the unions. By 1980 twenty states had passed these "right-to-work" laws. These states are indicated by the shaded areas in figure 5.2. The right-to-work states are overwhelmingly concentrated in the South Atlantic, the East South Central, the West South Central, and the Mountain regions.

These political and ideological initiatives by business helped to weaken labor's resistance to *all* forms of postwar corporate reorganization. They made it easier for management to change work rules in the older factories of the Frostbelt and to promote rationalization plans that closed down older productive capacity in order to free corporate resources for southern and global expansion. With labor's leadership internally divided, an overriding Cold War climate, and media campaigns describing the new multinational corporations as the world's greatest "engine of progress," the trade union movement lost a good deal of its momentum. As Solomon Barkin wrote about this period:

FIGURE 5.2

States Having Right-to-Work Laws in 1980, by Region

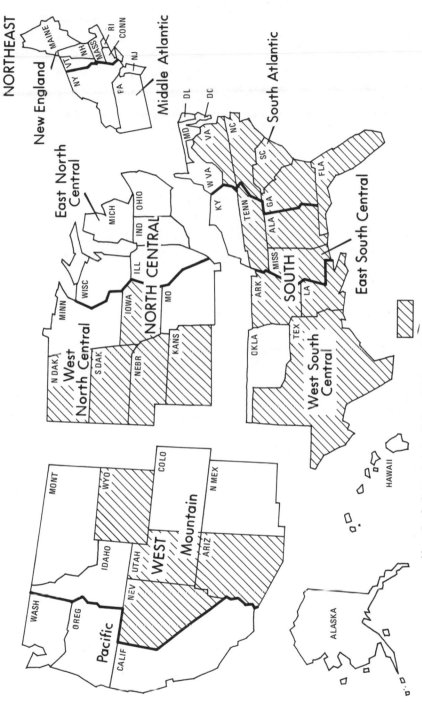

NOTE: Pacific division includes Alaska and Hawaii. Right-to-work states are shaded.
SOURCE: U.S. Bureau of the Census, *Statistical Abstract of the United States, 1980* (Washington D.C.: U.S. Government Printing Office, 1980), p. 429.

> The pressures of intensified competition and rising unemployment are limiting union power, and public disapproval of strikes is making trade unions more amenable to the conciliatory processes provided by public intervention, thereby diminishing their own bargaining leverage.
>
> Legislators and judiciary have become increasingly responsive to pressures from business interest desirous of undermining union power and its internal strength. They have yielded to demands for laws and interpretations that restrain trade unions. The pendulum has already swung so far as to halt the growth of the labor movement and actually constrict it.[40]

Indeed, after 1954 the proportion of workers belonging to unions began to fall in every region of the country, from an average of 35 percent in that year to only about 24 percent in 1978.[41]

With the difficulties of organizing new workers, particularly in the South, the labor movement shifted its emphasis to improving the wages and working conditions of its existing membership. This was a much easier task to accomplish, especially in those industries such as automobiles, steel, aerospace, and rubber that were benefiting from the postwar economic expansion. From capital's point of view, this was an attractive development. Thus, between *organized* labor and big business, a "new social contract" began to emerge, admittedly with a good deal of strife.

> When the United States emerged victorious from the war, with a much greater degree of economic concentration than had been the case prior to the Great Depression, the large corporations were in a position to offer a new type of deal to the unions. *If* the unions would enforce labor discipline, supply labor stability, accept longer contracts, purge the radicals, set up grievance procedures which removed the handling of grievances from the rank and file as much as possible, stay within the two-party system, leave price and other social decisions alone, etc., *then* the employers would recognize the unions, provide dues check-off, increase wages [in some unionized industries] substantially, not resist too strenuously certain types of legislation favorable to labor, grant seniority rights, etc.[42]

What the corporations won with this cease-fire was the avoidance of unacceptable levels of economic disruption at home during a period when American capital had an unprecedented opportunity to expand abroad.

Jack Metzgar calls the result—an amalgam of tacit understandings and formal rules embodied both in the Wagner and Taft-Hartley acts and in various court rulings—the system of "negotiated class struggle." What the corporations were really offering to labor was sustained economic growth and, with it, the promise of both steadily rising real wages and an increase in the social autonomy of the working class.

> The freedom to live in its own way within a steadily expanding range of choices was the principal benefit for the working class of the social contract between capital and labor. It seemed a small price to pay for these increases in social autonomy to allow "the company" to make the larger decisions. . . . Whether and where a company does business, the overall direction of an industry and the conditions of the economy are some of those larger decisions.

In particular, "shutdowns and cutbacks are not negotiated. They are announced."[43]

Conclusion

The extent to which capital as a class deliberately and consciously *decided* to call a cease-fire with organized labor during the Eisenhower years can be exaggerated. Managers might more accurately be described as having grudgingly accepted the collective bargaining process, considering the apparent benefits that union cooperation in the management of stable industrial relations gave to them.

But it is crucial to recognize that whatever the interpretation, both the new social contract with organized labor in particular and the extension of the social wage in general were clearly predicated on more or less continuous economic growth that in turn depended on the *Pax Americana* in global affairs. As the conditions underlying that growth fell apart in the late 1960s and early 1970s, it was inevitable that both the willingness of capital to honor the social contract and the ability of the U. S. economy to afford a large and growing social safety net would come to an end. And that, of course, is exactly what is occurring now.

Chapter 6

Managerial Capitalism and

the Economic Crisis: 1971–?

> It was easy in the pre-Vietnam days to look at an area on a map and say, "that's ours" and feel pretty good about it. That's no longer the case, as Iran has made so terribly clear. American investment . . . is going to happen at a reduced rate until we can redefine the world.
>
> Prediction by the Middle East chief of a major U. S. bank, quoted in *Business Week*, 12 March, 1979.

THE "GOLDEN AGE" of the 1950s and 1960s was not to last. Challengers to the global hegemony of American corporations began to emerge from behind every bush. In one industry after another—steel, rubber, textiles, automobile, electronics, and footwear—Japanese and European competitors arose to challenge U. S. supremacy. Between 1960 and 1970 the American share of world trade declined by 16 percent—and would fall during the decade of the 1970s by another 23 percent.[1] In support of their own multinational corporations—many of them state-owned enterprises—the other capitalist governments of the world refused to abide any longer by the Bretton Woods accords. The collapse of the accords in 1971, symbolized by the Nixon administration floating the dollar free of the twenty-five-year regime of fixed currency exchange rates, signaled the end of the *Pax Americana*.

Long-developing tendencies within the global economy compounded the troubles felt so keenly in the United States. None was more disruptive than the chronic stagflation: the trend toward long-run inflation combined with high unemployment. Stagflation seemed to be related to the basic institutional facts of life in the new global capitalist system. It was certainly fueled in part by the pricing behavior of giant oligopolies. It was exacerbated by the increased interdependence brought about by the multinational investment policies of these same oligopolies, which contributed to the growing synchronization of business cycles across nations. And it was reinforced by the inclination of democratically-elected welfare states—especially the United States—to finance military interventions by running huge deficits rather than by taking the fiscally responsible, but politically unpopular, tack of raising taxes or reducing the social wage.

By the 1970s governments found that their ability to deploy Keynesian policies to "fine-tune" their economies had been seriously undermined. In the United States, above all, the result was slower growth, soaring prices, more frequent recessions followed by "flatter" recoveries, and an increasingly impotent central government. For industry, all of this meant greatly heightened international competition and a sharp squeeze on profits.[2] How capital reacted to this situation explains in large measure the deindustrialization of America.

The New International Competition

In the years just after World War II, the major surviving European and Japanese corporations, as well as newly formed ones, were preoccupied with rebuilding their domestic capacities. The Allied proscription against German and Japanese remilitarization after the war contributed significantly to this reconstruction by effectively forcing those two countries to plow back virtually all of their domestic savings into research, development, and new plant and equipment for the production of marketable commodities.

For a while, this left a substantially clear field for American firms in the postwar global economy. Not until the 1960s could foreign corporations afford to undertake major, direct overseas investments again. But when they *did* begin to compete internationally, it was from a modern, tightly-managed capital base, under conditions of relative domestic political stability and backed by a wide consensus about the desirability of active government indicative planning.

To be sure, direct foreign investment by American corporations continued to increase even after Nixon's landmark action on exchange rates in 1971. It expanded from a rate of $2.2 billion per year in 1966 to about $6 billion a decade later.[3] But the investments of other countries' multinationals grew much faster. As a result, U. S. corporations' share of the total direct foreign investment flows of the thirteen countries in the Organization for Economic Cooperation and Development (OECD) which keep such records (including the United States, Japan, Canada, Australia, and nine Western European nations) fell by one half, from an average of 61 percent during 1961–67 to 30 percent during 1974–78.[4]

Individual U. S. corporate giants increasingly had to share the world stage. In 1959, according to a study of twelve manufacturing industries and international commercial banking, the United States was "home" for 111 out of the world's 156 largest multinational corporations: a share of 71 percent. By 1976 only 68 out of the largest 156 (43 percent) were American based. Moreover, the competition was across the sectoral board. The U. S. share of the dozen top companies in each of the thirteen industries in the study declined in twelve of those industries.[5]

The story that is often told of this dramatic turn of affairs is how the efficient Germans and the hard-working Japanese labored, albeit with aid from the American government, to build economies that were able to successfully compete with the United States. What that story leaves out is just how much these economic miracles owe to the direct involvement by American corporations in their affairs.

The fact is that, from the middle years of the *Pax Americana,* American corporations frequently pursued their objective of gaining access to overseas markets by granting licenses to foreigners to enter the industry, using technologies developed by the American pioneer, in return for a royalty.[6] On other occasions, the American corporation moved abroad by implementing a joint production arrangement with a foreign firm, sometimes involving the construction of a "turnkey" plant that would subsequently be turned over to the host country.[7] Direct investment by American companies in the stock of foreign firms constituted still another form of global interdependence between ostensibly independent, competing firms. Indeed, in all three cases, it is no exaggeration to say that American corporate management policy during the 1950s and 1960s actually helped to create its own future competitors.

For example, an analysis of American corporate reports and Japanese government documents reveals that General Electric first bought into Toshiba stock in 1953 and by 1970 owned the single largest block of shares in that Japanese electronics firm: 233 million. GE also owns 40 percent of the subsidiary, Toshiba Electronics Systems Co., Ltd. and has twenty-four licensing agreements with both companies to make products that GE used to export from the United States—radar, generators, lamps, and boilers—many of which are sold internationally under the GE label. In 1969 during a big strike against GE in the United States, Toshiba provided its nominal competitor with crucial electrical and electronic parts, something that the unions in other American plants were able to prevent *their* employers from doing.

Westinghouse negotiated its first licensing agreement with Mitsubishi in 1923 and by 1970 was a principal shareholder. The relationship was so non-competitive it compelled the Justice Department to sue Westinghouse for conspiring with Mitsubishi to deploy patents and technology agreements in violation of U. S. anti-trust laws. One of many other examples is that as of 1970, GE alone had licensing agreements with over sixty Japanese companies. As one researcher put it: "Japanese competition is by no means an independent force but operates, in many cases, as a co-partner of American capital."[8]

Since the American electric-products industry invested so heavily abroad during the 1950s and 1960s, via both licensing and direct financing arrangements, it should not be surprising that, over the period of 1968–75, electric-products imports into the United States exceeded exports by a wide and growing margin. This was especially true for electrical equipment, computer chips, and transistors. These imports displaced large numbers of domestic workers in the industries that produced these products and cut deeply into the membership rolls of the three unions representing them.[9]

In the late 1970s the number of financial devices used for transferring technology and jobs abroad grew dramatically. In some cases these were still volunteered by American firms attempting to penetrate foreign markets for sales or to achieve lower costs of production. In other cases, however, foreign countries demanded agreements which made them a co-producer of an American product.

Consider, for example, the aircraft industry. For many foreign governments, the balance of payments and desire for job creation are important considerations in the awarding of procurement contracts. Since most foreign air carriers are government owned, it has been relatively easy for those countries to demand that U. S. producers manufacture or assemble a portion of the final product in the purchasing country as a condition for a successful contract bid. In effect, American manufacturers are forced to compete on quality, price, *and* the co-production percentage. Some recent contracts carry up to a 59 percent co-production responsibility. Both the companies and the unions in the aerospace industry agree that if it were not for these particular non-tariff trade restrictions, much more production would be carried out domestically.

A particularly ironic twist underlies one of the largest of these co-production agreements, between GE and the French national combine SNECMA. Faced with—as it turned out, temporarily—declining military sales to Washington in the wake of the Vietnam War, GE managers were under great pressure to find new customers for their jet engines. But not even GE could finance the development of such expensive new capital goods by itself, in the absence of lucrative, cost-plus American government contracts. Thus, GE turned abroad for financing and in 1973, struck a co-production agreement with SNECMA. GE provided the technology for the engine's "hot core" (the compressor portion, originally developed for the American B-1 bomber, now modified for the European fleet), and SNECMA contributed one-half of the necessary capital.[10]

The sale of F-16 fighter jets to NATO provides another example of the co-production strategem. In the NATO deal, General Dynamics and Pratt & Whitney Aircraft promised, as part of their contract bid, that industries in the European countries ordering the plane would produce 40 percent of the value of the 348 F-16s they were purchasing, 10 percent of the value of the 650 to be bought by the U. S. Air Force, and 15 percent of the value of those sold to other nations.[11]

"Offset" agreements are also being used as sweeteners in order to secure international contracts. Here the seller agrees to procure markets for the purchasing nation's products as a condition of sale. Thus, when Belgium held out on the NATO F-16 deal, General Dynamics convinced the U. S. government to purchase $30 million worth of machine guns from the Belgian arms firm, Fabrique Nationale. This turned out to be just the gesture needed to win Belgium's vote on the U. S. fighter. Fabrique Nationale was happy; so was General Dynamics.

Goodyear Tire and Rubber is another American corporation that has become deeply interdependent with its competitors. Figure 6.1 depicts the variety of ways in which Goodyear and four other ostensibly independent multinational tire corporations are linked to one another on the supply side, even as they compete for market share in the world— and, increasingly, even inside each other's countries. Thus, Goodyear and Michelin may be rivals for the attention of consumers of automobile tires, but that has not stopped them from cooperating in the co-production of synthetic rubber. Similarly, Goodyear shares technology with its principal Japanese competitor, Bridgestone.

Another example of the interdependence among ostensibly competing industries of different countries has recently come to light. A new study of the restructuring of the American steel industry dramatically illustrates the contradictory nature of the claims that U. S. capital is being "out-competed by foreigners"—claims that are continually articulated by some of the very same American companies that turn out to be deeply involved in financing their own competition abroad.[12]

The contractions in the domestic steel industry during the 1970s— including the highly publicized shutdown of the Youngstown Sheet and Tube Company in Ohio— were caused in part by the inability of some of the companies to finance modernization plans. In that case, three of the principal bankers of the conglomerate parent, the Lykes Corporation, began withdrawing their support in the mid-1970s. At the very time they were doing so, these same banks were significantly increasing their investments in the Japanese steel industry. Between 1975 and 1977 alone, Citibank increased its loans to Japanese steel from about $59 million to over $230 million. Chase Manhattan's investments in Japanese steel rose from $59 million to over $204 million. And the loans from the Chemical Bank of New York increased more than five times, from $15 million in 1975 to over $82 million just two years later.

Publicly, the domestic steel industry, led by U. S. Steel, loudly cried that foreign—especially Japanese—companies were "dumping" excess steel output on the U. S. market, at prices below the cost of production. The Carter administration responded in 1977 by introducing a "trigger price" or minimum floor for steel. Any importation of steel at a price

FIGURE 6.1
Interlocking Relationships Between Major Tire Companies

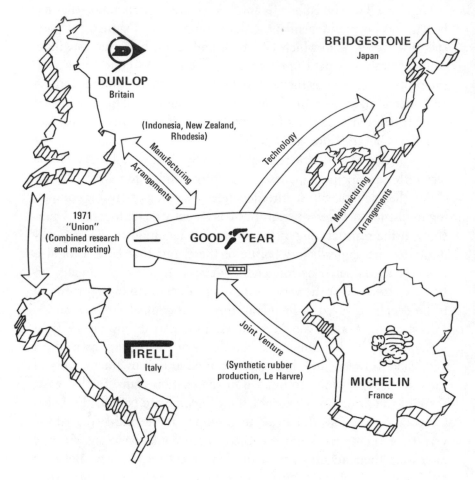

SOURCE: Edward Kelly and Lee Webb, eds., *Plant Closings: Resources for Public Officials and Activists* (Washington, D.C.: Conference on Alternative State and Local Policies, May 1979), p. 10.

below that floor would call forth an investigation from the Justice Department.

Yet even as the U. S. Steel Corporation was expressing concern about unfair competition from abroad, *it* was investing in overseas operations linked directly to that very competition. Thus, U. S. Steel's 1979 Annual Report lists partial ownership of eleven foreign companies operating on five continents, including four mining and mineral processing businesses in South Africa, in which it held shares ranging from 20 to 49 percent. This might not have been a problem except that these processing companies work closely with the South African Iron and Steel Corporation (ISCOR), a state-owned enterprise that produced nearly three quarters of the steel used in South Africa during the 1970s. Between 1972 and 1978, ISCOR also received almost $538 million in loans from American banks. Almost 90 percent of that total came from Chase and Citicorp, both of which were among those banks that were refusing to provide investment capital to upgrade the domestic U. S. steel industry.

And who were ISCOR's principal foreign customers for iron ore and other minerals—dolomite, coal, zinc, and tin? None other than those same Japanese steelmakers who had received such enormous loans from the very U. S. banks that were disinvesting in Youngstown. Finally, to complete the circle, in 1979, according to U. S. Department of Commerce records, ISCOR's rapid growth made South Africa the fifth most important exporter of *processed* iron and steel to the United States.

Economic Crisis and the Squeeze on Profits

The upshot of all these developments was the dramatic erosion of the inflation-adjusted, after-tax rates of profit of American corporations. According to a careful study by Daniel Holland and Stewart Myers, the real rate of return for all non-financial corporations in the United States fell from 15.5 percent in the period of 1963–66 to 12.7 percent during 1967–70. As if this were not bad enough, the rate fell to 10.1 percent in 1971–74 and finally to only 9.7 percent for the period through 1978.[13] Since it hardly makes sense to borrow money at 15 percent to invest in new capital that yields a profit of only 10 percent, new capital investment naturally declined.

The fall off in profitability was especially noticeable in America's key industries. Using Internal Revenue Service data on corporate earnings, we have calculated the average rate of return on total assets for the periods of 1963–68 and 1969–75. These pre-tax profit rates are shown in table 6.1. Those sectors that have suffered the Japanese "invasion" the most—radio and television equipment (consumer electronics) and motor vehicles—show the greatest loss. In both cases industrywide profitability fell by nearly two thirds. The average slump across all twelve manufacturing industries cited in table 6.1 exceeded 46 percent. It is little wonder then that an economy whose engine is fueled by profit began to sputter.

For the managers of American industry, there appeared to be only two things to do to reverse this trend. They could identify new, more profitable uses for their capital. Or they could find ways to cut production costs in their existing activities, either to restore profit margins directly—if they thought they could retain their markets in the face of the heightened global competition—or to enable them to shave their prices, thereby hopefully becoming more competitive without having to forego further profits.

During the 1970s the managers of American corporations pursued both sets of strategies. They sought new, typically "quick-fix," profitable opportunities. And they radically restructured the geography of their production arrangements in order to escape high labor-cost business "climates." Both strategies required that they move mountains of capital between economic sectors and among regions.

TABLE 6.1

Net Pre-Tax Profit Rates in Selected Manufacturing Industries: 1963–75
(in percent)

Industry	1963–68	1969–75	Percentage Change
Rubber products	9.1	6.1	−36.2
Glass products	12.0	7.9	−34.2
Steel industry	7.3	4.4	−39.4
Fabricated metal products	8.0	6.4	−20.4
Radio, television equipment	12.2	3.8	−69.2
Machine products	13.9	9.3	−33.4
Farm machinery	8.4	4.1	−51.4
Machine tools	12.9	6.1	−53.1
Electrical equipment (heavy)	13.2	7.7	−49.1
Motor vehicles and parts	16.3	6.7	−64.8
Shipbuilding	5.8	3.1	−47.0
Railroad equipment	7.8	3.4	−56.9
Average for the twelve industries			−46.3

SOURCE: U. S. Department of the Treasury, U. S. Internal Revenue Service, *Sourcebook of Statistics of Income,* Publication 647, (Washington, D.C., U. S. Government Printing Office), 1963–75.
NOTE: Net profit rate = net pre-tax corporate income (less deficit) divided by total assets.

What followed might well turn out to have been the most frenzied period of capital shift in American history. Conglomerates bought and sold subsidiaries at a feverish rate, often running down and finally closing profitable enterprises after milking them of their cash to finance investment elsewhere. Traditional product-oriented companies began to emulate the conglomerates, using key industries such as steel, transportation equipment, metalworking, and petroleum exploration and refining as "cash cows" to finance diversification. By the end of the decade, the entire private sector seemed to be engaged in buying, selling, or devouring parts of its own corporate anatomy in a madcap race to enhance or protect the "bottom line."

Conglomeration and the "New Managerialism"

It is a central tenet of modern industrial organization theory that large corporations are under constant pressure to grow and to expand their market share. "History suggests," wrote Paul McCracken, the head of President Ford's Council of Economic advisors, in a letter to the chairman of K-Mart, "that companies which decide to 'take their ease' are apt to be on the route to decay."[14]

This advice poses serious problems for the corporation caught in a profit squeeze. Where is it to find the capital for expansion? With its own retained earnings in a slump, it must turn to outside sources of funding. In normal times, it goes to the bank for this purpose. But when interest rates become so high that they seriously discourage external borrowing, it becomes even more urgent than usual for corporations to attract equity capital from investors. Since the latter make their money mainly from capital gains realized when they sell their stock, corporate managers are forced to pay close attention to the selling price of their shares. To most investors, it is the spread between a stock's selling price and its expected yield—or earnings—that matters: its so-called multiple. To companies trying to attract these investors, maintaining high "price/earnings (P/E) ratios" becomes the key objective of financial management.

During the crisis years of the 1970s, some of the most (in)famous conglomerates developed a degree of notoriety for engaging in what was euphemistically called "creative accounting," in order to fool Wall Street into validating the firm's quest for high P/E ratios. Many of these methods involved unsound and sometimes illegal procedures to inflate the value of a firm's assets. In our own interviews with former officers of a well-known conglomerate, we found that the managers had simply reported the worth of one particular subsidiary's inventory at 150 percent of its true market value! In another case, $250,000 out of $375,000 worth of samples advanced were in the hands of salesmen who were no longer even with the business in question. Yet the parent conglomerate counted this as a recoverable asset—and therefore as an increment to net worth. This same subsidiary had also purchased a building for $1.8 million before being acquired. After acquisition, the parent conglomerate "sold" this building to its nonprofit, non-taxable charitable foundation for $3 million (obviously a purely paper transaction) and reported the $1.2 million difference as an operating profit of the subsidiary. All this was done in an effort to trick the market into bidding up the P/E ratio on the conglomerate's stock.

Stories like this may be amusing, and they are fairly ubiquitous. But of far greater significance for the deindustrialization of America are the many thoroughly legal, aboveboard conglomerate strategies that make up what is sometimes called the "new managerialism." The basic policy —to emphasize cash management over a commitment to any particular product line—was codified by the Boston Consulting Group (BCG), a prominent management consulting firm originally affiliated with the Harvard Business School.

In the early 1970s, BCG proposed that the optimal portfolio of a diversified company could be described in terms of a matrix arraying the market share of each of the corporation's product (or service) lines against the sales growth rate of each activity.[15] Lines with both low market shares and low growth rates were nicknamed "dogs." BCG recommended that they be abandoned, even if they were nominally profitable, on the grounds that they would probably require reinvestment of any cash surplus in order to maintain market share. (To BCG, the ability to move surplus cash around is the *sine qua non* of sophisticated management.)

Branches or subsidiaries with high market share but low growth rates would typically be found in more mature industries. These were the famous "cash cows," expected to generate large positive cash flows that corporate headquarters should "milk," in order to provide investment funds for rapidly growing but still low-market-share product or service lines (the so-called "problem children" or "question marks") or to acquire altogether new subsidiaries.

The fourth category—the high-share, high-growth "stars"—should be allowed to go their own way for the time being. They would probably need all of their retained earnings while they were in this mode, and so could not yet be expected to make regular, sustained contributions to the corporate "cash box."

There are literally endless examples of the practical application of these categories and investment rules during the 1970s. The problem is that many of them led to questionable, and in some cases, incredibly inept management decisions that actually destroyed viable businesses and generated much of the capital disinvestment discussed in chapter 2.

For example, some corporate headquarters required that their branches or subsidiaries (including those that were formerly successful independent businesses) meet minimum profit targets, known in the trade as "hurdle rates of return." Division and local managers' executive perks—not to mention fresh financial resources for the subsidiary itself—were often made to depend on whether these targets were met. Many branches and previously acquired businesses were thus ultimately shut down, not because they were unprofitable, but because they could not achieve the parent corporation's current (and often arbitrary) hurdle rate of return.

At Cornell University, William F. Whyte and his colleagues have been studying cases of conglomerate destruction of viable businesses. Among their findings are numerous examples of abandonment of going concerns by conglomerates whose target rates of return were not met. For example:

> The Herkimer [New York] plant, producing library furniture, had been acquired by Sperry Rand in 1955. The plant had made a profit every year except one through the next two decades, and yet Sperry Rand decided to close the plant [in part because it] was not yielding a 22% profit on invested capital. That was the standard used by this conglomerate management in determining an acceptable rate of return on its investments.[16]

Similarly, Genesco, a major clothing conglomerate with holdings throughout the East, is known to have once imposed a 25 percent hurdle rate on its various companies—three times the average rate of profit earned in its industry.[17] And there are many more examples like these.

But whatever the particular value of the target in any particular company, the principle of the corporate hurdle rate means that viable businesses can be closed because, although they are making a profit, it is simply *not enough of a profit* to satisfy company policy.

Probably the most famous modern conglomerate-related plant closing in America was the 1977 shutdown of the Youngstown Sheet and Tube Company in Ohio. In 1969 Sheet and Tube, then the nation's eighth largest steelmaking firm, was purchased by a New Orleans-based conglomerate, the Lykes Corporation. The acquisition was financed mainly by a loan that Lykes promised to pay off out of Sheet and Tube's very substantial cash flow. During the next eight years, Lykes used Sheet and Tube's cash to amortize that debt and to expand its non-steel operations. Figure 6.2 shows pre- and post-merger annual capital investment in Sheet and Tube. In the decade before the merger, investment in plant and equipment averaged $72 million a year and increased each year at an average rate of $9.3 million. After the acquisition by Lykes, the average fell to about $34 million per year and would have had a *zero* growth trend if not for a few investment projects begun in 1975 and then quickly abandoned. Figure 6.2 shows that, in the years immediately following the acquisition, Lykes pursued a strategy of planned disinvestment in its recent acquisition. By the time changing market conditions had convinced Lykes that it might make sense to remain in Youngstown after all, there were no longer sufficient reserves to finance the necessary retooling.

It is also true that Lykes's bankers were redlining both the company and the town by this time—refusing to invest in either. Nevertheless, most financial analysts seem to agree that "Lykes must bear responsibility for a good deal of the failure at Youngstown Sheet and Tube."[18] As *Business Week* said in its 3 October 1977 issue: "The conglomerators' steel acquisitions were seen as cash boxes for corporate growth in other areas."

In a rather absurd postscript to the closing—which, as we have seen, cost 4,100 Ohio workers their jobs—Lykes merged in 1978 with the

FIGURE 6.2

*New Capital Investment in the Youngstown Sheet and Tube Company,
Before and After its 1969 Merger with the Lykes Corporation: 1961–75*

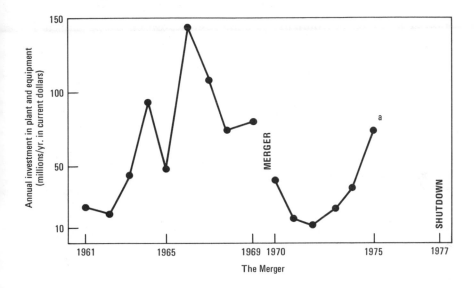

The Merger

SOURCES: U. S. Senate Committee on the Judiciary, *Mergers and Industrial Concentration,* Hearings before the Subcommittee on Anti-Trust and Monopoly, 95th Congress, May 12, July 27, July 28, and September 21, 1978, (Washington D.C.: U.S. Government Printing Office, 1979), p. 344; and William Hogan, S.J., *The Economic History of the Iron and Steel Industry in the United States* (Lexington, Mass.: D. C. Heath, 1971), p. 1835.

[a] Investment project undertaken only after two consecutive years of unexpectedly high worldwide demand for steel. Project was abandoned during the 1975 recession.

conglomerate Ling-Temco-Vought (LTV), owner of the nation's *next* largest steelmaker. The argument used in court by Lykes and LTV to overcome antitrust objections to the merger was that their steel business was "failing" and could only be rescued by achieving financial scale economies through merger! The now-completed merger makes Lykes-LTV the nation's third largest producer of steel. Such is the history of how an industry "naturally" becomes more concentrated.

Centralized control by a home office can impair the profitability of a newly acquired branch or subsidiary in a number of other ways as well. Some of these costs have been so great that they actually turn a once-profitable subsidiary into a loser.

Sometimes, the home office requires its new acquisition to carry additional management staff sent from headquarters—personnel not previously needed by the subsidiary and that market analysts feel are

153

superfluous. For example, a recent issue of a New England trade magazine cited one case of a small manufacturer, with 40 percent of the domestic hypodermic-needle market, which was put up for sale by its conglomerate parent. A market analyst noted that "the parent corporation, a *Fortune* 500 company . . . has imposed an excess of staff and other requirements which add non-productive costs to the operation. A *pro forma* [simulated balance sheet] eliminating this overlay of corporate expenses shows a much better picture."[19]

This practice was also present in the case of the Sheller-Globe Corporation's acquisition in 1974, operation of, and subsequent closing in 1977 of the Colonial Press in Clinton, Massachusetts. The Press was charged $200,000 some months and a yearly average of $900,000 in corporate overhead costs. There was little justification for these. The Press was being forced to pay the costs of larger corporate activities from which it did not benefit. Sheller-Globe primarily makes automobile parts, school buses, and ambulances and had acquired this book-printing firm incidentally, as part of a larger acquisition of an automotive competitor that had itself bought the Press earlier. Sheller-Globe's previous experience was in its big-city auto-parts plants, where physical security of the premises is important. Sheller-Globe had an entire department solely responsible for security. This centralized corporate-security department applied the same protective systems to all divisions —including the Colonial Press, located in a bucolic New England mill town! Sheller-Globe built a link fence around three sides of the Colonial Press plant and hired twenty-two security guards. Upon leaving the plant, employees would be searched for stolen goods. The level of theft occurring at the Press could not possibly have justified such outlays. Yet the Press was forced to bear part of these costs.[20]

Taxing a subsidiary in order to subsidize headquarters operations or corporate allies is destructive enough. But perhaps most serious of all are the cases where home-office policy actually *creates* the unprofitability of a previously-profitable subsidiary through clumsy interference with the local managers who know the situation best. William Whyte's case study of the Herkimer, N. Y. library furniture plant revealed just such a problem.

> The plant had always had its own sales force and was not dependent upon Sperry Rand for its market. In fact, being part of the conglomerate imposed

serious barriers in marketing. For example, it was a rule of Sperry Rand that the Library Bureau salesman could not call on any customers served by Sperry Rand. While this left the Library Bureau its main markets with public and educational institution libraries, the rule barred the plant from selling to a large number of industrial and business firms that used library equipment. The [subsidiary] could only enter these markets through Sperry Rand salesmen who were unfamiliar with Library Bureau products and had more important things to sell. The handicaps were similar in the export field . . . [According to the former] head of sales for the Library Bureau . . . "We were not officially barred from exporting, but to sell anything outside of the country, we had to send our proposal to the international division, and it would just die there. We would never hear anything back."[21]

Similarly, Sheller-Globe immediately brought outside management into its Colonial Press subsidiary who were, with the exception of the newly installed president, totally without experience in the publishing industry. Nevertheless, this outside group was given control over the most important decisions. Flexibility with respect to publication schedules for such prestigious customers as Reader's Digest and Random House was reduced. Not only was the Press no longer allowed to offer free warehouse space to publishers, but the customer service and order departments were also merged to the point where "orders were misplaced and the relations with customers deteriorated." A fancy and overblown computerized management information system was installed at great expense, which so fouled up operations that "books were lost and there was often general confusion about what materials there were and where they were located." Publishers were no longer given itemized cost estimates. Not surprisingly, "customers became alienated, large accounts (such as Random House) were lost, and sales declined. . . . Decisions which were appropriate to the automotive industry proved disastrous in the book-printing industry."[22]

The success of the conglomerates at maintaining their cash flows well into the worldwide economic crisis of the 1970s—albeit at the expense of workers and communities hit by one plant closing after another—prompted imitation by many older, more established firms. By the end of the decade, corporations long identified with particular products—many of them vital to the economic well-being of the whole society—were vigorously milking their more lucrative operations or running down their oldest facilities rather than upgrading them, in order to finance diversification.

Thus, for example, the Mobil Oil Corporation used part of its post-1973 inflated international oil profits, not to expand badly needed domestic petroleum production, but to purchase Montgomery Ward, a well-established department-store chain.[23] This was just the beginning of Mobil's diversification drive, as will be seen later.

Throughout the last decade, many of the nation's leading steel companies used the profits from their existing operations—profits enhanced by the savings derived from not reinvesting in new, modern equipment for existing mills—to acquire non-steel businesses. Between 1970 and 1976, the steel industry as a whole paid out 43 percent of its after-tax profits in dividends (a rate above the average for all industries) at a time when steel-company spokespersons were loudly complaining that pollution control expenditures required by law were preventing them from upgrading their old plant and equipment. Some Wall Street analysts saw this as a strategy for buying time, holding the investors' confidence, while management developed a plan for diversifing into new fields.[24]

In the late 1970s the entire industry did just that; it shifted capital into cement, petrochemicals, coal, natural gas, nuclear power plant components, containers and packaging, and real estate. Between 1976 and 1979 the ratio of new capital spending to depreciation in the steel operations of U. S. Steel fell by 50 percent. So far had this diversification progressed that, by 1978, of that corporations's total worldwide assets 44 percent were in businesses outside of steel.[25] Symbolically, in the middle of 1978 another major producer, Armco Steel Corporation, legally dropped "Steel" as its middle name.

Still another example of massive corporate disinvestment to finance diversification is provided by the withdrawal of Pullman Incorporated from the business of manufacturing rail passenger cars, thus leaving only a single domestic producer, the Budd Company (now a subsidiary of Thyssen, a German steel firm). Pullman's new parent firm, Wheelbrator-Frye, will allow it to continue to manufacture freight cars, along with many of the products into which Pullman's managers diversified during the 1970s: oil, petrochemical, fertilizer factories, and truck trailers. Ironically, this occurs at a time when "the energy crisis, environmental problems, deterioration of the central city, and congestion of the highways all point to the need for a dramatic increase in railroad service."[26]

Unhappily, these are anything but isolated examples. Recall the findings by Roger Schmenner (reported in chapter 2) on the investment transactions of the *Fortune* 500 during the 1970s. To recapitulate: two out of every three "new" manufacturing plants added to the empires of these corporations after 1972 were in fact not new at all, but rather pre-existing facilities acquired during the decade. During the same period, they physically expanded only one seventh of all their plants.

Moreover, as we move into the 1980s, the tendency toward conglomeration—the extraordinarily pervasive "urge to merge"—continues. Even foreign capital coming into the United States is now going principally into the acquisition of already-existing American companies rather than into the creation of new enterprise and jobs.[27] On the East Coast, it is principally Dutch, British, and Canadian money; on the West Coast, it is Middle Eastern and Japanese capital. All of it reflects the continuing urge to merge.

The very largest multinational corporations are now displaying the strongest merger tendencies. Not surprisingly, the oil companies lead the pack. In 1972, even before OPEC began to openly resist Western control over the pricing and allocation of Middle Eastern oil, John Blair could write:

In 1968, 6 of the 10 largest and 9 of the 20 largest industrial firms were oil companies. But the oil companies are leaders in merger activity not just because of their size, but because of the pressure of their immense internally generated funds for effective utilization. Reflecting the tax advantages enjoyed by the industry, particularly the foreign tax credit and the depletion allowance, the cash flow of oil companies in 1968 totaled $9.6 billion, consisting of $5.8 billion in net income after taxes and $3.8 billion in depletion and depreciation reserves. This is equal to the assets of more than 60 percent of the total number of all manufacturing corporations . . . between 1956 and 1968 . . . the 20 major [oil] firms absorbed 20 others primarily engaged in petroleum refining.[28]

In 1976 Mobil Oil took the lead when it acquired Marcor Corporation (itself the result of a merger of the Montgomery Ward department-store chain and Container Corporation of America). Three years later, the largest oil company, Exxon, showed that it, too, could take a lesson from the conglomerates when it acquired the Cleveland-based

Reliance Electric Company, the nation's third largest manufacturer (behind only G.E. and Westinghouse) of electric motors. In making its takeover bid, Exxon paid Reliance's stockholders more than 200 percent of the prevailing market value of their stock. All of this furious buying and selling led Harold Williams, then Chairman of the Securities and Exchange Commission, to complain to a subcommittee of the U. S. House of Representatives:

> It has become acceptable to assume that corporate control may change hands with no greater concern about the consequences than accompanies an exchange of property deeds in a game of Monopoly.[29]

In 1981 Mobil was back in the news in connection with what turned out to be the two most expensive merger transactions in history. Throughout the first half of the year and into the summer, Mobil, DuPont, and Seagrams Distillers fought it out for the right to acquire Conoco Inc., then the nation's ninth largest oil company. In August, Dupont won, paying a record $7.4 billion. Less than five months later, a furious, often tempestuous bidding war between Mobil and U. S. Steel over the acquisition of Marathon Oil came to an end when the courts ruled, in early January 1982, that a merger with Mobil would violate the anti-trust laws. This left U. S. Steel free to begin buying up a controlling share of Marathon's stock. In a last-minute fit of pique, cash-rich and twice-denied Mobil threatened to have its way after all —by buying a major share of U. S. Steel! The Marathon buy-out even topped the bidding war for Conoco. Although U. S. Steel's Chairman of the Board David M. Roderick promised that the acquisition of an oil company "would in no way diminish [our] commitment to [our] steel operations," the *New York Times* predicted that a new "storm of criticism" would be forthcoming from Wall Street for the corporation's decision to diversify rather than modernize.[30]

But if investors are pleased with the potential money profits gained from the exercise of their merger mania, the social crisis associated with the deindustrialization of America has certainly not been ameliorated. Indeed, it has almost surely been exacerbated by all this merger activity.

For one thing, the manipulations necessary to *finance* such expensive mergers are likely to add to inflation. Between 1975 and 1980, more than $100 billion of corporate cash reserves were diverted toward supporting tender offers alone. And during a two-week period in July of 1981, six oil companies arranged lines of credit totaling $28 billion —all for the purpose of financing takeovers.[31] According to the House Banking Committee's Chairperson Fernand J. St. Germain of Rhode Island:

> The[se] massive credit lines secured by companies . . . could put upward pressure on interest rates . . . and make it difficult for other sectors of the business community to obtain credit. . . . Privately, one Federal Reserve official acknowledges that the enormous credit caches could cause macroeconomic trouble. Much of the money is apparently being secured in European credit markets, where some $735 billion in greenbacks have piled up subject to no U. S. banking regulations. The unexpectedly massive infusion of these funds into American financial markets could complicate the Fed's efforts to control the U. S. money supply. If so, the central bank's only recourse would be to put even stiffer brakes on domestic money growth.[32]

Dupont's expenditure of more than $7 billion to purchase Conoco took place during the very same week that President Reagan signed a bill giving $60 billion in tax cuts to American industry for the announced purpose of "stimulating new investment in plant and equipment and creating jobs." But, at least in the short-run, the acquisition of Conoco creates *no* new productive capacity or directly productive (as compared with managerial) employment, whatever DuPont chooses to do with its new property later on.

All this furious buying and selling and wheeling and dealing has meant a huge increase in the size of corporate bureaucracies. This has been especially true in those conglomeratelike firms that are decentralized into individual profit centers, each with its own managerial hierarchy. The growth of these bureaucracies, used to control widespread corporate empires and to maintain discipline within the work force, adds layer upon layer of management, all of which adds to the cost of production but not necessarily to real output.

In fact the mushrooming of *corporate,* as distinct from government, bureaucracies may explain much of the productivity decline that has caused so much concern to the country. Between 1950 and 1980, the ratio of "overhead" personnel—managers, their secretaries, and so forth—to all employees in U. S. manufacturing rose from 18 percent to over 30 percent.[33] Economist David M. Gordon, writing in the *American Economic Review,* reports statistical evidence showing that the increase over time in this ratio contributed significantly to the decline in productivity during the 1970s. Indeed, in Gordon's model, an index of the effectiveness of "bureaucratic control," based on this ratio, accounts for over 85 percent of the measured retardation in labor productivity between 1954–73 and 1974–78.[34]

Centralization, Conglomeration, and Community Economic Instability

These unrestrained acquisitions and divestitures, along with the use of the profits from basic industry to finance diversification, help to explain those shutdowns and relocations that were discussed in chapter 2. Every wave of conglomeration and diversification seems to be followed in short order by a "shake-out"—the most dramatic symptoms of which are plant, store, and office closings. And because of the way it is at least partly financed—that is, by running down older productive capacity—corporate diversification policies seem always to leave industrial plant closures in their wake.

Centralization is the aspect of modern capitalist development that gave rise to the process of conglomeration. But centralization has also undermined the economic stability of communities across the country indirectly, through its tendency to increase the degree of absentee control of a community's economic base. All of these shifts of facilities or transfers of ownership during the 1960s and, with greater intensity and at a more rapid pace in the 1970s, have radically altered what some have called the "geography of industrial organization."

In particular, as the ownership and control of productive assets became increasingly centralized, it was inevitable that more and more business establishments in a typical American community would directly or indirectly come under the influence of "absentee landlords" —central managements headquartered elsewhere. The significance of this trend is that, whether or not any particular "remotely-controlled" business is actually reorganized or shut down by its absentee owners, the *potential* for this (or any other management decisions deleterious to the local economy) is greatly enhanced by the very fact of absentee control.[35]

In his fascinating Cook's tour of New England, writer Neal Peirce noted:

> During the 1960s, the national conglomerates had a field day snapping up family-owned businesses, especially in northern New England. By the early 1970s, 19 of the 22 Vermont plants with more than 500 workers were owned by out-of-state corporations. In Maine, all of the six firms with 2,000 or more workers were absentee-owned. The same applied to 16 of New Hampshire's largest firms.[36]

David Birch has discovered a similar result for the southern states. In the manufacturing sector, at least, they, too, are "colonized" by corporations based outside the region. Whereas over the period of 1969–76, nearly nine tenths of the new jobs created in manufacturing branch plants located in the North had corporate headquarters also based in the North—principally in New York, Chicago, Pittsburgh, St. Louis, Stamford, and the greater Philadelphia area[37]—fewer than one third of the new jobs created over the same period in southern manufacturing plants belonged to southern-based corporations. Putting it the other way around, in recent years 70 percent of the South's net job growth in manufacturing corporate branch plants has been controlled by Frostbelt firms. Moreover, nearly 100 percent of the net growth of employment in those southern manufacturing establishments that were conglomerate subsidiaries belonged to conglomerates based in the North.[38]

Between 1955 and 1968, the Federal Trade Commission (FTC) gathered information on the location of the corporate headquarters of both the acquired and acquiring companies involved in nearly 18,000 mergers. Using these data to map the "geography of remote control of capital" during this period, British researcher Peter Dicken observed that "four out of every five states experienced an outward shift of corporate control" as more and more of their businesses were acquired by outside corporations.[39] (During the study period 1955–68, *all* the southern states were net losers of control over their own businesses. This is the history that led to the outcome measured by Birch for 1969–76.) The vast majority of the control is located where it has always been located in this century: in the North. Unfortunately, the FTC no longer releases data on the location of the parties in merger activities.

Another enterprising researcher, Berkeley geographer Allan Pred, collected his own data by interviewing officials in corporate home offices in several Western cities to find out where their branch plants or subsidiaries were located in 1974–75. For example, in that year 181 multilocational business organizations headquartered in the San Francisco Bay Area employed more than a million people worldwide. Only one quarter of those jobs were located within the Bay Area itself (San Francisco-Oakland-San Jose). Sixteen percent were employed in foreign countries. And 59 percent were employed elsewhere in North America. These San Francisco/Oakland-based corporations controlled 23,000 jobs in New York, 92,000 in Los Angeles, 13,000 in Dallas-Fort Worth, 12,000 in Chicago, 8,000 in Washington, D. C., and 3,000 in Atlanta. More than one half of the 59 percent of the jobs in the United States and Canada were located outside of the continent's seventy largest metropolitan areas, in smaller cities, towns, and rural counties.[40] In such places, as was shown in chapter 3, a major plant closing or permanent cutback can have an especially devastating effect on the local economic base.

Large corporations and conglomerates unquestionably have the financial capacity to infuse any particular community with new job-creating capital. The question is whether or not—and how—this capability is employed. On this score, researchers at Temple University in Philadelphia recently found that, during the decade of the 1970s, between 58,000 and 84,000 jobs (3 to 5 percent of the employment base in 1969) disappeared from that city through identifiable shut-downs or relocations of establishments with thirty or more employees. Absentee-owned corporations were responsible for 54 percent of all these plants and store closings and an estimated 64 percent of the job loss.[41]

This disproportionately high shut-down rate among establishments controlled by absentee-owned corporations occurred despite strong evidence that, at least in the 1970s, conglomerates tended to acquire "winners": independent firms that exhibited higher-than-average growth or profit rates.[42] What happens then to the employment growth of smaller, independent businesses when they are acquired?

Again using Dun and Bradstreet data, Birch has been able to identify about 6,000 business establishments that were independently owned in 1969, acquired between 1969 and 1972, and continued in their affiliated status during 1972–74. He compares the 1972–74 growth performance of these establishments with that of a sample of 1.3 million establishments that remained both "alive and independent" throughout the five-year period. The results are displayed in table 6.2.

A comparison of the upper and lower panels of the second column shows that conglomerate subsidiaries generally grew faster during 1972–74 than independently-owned businesses of comparable size. But this does not take into account the fact that conglomerates tend to acquire faster-growing businesses to begin with, which is confirmed by examination of the first column. The comparison that properly adjusts for this bias is contained in the third column, where it can be seen that the acquired establishments actually did somewhat *worse* than the independent establishments over the same interval of time. Birch's own conclusion is that "the acquisition process . . . has certainly done little

TABLE 6.2

Average Annual Percentage Employment Growth of U.S. Establishments by Size and Legal Status: 1969–72 and 1972–74

Employment Size in 1969	Employment Growth During		Change in Growth Rate
	1969–72	1972–74	
Independents Throughout			
0–20	8.5	3.5	−5.0
21–50	0.5	2.1	1.6
51–100	−1.0	1.4	2.4
101–500	−1.8	1.1	2.9
501 and over[a]	2.1	1.4	−0.7
Establishments Acquired 1969–1972			
0–20	14.2	3.4	−10.8
21–50	2.1	3.6	1.5
51–100	0.5	2.2	1.7
101–500	−0.8	1.7	2.5
501 and over[a]	−8.3	−2.6	−5.7

SOURCE: Prepared statement of David L. Birch, in Subcommittee on Antitrust and Restraint of Trade Activities Affecting Small Business, Committee on Small Business, U. S. House of Representatives, *Hearings*, 96th Cong., 2d sess., U.S. Government Printing Office, 1980, p.234.
[a]The sample consisted of only twenty-eight acquired firms, too few to permit reliable inference.

to increase [acquired companies'] growth performance relative to the independents from whom they have been culled."[43]

Other studies, on the experience in Maine, Wisconsin, Nebraska, and Iowa, come to similar conclusions. Absentee-controlled firms' payrolls grew more slowly than those of locally-owned companies, and the former were quicker to cut back employment during recessions. Acquired firms were typically forced to switch from using the services of local bankers, accountants, and lawyers to those in the parent corporation's home-office city.[44] Industrial relations issues, especially those involving the greatest degree of conflict, tended to be handled by lawyers sent out from corporate headquarters rather than by professionals living in the community where the conflict is occurring. Residents of the area found it increasingly difficult to hold the managers of these absentee-owned businesses accountable, even as the real political influence of the latter grew, for example, in local legislatures.[45]

The Break-Up of the Social Contract: Running Away from the Unions

Buying and selling entire businesses and transferring capital from one sector to another at the first sign of trouble constituted the most important corporate strategies for raising short-term profitability during the 1960s and protecting those profits in the face of the economic crisis of the 1970s. In the process, a great many profitable, formerly independent companies were shut down, and the social productivity embodied in skills and viable plant and equipment destroyed.

Capital's second strategy for coping with the crisis was to relocate —or more often, to differentially expand and contract—facilities to different parts of the country, and to different areas of the globe. If the search for profits is the prod that explains management's desire to relocate production, *which* locations are considered preferable to others?

For any particular firm, there may be a variety of "special cases" in which factors such as market access, the availability of cheap energy, or proximity to a particular skill center dominate the choice of location.

But it now seems to be a fair generalization that, for the most part, the geographic patterning of deindustrialization has to do with the proclivity of companies to shift capital out of older industrial areas to escape having to live with a labor force that, through the previous industrialization process itself, had become "costly" in the broadest sense of the term: acclimated to a higher standard of living and to a greater degree of influence on day-to-day workplace procedures.

To be sure, even as the post–World War II social contract was being developed, companies were violating the spirit, if not the substance, of the "agreement" by shifting operations (or differentially expanding) into the Sunbelt, non-union peripheries within the North, and abroad. During the 1950s and 1960s the practice of running away from the unions grew so much, that by the 1970s the northern-based industrial unions had been severely weakened. Their membership rolls in their older Frostbelt jurisdictions declined. The rolls in the Sunbelt states grew slowly, if at all, under various combined obstacles: insufficient union funds to sponsor organizing drives; cultural resistance in many places (especially rural areas); direct legal (sometimes even police) repression of attempts to organize Sunbelt workers; and the often lethargic attitude of some of the older, established, national trade union leaders toward the need to organize new members.

The business community fairly widely admits now that it consciously chooses locations in order to avoid unionization wherever possible. For example,

> Donovan Dennis, vice-president of Fantus Corporation, the well-known plant location consulting firm, was asked by the *Wall Street Journal* to name the single most important determinant of plant location. He responded, "Labor costs are the big thing, far and away. Nine out of ten times you can hang it on labor costs and unionization."[46]

From his information on the industrial location practices of the *Fortune* 500, Roger Schmenner concludes that an anti-union "climate" is an extremely important factor influencing industrial plant location managers. In particular, inside the United States,

> location is directed to the . . . right-to-work states, most of which are located in the Sunbelt and Plains States. . . . While only 34 percent of the [plants in his sample that remained in operation throughout the 1970s] were

located in right-to-work states, fully one-half of all the *new* plants were sited in them. These data support the contention that the edge for non-unionism in right-to-work states has triggered a more-than-proportional degree of plant openings there. . . . No other public policy carries anywhere near the location clout of the right-to-work law.[47]

The antipathy of (especially traditional) southern capitalists to unions is so great that some local development authorities are put under pressure to actively discourage companies in highly-unionized industries from moving in. The *Wall Street Journal* reports that "there are literally scores of companies that have been turned away from southern towns because of their wage rates or union policies." As the chairman of the Mississippi Industrial Foundation in Greenville put it, "there are a lot of companies we never see because they know better" [than to bring a union into Greenville].[48]

Over the years since the late 1940s, managerial strategies of shifting capital to avoid or shed unionization have become increasingly sophisticated, especially when practiced by large multiplant, multiproduct corporations. While runaway shops may still be important in the more highly competitive industries such as clothing, shoes, toys, furniture, and some segments of electronics, the new strategies typically involve the operation of multistate, multiregional systems of plants and subcontractors. Chief among these strategies are *parallel production* and *multiple sourcing*.

Under parallel production, major firms in the most powerful industries—automobile, steel, rubber, electrical machinery, aircraft, and machine tools—have created essentially duplicate production facilities for the same components and even for some assembly operations. This phenomenon is especially prevalent where the original facility is a union shop. Parallel production is often implemented even when it involves foregoing some economies of scale at the original site. The compensation to the company is that a strike or other form of disruption at the original shop can be met by redirecting more production to the non-union facility. In this way the firm can break a strike without ever committing a statutory unfair labor practice. Not only does parallel production shift jobs to other areas, thus immediately causing local job loss, but it also strengthens the hand of management back in the union shop.

The automobile and electrical goods industries are well known for their use of this tactic. What the United Auto Workers (UAW) calls General Motor's "southern strategy" was initiated soon after World War II, when GM began a concerted effort to circumvent the union's strength by locating new plants in what are primarily right-to-work states. The practice continued through the 1970s. In fact, between 1975 and 1980, GM opened a total of fourteen new plants, with eight located in the deep South and one in Mexico. Nine of the U. S. plants were placed in right-to-work states.[49] This permitted GM to effectively use the threat of shifting production to its non-union shops as a bargaining lever in its northern plant negotiations.

General Electric is also known for its use of this strategy, which began during the reign of Lemuel R. Boulware, the fiercely anti-union vice-president for labor relations. For years the company has pursued parallel production policies in a number of its lines. The most recent involves aircraft engine components manufacture. GE's main competitor, Connecticut-based Pratt & Whitney (the jet engine division of the United Technologies conglomerate), established parallel plants in rural towns in Maine and Georgia. General Electric's Aircraft Engine Group responded by constructing a component plant in the non-union town of Madisonville, Kentucky.[50]

What has been accomplished by this anti-union thrust in the major companies is being extended to smaller suppliers by the strategy of multiple sourcing. Increasingly, prime contractors are refusing to grant sole source arrangements to the independent shops that provide them with components. This is true even when the subcontractor is fully capable of supplying all the parts required and at a competitive price. This strategy enables the prime contractors both to assure on-time delivery of components and to play one vendor off against another. Local suppliers are forced to reduce production runs, lay off workers, and more strenuously oppose union organizing drives or demands. This accounts in part for the inability of unions to organize the supplier-shop constellations in the aircraft industry, and for the low or declining rates of unionization in other sectors of the economy, including metalworking and electronics.

Of course a multiplant firm has the option of gradually or, on some occasions, abruptly, phasing out the old high-wage, unionized facility altogether and shifting operations to the non-union, lower-wage southern or far northern plant. In the timber industry of the Pacific Northwest, such shifts have been taking place for several years. Companies in Oregon and Washington are shutting down their local mills—or are being forced out of the market by competitive bidding for timber supplies for export to Japan—and expanding their activities in the Southeast.[51]

The Brown and Williamson Tobacco Company's decision to shut down one of its older southern plants, and to cut back operations in another in order to consolidate production at yet a third southern site —unionized but with less restrictive work rules—provides evidence that helps to explain the high rate of southern plant closings reported in chapter 2. In early 1979, Brown and Williamson announced that it would phase out its 3,000-employee plant in Louisville, Kentucky, over a three-year period and cut back operations in its Petersburg, Virginia, plant. According to Carroll H. Teague, Jr., vice-president for Personnel and Labor Relations, production (and some of the more skilled workers) would be shifted to the firm's Macon, Georgia, plant. Why Macon? Because, Teague told the press,

> we had been extremely successful in negotiating restriction-free agreements in the Macon plant. We did not have [maximum allowable] machine speeds, manning ratios, or restrictive seniority provisions. We had only four labor classifications throughout the entire plant. We organized production in a way that permitted us to operate the machinery 24 hours a day—and not to shut down for lunch breaks.[52]

The effect of these interstate and interregional capital shifts on the power and solvency of the largest unions has been quite significant. Consider the electric products industry, the scene of so much violent confrontation throughout the twentieth century. Between 1958 and 1974 the principal unions—the International Union of Electrical Workers, the United Electrical Workers, and the International Brotherhood of Electrical Workers—managed to organize only one out of every four new production workers in the industry.

> Since employment [within the United States] has continued to grow, although fitfully, the union problems are not due to a decline in the number of workers available to be organized, but rather to the difficulties of enrolling workers in new [southern] plants as old, well-established [northern] locals shrink and even disappear.[53]

Some northern unions or union organizers have actively intervened to prevent companies from shutting down operations in their jurisdictions in order to expand in non-union areas. A dramatic example concerns Gould Incorporated's 1,500-person circuit-breaker plant in Philadelphia and its union, the United Auto Workers.[54]

The original ITE Circuit Breaker Company was a locally-owned family firm with a national reputation. A 1968 merger with a Chicago corporation created the ITE Imperial Corporation, the third largest producer of electric power and distribution equipment in the country. Then in January 1976, after a long merger fight, the new ITE was acquired by Gould, Inc., another large electronics corporation headquartered in Chicago. The UAW knew there would be trouble, for Gould's Chairman William T. Ylvisaker had just said as much to the New York Society of Securities Analysts: "We don't like unions, we fight them."

Gould had tried to shift production from the Philadelphia plant to facilities in Florida, Virginia, and Oklahoma, but UAW Local 1612, a holdover from the ITE days, had been able to stop them through the successful bargaining of contract language that made such capital transfers illegal. Acting on a tip from office workers, Local 1612 officers went to Wilmington, North Carolina, in September 1977, where they found an unmarked factory containing machinery that had gradually been moved from the Philadelphia plant. Subsequently, five more small plants in various states of completion were discovered in the Carolinas, Florida, and Oklahoma.

Local 1612 had caught Gould red-handed and forced the case to arbitration. In June 1979 an arbitrator ruled that Gould had indeed violated a job-transfer clause of the contract and would have to recall 215 laid-off workers, pay their back wages, and haul the equipment from North Carolina back to Philadelphia. In this case, however, the union won only a reprieve; in 1980 the contract ran out, and Gould began to (legally) transfer its capital to its Sunbelt facilities.

When unions have been successful in preventing a "runaway" plant, it is often because they have achieved widespread community support. But when it occurs, it is just such community support that makes the older industrial areas of the "Frostbelt" an "undependable" place in which to do business, and from which many companies want to run. For example, in 1979 the International Association of Machinists went on strike at the Olin Corporation's Winchester rifle factory in New Haven over company-mandated changes in grievance procedures with respect to new productivity norms. Neighborhood residents were active in picket lines, and anticompany feeling ran high in the community as a result of a long history of offensive behavior by Olin. In the eleventh week of the strike, Winchester announced that it would be importing scabs to begin production again and threatened to give them seniority over the striking workers. Facing 800 strikers and their neighbors and sympathizers gathered at the plant gates, New Haven Mayor Frank Logue invoked emergency powers and effectively locked out the strikebreakers by ordering the plant closed! He was overruled four days later by a Superior Court judge, and the strike was eventually settled.[55] Nevertheless, it is unlikely that Olin and other companies doing business in New Haven will forget the incident when making future investment plans.

International Investment and the Search for a Union-Free Environment

In seeking to escape a "pro-union" or "anti-business" climate inside the United States, Olin and other large corporations have another choice. It has been noted earlier that they can build, expand, or acquire facilities outside of the country altogether. In fact, all the strategic innovations devised by multiplant companies for playing off one group of workers within the country against another group—parallel plants, multiple-sourcing, and so forth—have become standard operating procedure in the global economy as well. If anything, the intensified competitive environment of the last decade has *increased* the proclivity of U. S. multinational corporations for employing these strategies.

There is no question that at least some of the enormous shift of American capital to Europe, Canada, and the Third World during the 1960s represented a response to the presence and (occasionally) to the power of American industrial unions. Thus, for example, in 1966, as an alternative to expanding its older, unionized television factory in Cincinnati, RCA opened a 4,000-employee facility in Memphis. When the Memphis workers organized a union, RCA closed *both* plants and moved all of its black-and-white television production to Taiwan.[56] Six months after the second of two strikes at its Ashland, Massachusetts, timer plant during the late 1960s, GE drastically cut back and then totally shut down the operation, shifting production to Singapore. As one former United Electrical Workers researcher put it: "The lesson intended is absolutely clear—GE can move, UE can't."[57]

One of the most dramatic examples of the runaway shop, explicitly supported by U. S. government tax and tariff policy, is found in the "export platform" phenomenon, first mentioned in chapter 5. The story begins on the Mexican border.

For many years, large American produce growers had access to cheap immigrant Mexican labor through the Bracero Program, which admitted specified numbers of Mexican farm workers to the United States for limited periods of time to work in the fields. The elimination of this politically embarrassing program in 1964 not only gave rise to the contemporary problem of the migration of undocumented Mexican workers to the United States but also produced enormous unemployment in northern Mexico.

This reserve army of labor, created in the first place by U. S.-Mexican economic policy, now provided the conditions for a new stage of development in the region. In 1965 the Mexican government again offered cheap labor to American business, this time on the southern side of the border. The new Border Industrialization (or so-called in-bond) Program allowed entirely foreign-owned companies to set up operations within a virtually tax- and tariff-free 12.5-mile strip of the border. The Mexican Minister of Commerce told the *Wall Street Journal,* "Our idea is to offer an alternative to Hong Kong, Japan and Puerto Rico for free enterprise." Through various U. S. tariff-code loopholes (discussed in chapter 5), American corporations could assemble products in this zone and import them into the United States, thus paying duty only on the value added in the assembly process, that is, only on the cost of the cheap Mexican labor.

The garment and electronics industries and toy companies were quick to respond. Among the pioneers were Litton Industries, Transitron, Motorola, Fairchild, Hughes Aircraft, and General Electric. Within two years after the program went into effect in 1969, licenses had been granted for seventy-two U. S. plants. By 1974 the number had reached 655.[58] Other multinational corporations operating *maquiladoros*—the word used by Mexican workers to describe these border assembly plants—included North American Rockwell, Burroughs, General Instrument, GTE Sylvania, RCA, Levi Strauss, Puritan, and Kayser-Roth. In a period of less than ten years, the *maquiladoros* came to employ almost 13 percent of -the border region's labor force.

The most recent additions to the *maquiladoro* program are seven General Motors and two Chrysler plants, all built in or around Ciudad Juárez since 1978. In these plants Mexican workers turn out wiring harnesses, seat covers, radios, instrument panel padding, electronic controls, and shock absorbers. Workers refer to these areas, just across the Texas border, as "little Detroit."[59]

Runaways in the electronics industry have continued as well. In September 1979, GE announced that it would shut down its Providence, Rhode Island, home appliance cord set manufacturing plant and transfer the operations to the border town of Nogales. There, in the words of a GE spokesperson, ". . . workers earn less than $2 per hour, compared with a $5.84 minimum in Providence."[60] Late in the summer of 1980, General Instrument Incorporated joined the bandwagon by shutting down its Jerrold Electronics cable TV equipment plant in Chicopee, Massachusetts, moving it to Nogales. At the very time of the move, in the company's 1980 Annual Report, the company's executive director Frank Hickey stated, "Our cable TV group had its best year by far, with a record year-to-year world-wide revenue gain and a profit increase of $23 million."[61]

The growth of strikes, together with high turnover that resulted inevitably from the monotony and health hazards of the work, caused some of the companies on the Mexican border to move farther south in the mid-1970s. Mexico itself opened three new tax- and duty-free areas in the central part of the country, which almost immediately resulted in the construction of new Burroughs Corporation computer facilities in Guadalajara and a General Electric plant in Chihuahua.

The idea behind the maquiladoras has now spread to other parts of the world. In response to special incentive programs, American firms have established offshore assembly operations in Haiti, El Salvador, and Colombia. The North African countries play the equivalent export-platform role for European manufacturers.

A related device, the free-trade zone, was pioneered in the 1950s and 1960s by other countries. The first free-trade zone was established at the Shannon Airport in Ireland in 1958. Taiwan announced the opening of another such zone in 1965. In 1967, the United Nations Industrial Development Organization began encouraging countries throughout the Third World to develop free-trade zones of their own. An evaluation of these zones shows them to be populated by companies paying the lowest possible wages accompanying the most miserable working conditions. Indeed, low wages and standards, and the absence of unions, are expressly designed into these trade zones, being precisely what is supposed to attract "foot-loose" international companies.[62]

Similiar areas were being erected in the United States. By 1976 nearly forty federally-licensed zones had been set up in American cities by municipal or state governments, public economic development corporations, or nonprofit subsidiaries of local chambers of commerce. Before 1950, in order to be free of the usual import duties, American companies located in free-trade zones could only transship the articles, that is, bring them into the country, store them, and then re-export them. The Boggs Amendment of 1950 permitted companies located within the zones to engage in light manufacturing and related processing. Activity in the zones increased steadily thereafter into the 1970s. Indeed, between 1971 and 1976 there was nearly a fivefold increase in both the value of goods received at and forwarded from zones located inside the United States.[63] The idea of the free-trade zone has been expanded into a proposal to create "urban enterprise zones," to be located in inner-city areas of Britain and the United States. This proposed experiment in "selective deregulation," which has become the Thatcher and Reagan administrations' major domestic economic development initiative, will be evaluated in chapter 7.

The inequality in the "bargaining" situation between a multinational corporation and a national labor union is especially uneven when that multinational is also organized as a conglomerate. Charles Craypo of Notre Dame University has conducted a detailed investigation of such a case, involving Litton Industries, one of the best known modern conglomerates. Ranked 249th among the *Fortune* 500 in 1960, by 1972 Litton had become the 35th largest corporation in the country.[64]

In 1965 Litton entered the typewriter market by acquiring Royal, then the second largest firm in the industry. Three years later, Royal merged with a German firm, Triumph-Adler, that had been about to introduce a new line of electric typewriters into the U. S. market. Following a strike in 1969 at the company's Springfield, Missouri plant, Litton transferred the production of the portable typewriter line to its plant in Hartford, Connecticut. Later that year, the Missouri plant was shut down entirely, and a production contract, together with the machinery from Springfield, were turned over to a firm in Portugal. Then, in August 1970 the manufacture of office electric typewriters was shifted from Hartford to Germany and England, where Litton also had a subsidiary. Finally, in January 1972 Litton announced that the production of all remaining models would be moved to England and the Hartford plant would be shut down altogether. The Triumph-Adler subsidiary was sold to Volkswagen. In five years, a company that had been a leader in its industry and a major employer in the cities in which it did business was no longer making any of its products inside the United States.

The Hartford employees had been represented by the United Auto Workers. In trying to bargain over the termination, to get the best possible arrangements for its members after the company flatly refused to discuss "what it might take for them to stay," the UAW found itself in a truly powerless situation. For one thing,

> Royal workers and their unions had no prior knowledge of these transfers of production (and jobs); on the contrary, they were often given press releases and other communication which proved to be inaccurate. Six weeks before the 1970 transfer of work from Hartford to England, for example, the president of Royal sent an encouraging letter to each member of the Hartford bargaining unit which stated: "We are entering an exciting era of new and better opportunities for the future. Our plans see Hartford continuing as our principal United States manufacturing facility and as our worldwide headquarters. . . . "[65]

When it came time to bargain over termination, union negotiators at Hartford did not even know where the company's European plants were located or precisely which product lines were being shifted to which locations. As a conglomerate, Litton was legally able to fold operating information on its Royal division into the consolidated corporate balance sheet and income statement, so that the union could not even tell whether the Hartford plant was making a profit. Nor did the plant manager, whom the local union members knew well, have much information himself, let alone the discretionary authority to engage in bargaining. All negotiations were handled by Litton headquarters. All in all,

> Litton transferred overseas the jobs of about 2,500 unionized workers without having to incur severance or termination payments, improved pension benefits, worker relocation and retraining benefits, or any of the other compensations often obtained by unions in negotiations accompanying plant relocations. The impact of conglomerate, multinational structure on collective bargaining is to give the employer, under certain conditions, the capacity to make the institutionalized bargaining system an ineffective method of resolving industrial disputes.[66]

Even when they cannot escape unions altogether, corporate parallel production and subcontracting policies ("outsourcing") can still increase the company's power over its workers by forcing the unionized work force of one country to compete for jobs with that of another. In the absence of sustained international labor solidarity, this strategy has proven to be quite successful. This is especially true in the case of the so-called world car.

The story—like that of the mass-produced automobile itself—begins with the Ford Motor Company. A wave of labor strikes, grievances, and absenteeism befell Western European businesses in 1968–69, and Ford was no exception. First, its Belgian plant was struck in 1968. Then, a 1969 strike against Ford of Britain directly interfered with the delivery of parts and subassemblies to the company's plants in Belgium and Germany.[67]

Ford tried several ways of reorganizing production in order to reduce its vulnerability to labor disruption in any particular plant within the overall system. Each plant was highly specialized in its function. Ford wanted to find a way to reduce that extreme specialization without greatly sacrificing production efficiency. The result of this experimentation was Ford of Europe's introduction in 1976 of the *Fiesta*, the company's smallest car. The engines were manufactured in two parallel plants located in Almusafes (Valencia), Spain, and in Dagenham, England. Final assembly was located in Spain, England, and in Saarlouis, Germany. Each plant was designed to operate normally below potential capacity, in order to be able to absorb additional orders in case of a work stoppage elsewhere. Gearboxes, transmissions and axles were single-sourced from plants in Bordeaux, France. One Ford executive said of this arrangement:

> In the three quarters of a century since its founding, Ford has built nearly 150 million vehicles. But, outside of the Model T, none seems likely to have such a long-lasting and decisive effect on the management of our world-wide operations as an 11-foot-long little car called the Fiesta. . . . [Fiesta] began a new chapter in multinational business cooperation with manage-ment implications far beyond the European continent or Ford.[68]

Thus, the manufacture of interchangeable components—the old "American system" that goes all the way back to rifle production in Springfield, Massachusetts, in the early nineteenth century—had been combined with the strategy of parallel production to provide a previ-ously unheard-of degree of managerial control. In Wall Street's own view:

> If, for example, the workers on the Fiesta line at Dagenham slow down or strike, Ford can increase output from its Fiesta engine line at Almusafes. And the longer supply lines dictated by the international integration of Fiesta production could prove to be an advantage despite high transporta-tion costs and possible shipping delays [since] stocks already in transit from Dagenham can supplement the increased output from Almusafes and thereby keep Ford's Fiesta assembly facilities operational despite a strike.[69]

The newest of Ford's world cars, a direct descendant of the *Fiesta,* is the extremely successful *Escort.* As table 6.3 vividly illustrates, by 1980 both dispersed sourcing and parallel production had been signifi-cantly expanded by the company. Parts were being made or assembled in sixteen countries on three continents.

Through 1980 Toyota and Datsun were still following a traditional, home-based production strategy, relying on extraordinarily resourceful advertising campaigns and on American consumers' belated interest in small cars to enable these Japanese multinationals to continue export-ing their product to the United States and other countries, many in the Third World. However, with the American automobile manufacturers now forced into the small-car market, and with growing U. S. political pressure on their government, even the Japanese are beginning to move

TABLE 6.3

Sources of the Components of the Ford Motor Company's European Escort

Country	Components
Austria	Radiator and Heater Hoses, Tires
Belgium	Hood-in Trim, Seat Pads, Tires, Brakes, Tubes
Canada	Glass, Radios
Denmark	Fan Belts
France	Seat Pads, Sealers, Tiers, Underbody Coating, Weatherstrips, Seat Frames, Heaters, Brakes, Master Cylinders, Ventilation Units, Hardware, Steering Shaft and Joints. Front Seat Cushions, Suspension Bushes, Hose Clamps, Alternators, Clutch Release Bearings
Italy	Defroster Nozzles and Grills, Glass, Hardware Lamps
Japan	W S Washer Pumps, Cone and Roller Bearings, Alternators, Starters
Netherlands	Paints, Tires, Hardware
Norway	Tires, Muffler Flanges
Spain	Radiator and Heater Hoses, Air Cleaners, Wiring Harness, Batteries, Fork Clutch Releases, Mirrors
Sweden	Hardware, Exhaust Down Pipes, Pressings, Hose Clamps
Switzerland	Speedometer Gears, Underbody Coatings
United States	Wrench Wheel Nuts, Glass, EGR Valves
England, Germany	Muffler Ass'y, Pipe Ass'y, Fuel Tank Filler
England	Steering Wheel
England, Germany	Tube Ass'y Steering Column, Lock Ass'y, Steering and Ignition
England, France	Heater Ass'y
England, Germany	Heater Blower Ass'y, Heater Control Quadrant Ass'y
England, Italy	Nozzle Windshield Defroster
England, Germany	Cable Ass'y Speedometer
Germany	Cable Ass'y Battery to Starter
England, Germany	Turn Signal Switch Ass'y, Light Wiper Switch Ass'y, Headlamp Ass'y Bilux, Lamp Ass'y Front Turn Signal
England, Italy	Lamp Ass'y Turn Signal Side, Rear Lamp Ass'y (inc. Fog Lamp), Rear Lamp Ass'y
England, Germany	Weatherstrip Door Opening, Main Wire Ass'y Tires, Battery, Windshield Glass, Back Window Glass, Door Window Glass, Constant Velocity Joints
France, Germany	Transmission Cases, Clutch Cases
England, Germany	Rear Wheel Spindles
Germany	Front Wheel Knuckle
England, Germany	Front Disc
England, France, Italy	Cylinder Head
England, Germany	Distributor
United States	Hydraulic Tappet
England, Germany	Rocker Arm
England	Oil Pump
Germany	Pistons
England	Intake Manifold
England, Germany	Clutch
Germany	Cylinder Head Gasket
England, Germany, Sweden	Cylinder Bolt
North Ireland, Italy	Carburetors
England	Flywheel Ring Gear

Source: U. S. Department of Transportation, *The U.S. Automobile Industry, 1980,* (Washington, D.C.: U. S. Department of Transportation, 1980), p. 57.

in the direction of developing "world cars" of their own. (Not surprisingly, this is being promoted by UAW President Douglas Fraser through his exhortations to the Japanese firms to locate assembly plants inside the United States.) Honda is the first of the Japanese firms to move in this direction, with plans to build an assembly plant in Ohio. Datsun is constructing a pickup truck plant in Kentucky. Volkswagen is already assembling cars in Pennsylvania.[70]

It is apparent that by the 1970s, U. S. corporate managers had found a way to respond to the crisis of competition, costs, and profits by reorganizing production on an explicitly interregional, international scale. Capital mobility itself, whether enacted or merely threatened, was becoming a mechanism for altering the very foundations of labor-management relations.

But it was doing much more than that. Combined with the use of widespread networks of subcontractors, these parallel plant and foreign-sourcing strategies, first deployed within the United States, are reversing a tendency that has characterized capitalist development since the eighteenth century: the relationship between the centralization of control over production and the concentration of productive activity in large, centrally located facilities. The permissive technological environment allows huge corporations to operate hundreds of smaller, geographically dispersed plants in place of a small number of politically vulnerable, large local complexes. General Electric's Lynn, Massachusetts aircraft engine plant, the Gary, Indiana works of U. S. Steel, and Ford's River Rouge complex in Detroit thus represent a spatial form of production from the distant past, the likes of which we will not see again.

Fight Along with Flight: The Direct Attack on the Unions

Even before the corporate demands for wage concessions ("givebacks") became the most prominent feature of industrial relations in the 1980s, an open assault on labor was becoming manifest in the form of repeated attacks on the trade unions. In earlier periods, particularly before

World War II, company efforts to keep out unions and to "bust" them when their organizers successfully made inroads into the plant or the community, were often characterized by physical violence, brought into play by private police or company-paid "goon squads."

By the 1970s the corporations' tactics had changed dramatically. The new "union busters" are specialized firms providing legal, psychological, and other technical assistance to management in all branches of industry. A thousand firms, with estimated aggregate annual revenues of as much as $500 million, now advise both private and public employers how to keep union organizers and sympathizers out of the workplace if possible; how to defeat the union when representation elections cannot be avoided; and, where unions have succeeded in winning elections, how to manage new elections to decertify them.

Paradoxically, partly as a result of the advice of these new white-collar (gray-flannel), anti-union consultants, the number of unfair labor practices cited by the National Labor Relations Board against American business *rose* by 300 percent during the 1970s. The reason is that many companies had learned that it was more profitable to break the law and risk paying a trivial fine than to allow unions to successfully organize their plants, stores, and offices.

Thus, where the odds of a union victory in a typical representation election were about three to two during the 1940s and 1950s, by 1978 they had fallen to only a little above one in three. Even more ominous for organized labor, during the decade of the 1970s, average annual decertifications of prior union victories rose from less than 240 to over 800. In 1978 unions were losing three of these contests for every one in which they were victorious.[71]

Even where unions thought themselves to be safely entrenched, many companies have begun to openly threaten plant shutdowns unless the unions will agree to re-open contracts and take wage freezes, or even provide the company with givebacks. This has now occurred so often —in seriously troubled companies like Chrysler; in firms such as Ford that earn much higher profits overseas than in their domestic operations; in major corporations engaged in long-term restructuring schemes like U. S. Steel; and even in healthy, profitable multiplant firms openly exploiting the times to depress Frostbelt labor costs to the levels in their Sunbelt locations—that it has taken on epidemic proportions.

In the public domain, the same assault on labor is taking place. To defeat labor-law reform and maintain the pattern of pro-business legislation upon which they have come to count so heavily, companies across the country have been forming nonprofit political action committees (PACs) to circumvent the laws (on the federal books since 1907) that made it illegal for private corporations to donate money directly to political candidates. Unions have organized PACs themselves, but their resources are greatly inferior to those available to private industry. Since the early 1970s, the growth of corporate PACs has been astronomical, far outpacing organized labor's efforts. Corporate PACs are also being used to pay for advertising and other public relations activities designed to influence popular referenda. Their potential power has been described by one observer as "staggering."[72]

Capital's Assault on the Social Wage: The Demand for a "Good Business Climate"

Running away from unions was one way for capital to escape the fetter on profit making which the postwar social contract had become, in the context of the heightened global competition and economic crisis of the 1970s. Another response was to fight the unions head-on over wages, work rules, and—with the help of the corporate consultants—the right of a union to represent any particular company's workers at all.

But precisely because so few American workers *belong* to unions, these managerial responses to the crisis were not sufficient to make really significant, long-term dents in labor costs. For that to happen, workers would have to have been made so insecure and desperate for work that they would be forced to become more "flexible," that is, more willing to accept management's new terms with respect to wages, working conditions, and discipline as industry underwent the process of restructuring technologies, plant locations, and job tasks. The only way for capital to achieve this degree of flexibility—that is, to produce the necessary amount of insecurity—was to attack the social wage itself. This is the historical context within which to understand the significance of that extraordinary 1974 *Business Week* editorial quoted in chapter 1, calling for the dismantling of the standard of living to which American workers had become accustomed.

The assault on the social wage began at the state and local level, giving rise to what *Business Week*'s editors have called "the second war between the states." In choosing where to locate their new plants, or where to move existing operations if the present site is somehow undesirable, managers often talk about the local "business climate." What do they mean?

Sometimes, this fuzzy but much used term is nothing more than a euphemism for the presence or absence of unions, or of a local tradition of labor militancy. But corporate managers are usually thinking about more than just unions when this mystifying but nevertheless ubiquitous concern for a "good business climate" is expressed in local newspapers, on television, or in hearings before legislative committees. They are referring to the extent to which the policies of state and local government promote or retard capital's ability to locate where they prefer, especially with consideration of local taxes; to produce as they wish (irrespective of any external costs that production might impose on the area, such as environmental pollution, or on their workers, as with on-the-job health and safety hazards); and to maintain control over the labor process on the shop (or office) floor.

It appears that companies also have in mind the whole panoply of government policies that provide social insurance, welfare and food stamps, and minimum wages. These shelters from the insecurity that comes with being totally dependent on the demands of capital represent the spoils of past political victories by workers and their unions. The social wage is costly to business, and increasingly they want out. *That* is what the corporate demand for a good business climate is mainly about.

In the United States, from the years immediately following World War II, the shifting of capital from the inner cities to the suburbs and the rural peripheries of the country, and from the North to the South and West has been accompanied by often surprisingly up-front demands by corporate managers—or by their advocates in the many private and public local economic development agencies across the country—for a good business climate as a condition for moving in, or staying put. Elected state and local government officials have at best felt helpless before these demands. But it is probably also fair to say that these officials have tended to see state and local tax breaks and other "incentives" to business as plausible development policies—"if we lower their costs of doing business, why *wouldn't* companies invest here?"

Whatever the rationale, the result has been a proliferation of tax breaks and other business subsidies, together with the weakening of pro-labor, pro-consumer regulations on industry. In a veritable orgy of "incentive" granting, state and local governments have been falling over each other to outcompete or, with the ubiquitous availability of such incentives, to just stay on a par with their rival jurisdictions.[73]

In one recent study by the Conference of State Manufacturers' Associations, the "goodness" of a state's "business climate" was defined in terms of low taxes, low union membership, low workmen's compensation insurance rates, low unemployment benefits per worker, low energy costs, and few days lost because of work stoppages—in that order. Mississippi ranked first in the nation on almost every criterion.[74] Texas, which also placed high on the list, has no corporate or individual income tax, no payroll tax, property taxes below the national average, and the lowest unemployment insurance tax rates in the country.[75] In such a climate, it is not at all remarkable for large companies such as J. P. Stevens to demand—and get—what amounts to a perpetual tax holiday (along with lax enforcement of brown-lung regulations) from the typically rural southern jurisdictions in which it has built its textile mills, while over the years gradually shutting down its operations in the North.

Bold demands by private corporations on state governments are of course hardly confined to the Sunbelt. From the earliest days of the *Pax Americana,* companies have been threatening to leave if the local social wage were not relaxed. One of the earliest examples involves a firm discussed before: the first of the modern era's conglomerates, Textron. Having bought up textile mills in Nashua, New Hampshire, and in other New England towns during World War II, the Providence-based corporation began to shift its capital to its southern properties after earning enormous profits by speculating in, and finally selling, the valuable stocks of raw cotton owned by acquisitions such as the Nashua Manufacturing Company (whose name was changed to Textron in 1947). When this policy of milking the inventories of what had been a viable enterprise was challenged by the Textile Workers Union and by the town of Nashua, Little and his senior managers offered to keep the mill open, provided that the union, the town, and the state of New Hampshire make "certain concessions" that became known as Textron's "Nashua Plan." The company demanded (1) the freedom to ignore seniority in implementing work force reductions of almost 1,500 employees in the mill; (2) a speed-up of the work load to match the much higher pace of production prevailing in the corporation's southern plants; (3) substantial reductions in local taxes; and (4) agreement by the community to accept the plan in its entirety. When the ultimatum was not accepted, Little shut down the mill.[76]

In the ensuing years, multiregional, multinational corporations have become more subtle in coercing jurisdictions to compete against each other. Once again, the needs, and the capabilities, of capital are pitted against the interests and the built-in immobility of communities. Two recent examples are provided by the behavior of General Motors in the Upper Midwest and by Goodyear in Oklahoma.

The relocation in 1979 of a $180-million Goodyear radial tire plant from Ohio to Oklahoma provides a clear illustration of the power that such an enormous corporation can wield over a small town. The company surveyed a large number of potential sites in the Oklahoma-North Texas region. The managers were searching for a place large enough to provide a skilled labor force of 1,400 employees, but small enough to be unlikely to attract any other *Fortune* 500 company that might come in and bid up wages. They were quite explicit about wanting to escape unionization. At one point, management actually placed want ads in the newspapers of different communities to "feel out" the availability of labor, even though at that stage there were no real jobs to be offered. Finally, Goodyear solicited bids from six jurisdictions and indicated quite bluntly that it would locate in the town that made the best bid. The "winner"—the town of Lawton, Oklahoma—made what a team of Harvard researchers called "some amazing concessions" in the process. Goodyear had interstate highways moved, access roads built, and even a school jurisdiction annexed so that the children of Goodyear managers could attend a school controlled by the Lawton City Council, over which the company would presumably have some influence.[77]

When cities are in deep trouble as, for example, is Detroit with its persistent double-digit unemployment rate and a nearly bankrupt city treasury, the concessions can be even grander. Such was the case with the now infamous "Poletown" GM plant. After announcing that it would close both of its remaining automobile plants—a multistory Fisher Body plant and a sixty-year-old Cadillac assembly facility— General Motors told Detroit's mayor and city council that it would be willing to locate an ultramodern assembly plant (built from the same plans as its sprawling, suburban facility outside of Oklahoma City) right in the middle of Detroit, so that it would straddle both an inner-city neighborhood and the surrounding Polish community of Hamtramack. General Motors' president said that the corporation would be willing to build the 6,000-employee plant if Detroit would meet its demands for land assembly, site preparation, and a substantial tax abatement.

In this highly unequal poker game, the city had a poor hand and GM held the aces. Everyone from the mayor to the most progressive members of the city council knew it, and therefore the city met the company's demands almost totally. Over four hundred acres were cleared, 3,200 people were forced from their homes in what had been one of Detroit's most socially integrated communities, churches were torn down, and 160 community businesses were closed. The city used its power of eminent domain to clear out the families and small-time entrepreneurs; it agreed to relocate on-off ramps for two of the city's expressways and finally gave in on a twelve-year tax abatement that may cost the city as much as $240 million in foregone revenues. Despite community opposition and a number of court battles, the plan is going ahead as scheduled. The number of jobs saved is likely to be small— certainly fewer than the number lost by GM's overall restructuring program. But the city elders were in no position to deny GM what it requested.[78]

The Poletown experience is being repeated across the nation. In the wake of the Sunbelt's head start, more and more Frostbelt states legislated a succession of subsidies, tax breaks, and deregulation incentives during the 1960s and 1970s in a desperate attempt to hold onto their existing plants and to attract new ones. The package of "Mass Incentives" offered by the Commonwealth of Massachusetts is typical. A 1980 newspaper advertisement, sponsored by the Massachusetts Department of Commerce, lists twenty-three ways the state is trying to be congenial toward business. Only a year before, the state was able to tell the business community that it had successfully reined in its unemployment compensation program by delaying benefits and had reduced its welfare case load by requiring general relief recipients to work for their welfare checks. Ironically, both sets of measures were instituted under Democratic governors after a Republican governor had, according to the leading bankers in the state, created the worst business climate in the nation by raising taxes to pay for things such as state aid to local schools, expanded mental health programs, and assistance to mass transit.

The interstate competition in concessions to business has been the subject of a good deal of recent research. But what seems to have been overlooked is that, so intense has the rivalry been, and so successful the corporate blackmailing, by the mid-1970s the interstate differential on business taxes had all but disappeared!

Our estimates of the state-by-state effective business tax rates in 1975 are presented in table 6.4.[79] By 1975 the actual differences between the Frostbelt and Sunbelt states amounted to no more than a single percentage point. For instance, corporate income taxes plus property taxes on business added up to about 1.98 percent of total business sales in depressed Rhode Island. In booming Texas, the rate was 1.31 percent—hardly a large enough difference to coax a firm to pack up its capital and set off for the Southwest. Even so-called Taxachusetts imposed a tax burden on its business community that in 1975 (before the advent of more "pro-business" gubernatorial administrations) was no more than 1.7 percentage points higher than in South Carolina, a state that has traditionally attracted Yankee capital by its claims of, among other things, pro-business-structured taxation.[80]

Despite all the newsprint about Taxachusetts, local business taxes are *not* the chief targets of groups like the Chamber of Commerce and the National Association of Manufacturers. Rather, the regulations that industry complains about most loudly and most often are those that intervene in the workplace relationship between labor and management—laws having to do with minimum wages, affirmative action, and health and safety—and state laws that provide for some form of income maintenance: unemployment insurance and food stamps for those who usually work, and welfare for those who often do not.

In this respect, the northern industrial states that first pioneered in the development of social benefits for workers and their families are the

TABLE 6.4

State and Local Effective Business Tax Rates[a] by State: 1975[b]
(in percents)

Region and State	Effective Tax Rate	Region and State	Effective Tax Rate
New England	2.46	East South Central	0.96
Maine	2.22	Kentucky	1.21
New Hampshire	2.45	Tennessee	0.94
Vermont	2.77	Alabama	0.63
Massachusetts	2.75	Mississippi	1.16
Rhode Island	1.98		
Connecticut	2.09	West South Central	1.24
Middle Atlantic	1.99	Arkansas	1.14
		Louisiana	0.96
New York	2.16	Oklahoma	1.34
New Jersey	1.99	Texas	1.31
Pennsylvania	1.66		
		Mountain	1.91
East North Central	1.54		
		Montana	3.41
Ohio	1.31	Idaho	1.92
Indiana	1.52	Wyoming	3.51
Illinois	1.50	Colorado	1.63
Michigan	1.71	New Mexico	1.64
Wisconsin	1.89	Arizona	2.01
		Utah	1.43
West North Central	1.74	Nevada	1.48
Minnesota	1.82	Pacific	2.22
Iowa	1.99		
Missouri	1.12	Washington	1.24
North Dakota	2.47	Oregon	1.69
South Dakota	2.96	California	2.43
Nebraska	1.99	Alaska	3.72
Kansas	2.20	Hawaii	1.72
South Atlantic	1.21		
Delaware	0.85	Average	1.69
Maryland	1.46		
Washington, D. C.	1.44		
Virginia	1.37		
West Virginia	1.16		
North Carolina	0.98		
South Carolina	1.09		
Georgia	1.10		
Florida	1.34		

SOURCES: Tax rate estimates based on data in Roger Vaughan, *State Taxation and Economic Development* (Washington, D. C.: The Council of State Planning Agencies, 1979), table 14, pp. 74–75 and data on manufacturing, retail trade, wholesale trade, and selected services, U. S. Bureau of Census, *Statistical Abstract of the United States, 1975* (Washington, D. C.: U. S. Government Printing Office, 1975), Tables 11, 1267, 1316, 1323, and 1331.

Notes: [a]Tax Rate = $\dfrac{\text{(Corporate Income Tax Revenue + Business Property Taxes)}}{\text{(Value of Manufacturing Shipments + Total Retail Sales + Total Wholesale Sales + Total Selected Service Industry Receipts)}}$

This "business tax rate" excludes unemployment insurance, workers' compensation, and special excise taxes imposed by state or local governments.

[b]Because of data limitations, the tax rates do not strictly correspond to a given year. Corporate income tax data are for 1977; business property tax revenue information corresponds to 1975; total value of sales/shipments/receipts is for 1972. Since the last of these values (at least in current dollars) has increased since 1972, the tax rates as calculated here *overestimate* actual 1975 tax rates. This should not seriously affect the differences between states.

ones that have come most under attack as being "anti-business." The legacy of those past struggles in state politics is reflected in the current interstate differentials in benefits and coverage. Unlike taxes, *these* differentials are quite large. This is particularly true of the welfare programs: Unemployment Insurance (UI), Aid to Families with Dependent Children (AFDC), and General Assistance (GA). The second war between the states is becoming mainly a struggle between those who would preserve these benefits and those who wish to roll back the social wage at the state and local level.

The actual beneficiaries of these programs have much to lose if the more generous states retreat to the standards set in the more miserly, usually southern jurisdictions. For instance, in 1979 the maximum benefit available to unemployed workers in Massachusetts was more than twice the level of that prevailing in Georgia and Alabama. The maximum tax on employers was as much as 50 percent higher in some Frostbelt states, due to a combination of stronger pro-labor support in northern legislatures, and to generally higher unemployment rates there.

Similarly, benefits under AFDC and GA vary enormously across the country, with the highest amounts of cash assistance in states such as Connecticut, Michigan, and California and the lowest in the South. By June 1979, as a direct consequence of each state being allowed to set its own AFDC benefit levels, the range in monthly payments in the continental United States extended from New York at $362.93 to Mississippi with a meager $79.87 per family. Within GA, a wholly state-financed welfare program, the benefits in some states were as much as *twelve times* greater than in others.[81]

To repair these disparities, the South might be thought to be most interested in federal welfare reform. In fact just the opposite is true. The congressional representatives from the southern states have traditionally been the most vocal opponents of any type of expanded welfare program. This is true despite the fact that reform would mean even larger federal subsidies to the lowest benefit states and would hold these states "harmless"—that is, require them to spend no more state funds than at present.

The reason for southern opposition goes to the very heart of the social-wage issue. While low-wage states do not wish to raise taxes and therefore signal a worsening business climate, their legislators are even more concerned about the possibility of providing grants so large that they might *compete* with the minimum-wage levels in their local labor markets, now being trumpeted as an inducement to employers. They fear that the supply of low-wage labor will be reduced by higher welfare benefits, and so they vote to keep welfare families at below-subsistence levels.[82]

What southern mayors and governors are trying to preserve, many northern elected officials are currently trying desperately to re-create. And the struggle goes far beyond welfare payments. Because capital is mobile and communities are not, the pressure is building in every part of the country for a general reduction in the social wage—and with it, the standard of living of *all* working people.

"Reaganomics" and the Social Wage

Along with, and perhaps even to some extent growing out of, the fractional, unplanned, often chaotic war between state and local governments to attract industry (or to hold onto what they already have), a *national* conflict has re-emerged between the leadership of American industry and working people as a whole—between *capital* and *community* on a grand scale. A concerted attack on the rights, privileges, and standards of living of the general public is underway. In a nutshell, capital has unilaterally ended even lip service to the great postwar social contract.

The election of Ronald Reagan to the presidency in 1980 is in this respect a major watershed in modern American history. For his administration is profoundly committed to "disciplining" labor by fundamentally undermining the social wage. While it is no doubt true that the tax, expenditure, and (de-) regulatory programs of the government are also greatly redistributing income in favor of the rich, the impact of these policies on corporate production and profitability over the long run is of far greater historical importance.

Take the tax program. The massive supply-side tax breaks for individuals are supposed to promote new savings that can be ploughed by institutions into new capital investment, while lower tax rates on businesses are expected to stimulate investment directly. We think this is unlikely to occur (and in any case, there is in fact no shortage of savings, as will be shown in the next chapter). But whatever the expectations about the stimulative effect of the program, there can be no doubt about its drastic impact on the capacity of the government to continue to finance the social wage.

In August 1981, the Treasury Department officially estimated that the cumulative revenue loss by 1986 resulting from these, and a few smaller, business tax breaks would be about $144 billion. State governments also stand to lose massive tax revenues as an indirect result of the federal policy. It has been estimated that, if the state governments do not rewrite their own tax laws to disassociate them from the new federal law, they stand to lose as much as $27.5 billion in tax receipts over the next six years, with an estimated annual tax loss of over $10 billion by 1986. This will cut further into the already rapidly shrinking state collection of business revenue resulting from the war between the states over industrial location and retention.[83]

In the area of deregulation, the policies that the conservatives are pursuing are supposed to unfetter "free enterprise" for a new wave of capital accumulation. But it is hard to see how—in the context of a slack economy within a global recession—the specific policies being followed will not actually exacerbate the problems treated in this chapter. For example, consider an amendment to the Clean Air Act called the Steel Industry Compliance Extension Act of 1981. It permits the steel companies to defer compliance with the laws limiting air pollution for three years, provided they use the savings to "invest in modernization." Unfortunately, nothing in the act requires them to modernize their *steel*-making facilities. And by not so stipulating, the act implicitly promotes continued diversification away from steel.

Take another example. In early November of 1981, the president signed into law a bill expanding the coverage provided by the U. S. Overseas Private Investment Corporation, a government agency which sells political risk insurance and other financial services to American companies investing abroad. This expansion of a policy that promotes overseas investment stands in marked contrast to the almost simultaneous sharp cuts in the budget of the Export-Import Bank, which subsidizes exports from domestic plants.

And as for the new administration's position on merger mania, just before Christmas 1981, the president's new anti-trust chief, William Baxter, unflinchingly told the Washington press corps, "There is nothing written in the sky that says the world would not be a perfectly satisfactory place if there were only 100 companies."[84] Just two weeks later, Baxter and his lawyers in the Justice Department kept their word when they dropped an anti-trust lawsuit against IBM that had been pending for twelve years.

Conclusion

Only if the supply-side incentives—pioneered during the new war between the states and now elevated to national policy by the Reagan administration—are seen in their relation to the cuts in social wage expenditures and to deregulation, does all of this begin to make sense. It seems that the main objective of the conservatives now in power is not so much to stimulate new economic growth as to deprive government of the revenues with which to finance the social safety net, whose very existence strengthens labor in its continuing struggle with capital. Public service jobs—at least as they were originally conceived by the Democratic leadership in the early 1970s, and even earlier, during the 1930s—provided a relatively high-wage alternative to poverty-wage-level jobs in the private sector. Unemployment insurance, food stamps, and welfare helped laid-off workers to hold out a little longer before being forced to take a job inferior to the one they had before. Health and safety regulations enabled workers, under some circumstances, to withhold their labor from employers who ordered them to perform dangerous or stressful tasks.

In sum, the erosion of the social wage threatens to weaken the power of labor, unionized or not. To the extent that the strategy is successful, capital faces the prospect of extracting more from labor—making greater profits, at least for a while—in an era when profits can be increased only by radically cutting costs. The question is: How far can these new policies be pursued before they call forth enough resistance to threaten the political stability of the system itself?[85]

PART IV

The Great
Reindustrialization
Debate

Chapter 7

What's Wrong with

Present Policy?

THE STRATEGIES adopted by corporate management to cope with international competition, organized labor, and the social welfare state have clearly taken their toll. More than 30 million jobs lost to plant closings and permanent physical contractions in a single decade, the virtual abandonment of older industrial cities, and the helter-skelter development of Sunbelt boomtowns are merely the most obvious manifestations of an economy that has failed to provide steady growth, secure employment, or stable prices, and that no longer competes effectively in the global market place. After traveling the length and breadth of the entire country, one foreign observer concluded that America's situation resembled that of someone suffering from acromegaly, a medical condition caused by hyperactivity in the pituitary gland. "Acromegalic man looks like a hell of a fellow; tall and broad-shouldered, with hands like hams. Yet appearances deceive; in reality he is dangerously weak."[1]

The United States continues to churn out an unparalleled gross national product, yet deep down there is a gnawing awareness that the very sinew of the production system is moving toward a state of atrophy. Daily news accounts and government reports that track the pulse of the economy provide statistical confirmation of the frustration and anxiety sensed at the supermarket check-out counter, at the factory gate, or on the unemployment line. It took nearly a decade to sink in, but by the 1980 elections people were alarmed enough by the perceived demise of the economy to chance a wrenching change in political regime.

As such, a generation from now, when historians look back on the decade of the 1980s, they may very well classify it in the annals of economic history alongside the 1930s. This is not because the current decade will necessarily bring another Great Depression—although responsible economic forecasters have soberly expressed that concern—but because the 1980s will almost surely mark a momentous turning point in the relationship between the public and private sectors.

"Laissez faire conservatism," Clinton Rossiter writes, "rose to prominence between 1865 and 1885, to ascendancy between 1885 and 1920, [and] to virtual identification with 'the American Way' in the 1920s."[2] Under Calvin Coolidge and, later, Herbert Hoover, the "business of government was business" and Edmund Burke's admonition that "that government which governs least governs best" served as the guiding principle of political economy.

The Great Crash in 1929 changed all that. Public confidence in the almighty business sector was shattered. The ensuing depression, which saw 25 percent of the labor force out of work by 1933, ushered in a whole new era. Within the first hundred days of the Roosevelt administration, the spirit of Hoover, Coolidge, and Burke was unceremoniously ousted from the White House to make way for a host of imaginative initiatives formulated to cope with the economic emergency. By the end of Roosevelt's first term in office, the relationship between the public and private sectors had been fundamentally realigned.

In the 1980s the debate over this relationship occupies center stage once again. But unlike the Great Depression, the stagflation that has gripped the nation for more than a decade is being blamed on too *much* government and too *little* laissez faire. Democrats have frantically joined Republicans in implicating "big government" as the ultimate culprit. In the first hundred days of his administration, a confident Ronald Reagan brought Coolidge back into the White House (his portrait and his policies!) and set in motion programs for "getting the government off the backs of the people," a euphemism for aiding corporate enterprise by eliminating entire chunks of the social welfare state. Reducing the scope and power of government—in effect reversing a half century of social policy—is Reagan's formula for re-creating the conditions necessary for rapid economic growth.

But Reagan is hardly alone in offering an unabashedly pro-business program for economic revitalization. State and local governments are being urged to create good business climates of their own to attract new industry or to encourage existing companies to stay put. All varieties of tax reduction and subsidized investment schemes are being promoted for this purpose. At the national level, financial experts like Felix Rohatyn, the Wall Street banker who designed the plan to save New York City from bankruptcy, are advocating the resurrection of the depression-era Reconstruction Finance Corporation (RFC) in order to infuse troubled industries with new sources of capital. In separate statements, Lester Thurow and the editors of *Business Week* have argued for the creation of new institutions that might encourage firms to further diversify their assets, "to move into new areas and out of old areas" even more rapidly with the prodding of government incentives.[3] Other suggestions include turning America into "Japan, Inc.," creating special inducements for small business, and developing urban "enterprise zones" in or near the inner-city ghettos.

Each of these schemes is being promoted as a way of encouraging more savings, capital investment, industrial innovation, and work effort —the key components, many believe, of any serious reindustrialization plan for America. Some advocate the Reagan approach of smaller government, while others see an even larger role for the public sector in economic planning. This clash of ideologies revolves around the central question of how best to motivate the kinds of social behavior necessary for triggering a new wave of economic growth.

But growth *per se* is not enough. Any lasting solution must also deal with the fundamental tension between the heightened mobility of private capital and the ways that very "hypermobility" undermines the personal security of workers, their families, and their communities. Any acceptable plan for revitalizing the American economy must embrace a commitment to greater security, along with a commitment to equity and the democratic process.

None of the proposals put forward so far can simultaneously deliver growth, security, equity, and economic democracy. Because they cannot, their desirability as a basis for reindustrialization must be questioned. But before they are rejected out of hand, their strengths and weaknesses must be examined.

The Conservative Strategy

Conservatives from George Gilder, author of the best-selling *Wealth and Poverty*, to Milton Friedman and Ronald Reagan share the belief that America's economic demise can be traced directly to the growth of the "welfare state." If it were not for a plethora of public insurance schemes and "social safety nets," people would presumably work harder, save more, and invest more in productive activity. Public programs ranging from cash assistance for the poor to auto emission standards have destroyed the incentive (called by Keynes the "animal spirits") for investment, killed entrepreneurial initiative, and devalued the very concept of honest work. High taxes have muted the gains from investment; government regulations have taken the excitement out of entrepreneurial activity; and welfare spending has made it possible—or so these people say—to live comfortably without ever working. In short, the welfare state has made people soft. As social commentator Irving Kristol writes, "dependency [on the State] tends to corrupt and absolute dependency corrupts absolutely."[4]

The currently most fashionable brand of conservative economics is that of the supply-siders who believe that tax rates have become so high that lowering them will produce an outpouring of new work effort so enormous that total tax revenues over time will actually increase.[5] Workers would like to work more but after they pay their taxes to the government, they are left with so little that it is not worth the effort. Similarly, investors would be willing to sink more into productive capital, but the after-tax rates of return are so meager it makes more sense for them to spend their savings on luxurious consumption or speculate in tax-sheltered nonproductive investments such as gold, pork belly futures, or antiques. In both cases, the current economic crisis, and the slow growth of the economy, can be blamed directly on the government's voracious appetite.

What's Wrong with Present Policy?

The formula for economic recovery prescribed by the conservative strategists is almost elegant in its simplicity. Cut taxes, slash the social safety net, abolish government regulations and—abracadabra!—savings, investment, and work effort will multiply. Essentially, the supply-side strategy calls for a return to an economy where the private market alone determines winners and losers. The winners are not denied the fruits of their economic prowess. The losers, presumably to provide a sobering example for everyone else, are denied access to the public sector for any form of assistance.

Although its proponents may not see it quite in these terms, this is a strategy that has adopted the theories of a rather disparate trio: Adam Smith, the eighteenth-century economist; Ivan Pavlov, the Russian psychologist; and Herbert Spencer, the father of social Darwinism. The new supply-side economics has brought together under one roof Smith's "invisible hand," the simplicity of the Pavlovian stimulus-response mechanism, and a commitment to Spencer's theory of the survival of the fittest. While supply-side economics looks new, it turns out to be nothing more than a revival of old-fashioned, conservative laissez faire.

There is no mystery why the new proponents of the free market have found themselves elevated from almost total obscurity to prominence on television talk-shows and important positions in government. The argument that Washington is responsible for the country's dismal economic performance appeals to enough people so that the supply-side medicine looks plausible. Its extraordinary simplicity, plus its promise of a "quick-fix,'" is quite alluring. Unfortunately, however, it will not work. Inadequate savings are not really the problem; corporate tax cuts will not spur investment; and personal tax cuts will not generate very much additional work effort.

While it is true that the personal savings rate has been depressed below the historical average for the past two or three years, most economists believe this is a temporary aberration. The dominant characteristic of the saving/income ratio is that it has no trend at all over the entire postwar period.[6] Savings rates were relatively low during the late 1940s as consumers spent out of their wartime savings to replace all of the consumer durable goods they could not purchase during the war. During the 1950s saving rates were typically between 6 and 7 percent, while during the 1960s the rates averaged a bit lower. During most of the 1970s the rate actually returned to the higher levels of the 1950s. As such, there is no secular trend whatsoever—down or up—as the supply-siders would lead us to believe.

Even more important, personal savings constitute only one source of total investment reserves and, at that, a minor one. All the supply-siders, without exception, focus their attention on this component, as does Thurow. Yet *more than three fourths of total gross savings is done by business!* In 1980 personal savings amounted to $104 billion compared with $333 billion in savings in the corporate sector,[7] consisting of undistributed profits and the reserves set aside for depreciation.

Unlike personal savings, the trend in corporate reserves is, if anything, *up,* and not down. As economist Paul Sweezy has demonstrated, from 1955 until 1974 total corporate savings as a percentage of gross domestic corporate product averaged about 13.5 percent. Since then —and precisely during the period when productivity was declining— the corporate savings ratio has averaged 14.3 percent.[8] There has consequently been no erosion of corporate savings in the past twenty-five years.

That inadequate capital for investment is not the problem has been known for some time, at least in some circles. In 1978 *Business Week* surveyed the nation's largest firms about their cash positions. What they found was that

> the nation's biggest corporations are sitting atop a record $80 billion pile of ready cash that could finance a grand boom in capital spending. . . . Instead the money is being fed out slowly, the pace of business investment remains sluggish, and top corporate executives and a good many economists concede that tax measures aimed at generating [even] more cash as a way to stimulate investment probably would not do the trick.[9]

Instead of going into capital spending programs to increase capacity and to upgrade the efficiency of existing plants, corporations all through the late 1970s were expanding their bank accounts or channeling their reinvestible funds into acquisitions of other peoples' businesses. The problem was *not* with the supply of capital funds, but rather the old Keynesian issue of inadequate demand for the goods and services that could be produced if investments in new plant and equipment were made. Why make new investments if only three quarters of existing capacity is being used in the first place?

The supply-side theorists also ignore the facts about labor supply. Cutting taxes by 25 percent, as Congress mandated under the Economic Recovery Act of 1981, will do nothing but depress tax revenues and generate the conditions for massive government deficits. This is the conclusion of many researchers, including Martin Holmer, director of income-security policy research for the U. S. Department of Health and Human Services. Using the most pro-Reagan assumptions possible about worker responses to tax cuts, Holmer finds that even a 30 percent tax cut (the magnitude envisioned in the original Kemp-Roth proposal on which the president campaigned in 1980) would increase total hours worked by only 2.3 percent. The increase in earnings from this slight boost in work effort is "so modest that it generates new tax revenue equal to only about one-fourth of the original $40.3 billion tax reduction."[10]

Upon reflection, this result is not very surprising. Consider what must happen to work effort for tax *revenue* to remain constant in the face of such huge cuts in tax *rates*. Suppose that you are currently making $200 per week and the government normally takes 20 percent of your earnings in taxes, or $40. Now the government cuts tax rates by 30 percent so that you face only a 14 percent levy. In order for the government to continue collecting $40 from you, your earnings must rise to $285 per week, a 43 percent increase. Unless your wage rate goes up miraculously, the government must count on your choosing to work 43 percent more if it is to get its $40. If you were working forty hours a week before the new tax law went into effect, all you have to do now is work fifty-seven hours! Ten hours a day, six days a week will do it.

This latest incarnation of supply-side theory (which turns out to have been around since the nineteenth century) does not provide much of a blueprint for running a modern economy. It proved bankrupt in the 1930s when the world was in many ways less complicated, and today its chances for success are even more remote. One reason has to do with what economists call "market failure"—the inability of the private market to produce sufficient amounts of collective goods like public health, or to curtail the production of "externalities" like pollution.

Consider, for example, the special problem of how future generations are to register their claims on current resources. Edith Stokey and Richard Zeckhauser of Harvard University's Public Policy Program point out that "future generations can hardly compensate us now for not destroying critical wetlands or not depleting the ozone layer."[11] Since there is no market through which current and future generations may conduct transactions, the public sector must be called upon to act in the interests of the unborn. This argument is hardly limited to those things that fall under the jurisdiction of the Department of the Interior. Surely future generations would pay dearly, if they could, for current investments in cures for cancer, heart disease, and diabetes, or for capital spending on more livable cities or better transportation systems that could be around for their use when it is their turn to inhabit the earth.

Coping with externalities is an even more common problem. Market externalities arise whenever the actions of one person (or perhaps a firm) affect the welfare of another, without the transfer having been compensated through a direct exchange of commodities (or money). A good example is found in Garrett Hardin's "Tragedy of the Commons":

> The parable of the commons is a tale of villagers who own a common grazing ground and use it for pasturing their cows. The grass is ample for a few cows, but once the number of cows rises above a certain level, the effects of overgrazing are felt. The cows grow scrawnier and the total output of meat drops. Yet each villager, seeking to maximize his own welfare, is inexorably drawn to pasturing as many cows as he can afford. All grow poorer and poorer.[12]

Although the most familiar forms of externalities relate to the environment, British economist E. J. Mishan reminds us that "the number of external effects in the real world are virtually unlimited."[13] The dumping of highly toxic wastes into New York's Love Canal provides only one of the more outrageous, and therefore newsworthy, examples of a serious externality that could never be ameliorated through the private market. In the same way that the residents of Love Canal, by themselves, could never have forced Hooker Chemical to stop their dumping and pay damages for the costs imposed on them, zoning is needed to restrict damage to residential house values, anti-trust laws are needed to prevent monopolies from overpricing customers, and the FCC is needed to keep one FM station from jamming another. As technology has become more complex, we have in the process all become more interdependent. Thus, a modern society requires *more* government intervention than an eighteenth-century one. The conservative strategy of taking people back to an earlier period in terms of economic policy simply ignores this technological fact of life.

It also fails to take into account the expanded need for "public goods": commodities as simple as sidewalks and schools that would not be provided in sufficient quantity unless public financial arrangements were made for supplying them. There is no doubt that with growing affluence and new technology, the range of public goods has increased enormously. Large cities require subways or modern bus systems in order to reduce highway congestion. New technologies make it possible to transform yesterday's science fiction into today's medical miracles if sufficient funds can be raised. In each of these cases, and in countless others, the private market fails because the gains from investment are collective and cannot be privately appropriated. Where would we be today in the struggle against cancer if medical research were to have been funded solely by the private sector? "The important lesson for public policy," Stokey and Zeckhauser write, "is that by their very nature public goods will not be produced if the task is left to individuals acting in isolation, even when it is to everyone's advantage to have them produced and hence clearly best for the group as a whole."[14]

If the only problems with laissez faire were that it failed to account for certain intertemporal markets, extreme cases of externalities, and the provision of socially desirable public goods, it still might be possible to construct an economy along strictly private market lines, using very limited regulations and user charges to deal with these special cases. But there are even more serious problems. History suggests that private markets have a tendency toward chronic instability and uneven development.

The economic historian Douglas F. Dowd has noted that between the year 1800 and the outbreak of World War II, the United States experienced more than two dozen recessions, depressions, and financial market panics lasting in some cases as long as a decade.[15] Major depressions occurred in 1808–1809, 1816–1818, 1820–1821, 1858, 1866–1867, 1874–1878, 1894–1897, 1908, and, of course, all through the 1930s. In almost every one of these cases, the depression was preceded by a wave of bankruptcies, a bank panic, and a stock market crash. What Dowd points out is that these fluctuations are not "defects," but essential for a capitalist economy's long-term health.

> We may think of the role of business fluctuations in a capitalist economy as comparable to the processes of inhaling and exhaling, of hunger and surfeit, of ingestion and digestion, in the human body . . . Thus, business fluctuations are inherent to a capitalist economy. To rid the economy of them would require ridding it as well of its basic institutional characteristics: private ownership of the means of production, and the right and will to use those productive assets to make profits at the decision of the businessman.[16]

By their very nature, laissez faire economies are *unplanned,* no matter how carefully each enterprise may do its own planning. Because the economy is complex (and is becoming more complex and specialized at perhaps a geometric rate), coordination—even through an efficient price system—takes *time.* Time must pass between the initial decision to invest and produce; and since market signals can change in the interim, the best-laid plans can go astray. Like falling dominoes, a mistaken investment can lead to cutbacks in the demand for capital and labor that then spiral on through the economy. It is not that the perfectly free market will never recover, but simply that it can take a long time. Unrecoverable resources, such as productive labor power, are wasted and the entire economy can suffer. Recessions "cleanse" the economy and prepare it for another round of growth, but the cost of the reconditioning process is truly heavy for society to bear—as was shown in chapters 3 and 4.

As a result, even before the Great Depression, labor *and* business turned to the State to *speed up* the process of recovery. A return to strict laissez faire, even if it were somehow miraculously to increase growth and productivity in the short-run, would quickly return the economy to a state of chaos—one in which the boom/bust cycle would be even more severe than it is today. This is the fundamental flaw in the logic of all those who advocate an unqualified return to a "more competitive economy."

A related issue has to do with the tendency toward uneven development within capitalist economies.[17] In the static theory of traditional economics, diminishing returns to any particular investment supposedly militate against perpetual inequality among sectors of the economy, or for that matter, between individuals or between groups in society. Theoretically, additional investment in any one region, industry, or firm will tend to become less and less profitable after some point, and those with investment resources will begin to shift their surplus savings to other sectors of the economy.

Even in pure theory, this would occur only in a system populated—as in most economics textbooks—by millions of small independent entrepreneurs, with labor free to move from one location or industry to another, regardless of national borders and totally lacking non-pecuniary attachments to particular "turfs." In a world where capital ownership is concentrated, and where labor is *not* so frictionlessly mobile, the textbook equilibrium models are simply not applicable. Rather a "secular deterioration" can often evolve between industries, regions, and social groups, something like the uneven development between rich and poor nations. There is an inherent tendency in such an economy toward a dichotomization between those who have and those who do not.

Without going into excessive detail, this occurs for two reasons. First, investment can change the *quality* of an industry, region, or individual to make further investments profitable, thereby overcoming the classical tendency toward diminishing returns. A college education makes the graduate a good candidate for going on to medical school. Similarly capital investment in a given product often increases the market value of the product, thereby temporarily increasing its profitability. Higher profits can then be used for research and development and for advertising that further expands the market for these goods. On the other hand, new capital, products, or for that matter, people, if they originally fail to meet the market test, seldom receive a second chance and consequently find themselves doomed to economic deterioration. Solar energy could become just such a commodity.

The second, and perhaps more salient, reason for uneven development derives from the potential redistributive effect of any given private investment decision. While it may be true that continued investment runs into diminishing returns, owners of private capital will tend to link profitability and distribution criteria in the reinvestment decisions they make. Private investors will reinvest their capital in areas that promise the highest economic return *only* if such investment does not alter the long-run income distribution in a manner that reduces their own relative standing. Owners of capital have both a psychological and political stake in an unequal distribution of income, and hence they often measure their success not by the absolute amount of their accumulation, but by the surplus they acquire relative to others. Where government is an important actor in the economy, the political stake is *particularly* important since influence over public policy is critical in securing profitable public sector contracts, special tax advantages, and government subsidies. The more concentrated the economic wealth, the smaller the circle with disproportionate influence in these decisions.

Private individuals will consequently tend to invest in their own, rather than contribute to the economic viability (and thus the political viability) of competing individuals and groups. It is for this reason that conglomerates will gobble up hundreds of capital-starved, smaller firms rather than extend lines of credit, and that rates of profit across industries remain unequal even when capital markets work smoothly.

Economic instability and uneven development have always existed in so-called free enterprise systems, but now the growing hypermobility of capital is exacerbating these tendencies. Recall that chapter 3 discussed how sections of the country were being devastated by runaway shops and the other less dramatic, but numerically more important, forms of capital flight. And chapter 4 described how even large influxes of new capital, as in the case of high tech in New England, can actually promote *greater* inequality in job opportunity and in income.

Finally, in trying to understand why conservative economic solutions have never had much success in the past, there is the issue of economic *fear.* The classic laissez faire system depends on the simple Pavlovian stimulus-response mechanism of carrots and sticks to encourage productive behavior. The supply-siders believe that by making the carrots juicy enough and the sticks painful enough, almost any level of work effort and savings behavior can be induced. The fittest will survive and prosper, making all of society better off.

There is an obvious problem with this simplistic view. Workers (and corporate managers) can respond to the economic insecurity of the unfettered private market in either of two diametrically opposite ways. The fear of economic failure can induce them to compete more vigorously in the market place, or it can make them seek restrictive forms of protection. The entire history of capitalism—from the seventeenth-century enclosure acts and early U. S. federal policy on banks, canals, and railroads to the twentieth-century array of market rules that run from milk price supports to every conceivable form of occupational licensure—provides evidence that the dominant response to heightened insecurity is protectionism, *not* more virulent forms of cutthroat competition.[18]

In this sense, laissez faire is a "dynamically unstable" system. Even if we could somehow magically institute a perfectly competitive economy, very soon it would begin to break down as groups of firms formed trade associations and workers formed unions to protect their own interests against the chaos of the market. Within a short period of time, a good part of the protective safety net that individuals and institutions have thrown up around them would be back in place. Unmitigated competition breeds perpetual fear. No one likes to live a life always looking backward to see who is about ready to overtake him. As a result, people choose group cooperation to meet their economic needs, not competition.[19]

In *The Zero-Sum Society*, Lester Thurow worries a great deal about this "rush for sheltering." But his mistake is to treat all demands for protection as the search for *privilege*. Some of it is. But the growth in sheltering is not the cause of America's deindustrialization; it is the consequence of it. When the economy stopped growing, people everywhere rushed for a seat as though the music had stopped in a game of musical chairs. The way to stop the rush is to add more chairs. Even better, redefine the rules of the game altogether, so that people do not need to each have their own individual chair.

For all of the reasons mentioned here, the conservative supply-side strategy will not lead to revitalizing the economy. It *cannot work* on technical grounds because it fails to deal with the problems of public goods and externalities and it will inevitably exacerbate economic instability and uneven development. What may be more important, it fails the test of political feasibility, because, not wanting to live in a society where the primary motivation is fear and insecurity, people *will not let it work*.

The Liberal Strategy

The standard liberal recipe for achieving a well-functioning economy has been to rely on the market as much as possible, but to use the government to temper whatever excesses and imperfections remain. In particular, liberals have tried to mitigate the extreme uncertainty and insecurity of the private market. The expansion of federal, state, and local regulation, modest redistributions of income through tax and transfer programs, protection from "unfair" competition, and an active fiscal and monetary policy have all evolved as a natural outcome of this process.

During the 1960s, the federal government embarked on an active stabilization policy to reduce unemployment and provide for smooth growth. It also developed the Great Society programs to transfer an unprecedented flow of resources to the poor. And it expanded its regulatory functions to provide for more extensive protection of the environment, workers' health, and equal job opportunity. In many ways, the results of these policies were remarkable.

The late Arthur Okun, Chairman of the Council of Economic Advisers under Lyndon Johnson, was able to write in 1969 that one of his most pleasant assignments

> was the responsibility for keeping straight the arithmetic on the duration of the nation's economic expansion. By January 1969, we were able to report that the economy had advanced for ninety-five months since the last recession ended early in 1961. Nobody asks me for that statistic any longer; but I still enjoy keeping score. As of this writing (November 1969), the nation is in its one-hundred-and-fifth month of unparalleled, unprecedented, and uninterrupted expansion.[20]

Indeed this was quite a record. Based on previous history, Okun calculated the odds against such a continuous growth in the economy at 512 to 1! Real family incomes grew by over one third during the decade and by 1969, aided by Vietnam War spending, the overall unemployment rate stood at a mere 3.5 percent.

There were also some impressive victories in the battle against poverty. The federal government spent more than $250 billion during the 1960s on a broad range of anti-poverty measures, including expanded cash assistance programs, new health, housing, and food entitlements, training allowances, and economic and community development projects.[21] The number of people below the poverty level fell from nearly 40 million to 24 million so that by 1969 only 12.1 percent of the population was classified as poor, compared with 22.4 percent a decade earlier.[22]

The impact of increased government regulation is harder to measure.

Still, there are some concrete statistics that suggest government intervention made a difference. For example, improved mine safety rules and stepped-up inspections contributed significantly to the fact that coal mine fatalities (per 1,000 employees) declined by three quarters between 1960 and 1978.[23] Air and water pollution were substantially reduced by reason of federal abatement measures. By 1979 hydrocarbon emissions from autos were down by 40 percent, carbon monoxide fell by 25 percent, and nitrogen oxides declined by 19 percent over the levels prevailing a decade earlier.[24]

Regulation of the physical environment and the work place continued to show impressive results all through the 1970s, but the rest of the liberal strategy began to unravel quite rapidly. When Okun wrote that there had been 105 months of uninterrupted expansion, he obviously failed to give his wood desk the standard precautionary knock. A month later that record came to an end. Since that time, it has been all downhill.

Why did the liberal policy fail? One possibility is that the technocrats entrusted with manipulating stabilization policy lost their touch. After a decade of carefully adjusting fiscal and monetary policy to assure full employment and stable prices, they inadvertently took their eyes off the gauges—some believe they were distracted by Vietnam—and accidentally stepped on the economic accelerator. Once the economy spun out of control, with both inflation and unemployment rising simultaneously, they could no longer stabilize anything.

Economists Raford Boddy and James Crotty offer another explanation.[25] Building on a theory put forth during the 1930s by the Polish economist Michael Kalecki, and using data from a St. Louis Federal Reserve Bank study, they have argued that sustained prosperity and the maintenance of corporate profits are essentially incompatible. Their argument is that continuous economic growth normally leads to tighter labor markets. With low rates of unemployment, the threat of job loss diminishes and workers can no longer be easily "disciplined" by their bosses. They demand higher wages and cannot be pressured as easily to accept changes in work rules that would add to productivity. As a consequence, the ratio of profits to wages falls dramatically after boom conditions have continued for a sufficient length of time. The only way for capital to reverse the decline in the profit share is to *stimulate a recession.*

In fact, by late 1969 the profit/wage ratio had declined to 9 percent from its peak of nearly 17 percent in 1965. What could be done to reverse this disturbing trend? Boddy and Crotty believe that the fiscal and monetary authorities were pressured by business to raise interest rates and slow government spending with the explicit intent of generating a recession, thereby providing the preconditions for a reversal in corporate fortunes. And sure enough, by the end of 1971, the profit/wage ratio had bottomed out and was on the rise again.

This theory of a "political business cycle" may have some validity, but there must have been more fundamental factors at work to undermine liberal strategy. These factors have to do with the main themes of this book. The rise of international competition and the increase in the velocity of capital mobility make the entire panoply of liberal policies ineffective, unaffordable, and ultimately unproductive.

In a world in which capital moves relatively slowly, government regulation can have some bite. Capital cannot avoid environmental protection requirements or work place restrictions. But when financial capital and even real plant and equipment can be moved with relative ease, jobs can be held hostage, thus forcing people to choose between industrial growth accompanied by unhealthy water and air, and environmentally wholesome but desolate ghost towns.

Equally critical is the impact of capital mobility on the financial ability of all levels of government to fund the social safety net and to provide the range of civilian public goods, from health research to transportation, that we have come to take for granted. This problem —the "fiscal crisis of the State"—first emerged during the 1960s at the local level. By the 1980s it has come to dominate the struggle over the federal budget.

Consider the public revenues now being lost because companies have been so successful in convincing governments to cut taxes. As noted in the previous chapter, the great "supply-side tax program" of 1981 is expected to cost the U. S. Treasury $144 billion in foregone revenue by 1986. The *ability* (whatever the willingness) of the federal government to finance social safety-net programs or to maintain such basic federal public goods as the national highway system will be seriously undermined.

Much of this is actually felt at the state and local level. For a long time the losses in revenue from business were made up by shifting the tax burden onto families, in the form of higher personal and property tax rates. Now with Proposition 13 in California, Proposition 2½ in Massachusetts, and tax-cut fever spreading throughout the nation, the revenue shortfall is being made up by sharp cutbacks in both state and local budgets for police and fire protection, public schools, mass transit, parks, social services, and public aid. The *Wall Street Journal* recently raised the specter that tax abatement fever may be "out of control," thus forcing severe cutbacks in public services and deepening the urban fiscal crisis in cities throughout the country.[26]

The war between the states for corporate capital is already sufficient to make existing social programs and public goods no longer affordable. Yet the situation is likely to become even more critical as Reagan's "New Federalism" shifts the burden for these expenditures onto state and local governments. According to the Reagan plan, the states will be required to assume all the costs of food stamps, aid to families with dependent children, and forty other federally-funded programs. By 1984, if Congress goes along, it is estimated that over $46 billion worth of welfare, health, nutrition, transportation, and training programs will be shifted to states in return for the federal government's agreement to pick up the full cost of Medicaid.[27]

Some liberals have endorsed at least the underlying principles of the New Federalism without altogether understanding the full implications. This swap of fiscal responsibilities will undoubtedly intensify the war between the states, forcing further cutbacks in the scope and size of the social safety net. Corporate pressure on individual states to restrict public spending will be enormous. Merely the threat of capital mobility will force states to cut program benefits in order to maintain a low tax profile and a good business climate.

Yet even if they manage somehow to get off the New Federalism bandwagon before becoming trapped by the contradictions of fiscal decentralization, the liberals' standard program of stabilization, regulation, and redistribution has been doomed by history. The expansion of international competition and the new technological breakthroughs that make rapid capital mobility possible have produced a set of conditions under which government can no longer coerce the private sector to cooperate in the regulatory process or to provide the necessary revenue for the provision of public goods and social redistribution. Unfortunately the ability to provide an adequate social safety net was impaired before the liberal policy could complete its task of delivering a cleaner, safer environment and ridding the nation of poverty. The liberals still want both a high degree of laissez faire *and* an adequate social wage—including many public goods. Unhappily, in an era of hypermobility, the two do not seem to mix very well.

The New "Corporatist" Strategy

The conservative supply-side strategy and traditional liberal policy differ sharply on the issue of the government's proper role in the economy. But by and large they share the belief that capital should be free to move wherever and at whatever speed private profit signals dictate. Before the rise of global competition, and before the technological barriers to extensive capital mobility had been overcome, reliance on the private market for capital investment seemed compatible with economic growth and modest income redistribution.

During the past decade, however, the luster of the private market has begun to tarnish. And as it has, a small but influential number of analysts, from universities and Wall Street, have tried to devise new schemes to "reindustrialize" America that go beyond the standard conservative and liberal prescriptions. These strategies are based on a new level of cooperation between the government, national unions, and business, and they favor a far greater measure of government influence over private sector investment decisions than America has seen at any time since World War II.

Felix Rohatyn has long been "a leading voice demanding fundamental change in the relationship between capital, labor, and government."[28] Outspoken in his support for aid to the deteriorating industrial Northeast, Rohatyn declared in one of his many articles in the *New York Review of Books* that

> America cannot survive half rich, half poor; half suburb, half slum. If the country soon wakes up, it will not do so by way of laissez faire; nor will it do so by way of the old liberalism which has proven incapable of coping with our present problems.[29]

What's Wrong with Present Policy?

The new road, according to Rohatyn, involves a coordinated political and economic strategy addressing itself "literally to survival." For the cities he advocates a program that contains changes in federal grant formulas to offset the regional shifts in national wealth (due to policies such as oil price decontrol), special tax credits to older industries, special financial assistance to unemployment-prone urban centers, and targeted government procurement to aid low-income areas.[30] Each of these programs calls for the federal government to redirect capital to where it is needed most in a "social sense" rather than where it would automatically go if only short-term profit signals were heeded. In that sense, the package is quite a radical departure from both conservative and liberal thinking.

For the country as a whole, Rohatyn has long advocated resurrection of the Reconstruction Finance Corporation (RFC). The old RFC was the brainchild of another investment banker, Eugene Meyer.[31] Established by Herbert Hoover in 1931 as the economy slid deeper into the Great Depression, the original RFC was set up to provide troubled firms with capital in order to keep them afloat. The new RFC would have much the same purpose as the old. Instead of relying on special federal legislation to bail out firms like Lockheed and Chrysler with guaranteed loans, it would be empowered to make significant equity investments in whatever firms the quasi-government corporation believed could be saved.

The RFC would not be a permanent investor in any one particular enterprise but instead would remain involved only until such time as it could safely divest itself of the firm and return it to the regular private market. "The RFC," argues Rohatyn, "should, in effect, become a revolving fund—hopefully a profitable one—which steps in where no alternatives are available and which steps out when the public interest has been served and normal market forces can again operate."[32]

According to political economist Alfred J. Watkins, Rohatyn's term as the architect of the New York City rescue mission in 1975 convinced him that the real strength of a quasi-government body such as the RFC lies in its ability to circumvent normal democratic channels in order to impose austerity and sacrifice on any financially troubled public or private enterprise. The price of an RFC investment would almost always include a commitment to wage cuts on the part of the workers in the failing firm and a demand for the implementation of whatever new work rules are required to boost productivity. For this reason Watkins views Rohatyn's RFC as a direct descendant of the 1930s doctrine known as *corporatism:* "a rejection of nineteenth-century laissez faire and parliamentary wrangling in favor of something not unlike the more settled, medieval society of estates, in which each knew its place and traded opportunity for security."[33]

In the political arena, there are generally three reactions to the Rohatyn RFC proposal. The standard conservative line is that the idea is simply the work of a born-again socialist, despite the author's lofty position in the investment banking firm of Lazard Frères. Nothing in the proposal appeals to such critics at all. Then there is the AFL-CIO, which supports the idea of bailing out the industries where their members are employed, but is somewhat troubled by the lopsided austerity measures that such a government corporation might impose.

Finally there are those like Lester Thurow who believe in the need for an industrial policy, but who fear that one designed to "prop up dying industries is a route to disaster."[34] According to Thurow, the United States will have to develop new industries and new techniques for managing the economy if it is to compete in world markets and survive into the future. The last thing the government should do is protect industrial losers. What the country needs is the equivalent of a public/private "corporate finance committee" that would not seek to plan the economy but would direct more of the economy's investment funds into new growth areas and out of declining ones.

The corporate finance committee would have the responsibility for picking "sunrise industries"—areas with a potential for rapid technological gain—and then investing in them by offering long-term debt capital at market interest rates. In effect, the public sector would become the country's leading venture capitalist, offering smaller firms having a good product, but no credit rating, the resources necessary to get off the ground. Staffed by recently retired businessmen, labor leaders, and government officials from the congressional and administrative branches, the national corporate finance investment committee would also act as a lobbying group for the sunrise industries. It would evaluate proposals from its beneficiaries regarding their needs for changes in government regulations (that is, with respect to anti-trust or the environment) and, if the requests seem reasonable, would recommend them to the larger society.

At first glance there appears to be much to recommend in both the

Rohatyn and Thurow approaches to reindustrialization. Something obviously needs to be done to inhibit the socially costly demise of the older industrial regions of the nation, and it seems equally obvious that America's potential growth industries could use an injection of additional capital in order to compete with Japan and Western Europe.

Yet there are a number of nagging questions. One has to do with which firms will benefit from the activities of the RFC or Thurow's corporate finance committee. The RFC of the 1930s was under constant criticism for its propensity to bail out the largest banks and railroads in the nation, thus earning the government agency the title of the "millionaires' dole." There was obviously something to this—its very first loan went to A. P. Giannini's Bank of America (today, the richest bank in the nation), while the second went to the Van Sweringen brothers, owners of a network of railway lines with a total of 28,000 miles of tracks, the most mileage of any railway system then operating in the United States.[35] Criticism of the RFC for its loan policies prompted America's greatest wit of the 1930s, Will Rogers, to muse:

> The Reconstruction Finance Corporation is made up of fine men, honest, and mean well [sic] and if it was water they were distributing it would help the people the plan was meant to help. For water goes down hill and moistens everything in its way, but gold or money goes uphill. The Reconstruction loaned the railroads money, medium and small banks money, and all they did with it was pay off what they owed to New York banks. So the money went uphill instead of down. You can drop a bag of gold in Death Valley, which is below sea level, and before Saturday it will be home to papa J. P. [Morgan.][36]

The criticism was a just one. Banks and railroads used RFC loans to repay debts and maintain their credit ratings rather than to create new employment.

There is no guarantee that a modern version of either the RFC or Thurow's finance committee would not end up doing the same thing. In fact, to the extent that government aid is tied to a city reducing its payroll, as was the case in New York, or is used to make investments in labor-saving technology, as is likely in the high-tech industries, the net impact on employment might very well be negative. The overall effect would be to boost private profits without necessarily improving the incomes of workers or their families.

The defect in these schemes is the continued reliance on private profit signals to determine where investment should be directed. This produces the biases in the types of investments that get made. It is a good bet that capital-intensive rather than labor-intensive projects will be favored under either scheme. Projects that pay off in the short-run, giving stockholders hefty dividends and proving to the government agency that its trust was well-placed, would dominate long-term investments that might actually be more socially valuable. And, of course, by depending on the private sector to rejuvenate the economy, critical investment in public goods—including needed social infrastructure—will be entirely overlooked. Moreover, the whole thing is extremely, and in Rohatyn's case, perhaps explicitly, antidemocratic. For these reasons we believe the RFC/corporate finance committee road to revitalization is at best a partial solution, and perhaps no solution at all.

"Japanizing" the American Economy

Many of the ideas proposed by Rohatyn and, even more so, by Thurow have been influenced by their frank admiration for the post–World War II state capitalism that has given our onetime military adversary the contemporary nickname of "Japan, Inc." Despite cultural differences between the United States and Japan, an increasing number of American managers, labor leaders, and government officials are asking what can be learned from our most successful competitor.

There seems to be particular interest in Japan's methods of industrial planning. In every way as capitalistic as we are, the Japanese government nevertheless has no qualms about encouraging business to invest in potential growth industries and to disinvest in declining ones. In this regard, the Ministry of International Trade and Industry (MITI) plays a number of roles.[37] Its officials consider it their responsibility to assist companies in declining industries to merge or go out of business, while encouraging new ones to move into these localities and employ the personnel who were laid-off. In some cases where an industry can be saved by reducing its size, MITI will work out a "depression cartel": an agreement among the companies in the industry to reduce production capacity equitably in each firm. Thus, for example, industry-specific legislation has been used to rationalize the chronically ailing textile industry and to soften the blow to the shipbuilding industry when the supertanker market collapsed following the first OPEC price hike in 1973.[38]

MITI also helps form consortia of Japanese firms to undertake large construction projects and will often encourage the country's private insurance companies to provide coverage for some of these ventures. MITI officials help to arrange funding for promising companies from the country's own Development Bank and Export-Import Bank, and from the Asian Development Bank. But generally it works to secure funding from the private banking system. Normally banks will compete eagerly to give loans to the companies that have MITI's blessing.

What is intriguing in all of this activity is that most of it is done through voluntary cooperation, rather than by directive. In reality MITI has very little direct power and can only succeed as long as companies are willing to go along with its recommendations. This high degree of cooperation is due to the fact that firms know that the government agency is interested in their welfare, that MITI provides superior information and analysis, and that its bureaucrats constantly meet with industry executives to develop mutual understandings.

To be sure, there are some direct ways that the central government encourages private sector development. This is particularly true in the "sunrise" high technology area. *Business Week* reports that

MITI and other Japanese government agencies continue to pour money into research in high-technology areas. MITI will lend private industry nearly $500 million in 1981 in no-interest loans through the Agency of Industrial Science & Technology. MITI's Association of Information Processing Companies will lend the industry an additional $25 million. The Development Bank of Japan [DBJ] will lend the computer and electronics industry $220 million and other high-technology industries a further $210 million for projects "that fall under some category of government policy." In a high-technology project, DBJ generally puts up 50% of the capital (with 40% lent by private banks and the remainder provided by the borrower), at a preferential interest rate of 7.5%, compared with the long-term prime rate of 8.9% that prevailed in November [1981].[39]

Altogether the twelve government-financing institutions ranging from the DBJ and the People's Finance Corporation to the Housing Loan Corporation and the Medical Care Facilities Finance Corporation channeled almost $60 billion in equity investments and loans into the economy in 1981.[40] This provides the Japanese with what Arthur D. Little consultant Jerry Wasserman calls "patient money." The Japanese can afford to take the long-term view because the private market is not perpetually hovering over each firm and demanding it make a profit and return a regular dividend. Hitachi, Matsushita, and Toshiba were able to turn themselves into major semiconductor suppliers in this way, while in the United States "General Electric, Westinghouse Electric, and RCA grew impatient with the slow payoff on their semiconductor investments, cut back, and never fulfilled their early promise."[41]

That the Japanese take the long-term view in their investment strategy is also reflected in both the attitudes of management and the nation's approach to labor-management relations. In the United States the typical relationship between workers and their firms is *temporary*. This applies all the way from the lofty ranks of upper-level management down to the blue-collar worker on the assembly line. Neither the incentive structures for managers nor the ease with which firms can use layoffs to adjust to changes in product demand is conducive to a long-term, secure relationship between employer and employee. As a result, it is not uncommon for a firm's annual employee turnover rate to exceed 25 percent or more.[42] American managers, more often than not, improve both their salaries and their social status by hopping from one company to another rather than by sticking around to move up through the corporate hierarchy.

In the major firms in Japan, this high degree of employee turnover is almost completely unknown. The Japanese are said to use a system of "permanent" or "lifetime" employment whereby certain "regular" employees and top managers remain in the same firm from the time they first enter after leaving school until retirement.[43] While there are no definitive studies of the differences in job tenure between U. S. and Japanese workers, survey research conducted by Robert Cole and Paul Siegel in Detroit and Yokohama indicates that in general the odds of spending a lifetime with your first employer in the Japanese city are at least four and one-half times as great as in America's automobile capital.[44]

The economic security that goes along with guaranteed employment has been extraordinarily beneficial for the Japanese economy in a number of ways. Since the economic success and social status of top managers is tied inextricably to the long-term financial success of their firms, managers' planning horizons are longer; they are much more likely than American managers to search for long-term security than short-term profits.[45] This provides the opportunity to think strategically rather than simply in terms of tactical expediency. Combined with "patient money," the Japanese firm is in a much better position to plan for future markets and to develop products that might not make money for the company for a decade or more.

The longer horizons also encourage greater investments in employee training. In the United States, the boom in defense spending has created a tremendous demand for Class A machinists in both the aircraft and shipbuilding industries. But given the lengthy apprenticeship required for this job and the uncertain long-term outlook for employment, neither firms nor workers are willing to make the large investments necessary. Without some guarantee of a long-term employment contract, the expected value of the training is simply not great enough to warrant the expense.[46]

In Japan the situation is very different. As Ezra Vogel of Harvard University points out, "Because employees tend to remain in large corporations until retirement, it is rational for Japanese companies to invest far more heavily in training than do Western companies."[47] Firms do not have to worry that their well-trained employees will be pirated away by another company, and workers, knowing full well that this investment will pay off in the future, can pay for a portion of their general training by accepting lower wages when they join the company.

Similarly, lifetime tenure is a strong motivation for economic productivity. The career-long commitment of major enterprises to workers provides the foundation for quality-control efforts, work redesign, career enlargement, and other practices the Japanese have developed "to diminish alienation and foster identification."[48] Moreover, it encourages workers to accept and even promote the introduction of new technology, since this tends to enhance their firm's viability without endangering their jobs. In this case it promotes worker flexibility. Vogel notes:

> Featherbedding and the reluctance of American workers to be flexible in performing various jobs in a company are problems for American industry

not only because workers are afraid of losing their jobs but because they want to protect their skill level. The Japanese worker concerned about the long-range future of his company eagerly seeks technological change and, because his status and future is less related to a special skill level, he is more willing to perform miscellaneous tasks and to assist fellow workers in different tasks as the need arises. The employer gets fuller and more flexible use of employees, and employees find the varied work less monotonous than their American counterparts who stick to the same work.[49]

Finally, because planning horizons are longer and "permanent" workers cannot be laid-off at will, the degree of capital mobility documented for the United States is not common to Japan. Managers do not see moving capital from one industry to another or between regions as a useful policy for disciplining labor. While American businessmen would consider the inability to shift labor from one industry to another in accordance with changing patterns of cost and demand as a serious impediment to productivity, the Japanese have been able to translate job guarantees into a source of economic growth.[50] For Japan, economic security provides a much more powerful inducement to productivity enhancement than economic fear.

The Japanese system of targeted investment and permanent employment has worked wonders for some of the Japanese. But the question of whether these mechanisms are culturally unique and therefore not transferable to the United States always arises. Here the evidence strongly suggests that at least as far as investment practices and job security are concerned, the Japanese are *not* unique. Indeed, they seem to have *learned* these practices relatively recently.[51] Presumably the United States could also. But before attempting to mimic the Japanese, it is worthwhile to ask whether this country would want to. There is a real question of whether *their* system is consistent with *our* basic democratic values.

Many Japanese intellectuals and Western scholars of Japan worry about the strong pressure for conformity in the Japanese system that can easily restrict dissent and stifle individualism. Big business has even more political power in Japan than it does in the United States, and it is not hesitant to use it. The government bureaucracy there tends to be more professional and therefore has more expertise. But it is also more independent of the electoral system and thereby more immune to the popular will. The central government has substantially more authority than local jurisdictions, which allows better coordination of industrial, transport, commercial, and recreation facilities. But such a high level of centralization detracts from the ability of individual communities to control their own destinies. The highly structured and autocratic education system turns out excellent technicians, but there is some doubt about how well it develops critical, creative, well-rounded individuals. In essence, the Japanese appear to have built an enormously productive and efficient economic machine, but at substantial political cost.[52]

There is also the problem of who actually benefits from the Japanese system. While there is no question that nearly everyone in the nation has gained indirectly from the expansion of the economy, those covered by permanent employment comprise at most one third of the labor force.[53] No more precise estimate exists because permanent employment is not a formally guaranteed right, but rather informal company policy. Permanent employment is less pervasive in the small-scale private sector where working conditions tend to be poor, product demand unstable, and capital funds in short supply. White-collar employees and managers are better covered than regular blue-collar workers. Moreover, the system is basically limited to men; women generally do not yet have access to permanent employment.

In fact, to make the job-guarantee system work, a "dual economy" has been more or less explicitly created in Japan. The core of a large firm's employment is covered under the system. But fluctuations in demand are handled through the hiring and dismissing of "temporary" workers who do not share these benefits. In times of temporary growth, the number of such workers expands, usually through the employment of housewives and recent retirees. During economic recessions, these temporary workers are released and permanent employees reassigned to their tasks. If the situation becomes very severe, work ordinarily done by subcontractors will be brought back into the main plant to ensure jobs for "permanent" workers. In this way, employees in the smaller shops bear the full burden of cyclical downturns. Given that a company like Toyota normally purchases about 80 percent of the value of production from its suppliers, this "loophole" in the permanent employment system is by no means minor.[54]

What makes matters worse is that the typical Japanese company makes it clear to its employees that while employment may be guaranteed, job benefits are not.

Benefits are not distributed automatically by contractual agreement to anyone simply because he is a company member or because he falls into a certain category of age, status, and length of service, for leaders believe flexibility of rewards is needed as a critical leverage to maintain discipline.[55]

Those outside the major firms are at even a worse disadvantage because of Japan's low level of social security benefits. Workers are almost wholly dependent on the company for retirement pensions and often housing. As a result, the benefits of being a permanent employee and playing according to the rules are substantial; the costs of being "outside" the system or of becoming known as a dissident are enormous. As Robert Cole points out, the central benefit that induces workers to tolerate a regimented, confining industrial system is job security. "We might better speak of worker acquiescence than worker acceptance of permanent employment." Or as John Junkerman writes, "Without the promise of job security, Japanese workers [might] not submit to singing the company song."[56]

The Japanese system is therefore a two-edged sword. It offers economic prosperity and material progress. But it exacts a price in terms of regimentation, autocracy, and institutionalized inequality. Such a form of social organization is surely not what we want for the United States, even though there is much to learn from the Japanese about the technical coordination of financial and production planning and the efficiency of a system based on some form of built-in job security.

Targeting Economic Development Policy to Small Business

Just as the fascination with "Japan Inc." as a model for American economic development turns out to be naïve, so do two policy proposals that are currently receiving widespread attention in Britain and the United States. Actually, the two are closely interrelated. Advocates of a development strategy aimed at small companies see *size* as the most important factor determining the likelihood of generating new jobs. And what the architects of the "urban enterprise zone" policy want to do is to use both tax subsidies and deregulation to channel the hoped-for small business growth into areas where the resident work force best "fits" the kinds of jobs being created.

Recently, a number of policy analysts have rediscovered the numerical importance of the small business sector. In an economy so permeated with the free enterprise ethic, it should be no surprise that so many small entrepreneurs are continually risking everything to get into business. Every year, tens of thousands of new entrepreneurial firms are born. In the present economic climate, the political attractiveness of any research finding of the "robustness" or "liveliness" of this sort of investment activity is treated as a godsend by the ideologues of laissez faire. After all, they can say, things cannot be as bad as they appear; look at the energetic growth of small business!

Thus it would be hard to exaggerate the excitement that has been generated among both traditional conservatives and recent converts by the most recently published research of David L. Birch. Using the same Dun and Bradstreet data relied so heavily upon in chapter 2 of this book, Birch has written that:

> Of all the net new jobs created in our sample of 5.6 million [establishments] between 1969 and 1976, two-thirds were created by firms with twenty or fewer employees, and about 80 percent were created by firms with 100 or fewer employees.[57]

This has been picked up by the media in the United States, Canada, and Great Britain and repeated endlessly by advocates of a policy of switching the focus of publicly-subsidized development programs from large corporations to the "small business community." As a development strategy, it is precisely the opposite of "Japanization."

In the light of the central finding of *this* book—the tendency toward deindustrialization among large corporations through foreign investment, diversification, and merger—it should not be too surprising to learn that what growth *did* occur during the 1970s took place mainly by default in smaller establishments. But it hardly follows that economic development policy *ought* to be targeted to subsidizing this sector.

Indeed, there is good evidence that, relative to larger entities, small businesses (certainly those that employ twenty or fewer workers) pay low wages, offer unstable or only part-time jobs, often practice overt race and sex discrimination in hiring and wage policy, and exhibit arbitrary or capricious discipline over workers. In short, small firms tend to fall squarely into what economists call the "secondary labor market."[58]

Although job creation is unquestionably an appropriate social objective, when the *quality* as well as the quantity of the employment being created is examined, there are dramatic trade-offs. For example, as Birch has acknowledged, the stability of employment in small companies is highly precarious. Newly created small firms tend to grow for short spurts and then decline. Their failure rates are extremely high.

Harvey Garn and Larry Ledebur, drawing entirely upon Birch's own data, have constructed an especially vivid illustration of this. Table 7.1 shows the proportion of firms that survive beyond 4, 9, and 10 years after starting up, as a function of the original size of the firm. Thus, while firms with more than 500 employees have a 35.7 percent chance of surviving beyond 10 years, those with between one and twenty employees initially face chances of surviving that long of only 8.6 percent—odds of only one in twelve. Clearly the chances of surviving are lower, the smaller the firm. Moreover, the differences between large and small firms grow over time—for example, the largest firms are almost twice as likely to survive for at least 4 years as the smallest firms, and over four times as likely to last for more than 10 years. Finally, the size category favored by Birch (1–20 employees) is dramatically worse off than the rest; even companies with only twenty-one to fifty employees behave more like the largest corporations (in terms of "survivability") than those small businesses that some would place at the center of a new economic development policy for the nation.

There is another criticism to be made of the uses to which Birch's research have been applied. The implication most often drawn by conservative ideologues, especially Republican policy makers in Washington, is that the relative importance of *small* firms as net job-generators during the 1970s points to the desirability of policies to promote *independently-owned* businesses, that is, petty capital. The leap is from Birch's famous "66 percent of the new jobs are in *small* companies" to the celebration and advocacy of *entrepreneurship*.

It is certainly true that during the 1970s, on the average, about half the jobs in the private sector were to be found in independently-owned, single establishment enterprises. But at the margin, if one looks at

TABLE 7.1

The Proportion of Firms That Survive Beyond 4, 9, and 10 Years After Start-Up, as a Function of Initial Employment Size

Initial Size (Employees)	Beyond 4 Years		Beyond 9 Years		Beyond 10 Years	
	Proportion that Survive	Index*	Proportion that Survive	Index*	Proportion that Survive	Index*
1–20	.374	1.00	.173	1.00	.086	1.00
21–50	.536	1.44	.352	2.03	.262	3.05
51–100	.557	1.49	.364	2.10	.274	3.10
101–500	.564	1.51	.368	2.13	.283	3.29
500 and over	.677	1.82	.425	2.46	.357	4.15

SOURCE: Harvey A. Garn and Larry C. Ledebur, *The Estimation of Development Impacts* (Washington, D. C.: The Urban Institute, March 1981), p. 26; calculated from table 4–6 in David Birch, *The Job Generation Process*, (Cambridge, Mass.: MIT Program on Neighborhood and Regional Change, 1979), based on data for 1969–76.
*Ratio of larger size classes to the 1–20 class

private investment in *new* facilities (not acquired companies), the growth rates of jobs found in small plants, stores, shops, and offices owned by multiunit *corporations* were much greater than among independent small entrepreneurs. Let us define "small" more charitably, as establishments with fifty or fewer employees in 1969. Table 7.2 shows the growth rates of small New England independently-owned establishments versus corporate facilities over the seven-year period from 1969–76. The gap between the performance of the two sectors actually increased as the decade wore on.

With respect to the nation as a whole, Birch has found the same

TABLE 7.2

Jobs Created in New England by New Births of Establishments With Fifty or Fewer Employees, by Ownership: 1969–76

Type of Ownership	Employment in 1969 in the New England Sample (000)	Percentage Change in Employment Associated With New Births		
		1969–72	1972–74	1974–76
Independent	1,197	10.6	6.6	4.6
Corporate	1,118	16.6	14.0	10.5
Ratio	—	1.6	2.1	2.3

SOURCE: Authors' calculations from an extract from Dun's Identifiers' File, prepared for the authors by David L. Birch.

thing. In 1969, he reports, new independently-owned (as opposed to corporate-owned) establishments were responsible for creating about 40 percent of all new jobs in the economy. By 1976 this share had fallen to 23 percent.[59]

In short, at least with respect to investment in *new* start-ups, it is very misleading to treat the growth of "small" factories or stores as indicative of the dominance of "small business." In fact, what investment growth did occur during the 1970s seems to have increasingly involved corporations switching to smaller plants. According to Roger Schmenner, during the 1970s new manufacturing branches were on the average 60 percent smaller than older plants in the same industries.[60]

Why corporations are pursuing such a strategy may be guessed. In their sometimes desperate efforts to cut costs and increase labor discipline during an era of global economic crisis, managers may be discovering that smaller workplaces are easier to control, whether it be a matter of introducing new technology (and the work rules that go with it) or of trying to avoid being unionized.[61] Moreover, the supposed trade-off in terms of lost efficiency due to foregone economies of scale may have become less severe with modern technology. "For most industries," writes Schmenner, "scale economies either [no longer] exist or are comparatively modest."[62]

Thus, it can be concluded that, while the "small business" sector is indeed large and visible—especially in an era of a domestic "capital strike" by the *Fortune* 500—it is still the corporate sector, and especially the smaller corporation, that is responsible for most of the jobs created by investment in new plants and stores—not independent entrepreneurs. This fact has been obscured to some extent because corporations across the board are shifting toward a strategy of abandoning their older and larger facilities while constructing (or acquiring) smaller ones.

Urban Enterprise Zones

The other "quick-fix" policy now being trumpeted by conservatives (with the surprising support of some liberal politicians) is the designation of urban "enterprise zones": selected areas in which business would be encouraged to invest, under conditions of reduced income and property taxes, lower direct and indirect labor costs, and—in the most ambitious designs—extensive relaxation of environmental, health, safety, and other regulations. The ostensible objective is to stimulate new small business development in the inner city and, with it, additional employment for hard-pressed, low-income residents of the designated areas.

The idea of applying the international free-trade zone (or "freeport") idea to an Anglo-American setting has been widely attributed to a British city planner, Professor Peter Hall. In an address in June of 1977 to the British Royal Town Planning Institute, Hall put forth a proposal by which

> small, selected areas of inner cities would be simply thrown open to all kinds of initiative, with minimal control. In other words we would aim to recreate the Hong Kong of the 1950s and 1960s inside inner Liverpool or inner Glasgow.[63]

The areas would ideally be set up as freeports, with neither customs duties nor taxes. Moreover, they "would have to be zones of fairly shameless free enterprise . . . outside the scope of taxes, social services, industrial and other regulations." Hall conceived of it as a great social experiment, "an industrial policy based not on support of declining industries, but on encouragement of industrial innovation. France and (above all) Japan have followed that route with conspicuous success."

At the same time, Hall recognized that the "redundancy" (unemployment) of older workers caught with outmoded skills, and of younger native and immigrant workers with no skills at all, had become serious sources of political instability in the United Kingdom. For these workers, the zones offered two prospects:

> one not so good (but better than nothing), one much better (in fact, positively good). The not-so-good way would be the movement into the zones of multi-locational large corporations seeking cheap labor: in other words, doing in Liverpool what they already do in Singapore or in Mexican border cities. . . . This however would be acceptable only as a short term outcome; the case for the zones in that instance would be that, once started in gainful employment, inner city residents could begin to climb the ladder of skill and income, so that their economy could transfer progressively into sectors and products with higher value added.[64]

The "much better" possibility would be that, freed of most regulatory restraints, petty capitalists might invest in a host of innovational small enterprises, especially in the manufacture of scientific instruments and electronics, at least initially involving little technical skills. This sector would therefore provide both much-needed jobs to inner-city residents and a fresh burst of innovative enterprise for the British economy.

By starting small, and utilizing unskilled labor, these enterprises would "match" the present capabilities of the labor force. Gradually, the more successful of the enterprize zone firms would upgrade their technical requirements and demand more skills from their employees as they went along. Because on-the-job training would have taken place over this maturation period, the requisite skills would be created in balance with the firms' needs for them. It would be a development path in which "demands for labour and the supply of it are in some kind of equilibrium: as the economy demands more skilled workers, so they become available."

The idea appealed to (then) Conservative opposition economics spokesman, Sir Geoffrey Howe. In 1978–79 he began to advocate such an experiment for Great Britain with, to be sure, a number of differences from Hall's original model. In particular, while Hall saw the zones as "extremely last-ditch solutions" to be tried "only on a very small scale" in areas that had become "largely abandoned," Howe was interested in attracting private capital to the populated core of the British urban ghettos.[65] When Margaret Thatcher was elected prime minister in 1979, Howe became Chancellor of the Exchequer. Immediately, eleven sites for new enterprise zones were designated by the new government. The first of these was formally opened in the summer of 1981.

The concept seems to have been imported into the United States by the Washington-based, conservative Heritage Foundation, in conjunction with the Reagan presidential campaign. Congressman Jack Kemp (R-N.Y.), a close advisor to the candidate, became its most visible (and audible) spokesperson. The "Kemp-Garcia Urban Jobs and Enterprise Zone Act" became Reagan's urban policy and remains (in early 1982) his only positive (albeit rather lukewarm) proposal for new urban economic development.

The latest version of the Kemp-Garcia Act would designate a large number of urban, and some rural, areas as enterprise zones. Within their borders, capital gains taxes associated with new investments would be eliminated. Half of all income earned by enterprises operating within the zone, and half of all interest income earned on loans made to zone enterprises, would be sheltered from taxation. Employers would receive tax credits for each eligible—basically low-wage, unskilled, or nonwhite—resident they hired. Free-trade zones would be established "wherever possible." For the moment, in deference to the unions, no deregulation would be pursued, although it seems taken for granted that that *is* a long-term objective. (Even so, the AFL-CIO has still attacked the proposal as "little more than a localized version of 'trickle-down' economics" and an open invitation to runaway shops.)

At the same time, twenty states have begun to consider their own enterprise-zone legislation. An Illinois bill may be a harbinger of things to come. It passed both houses of the state legislature but was vetoed by the state's liberal governor. The state senate then quickly repassed the bill over the veto. This Illinois proposal would suspend all zoning and building codes, eliminate state-imposed minimum wages, abolish property taxes, institute a state right-to-work law to prevent unions from undermining the "pro-business climate," and gradually weaken environmental, health and safety regulations.[66]

At least with respect to the tax and wage subsidies, Americans have actually seen much of this before. During the late 1960s, in the wake of the urban, black working-class riots, there was a good deal of public debate over whether, and how best, to use public policy to induce private investment capital into the "black ghetto."[67] The idea of directing the tax breaks to outside groups who earn enough profits to make use of them, in return for their investing in inner-city entrepreneurs, was first tried during the Nixon years—with very little success.[68]

The current proposals are extraordinarily naive about the relationship between the management of technological change in the capitalist firm, on the one hand, and hiring and plant location policies, on the other. As managers introduce new machinery or production processes, they tend also to alter work rules and, as a result, make new decisions about whom to hire to perform the new jobs and (sometimes) where to do the producing.[69] This makes Hall's vision of a smooth link between the technical upgrading of the typical small firm's labor requirements and the upward mobility of the zone's initially unskilled workers most unlikely as an outcome.

At best, if the enterprise-zone policy actually succeeds in cheapening labor costs, it may marginally promote the expansion of the secondary labor market. Employers who offer low-wage, low-productivity jobs and who follow authoritarian or arbitrary personnel practices, are the most likely to benefit from an enterprise-zone policy. All the criticisms directed in the previous section against a too mechanical pursuit of the small enterprise development strategy apply here as well. Hall, in particular, ignores the often profoundly sexist organization of work and the meager possibilities for on-the-job training and "upward mobility" in these sorts of enterprises that include the very electronics shops—many of those making semiconductors—he so admires.[70] Indeed, there is good reason to expect that the zones could become havens for a revival of old-fashioned sweatshops (albeit some with modern equipment like computer numerically-controlled sewing machines or high-tech plastics extrusion molds). If this expectation is correct, then Hall's admonition that the "freeport" policy not be used to prop up declining industries becomes rather paradoxical, and his invocation of Japanese and French planning (which are aimed at developing industries like robots and jet aircraft) just a bit ludicrous.[71]

What is certain is that no one, besides the most devout supply-sider, really believes that the tax breaks in the Kemp-Garcia bill will change anything—not even Representative Kemp, who admits that "it is hard in practice to avoid windfalls."[72] When it comes to promoting new small-business start-ups, which both Kemp and Hall express as their primary objective, tax breaks simply are not very helpful until a company has grown large (and successful) enough to have any profits to tax! Instead, if they need anything at all, small entrepreneurial start-ups need long-term venture capital: that "patient money" that the Japanese manage to spread around so well.[73] Yet Kemp himself has insisted repeatedly that he has no intention of increasing the cost of his bill by proposing the subsidization of start-up capital.

Coming as it does from an administration so strongly committed to reducing government spending, the enterprise-zone proposal also has a somewhat disingenuous flavor to it. Significant new economic development, in inner-city neighborhoods or elsewhere, is going to require major *public* investments in physical infrastructure (roads, street lights, bridges, and sewers) and services (police, fire, job training, and maintenance of all that infrastructure). The rapid deterioration of these public goods in the older cities—and their unfinished status in the new cities of the Sunbelt—has become a serious bottleneck to further private investment there.[74] Thus, the fiscal crisis of the State directly contradicts the developmental objectives of the whole enterprise-zone concept.

The criticism so far has been largely in the nature of a forecast of the likely impact of the zone proposal in American urban economies. But in fact there are already two decades of Third World experience with free-trade zones that provide *evidence* of their impact. To summarize the conclusions of a number of evaluative studies—Milton Friedman's worship of Hong Kong notwithstanding—life in these zones for most workers is barely tolerable. And because of this, the zones are surely not a stable political form.[75]

In any case, as William Goldsmith points out, the whole thing is basically absurd—precisely because of the new international division of labor itself.

> Hourly wages for unskilled manufacturing workers in branch plants in 1975 were about 15 cents or less in India, the Philippines, Thailand, Mauritius, and Haiti; they were 25 cents or less in Indonesia, Malaysia, Taiwan, Lesotho, Liberia, Swaziland, Colombia, and Honduras. Add it up: 25 cents an hour is $10 a week, hardly more than $500 a year for the best of these cases! Even in nearby Mexico these wages were as low as 56 cents an hour. . . . Can wages in the U. S. be cut so low, even in enterprise zones, that workers can effectively compete with their counterparts in foreign, Third World, platform economies? I think not, if only because costs of living in the U. S. are relatively too high. But there is a stronger reason, which is that social and political resistance, even among isolated minorities in central cities, is likely to be substantial. In the long run, [such] inhuman conditions simply won't be tolerated.[76]

Conclusion

All of the proposed solutions reviewed in this chapter have one thing in common: they rely fundamentally on the private sector and the profit motive, even when they call for modest forms of government planning. Unpopular as this criticism may be at the present moment, there is good reason to think that the exigencies of global competition and capital mobility vitiate *any* strategy that relies on individual corporations to act in the public interest.

Supply-side regressive income redistribution, liberal Democratic tax reform, corporatist emulation of some stylized image of Japanese planning, the promotion of small-business entrepreneurship, and the targeting of business subsidies to designated low-income areas—all share a studied unwillingness to question the extent to which conventional private ownership of industry and the more-or-less unbridled pursuit of private profit might be the *causes* of the problem. At the very least, it is necessary to ask whether other options can even be imagined. That is the task of the last chapter of this book.

Chapter 8

Reindustrialization with a

Human Face

WE HAVE come a long way in our examination of the causes of the contemporary crisis in the American economy and of how the managers of industry have both contributed to, and in turn been trapped by, the new economic rules of the game. At the center of the analysis has been the phenomenon of the hypermobility of capital—management's urge to take advantage of every possibility for squeezing out an extra ounce of profit by shifting resources from one activity or location to another—as a response to these new conditions. And there has been graphic and often tragic evidence of how this accelerating race to regain the profit rates of the 1960s is destroying social productivity, jobs, incomes, and the very material basis for a stable political community.

If neither supply-side reliance on the wonders of the "free market" nor corporatist models of consensual planning after the manner of Japan can be expected to achieve the *democratic* reindustrialization of the American economy, what can?

The immediate answer—the first step in what is going to be a long process of radical political change in this country—is easy to specify. The growing insecurity of workers, their families, and the communities in which they live must be reversed. The supply-siders argue that insecurity is the motor that drives the capital accumulation process. It is, they say, *too much* government-guaranteed security that undermined savings, work effort, and productivity in the first place.

This is nonsense. This book has argued that productivity is a *social* relation. To promote it requires *more,* not less, social security. Only as the fear of poverty, disease, and joblessness recedes can human energies be totally released for creative, truly productive effort. Thus, before Americans can embark on any major planned structural transformation of the economy, they must reject the claims of those who would deliberately promote insecurity as a matter of policy, find ways to re-establish the social safety net, and *extend* the range of the regulatory system to make that net even more secure for more groups in the population. These are the preconditions for any fundamental restructuring of the American economy.

Given that the United States has moved away from even the most tentative experience with economic planning such as characterized the years of the Roosevelt coalition in the 1930s and the command economy of 1941–45, what that "fundamental restructuring" should be is now much harder to specify.[1] More important, under any sort of truly democratic planning (which the New Deal decidedly was not), the actual day-to-day tasks would be performed by those most closely involved with economic affairs: workers themselves, and their own designated representatives. Only in this way can that planning be made socially responsible. The absence of even the slightest concern for the need for such accountability is the greatest single danger posed by the corporatist models of Rohatyn and Thurow.

It follows that elaborate paper plans, written outside of the process of *making* radical social change, are not likely to be worth a great deal —even if they come from the most well-intentioned and expert of groups. Nevertheless, it seems useful to at least indicate some of the principal issues that any democratic planning system emerging out of the present impasse in economic affairs will have to confront. That is the purpose of this chapter.

The Immediate Agenda: Rebuilding the
Social Safety Net

The first piece of business is to re-establish a public commitment to the maintenance (and indeed, to an *expansion*) of the social wage. *More,* not fewer, people need to be brought under its protection. In thinking about how to do this, it must be recognized that some of the relevant issues are not new at all. Rather, they are old ones that need to be brought back onto center stage of public debate, and rescued from the premature burial given to them by the new conservatives.

One example is the distorted allocation of resources that is once again feeding a bloated, inefficient, and wasteful military machine. Even the most dispassionate cost-benefit analysis of the federal budget would conclude that $1.6 *trillion* for defense over a five-year period (the current Reagan proposal) amounts to incredible overkill, especially when the already small budgets for things like mass transit, school-lunch programs, and alternative energy systems are being gutted to pay for it. What kind of government policy increases a $16.5-billion budget for military research and development by 20 percent, while adding only 2 percent to the $3.6 billion R & D budget for the National Institutes of Health where the research involves trying to find cures for heart disease and cancer?[2]

Another good example is true progressive tax reform. Major changes are needed in the personal income tax to remove inequities, particularly in the treatment of non-labor income vis-à-vis earnings. Ordinary working people feel only cynicism and resentment for the disastrously inequitable system that exists today—a system in which a fifty-year-old bricklayer can actually pay more taxes than one of the five largest banks in the country.

Changes in corporate taxation are even more urgent. In particular, the long history of postwar zero-interest, long-term loans and grants from the U. S. Treasury to private corporations, via the Internal Revenue Code, must be ended. That is, we should stop granting IRS business-tax incentives of any kind, and for any purpose. It is clear that these "incentives" produce practically no new economic growth that would not have been forthcoming in their absence. But they *do* force the public to bear an immense loss in revenues that have productive and important alternative uses.

Instead of continuing to plunge headlong into an evermore intense war between states, in which one local government is played off against another by companies demanding a "good business climate," and as an alternative to the continued erosion of the federal income tax revenue base through new concessions to industry, it is necessary to completely revamp our tax system. Without those additional revenues, a strong and broad-based social safety net cannot be financed, especially at the local level.

Organizing is taking place around this question, especially outside of Congress. To cite but one example, the Multistate Tax Commission is helping states to cooperate with one another to recover a volume of corporate taxes that is based upon a carefully assessed estimate of the share of each corporation's worldwide business conducted in each state. In 1980, in a 6–1 vote, the U. S. Supreme Court decided that such a principle of state taxation of multiregion corporations was indeed constitutional and equitable. In *Mobil Oil Corp.* v. *Commissioner of Taxes of Vermont,* the Court ruled that Vermont had the right to tax Mobil's net dividend income from all its domestic and foreign investments, including the returns on its Saudi Arabian subsidiaries, at a rate equal to the proportion of Mobil's worldwide sales that took place within Vermont.[3]

Some economic advisors to the Democratic Party are proposing new forms of taxation such as the value-added tax to make up the revenue shortfall. Others are calling for at least a partial repeal of the provisions of the 1981 Tax Recovery Act. This is mere tinkering. If new revenue is to be generated for the maintenance and gradual expansion of the social safety net, ways must be found to close tax loopholes that allow various forms of investment income to escape taxation, in some cases entirely. More complete taxation of capital gains and the elimination of tax shelters on real estate, mineral rights, and foreign income is one step in this direction. *If* the tax code can be rewritten so that stockholders are fully taxed on the corporate earnings of the companies in which they hold stock, it may even be efficient to eliminate the present corporation income tax in favor of more steeply progressive personal taxation on investment income.[4]

Extending the Social Wage: Plant-Closing Legislation

As discussed in chapter 5, there is a long history of attempts by the labor movement to both promote public policies that would more fully protect working people from arbitrary and capricious treatment at the hands of their employers, and to struggle for a more expansive and widely-shared social wage. The conflict with industry over business' right to shut down an establishment precipitously or to abandon a community and its work force for another location is only the most recent attempt by labor to cope with the contradiction between capital mobility, on the one hand, and personal security and community stability on the other.

For workers who belong to unions, the first defense against precipitous dislocation is the negotiated contract with the company. In recent years, some unions, including the United Food and Commercial Workers and the Amalgamated Clothing and Textile Workers Union of America, have made significant breakthroughs in negotiating protection for workers' jobs, wages, and severance benefits. Nevertheless, quite apart from the fact that three quarters of the American labor force has no direct union protection at all, those whose jobs *are* covered by collective bargaining agreements receive relatively little—or very weak—protection from job loss related to shutdowns or large cutbacks.

The most recent data refer to 1978. In that year, three quarters of the 400 American collective-bargaining agreements contracts surveyed by the Bureau of National Affairs (BNA) made some provision for prenotification to workers. But 81 percent of these provided only *one week's notice or less!*

Moreover, the record for large manufacturing companies is much worse than the BNA averages suggest. According to the U. S. Department of Labor, of 826 contracts active on July 1, 1976 covering 3.4 million workers in manufacturing plants with 1,000 or more employees, only 111 contracts (covering 353,000 workers) provided for any sort of advance notification. That amounts to only 13 percent of the contracts, covering only 10 percent of the workers.

Provision for adequate income protection or severance pay is just as rare. In 1977–78, half of all American workers covered in some respect by a contract received no income protection of any kind. Only one sixth of all workers were even eligible in 1978 for Supplemental Unemployment Benefits—long-term company-paid unemployment insurance, negotiated as part of the contract.[5]

Another problem of growing concern to the labor movement has to do with what is called *successorship.* In 1964 the U. S. Supreme Court ruled that unions had the right to bring grievances before the National Labor Relations Board when an employer "disappeared by merger" and the "new" employer refused to recognize the union. As seen in chapters 2 and 6, this sort of "disappearance" of firms has become increasingly common in the past twenty years, and another merger wave, led this time by the computer and software industries, appears to be in the offing in the 1980s.

In 1972 in the *Burns* decision, the new Burger Court effectively reversed the previous Warren Court ruling, arguing that a successor's honoring the contract

> does not ensue as a matter of law from the mere fact that an employer is doing the same work in the same place with the same employees as his predecessor . . . a potential employer may be willing to take over a moribund business only if he can make changes in corporate structure, composition of the labor force, work, location, task assignment, and nature of supervision. Saddling such an employer with the terms and conditions of employment contained in the old contract may make these changes impossible and may discourage and inhibit the transfer of capital. . . .[6]

Some liberal legislators have tried to amend the Taft-Hartley Act to make it an unfair labor practice for an employer who assumes ownership or operation of an ongoing business to refuse to assume all of the terms and conditions of a predecessor contract. But so far, the legislation has had no success.

There are at least three problems with trying to rely on the collective-bargaining system—however "reformed"—to deal with economic dislocation. First, the case-by-case contractual approach cannot reach every worker directly at risk, since so few are unionized. Second, protection needs to be extended beyond those workers immediately affected by company rationalization strategies to cover everyone whose income security is threatened. And finally, collective bargaining is incapable of providing for the rebuilding of the local economic base in the wake of major shutdowns. Thus the need for legislation that addresses the whole range of problems created by plant and store closings and cutbacks.

In June 1978 a delegation made up of officials of three American unions and several government agencies visited Sweden, West Germany, and England to study how their governments and unions were dealing with what is, after all, a problem in all of the industrial capitalist countries. Led by the United Auto Workers, the Steelworkers, and the Machinists, the delegation found:

> In all three countries, corporations are legally obligated to give advance notice [to] workers, unions, and the national employment service before closing a plant or dismissing workers for economic reasons. Before initiating layoffs, moreover, a company must first negotiate the matter with its employees' union or the plant's works joint labor-management council. . . . The time gained gives affected workers and potential new employees the chance to arrange for alternative employment . . . advance notice triggers into action labor market boards at the national, regional, local (and in some cases, workplace) levels.[7]

The Swedish have the most highly developed programs for relocating workers; for example, they bring employment service computer terminals inside the old plant as soon as notice of the eventual closing is given, and statutorily *require* all employers to list vacancies in these computerized files. (This is quite a contrast to the American employment security system, where filing is essentially voluntary and has been shown again and again to be highly selective and often racially biased in its outcomes.) Moreover, the Swedish have a wide variety of programs for *replacing* the eroded local job (and tax) base through both direct public enterprise and grants and loans for new private sector start-ups. In West Germany, a firm contemplating a shutdown is required to give its reasons to the local works council, and to open its books so that the council will have free access to all corporate data relevant to evaluate the decision and its likely impact on the region in which the plant is located. The Co-determination Act of 1976 requires West German businesses to give one-year's advance notice of intended plant or store closings.

In the United States there has been similar legislation, but it has never been passed into law. As early as 1974, then Senator Walter Mondale (D-Minn.) and Congressman William Ford (D-Mich.) introduced the National Employment Priorities Act (NEPA) into Congress. The bill, which even supporters considered to be seriously flawed in several respects, was never even reported out of committee.

When the Ford-Mondale bill failed, the effort to organize plant closing legislation shifted to the states, led by the efforts of the Ohio Public Interest Campaign (OPIC).[8] In July 1977 a new plant closing bill drafted by OPIC was introduced into the Ohio Senate by Senator Michael Schwarzwalder (D-Columbus). At a rally to publicize the new Community Readjustment Act, the head of the International Union of Electrical Workers, David Fitzmaurice, charged that companies were "exhibiting the worst form of corporate selfishness" and would have to be made "responsible" for the costs they imposed on communities left behind in the wake of major shutdowns.

The OPIC-Schwarzwalder bill contains six provisions, designed around three basic principles: *advance notification, income maintenance,* and *job replacement* through local redevelopment:

- prior notification of major cutbacks and total shutdowns
- discharge or severance payments for all workers, whether or not they are unionized
- continuation of health insurance coverage for some period following the layoff, paid for by the company
- increased rights of transfer to other plants or stores in the company's system (if any)
- lump sum payment to the local municipality, to help finance economic redevelopment
- preparation by joint company-union-government committees of economic impact statements, to facilitate the redevelopment effort

Although the bill has yet to become law, in spite of active statewide organizing for its passage, the effort in Ohio has become the model for many similar bills that have appeared in other states. By early 1982 eleven states were actively considering various forms of this sort of legislation, while two—Maine and Wisconsin—already had some form of plant-closing laws on the books and several more were gearing up for the introduction of new bills. Behind the effort is a growing number of labor/community organizing committees such as the Coalition to Save Jobs in Massachusetts, the Delaware Valley Coalition for Jobs in Pennsylvania, the Community-Labor Organizing Committee in Rhode

Island, and the Coalition to Stop Plant Closings in Los Angeles. The Washington-based Conference on Alternative State and Local Policies provides technical assistance and informational support for the movement.

The rapid growth of activity at the local level, and the worsening economic situation in the country as a whole, provided the impetus for a new initiative in Washington in 1979. After long consultations with the UAW Research Department, Michigan Congressman Bill Ford reintroduced a drastically redesigned bill into the U. S. House of Representatives. Co-sponsored by Senator Don Riegle (D-Mich.) and fifty-eight others, the National Employment Priorities Act of 1979 began to attract attention through hearings around the country, and, more recently, as a result of a growing and vocal opposition, in the business press. The main provisions of Ford-Riegle cover prenotification in order to buy time for workers and communities to plan for readjustment, severance pay, regulations concerning successorship, transfer rights, the protection of benefits for a period of time following a shutdown or mass layoff, grants and loans to "failing" businesses under certain specified circumstances, economic redevelopment assistance to local governments, and assistance to workers to buy out closing businesses.

So far, liberals have been unable to move the legislation toward passage in the conservative congressional climate of the early 1980s. This is true despite the fact that the need for such legislation has now been heightened by a U. S. Supreme Court decision that can only be considered a setback for the plant-closing movement. In June 1981 in *First National Maintenance Corp.* v. *NLRB,* the court ruled 7–2 that a company may close a plant without bargaining with its union (in this case, District 1199 of the Health and Hospital Workers), provided the shutdown is "partial" (one of several plants or units in a multiunit company, but not the entire firm) and "purely for economic reasons" (as opposed to "anti-union animus"). In so deciding, the justices overturned a lower-court ruling that unions did have a right to be informed in advance, so that they might choose to negotiate a new contract that could conceivably *change* the "economic reasons" for the closure.[9]

Corporate Opposition to Plant-Closing Legislation

Business executives, lobbyists, management consultants, and their elected supporters are taking these legislative initiatives very seriously. A whole wave of books, magazine articles, and public speeches have denounced the efforts of labor and community groups to—as business spokespeople put it—hold industry for "ransom."

Management's standard threat is that it will stop expanding operations in states that pass legislation regulating the mobility of private capital. Moreover, it argues, no new companies are likely to build in such places. A typical statement is that of Bill McCarthy, an official of the corporate lobbying group, Associated Industries of Massachusetts (AIM). At the time of the first plant-closing legislative hearing in the Massachusetts State House, McCarthy warned: "Even serious consideration of this bill would be raising a sign on the borders of this state that investment isn't welcome here. A firm with divisions in other states would have one more incentive to expand elsewhere."[10]

This is hardly a new position for Mr. McCarthy's organization to be taking. As far back as the 1922–23 legislative sessions in Massachusetts, early AIM officials were making the same threats. For example:

> By far the most serious menace which confronts the industries of our section today is that growing out of a public misconception of the proper obligation of business enterprise to society.
>
> Colonel Gow, President of
> AIM, July 1, 1922.

> The community must see to it that legislation shall not unduly hamper business management.
>
> Frank Dresser, AIM
> staffer, December 29,
> 1923.

> It cannot be hoped that, with these great industrial plants once driven out of New England, others would come in to replace them, when competing Sections . . . offer such attractive advantages.
>
> AIM editorial, March 3,
> 1923.

All three quotations come from AIM's official magazine *Industry*. The Dresser statement was part of an article entitled "What Can We Do to Prevent Unwise Social Legislation?" And what was the "unwise social legislation" being debated in the state capitol which prompted these thinly-veiled threats?—minimum wages, workmen's compensation, and child labor laws!

This corporate opposition to plant-closing legislation is closely connected to the ongoing battle over the social wage. Richard McKenzie of the American Enterprise Institute captures this when he writes:

> Restrictions on business mobility will hinder the response of businesses to tax increases imposed by local governments. To the extent that this occurs, relocation restrictions increase the power of governments to raise taxes and reduce the quality of services they provide. Consequently, the enactment of relocation rules is likely to lead to higher taxes and lower quality services in many jurisdictions.[11]

But the simplest, and perhaps the most honest, demurrer of all was sounded by William Carroll, an aide to the governor of Rhode Island. When asked by the press why the governor was opposing that state's new plant-closing bill, Carroll said, "Industry doesn't like government telling them what they can do and what they can't do."[12]

Probably no measure in the proposed legislation is more violently opposed by business than the requirement for advance notification of major cutbacks or total shutdowns. In a 1977 letter to the study group that subsequently drafted the first Massachusetts bill, the Commonwealth's commissioner of Commerce and Development asserted that he had "discussed this with several people" and concluded that it would be "impractical" for a firm to be asked to announce such a decision in advance. Besides, he noted, for most businesses "the decision is often abrupt," so that anything like a six-month to two-year lead time wouldn't even be possible, let alone "practical."

But the case studies in chapter 6 and other research encountered along the way make it clear that a great many shutdowns are either explicitly planned far ahead, or are fairly predictable by the parent corporation's measurable disinvestment in the plant or store. Moreover, as the union team studying in Europe discovered, a number of American companies seem able to live with prior notification clauses in their labor contracts. Certainly most European firms have had to accommodate to the principle of prenotification.

Nevertheless, American corporations are generally unprepared and unwilling to deal with the social costs imposed by their actions. In the words of another management counselor, McNeill Stokes of Atlanta, "I say, if a state or municipality is so messed up that it can't compete —then let it fall."

> Business leaders clearly regard plant closing regulation as a priority threat. . . . The battle over plant closing controls may well set the tone of labor-management conflict in the new decade.[13]

Early Warning Systems

In the short run, the key element in all of the proposed plant-closing bills reviewed here is the requirement that a firm's management provide prenotification of a planned shutdown or major cutback. Without advance notice, a hardship is imposed on workers, as well as an overload on the local employment service office that has the responsibility for helping displaced workers find new jobs. Additionally, orderly planning for possible new uses of the facility being abandoned, or even (if necessary) for rescuing the existing operation through government subsidy or targeted procurement, becomes almost impossible.

Suppose, in contrast, that a shutdown notice has been issued. In order for workers, unions, local governments, and federal planners to assess the probable impact and to intelligently consider alternative responses, several key pieces of information will be needed. These include *quick* information on total payroll and employment at the time of the announcement; a breakdown of employment by age, race, sex, and occupation; total sales and the identification and location of the firm's main customers—including the government; the volume and type of goods and services that the plant or store or office purchases from local sources; the taxes presently paid to local, state, and federal treasuries; and the company's plans—if any—for transferring or otherwise assisting its own employees after the layoff.[14]

The federal government could help planners and researchers to determine which areas of the country show the highest risk of future redundancy through shutdowns by developing statistical reporting programs that flag unemployment explicitly traceable to layoffs resulting from establishment closings. This assistance would be a simple matter of (1) requiring the state employment security offices to keep and publish records on unemployment insurance claimants whose plants or stores had closed, and (2) having the Bureau of Labor Statistics in Washington add a question to the monthly Current Population Survey, asking the unemployed household members regularly interviewed whether their situations resulted from a shutdown.

Even *before* a company made its public announcement of a closing —or in the interim before prenotification legislation can be put in place —it might be possible for planners and labor union researchers to predict the probability of a particular firm in sufficient financial difficulty contemplating capital restructuring or even bankruptcy. Financial experts have already developed statistical models for just this purpose, although they are generally applicable to whole companies rather than to individual plants *per se*. [15]

In the meantime, workers need not wait for a government agency or a business disclosure law to hand them the necessary information. For, in truth, the best "early warning system" is a vigilant work force. Indeed, several unions are already considering ways to train "key reconnaissance personnel" in the plant or office to watch for signs that management is implementing, or at least contemplating, major disinvestment. Workers in the parts department of a plant know when replacement orders are being cut. Machine repair people are the *first* to become aware when management is cutting back on programmed maintenance, because it is their ingenuity that is called upon to keep the old equipment functioning. Key personnel in a firm's real estate department can tell when the company has stopped searching for local space for expansion, or is actually beginning to sell some of its property. Some unions and citizen-labor coalitions are beginning to write "early warning system" manuals for one another's use. This is a development of the greatest importance as workers themselves prepare for playing a key role in the great reindustrialization debate.

Toward a Radical Industrial Policy

The restoration of the social safety net, and its extension through plant-closing legislation, should not be confused with more fundamental social change. At best, the struggle for a more secure social wage can re-animate many people, encourage them to ask difficult questions, and help them to take chances that, in the present political climate, most working for a living dare not risk.

The truly far-reaching *structural* change comes when serious thought is given to economic planning. At this point, for reasons expressed earlier, any sketch of a radical industrial policy can (and should) be only extremely tentative. Even the most tentative discussion, if it is to be anything more than a purely academic exercise, would have to presume that a broad-based political movement will emerge during the 1980s and 1990s in response both to the destabilization of communities by hypermobile capital and to the attempts by the Right to dismantle the social wage in support of the long-term profit requirements of that capital. This book indeed makes that presumption.

If radical reindustrialization rejects private profit as the sole criterion for designing and managing a progressive industrial policy—and that seems to be an absolutely essential first principle—then to what goals *do* we subscribe? First and foremost, there must be *a rising standard of living for working people, more equally shared.* A corollary concern is that there be the *adequate supply of useful goods and services, whether or not they can always be made at a profit.* From the point of view of working people, profit is at best a means to the end of improving the quality and stability of their daily lives. Profit making may or may not be consistent with these concerns in any particular instance and seems fundamentally opposed to them at the level of the system as a whole.

The process of reindustrialization—the organization of the activities to be developed, renewed, rescued, or revived—should aim toward *creating more hospitable, more interesting, less authoritarian, and safer work environments.* If Marx was right in conceiving of work as the most fundamental way in which human beings express their humanity—their creative potential, their unique capacity for integrating emotional, intellectual, and physical forms of expression and action—then the *humanization* of the workplace should be a major objective of any truly democratically planned restructuring of the economy.

To assure that the planning process adheres to these goals, it will be necessary to radically *transform the nature of active popular participation in the day-to-day running of the basic institutions of the economy and the society.* This principle of "economic democracy" must be applied at every level of the system, from the factory (or office) through the neighborhood, the municipality, the statehouse, regional organizations, and ultimately to the national government itself.[16]

With these objectives in mind—economic growth, production for use, a humane work environment, and economic democracy—some general principles for a policy of reindustrialization with a "human face" can be identified. There seem to be four relatively distinct classes of industrial planning problems, each of which will require a different mix of a few basic policies (public subsidy, public ownership, and workers' control). What follows are only the most tentative guidelines for thinking about each category of planning problem.

Developing the "Sunrise" Industries

In any era, there will always be a number of new products (and related services) that private entrepreneurs and corporations very much *do* want to make. From these at least a potential competitive profit can be earned, but their profitability—especially in an increasingly international market place—depends on the producers achieving technical or financial economies of scale (or both). In the 1980s the most frequently mentioned examples are large memory semiconductors, industrial robots, electricity co-generation equipment, and all sorts of biological and biochemical research apparatus.

Given the desirability of mass production of these products, advocates of government support for high-tech industries argue that, unless the government provides financial grants or loans to U. S. firms and relaxes anti-trust restrictions to promote Japanese-like cartelization of these industries, American firms will not be able to compete with the government-subsidized firms of other countries. These advocates propose some form of "public-private partnership" between the companies manufacturing products for which there are potentially profitable growing markets and the government that "targets" financial and regulatory policy to help those companies to grow.[17]

In fact, there is nothing at all new about this sort of relationship. As John Kenneth Galbraith and others have often noted, since World War II much of the production of military equipment like jet planes, high fixed-cost, civilian spin-off products like commercial aircraft, and the research and development of new industrial technologies like computers or numerically-controlled machine tools has taken place in private, "for-profit" companies such as General Dynamics, Lockheed, IBM, and General Electric. But to call these firms "private" is stretching the term a great deal, since all are highly subsidized by the government, either through cost-plus procurement contracts or low-cost—if not completely free—rental of land, buildings, and machinery.

Most other capitalist countries have long since recognized the essentially public nature of this relationship. Thus, in Canada and throughout Western Europe there exists an entire sector consisting of "public enterprises": partly or wholly-owned government corporations that engage in the production of a wide range of basic industrial and consumer commodities. In most cases, there is nothing especially "socialistic" about these public enterprises in their operational objectives, in their day-to-day management, or even in the character of those who run them. Rather, they represent a mature form of what is often called "state capitalism."[18]

In the United States, the currently fashionable concept of the "public-private partnership" surely can be made more substantive—and the public can recoup part of its investment in the (risky) growth potential of new high-tech companies—if the government were to insist upon acquiring at least a minority equity position in any private firm that received more than a specified volume of assistance or qualified for some significant deregulation.

Partial public ownership of subsidized private corporations is a minimum requirement. In and of itself, mixed ownership is unlikely to do more than redistribute part of the profits back to the U. S. Treasury. This is desirable and fair, as far as it goes. But in terms of the planning objectives set out earlier, it does not go far enough. The lesson from a quarter of a century of European experience with even 100 percent government stock ownership is that the change of ownership from private capital to the state will not in itself transform the criteria or general use of resources in society. Control itself has to be transformed. . . . Without a socialization of control, with new forms of industrial and economic democracy, and new negotiations of changed ends for the use of resources, the institutions of state ownership and planning would tend to mean corporatism or state capitalism, rather than a transition to socialist planning and socialized development.[19]

Considerable experimentation should take place with respect to the creation of what Stuart Holland calls "planning agreements" between the public and private "partners," on policies concerning pricing, location (and relocation), sourcing, automation, affirmative action in hiring and promotions, health and safety, environmental protection, and the maintenance of a workplace environment conducive to greater experimentation with new forms of internal economic democracy. Unless they made a legally binding commitment to such experimentation, the managements in the potentially expanding sunrise industries should be made to forfeit the government assistance they say they must have in order to compete in the global marketplace.

Public Goods (and Services)

Mass transit and neighborhood health clinics differ from semiconductor and jet engine plants. By and large, private business cannot make a competitive profit from the former two. Either construction entails assuming very high front-end costs well in advance of any reliable knowledge of whether there will be sufficient demand, or else profitability requires pricing the good or service beyond the ability to pay of many needy users. Other services in the same category are pure public goods in that at least some users can find a way to use the service without paying for it at all, for example, people passing by a city park and enjoying its greenery or benches.[20]

Anybody's inventory of unmet needs in contemporary American society will include a host of public goods. One such inventory was constructed in 1976. At that time, the Institute for Policy Studies in Washington, D. C. assembled a series of papers aimed at identifying priorities for a major full employment program (a "social reconstruction") based on a radical overhauling of the federal budget. In that comprehensive study, four sectors were identified as especially in need of massive new investment: housing, energy, health care, and both freight and passenger transportation.[21]

Private sector involvement in the production of building materials, solar collectors, drugs, medical equipment, and motors for rail vehicles is likely in any such program. But the design, management, financing, monitoring, and actual service delivery will have to be lodged in the public sector to assure adequate supplies in the right places and an equitable distribution of the services. But "in the public sector" does not have to mean solely in or through giant, Washington-based government bureaucracies. A key element of the Institute for Policy Studies full-employment budget (a plan, by the way, that is as remarkably fresh and relevant today as when it was written, during the 1976 presidential campaign) is the insistence of its authors on lively experimentation with different organizational forms for both the production of the hardware and the delivery of the actual housing, energy, health, and transportation services.

For example, "public" enterprises might be locally, even municipally, owned. Producers' cooperatives would be encouraged, along with neighborhood-based community development corporations. As a way of eroding the often authoritarian doctor-patient relationship that permeates American medicine, health clinics could be "owned" and— as Holland says, even more importantly—*controlled* by the residents who utilize them. This is a concept that U. S. Congressman Ronald Dellums (D-Cal.) has championed for many years.

Especially in the production of expensive capital equipment, where private firms are unable or unwilling to provide a reliable flow of high-quality products at affordable prices, selective nationalization would be the appropriate policy. For example, in 1976 former Senator Adlai Stevenson III proposed the creation of a government oil corporation, whose chances to compete successfully against huge, established, private multinationals like Exxon, Mobil, and Shell might be helped by granting it a monopoly over U. S.-owned offshore oil. This would be an alternative to the current policy of leasing that oil to the big private companies. Such a public oil corporation could (Stevenson hoped) at the very least be held accountable by Congress for publicly reporting its true operating costs, thereby keeping the private companies honest about the true cost of drilling, refining, and shipping the product.

In another sector, Senator Edward M. Kennedy (D-Mass.) has proposed legislation that would divest General Motors of its mass transit-producing facilities, on the grounds that it has always subordinated these activities to its priority of ensuring a market for its private automobiles.[22] Kennedy would establish a national public trust that would own and operate the rail locomotive and other production facilities for a period of at least ten years. The long-term goal would be to gradually turn over ownership to the employees in the factories actually manufacturing the equipment, or to the communities where the plants were located.[23]

Policies for the "Sunset" Industries

A third class of industrial policies is being debated these days. It concerns those industries, products, activities, and companies that *used* to be profitable but that the private sector is now either rationalizing or abandoning altogether because they are no longer profitable *enough*. These are the so-called sunset industries.

Before forming a judgment on the kinds of policies most appropriate for dealing with these industries, a number of questions must be answered: How did they *become* unprofitable? Has the product become obsolete—the proverbial "buggy whip"? Have foreign competitors underpriced U. S. firms so as to clearly drive them out of the market? Or did myopic U. S. corporate planning, of the sort studied in chapter 6, run the industry into the ground, with those myopic planners now crying "abandon ship?"

Experience (and the simple logic of corporate self-interest) suggests that the business community cannot be trusted to answer these questions truthfully—if indeed their representatives are willing to say anything to their workers or to the public at all. Therefore, what is needed is a systematic, detailed monitoring of corporate investment and disinvestment decisions by government agencies, unions, and community organizations. And what might such "public" research indicate?

It will undoubtedly often be the case that the product being abandoned truly *is* unneeded, or technologically obsolete, based on criteria worked out by community (and union) researchers, together with advisory councils of rank-and-file workers and consumers. If so, it makes good sense to direct investment away from further production of such buggy whips. However, that is hardly the end of the story. Indeed, this is precisely where democratic social planning of investment departs from private practice, for the latter by and large *does* end with management's decision to abandon ship.

First, planning is necessary so that the cost of the economic dislocation is not suddenly and exclusively borne by the work force in that plant, company, or industry, or by the communities where the plants are located. This is where the political work of the plant-closing movement that has sprung up in different sections of the country fits into the development of industrial policy *per se.*

Second, the democratic decision to abandon a particular product does not necessarily mean abandoning the plant or equipment in place. It may be possible to convert the older facilities to new uses. For many years, the peace movement has advocated the conversion of defense plants to the production of useful civilian goods and services. The idea of recycling older plants in general makes good sense. Obviously, not all capital goods are sufficiently flexible to allow such conversion. But whether and to what extent conversion *is* a possibility can best be determined in any particular case by policies that enable the people who know the plant best—the workers and the industrial engineers designated by them—to undertake systematic conversion studies.[24]

One of the most dramatic examples of how creative such a worker-initiated conversion plan can be is the attempt by the shop stewards in a London-based British firm, Lucas Aerospace, to identify an alternative product mix for the company. Lucas's sagging military sales in the late 1970s had led management to plan the closing of several plants. Machinists, technicians, and designers from the firm's seventeen plants throughout England proposed instead that management shift production (in the same plants) into about 150 new product lines, ranging from a new type of kidney dialysis machine to a revolutionary road-rail vehicle for use in transportation-deficient Third World countries.[25] The "Lucas Corporate Plan," which also proposed new, more democratic forms of task organization on the shop floor, was subsequently rejected by the company's management.

The idea has caught on, however, within the Scandinavian shop stewards' movement and, more recently, within the International Association of Machinists (IAM) in the United States. The IAM has created a training program to bring rank-and-file machinists from several different sites together with academics and engineers in order to learn how to formulate plans for converting military and obsolete non-military facilities to productive civilian uses. IAM President William Winpisinger has said of this project:

> The Lucas workers have shown us that defense conversion and [democratic product] planning for full employment are not impractical or Utopian and that people working together creatively can develop new solutions to problems which many of us have been led to accept as insolvable or inevitable.[26]

This is the first time since 1945 that any major American trade-union leader has openly called for planned conversion of private industrial capacity according to specifications initiated by the workers. Back then, faced with either mass shutdowns of defense plants by the government or selling these facilities to the largest corporations at a discount, UAW president Walter Reuther called for the creation of major public enterprises to utilize World War II factories to produce inexpensive housing and railroad equipment. Government-owned or leased plants had capabilities in engine production and in the making or processing of magnesium, aluminum, electrical equipment, and ball bearings. Neither plan was ever put into practice, but the mere mention of it sent shivers through the business community. *Business Week* declared it to have "socialistic overtones." The editors wondered why anyone would seriously propose "that resumption of civilian goods output should be conditioned by social needs rather than free competition."[27]

The Lucas plan failed primarily because the British government was unwilling to provide either financing or procurement contracts for the new products, useful as they appeared to be to every government analyst who studied the plan. The lesson for the United States is clear. Public financial investment in the conversion process, especially via targeted government procurement, must be part of any industrial policy toward the democratically planned restructuring of sunset industries.

In many cases, a supposed sunset industry is not a sunset industry at all. Investigation of a given industrial situation will often reveal that the private corporation abandoning a particular site is not, after all, quitting the industry, but rather choosing to produce essentially the same product at another location. In Staughton Lynd's terms, management is opting for a "greenfield" rather than a "brownfield" investment strategy.

From the perspective of democratic industrial policy, the question is: Why? Are there valid technical or perhaps resource-availability reasons why continued production at the old site really is unfeasible? Or is management simply seeking to shed its older, more experienced, higher-paid, often unionized work force? This possibility must at least be considered in light of the finding that virtually all academic researchers—and even spokespersons for the business community—agree that when companies *do* relocate plants, "nine times out of ten" it is to reduce labor costs or to increase workplace discipline.

It is to slow down these unwarranted and socially wasteful greenfield investment shifts by managers that the plant closing legislation is particularly addressed. And it may well be that even more severe locational restrictions on private disinvestment are called for, when it can be established that the corporation is abandoning the site but not getting out of the industry.

As an alternative to using public policy to force the company to stay in a viable business at the old site, it might be more efficient (as well as politically more attractive) to help the workers take over and run the business themselves. Operationally, this means requiring companies to offer the older plant for sale and providing financial and technical assistance to workers, their unions, and perhaps the municipal government. As before, federal government contracts might be helpful in providing a transitional market for the (now) worker- or community-owned venture.

Chapter 6 explained the process by which, during the 1970s, capital began the restructuring of the domestic steel industry. The plight of one city—Youngstown, Ohio—became a symbol of the crisis for workers. A major shutdown, of the Campbell Works of the Youngstown Sheet and Tube Company, was the direct result of the conglomeration process. The response of the steelworkers, their families, advisors, and local elected officials was to organize in Ohio's Mahoning Valley a movement whose demands included several concrete proposals for worker ownership of the mill. Although the plans were ultimately blocked by ambivalent bureaucrats in the federal government, without whose assistance the scheme for worker control of steel making in Youngstown could not succeed, the story is instructive.

When the New Orleans-based conglomerate, the Lykes Corporation, first announced the Campbell shutdown in September 1977, instead of railing against Lykes, foreign imports, or government regulations, a group of local clergymen and trade unionists formed a new political organization, the Ecumenical Coalition to Save Mahoning Valley. From the beginning, their objective was a community takeover of the plant. After pledging their own savings to purchase stock in such an enterprise, they were able to convince the U. S. Department of Housing and Urban Development to grant them $300,000 to finance a detailed technical feasibility study. The contract was given to the National Center for Economic Alternatives (NCEA), whose interim findings were becoming clear by late spring 1978 (the final report itself was not released until September). The NCEA researchers, led by Gar Alperovitz and Jeff Faux, concluded that a profitable community takeover could work if the federal government would provide $15 million in front-end grants, and $394 million in federally guaranteed loans and procurement guarantees, and if the new enterprise could gain access to Sheet and Tube's old customer list.

Carter Administration officials, particularly White House advisor Jack Watson, had initially pledged support "in principle." But as the proposal became more concrete, the administration backed off. Then in June, against the advice of his own anti-trust division, Attorney General Griffin Bell approved a merger between Lykes and LTV, whose steel-making subsidiary, Jones and Laughlin, thereby acquired Sheet and Tube's customer list. The merger meant that Lykes would still indirectly be in the steel business and so be unwilling to sell the Campbell works to the Coalition. In any case, later that summer, the U. S. Economic Development Administration and the White House rejected the grant and loan proposals, thus killing the plan for good.[28] Without *some* short-term aid, embryonic worker- or community-owned enterprises are almost impossible to get off the ground, no matter how many jobs they might save.

The problem is at least partly a legal one, too. For in the absence of federal legislation, even appeals to the courts for assistance have no standing. When workers at U. S. Steel in Ohio went to court to try to get their plants reopened in early 1980, the trial judge, Thomas

Lambros, found the workers' case compelling but ruled that he could provide no remedy until plant-closing legislation was passed.

> This Court has spent many hours searching for a way to cut to the heart of the economic reality, that obsolescence and market forces demand the closing of the Mahoning Valley plant, and yet the lives of 3500 workers and their families and the supporting Youngstown community cannot be dismissed as inconsequential. United States Steel should not be permitted to leave the Youngstown area devastated after drawing from the life blood of the community for so many years.
>
> Unfortunately, the mechanism to reach this ideal settlement, to *recognize this new property right,* is not now in existence in the code of laws of our nation. [Italics added][29]

So far, two categories of "sunset" industries have been considered: those where the product truly is obsolete or unneeded, and those where the company is abandoning a particular site—but not the product *per se*—in favor of another. But suppose the firm *is* bailing out of a useful product line altogether, either because the managers cannot make a dollar at all or else because they (or the parent conglomerate) think they can make *more* profit in some other activity?

During the 1970s, groups of workers and local managers in a number of communities across the country decided to buy out and subsequently rehabilitate both "failing" businesses and companies originally acquired by conglomerates, milked of their profits, and then mismanaged into the ground. Saratoga Knitting Mills, Vermont Asbestos Group, Jamestown Metal Products, and South Bend Lathe are the names of only a few companies where this has occurred.

While subject to a number of serious objections, worker buy-outs are surely one reasonable response to conglomerate divestiture. But in spite of all of the heroic talk about "self-help" and "local effort," the success of all but the smallest of these ventures is going to depend on the availability of public financial, marketing, and management assistance. Instead of having to jury-rig such assistance on a case-by-case basis, typically with long lags that themselves work against the buy-out, what is clearly needed is to make such assistance a structured, orderly, regular part of any industrial policy toward sunset industries.

Worker-run takeovers are not the only solution to redeveloping those sunset industries producing still-useful products. Planning agreements with private companies, and, in a few cases, outright public ownership have a role to play. But the experience of the last dozen years is pointing . strongly toward the conclusion that unless workers, community development corporations, and municipalities are supported in their eager attempts to revive these basic industrial activities, the deindustrialization of America is going to continue unabated.

Corporate Bail-Outs

Finally, there is a fourth class of targets for a systematic industrial policy, one that has become as controversial in its own way as those "socialistic" proposals by Reuther and Winpisinger for substituting social utility for "free competition" as the criterion for deciding what to produce. This is the situation where a major private corporation clearly *does* want to remain in a particular activity, has somehow become "uncompetitive" vis-à-vis other (especially foreign) firms in the industry, and is demanding that the government (or, more and more frequently, its own workers) bail it out by selective deregulation, low interest loans, or wage and benefit "givebacks" or "takebacks." Or perhaps the public may feel that, quite apart from the jobs involved, the company is part of a sector of strategic importance in enabling the country to maintain other vital activities. For example, the preservation of a healthy domestic metalworking sector, with its ability to train skilled machinists and technicians and having products crucial to the performance of many other industries, is legitimately an object of social concern that transcends private pecuniary profitability.

Since none of the subsidies such companies request is likely to do anything to directly improve productivity or sales in the short term, many experts are extremely skeptical that such bail-outs can really restore a failing company's international competitiveness. In the most extreme case, these policies represent a straightforward redistribution of income from labor to capital.[30] On the other hand, companies—notably those in the auto, aircraft, and steel industries—claim that these cost reductions in wages, interest payments, contributions to pension funds, and outlays for meeting environmental or health and safety regulations will enable them to finance investments in new technology such as robotics and in replacing, if not upgrading, their older facilities.

Here again, democratic social policy meets the greenfield-brownfield trade-off. So far, the managers of companies seeking bail-outs have generally been unwilling to guarantee that any long-term restructuring scheme they might undertake will be designed to replace even a fraction of the jobs lost at the old sites. Unions are asking for such a provision in their "giveback" bargaining talks, but only a few companies are willing to consider them. And with their greatly enhanced mobility, there is really nothing in the present system to pressure them to do so.

The short-term social objective of preserving jobs is valid and important. Chapters 3 and 4 weighed the personal and community costs associated with economic dislocation and found them to be unacceptably high for a society concerned about overall productivity and equity. The long-term goal of restructuring basic industry along democratically planned lines is perhaps even more pressing. Thus, like it or not, progressives are going to have to take the bail-out strategy seriously.

But that does not mean that some basic principles of fairness and social efficiency cannot be applied to this category of industrial policy, as well. By now, these principles have been mentioned several times. They include, at a minimum:

- spreading the burden over *all* the citizens of the society, rather than loading it all on the workers in the particular company or industry requiring the bail-out
- public disclosure of company data to enable democratically constituted bodies to decide for themselves whether and to what extent assistance is really needed
- research by and consultation with workers in the affected plants and advisors of their own choosing
- planning agreements with companies receiving bail-outs, specifying a *quid pro quo* with respect to increased democratic management of production, restrictions on the subcontracting of components or supplies to non-union or foreign shops, the phasing in (and control over the use) of new technology, new plant location, and product pricing
- a government equity position in the subsidized corporation to ensure that the public obtains some financial return on its investment in the business

The general principle that unifies these ideas has been expressed succinctly by Ohio labor lawyer Staughton Lynd, in a number of (unpublished) speeches. Labor, says Lynd, should make no concessions unless the company's concessions are at least as tangible and enforceable at law.

Even with all of these safeguards, the chances for what journalist Andrew Kopkind has called "lemon socialism" are very great. In an era of continuing economic crisis, private corporations whose managers have gotten themselves into financial hot water will be increasingly tempted to cry for bail-outs as a short-term solution for keeping their companies (not to mention their own careers) afloat. The erection of new entitlement programs for corporate welfare is *not* the optimal solution to the deindustrialization of America. Nevertheless, the architects of a new industrial policy are going to have to confront this issue in the years ahead.

Worker Ownership

At several points in this chapter, it has been proposed that worker or community ownership has a role to play in any policy dealing with plant closings in particular and with industrial restructuring generally. Let us now examine this option a bit more closely.

Worker and, to a lesser extent, municipal ownership of industry are in fact part of a long-standing, if not much discussed, American tradition.[31] Organized labor's involvement in the direct ownership of enterprises can be traced as far back as the 1880s. It was then that the Knights of Labor created 135 cooperatives in the mining, shoe, and other industries, complete with a back-up General Cooperative Board to perform the tasks of "educating members to the dangers and pitfalls involved, of issuing instructions concerning management and credit, and of recommending financial aid" to the small-town mechanics, shopkeepers, and farmers who ran the cooperatives.[32]

Throughout the 1920s and 1930s, workers focused their energies on the struggles to win union recognition and workplace benefits. As seen in chapter 5, the fruits of these earlier struggles had become fairly well institutionalized by the 1950s, after which workers (or at least the leaders of their unions) traded off further demands on management prerogatives for the promise—made by capital, but realized through the new Welfare State—of a continually increasing private and social wage.

During the 1970s with the onset of the economic crisis, the movement for worker ownership revived. In the five years between 1974 and 1979, at least seventy substantial private businesses in the United States were bought either by their employees or by various community organizations. About 70 percent of these purchases came in the wake of closings related to corporate or conglomerate divestiture. Overall, by 1979, more than 1,000 employee stock-ownership plans were in operation in different companies, with workers owning the majority interest in probably 100 of these.[33]

A small number of the employee-owned businesses in America are full-fledged producers' cooperatives. As in the case of a network of eighteen plywood companies in the Pacific Northwest, some of which were started up as far back as the Depression, workers really do control as well as own these enterprises. This is due basically to the enforcement of the cooperative principle that each active worker may own— and vote—only one share of stock.[34] Workers either hire outside boards of directors or elect their own members to these positions. All management personnel are hired by, and are directly responsible to, these boards.

Currently, both here and in Great Britain, some workers are exploring the desirability of creating integrated complexes of industrial co-ops, modeled after the remarkably successful Mondragon system located in the Basque region of Spain. Mondragon consists of eighty-two manufacturing and service establishments, owned and run by their workers which in turn cooperatively own their own development bank, credit union, schools, research and development installation, leisure clubs, worker housing, and even an agricultural extension service.[35]

In this country, however, the vast majority of worker-owned enterprises are run not on cooperative principles such as minimizing the wage differential between managers and the lowest-paid workers, or breaking the link between the ownership and control of capital. Rather, the most common form of worker ownership of industry in the United States is the Employee Stock Ownership Plan (ESOP), whereby a company deposits part of its profits in an employee trust managed by some reputable fiduciary.[36] Gradually, these profits are "vested" in the workers who purchase shares of the trust with their holdings in proportion to their wages. The workers finance their share purchases either out of current wages or—in a disturbingly large number of cases, as with the employee rescue of the Republic Hose Manufacturing Corporation in Youngstown, Ohio, from a shutdown engineered by the parent conglomerate, Libby-Owens-Ford—by agreeing to the dismantling of the company-paid, union pension fund.

Because the vesting process takes time, employee "ownership" in most of these enterprises is at best partial. One study estimates that hourly workers own a majority of the stock in less than one tenth of all ESOP companies and that perhaps three fourths of such "worker buy-outs" will *never* transfer majority ownership to the employees. In any case, in almost every instance, whatever the vesting arrangements may be, *control* over day-to-day decisions in these companies has so far tended to remain in the hands of the firm's original managers.

Nevertheless, a growing number of workers have expressed an interest in becoming "mini-capitalists" as a way of saving their plants from shutdown. And a whole infrastructure of technical support groups has emerged to assist them, including Action Resources West in Salt Lake City, the Program on New Systems of Work and Participation at Cornell University, and the Washington-based National Center for Employee Ownership. The Industrial Cooperative Association in Somerville, Massachusetts explicitly promotes and works closely with producers' cooperatives.

Federal legislation to provide both technical and financial assistance to workers and communities seeking to purchase existing plants and stores through ESOPs has been introduced repeatedly into both the House and the Senate. In 1980 Congress passed, and President Carter signed, a bill authorizing the Small Business Administration to make all of its technical and loan guarantee services available to employee organizations seeking to purchase businesses that would otherwise close or relocate. Still on the drawing board in the House is a much more far-reaching bill by Congressman John Conyers (D-Mich.) that would help community groups "buy and operate local concerns that are relocating, shutting down, or being purchased by foreign interests, where major unemployment and local economic dislocation would result."

Producers' cooperatives would be explicitly eligible for support under the Conyers bill.

Productivity and employee job satisfaction have consistently been found to be higher in businesses bought by their workers. And in a sample of establishments drawn and analyzed by the Survey Research Center of the University of Michigan, the profitability of such businesses was found to be actually greater when the share of the total equity owned by the employees was larger.[37] These findings with respect to profitability should perhaps be deflated somewhat, to the extent that the post-ESOP profit figures include those diverted pension fund dollars that are no longer to be counted as a cost item. Nevertheless, there seems to be little question that, for at least some period following the buy-out, worker ownership *does* generate increased motivation, reduced absenteeism and vandalism, and a generally positive environment.

Still there are numerous pitfalls associated with worker buy-outs. For one—as the workers who purchased the GAF Corporation's asbestos-mining operation in Vermont learned at their great expense—when individuals own unequal amounts of stock, market forces can make it virtually impossible for those with large holdings to resist selling out to entrepreneurs who show up with large cash offers after the workers have turned a declining operation around.[38] For another, established corporate interests may try to undermine any worker-owned ventures that *are* successful. This lesson was learned a century ago by the Knights of Labor:

> In part the very nature of such enterprises worked against [the Knights]. The successful ventures became joint stock corporations; the wage-earning shareholders became owners and managers hiring labor like any other industrial unit. In part the cooperatives were destroyed by . . . squabbles among shareholders [but] just as important was the attitude of competitors. Railroads delayed the building of tracks, refused to furnish cars, or refused to haul them. Manufacturers of machinery and producers of raw materials, pressed by private business, refused to sell their products to the cooperative workshops and paralyzed operations. By 1888 none of the order's cooperatives were in existence.[39]

In all too many recent worker buy-outs, managers have retained (or been granted) far too much power—freezing out the shopfloor worker-owners, taking high salaries for themselves, devising ways to intimidate or eliminate opposition from the board of directors, and even (in the case of the president of South Bend Lathe) chairing business committees that advocate right-to-work legislation and support union decertification drives![40]

Finally, many unions are discovering that the terms to which they agreed in financing the buy-out—especially the defunding of their pension plans (or freezing of further company contributions), the elimination of cost-of-living allowances, and the wage and vacation givebacks—have greatly increased their members' personal insecurity. This is an especially serious concern for older workers.

For all of these reasons, the unions—and especially their national executive leadership—have been circumspect, if not downright hostile, to worker buy-outs of any kind. Their greatest expressed concern has been over the dismantling of often hard-won pension provisions as the basic source of capital for financing the buy-out. Some union officials have also warned that, since very few of these companies actually float their stock on the market, its value, which would ultimately determine the retirement benefits of a fully-vested employee at the time that she or he retires, is completely arbitrary and subject to manipulation by the managers.[41] Finally, many union officials fear that the traditional adversarial relationship between labor and management is thrown into limbo when workers also own the plant. How, they ask, can trade unionists collectively bargain with themselves?

There is another, more self-serving, aspect to that criticism. Some have suggested that union officials fear that in an environment of increased workplace democracy there will be an increase in the number of rank-and-file local challenges to the authority of union executive councils. In other words, decentralized control threatens union bureaucrats as much as it does conservative ideologues, though for very different reasons.[42]

It is impossible to give definitive answers to all of the totally legitimate questions that even the most sympathetic critics have raised about the contradictory nature of worker buy-outs in a time of general economic crisis. As with other essentially populist programs to decentralize the production and distribution of goods and services—such as the low-income urban and rural community development corporations (CDCs) that have come to play a small but important role in the economic lives of selected communities across the country—the possibilities are exciting, but the room for everything from honest failure to bold-faced rip-off is very great.

But since the directors of neighborhood CDCs and the delegated officials running worker-owned businesses hardly have a monopoly on either myopia, incompetence, or a taste for graft among their managerial brethren, it would be elitist to exclude local ownership from the design of a new, more democratic reindustrialization strategy for the United States. We will simply have to find better ways to build both the interests of workers and the mechanisms for their direct and *continual* control over the management process into our future experiments with worker and community ownership.

Where Do We Go From Here?

We have tried to outline a set of basic principles or guidelines for thinking about a program of democratic socialist reindustrialization. Its key elements are: an alternative set of planning objectives to the narrow pursuit of private profit; recognition of the need for particular strategies to deal with the development or restructuring of sunrise industries, sunset industries, public goods, and corporate bail-outs; a new, more democratic, participatory approach to the management of productive enterprise; and a belief in the principle that any private industry seeking assistance from the public must stand ready to negotiate a *quid pro quo* that would lead to sharing the benefits, along with the costs, from the revitalization of a company. In the context of a renewed commitment to using national policy to enhance the social and personal security of working people and their families, through a strengthening of the social wage and its extension into the realm of public regulation of capital mobility, such a program offers some chance for the re-creation of the conditions for productive economic growth on terms consistent with the needs and aspirations of the great majority of ordinary people.

This discussion obviously has left *a lot* of very big questions unanswered. What about inflation? How will such a radical program be financed? What is to prevent private industry from going on a truly massive strike—withholding its capital—in an attempt to blackmail popular forces into backing down? How are these grandiose, and still somewhat vague, ideas to be concretized and operationalized? And where do we start?

To all but the last question, there *are* no answers at this point—and that is as it should be. Detailed paper plans for economic revitalization are becoming a dime a dozen. Any concrete work plan is going to emerge out of the ideas and experience of working people themselves. As labor reporter Bob Howard writes: "Labor's alternative won't suddenly appear ready-made, the product of union research departments, meetings of the AFL-CIO executive council, or, least of all, labor's new political consultants in Washington. It will be the legacy of a multitude of confrontations between unionists across the country and the concrete problems of their working life. . . . "[43]

Where to *start* is easier: in the unions, in non-unionized workplaces, and in the labor-community-church coalitions that have sprung up in areas such as Ohio, California, Rhode Island, Pennsylvania, and Connecticut. People need to systematically monitor their companies' investment and disinvestment activities, beginning with the development of shopfloor early warning systems. Local, and especially national, popular information campaigns need to demand a redefinition of previously sacrosanct "management prerogatives" to allow explicit debate over subcontracting, the size of a company's overhead staff relative to the number of production (hourly) workers, plant location, diversification versus reinvestment in existing facilities, and even the pricing of the commodities being produced. And finally, the unions, labor organizers in general, and researchers within (or affiliated with) the unions have to follow capital and "go multinational" themselves, organizing across national borders and pursuing cooperative, collaborative research projects on an explicitly international basis.

Outside the labor movement itself, the public at large needs to become actively engaged in the great reindustrialization debate. At this point, all opinions are needed. New ideas should be encouraged, and an opportunity for them to be heard should be assured. Unions, community organizations, schools, the media, legislative hearings, international conferences—all are valid settings for the kind of continual public forum we envision. It does not cost anything to read, to meet together, and to talk.

If we are to turn around the deindustrialization of America, and the continued destabilization of all our community institutions in the wake of the increasingly unrestricted mobility of private capital, *organizing* is where we have to go from here. The steps after that will reveal themselves in good time.

Appendices

TABLE A.1

Jobs Created and Destroyed by Openings, Closings, Relocations, Expansions, and Contractions of Private Business Establishments in the United States, by State and Region: 1969–76

State Region	Number of Jobs in 1969[a] (1)	Jobs Created by Openings and Inmigrations (2)	Jobs Destroyed by Closings and Outmigrations (3)	Change (Jobs Created Minus Jobs Destroyed[d]) (4) = (2) − (3)	Ratio of Jobs Destroyed to Jobs Created (5) = (3) ÷ (2)
		Employment Change Associated With Establishment Openings, Closings, and Relocations: 1969–76[b]			
Connecticut	1043200	298836	335770	−36934	1.12
Maine	265700	98942	115129	−16187	1.16
Massachusetts	1958000	641331	730593	−89262	1.14
New Hampshire	223700	80375	91868	−11493	1.14
Rhode Island	293600	93211	116500	−23289	1.25
Vermont	121100	38506	47363	−8857	1.23
New England	3905300	1251201	1437223	−186022	1.15
New Jersey	2147800	846274	894395	−48121	1.06
New York	6006000	1689034	2338944	−649910	1.38
Pennsylvania	3765500	1153874	1210960	−57086	1.05
Mid Atlantic	11919300	3689182	4444299	−755117	1.20
Northeast	15824600	4940383	5881522	−941139	1.19
Delaware	180000	55725	61043	−5318	1.09
District of Columbia	320600	114034	167425	−53391	1.47
Florida	1692000	1357937	962199	395738	0.71
Georgia	1245600	1067721	579345	488376	0.54
Maryland	1032900	489521	367294	122227	0.75
North Carolina	1492700	556818	549958	6860	0.99
South Carolina	679000	286316	256620	29696	0.90
Virginia	1144000	552302	441417	110885	0.80
West Virginia	417300	170805	162580	8225	0.95
South Atlantic	8204100	4651179	3547881	1103298	0.76
Alabama	795500	417662	362373	55289	0.87
Kentucky	729100	358573	244876	113697	0.68
Mississippi	445000	264081	206676	57405	0.78
Tennessee	1095600	477916	397093	80823	0.83
East South Central	3065200	1518232	1211018	307214	0.80
Arkansas	432900	212482	173977	38505	0.82
Louisiana	823800	461612	357225	104387	0.77
Oklahoma	572800	287415	241106	46309	0.84
Texas	2945700	1803259	1293101	510158	0.72
West South Central	4775200	2764768	2065409	699359	0.75

TABLE A.1

	Employment Change Associated With Establishment Expansions and Contractions: 1969–76c				Overall Net Employment Change 1969–76	Dunn and Bradstreet Counts as a proportion of U. S. Department of Labor Estimate of Total Private Employmenta		
Jobs Created Through Expansion of Existing Establishments (6)	Jobs Destroyed Through Contractions of Existing Establishments (7)	Change (Jobs Created Minus Jobs Destroyed)d (8) = (6) − (7)	Ratio of Jobs Destroyed to Jobs Created (9) = (7) ÷ (6)	Ratio of Jobs Destroyed to Jobs Created (10) = $\frac{(3) + (7)}{(2) + (6)}$		1969	1972	1974
280308	260801	19507	0.93	1.03		.671	.712	.758
95738	64665	31073	0.68	0.92		.658	.770	.829
546599	468569	78030	0.86	1.01		.632	.685	.820
78060	60860	17200	0.78	0.96		.703	.722	.809
91127	69841	21286	0.77	1.01		.716	.744	.823
39176	27349	11827	0.70	0.96		.614	.656	.731
1131008	952085	178923	0.84	1.00		—	—	—
599367	537143	62224	0.90	0.99		.677	.683	.787
1586264	1297579	288685	0.82	1.11		.557	.611	.775
1030850	802148	228702	0.78	0.92		.648	.700	.801
3216481	2636870	579611	0.82	1.02		—	—	—
4347489	3588955	758534	0.83	1.02		—	—	—
38804	35009	3795	0.90	1.02		.610	.581	.797
90288	75233	15,055	0.83	1.19		.460	.599	.745
829159	523651	305508	0.63	0.68		.502	.578	.687
426802	292368	134434	0.69	0.58		.624	.698	.846
296258	235148	61110	0.79	0.77		.550	.669	.749
490158	314230	175928	0.64	0.83		.617	.669	.745
222105	156981	65124	0.71	0.81		.712	.754	.852
398269	313203	85056	0.79	0.79		.624	.669	.726
121131	68418	52713	0.56	0.79		.598	.646	.776
2912974	2014241	898723	0.69	0.74		—	—	—
275801	138897	136904	0.50	0.72		.601	.691	.789
258522	150795	107727	0.58	0.64		.632	.671	.718
174859	81790	93069	0.47	0.66		.634	.726	.794
380721	260380	120341	0.68	0.77		.697	.726	.810
1089903	631862	458041	0.58	0.71		—	—	—
169579	93103	76476	0.55	0.70		.666	.727	.798
304373	181866	122507	0.60	0.70		.593	.674	.694
243336	125715	117621	0.52	0.69		.644	.752	.835
1244385	756464	487921	0.61	0.67		.536	.677	.742
1961673	1157148	804525	0.59	0.68		—	—	—
5964550	3803251	2161299	0.64	0.71		—	—	—

TABLE A.1 (continued)

Jobs Created and Destroyed by Openings, Closings, Relocations, Expansions, and Contractions of Private Business Establishments in the United States, by State and Region: 1969–76

State	Region	Number of Jobs in 1969[a] (1)	Employment Change Associated With Establishment Openings, Closings, and Relocations: 1969–76[b]			
			Jobs Created by Openings and Inmigrations (2)	Jobs Destroyed by Closings and Outmigrations (3)	Change (Jobs Created Minus Jobs Destroyed[d]) (4) = (2) − (3)	Ratio of Jobs Destroyed to Jobs Created (5) = (3) ÷ (2)
South		16044500	8934179	6824308	2109871	0.75
Illinois		3760500	1587158	1244000	343114	0.78
Indiana		1599400	597812	498285	99527	0.83
Michigan		2591400	928181	815376	112808	0.88
Ohio		3342500	1129966	1040229	89737	0.92
Wisconsin		1269800	427464	364703	62761	0.85
	East North Central	12563600	4670581	3962593	707947	0.85
Iowa		701700	320891	251933	68958	0.79
Kansas		536800	243405	191315	52090	0.79
Minnesota		1075700	412991	406867	6124	0.99
Missouri		1139600	504157	484547	19610	0.96
Nebraska		373500	105626	78102	27524	0.72
North Dakota		109400	63248	45328	17920	0.72
South Dakota		119900	60231	49541	10690	0.82
	West North Central	4313000	1710549	1507633	202916	0.88
Midwest		16876600	6381130	5470226	910863	0.86
Arizona		403800	238458	211906	26552	0.89
Colorado		553800	396377	287745	108632	0.73
Idaho		154600	77092	82616	−5524	1.07
Montana		143400	79273	62256	17017	0.79
Nevada		157700	112387	91664	20723	0.82
New Mexico		201200	143873	86269	57604	0.60
Utah		248600	111481	117401	−590	1.05
Wyoming		78800	67113	38051	29062	0.57
	Mountain	1941900	1226054	977908	248146	0.80
Alaska		53500	48005	30690	17315	0.64
California		5539800	3004818	2493596	511222	0.83
Hawaii		204800	107048	99163	7885	0.93
Oregon		567700	237220	220387	16833	0.93
Washington		882700	402498	304489	98009	0.76
	Pacific	7248500	3799589	3148325	651264	0.82

TABLE A.1 (*continued*)

	Employment Change Associated With Establishment Expansions and Contractions: 1969–76c				Overall Net Employment Change: 1969–76	Dunn and Bradstreet Counts as a proportion of U. S. Department of Labor Estimate of Total Private Employmenta		
Jobs Created Through Expansion of Existing Establishments (6)	Jobs Destroyed Through Contractions of Existing Establishments (7)	Change (Jobs Created Minus Jobs Destroyed)d (8) = (6) − (7)	Ratio of Jobs Destroyed to Jobs Created (9) = (7) ÷ (6)	Ratio of Jobs Destroyed to Jobs Created (10) = $\frac{(3) + (7)}{(2) + (6)}$	1969	1972	1974	
5964550	3803251	2161299	0.64	0.71	—	—	—
1013760	753557	260203	0.74	0.77	.591	.686	.819
481841	367409	114432	0.76	0.80	.636	.694	.771
765486	629756	135730	0.82	0.85	.597	.704	.766
897617	629313	268304	0.70	0.82	.621	.700	.760
423092	271663	151429	0.64	0.75	.631	.686	.738
3581796	2651698	930098	0.74	0.80	—	—	—
266302	142533	123769	0.54	0.67	.673	.669	.737
238651	132801	105850	0.56	0.67	.551	.643	.732
381886	245400	136486	0.64	0.82	.534	.614	.656
409607	323538	86069	0.79	0.88	.559	.641	.705
141603	75960	65643	0.54	0.62	.592	.735	.801
54177	26146	28031	0.48	0.61	.483	.550	.590
48924	25082	23842	0.51	0.68	.547	.607	.669
1541150	971460	569690	0.63	0.76			
5122946	3623158	1499788	0.71	0.79	—	—	—
206153	106831	99322	0.52	0.72	.575	.569	.621
285702	164082	121620	0.57	0.71	.514	.615	.676
74611	34214	40397	0.46	0.77	.503	.545	.571
58098	35266	22832	0.61	0.71	.522	.583	.633
69736	26986	42750	0.39	0.65	.460	.496	.565
91493	44346	47147	0.48	0.55	.491	.603	.682
122610	53629	68981	0.44	0.73	.523	.572	.603
45160	15669	29491	0.35	0.48	.438	.555	.660
953563	481023	472540	0.50	0.67	—	—	—
34110	11730	22380	0.34	0.52	.495	.575	.533
2025166	1284734	740432	0.63	0.75	.533	.596	.667
87035	56539	30496	0 65	0.80	.585	.658	.709
241913	129968	111945	0.54	0.73	.609	.754	.822
279346	203797	75549	0.73	0.75	.521	.651	.666
2667570	1686768	980802	0.84	0.83	—	—	—

TABLE A.1 (*continued*)
Jobs Created and Destroyed by Openings, Closings, Relocations, Expansions, and Contractions of Private Business Establishments in the United States, by State and Region: 1969–76

State Region	Number of Jobs in 1969[a] (1)	Jobs Created by Openings and Inmigrations (2)	Jobs Destroyed by Closings and Outmigrations (3)	Change (Jobs Created Minus Jobs Destroyed[d]) (4) = (2) − (3)	Ratio of Jobs Destroyed to Jobs Created (5) = (3) ÷ (2)
		Employment Change Associated With Establishment Openings, Closings, and Relocations: 1969–76[b]			
Frostbelt	32701200	11321513	11351748	−30235	1.00
Sunbelt	25234900	13959822	10950541	3009281	0.78
U. S. as a Whole	57936100	25281335	22302289	2979046	0.88

Appendices

	Employment Change Associated With Establishment Expansions and Contractions: 1969–76[c]				Overall Net Employment Change: 1969–76	Dunn and Bradstreet Counts as a proportion of U. S. Department of Labor Estimate of Total Private Employment[a]		
Jobs Created Through Expansion of Existing Establishments (6)	Jobs Destroyed Through Contractions of Existing Establishments (7)	Change (Jobs Created Minus Jobs Destroyed)[d] (8) = (6) − (7)	Ratio of Jobs Destroyed to Jobs Created (9) = (7) ÷ (6)		Ratio of Jobs Destroyed to Jobs Created (10) = (3) + (7) / (2) + (6)	1969	1972	1974
9470435	7212113	2258322	0.76		0.89	—	—	—
9585683	5971042	3614641	0.62		0.72	—	—	—
19056118	13183155	5872963	0.69		0.80	—	—	—

SOURCE: David Birch, *The Job Generation Process* (Cambridge, Mass.: MIT Program on Neighborhood and Regional Change, 1979), appendix A. Based on records from Dun and Bradstreet Inc.

NOTES:

[a] D & B counts constitute a nonprobability sample of employment at the end of the years 1969, 1972, 1974, and 1976 in each of the businesses on which the credit service compiles records. There is no strictly "correct" way to estimate the true population flows from these D & B counts. What we have done is to use as a benchmark the annual average number of employees on payrolls of nonagricultural private establishments for 1969, 1972, and 1974 reported in Bureau of Labor Statistics, U. S. Department of Labor, *Employment and Earnings in States and Areas*, Bulletin 1370–13, 1981. We multiply each of the D & B-base flows (closings, openings, and so forth) in Birch by an "inflation factor" equal to the ratio of the U. S. Department of Labor numbers to Birch's D & B-based numbers for the corresponding time period (1969–72, 1972–74, and 1974–76). The sample fractions are given in the last three columns of the table.

[b] We aggregate "openings" with "inmigrations," and "closings" with "outmigrations," for the following reason:

Technically, a firm moving a pre-existing plant into an area would already have an i.d. (or DUNS) number for it, while a true start-up would have to be assigned a new number, and that distinction should allow us to tell new plants from movers. Unfortunately, the retention of old i.d. numbers for movers depends on actions taken by local D & B officers, who are inconsistent in this practice, having a tendency to perfunctorily assign new numbers, thereby coding a "new" activity as a birth and not an inmigrant. This implies that Birch's inmigrant variable understates the true incidence of plant migration.

The same holds for closings and outmigrations. Therefore we aggregate these categories. As before, Birch's outmigrant variable understates the true incidence of plant outmigration. Also, it should be noted that at least some of these closed establishments were undoubtedly opened up again at the same site—indeed, often with the same physical plant—under new ownership. That will be captured under our category "start-ups," although the data do not allow us to distinguish between such re-openings and the births of wholly new establishments. While we know that the incidence of physical relocation is very low (ranging between 0.2–2.0 percent of net job change among the states), the frequency of such reorganizations *in situ* is frankly unknown.

[c] The underlying D & B data are available for three periods: 1969–72, 1972–74, and 1974–76. If an establishment was opened in a particular state *after* 1969, its employment at the end of the period during which it was opened is counted under "openings" column (2). Any subsequent expansion or contraction or closing is then allocated to columns (6), (7), or (3), respectively. For example, suppose a corporation opens a branch plant in 1970. Its employment at the end of 1972 is 500. During 1972–74, it expands by 200. During 1974–76, it contracts by 150. For this plant, 500 would be added to column (2), 200 to column (6), and 150 to column (7).

[d] Because employment change associated with recorded relocations (inmigrations and outmigrations) is so small, there is some, but very little, double-counting in these totals. Because most relocations tend to be short-distance, whatever double-counting is present is probably relatively smaller for individual states than for the regions, and largest for the country as a whole.

TABLE A.2

The Proportion of Establishments in Existence in 1969 That Were Out of Business by the End of 1976

Region in 1969 and Industrial Sector	Number of 1969 Establishment in the Sample (000)	Size of Establishment in 1969, by Reported Number of Employees on December 31				
		1–20	21–50	51–100	101–500	Over 501
Northeast						
Mfg.	76	.53	.40	.37	.33	.21
Trade[a]	295	.60	.35	.34	.36	.57
Services	51	.61	.42	.43	.39	.29
Total[b]	514	.59	.37	.36	.33	.26
North Central						
Mfg.	63	.48	.30	.27	.27	.15
Trade[a]	296	.57	.33	.30	.28	.27
Services	56	.60	.39	.38	.41	.30
Total[b]	519	.56	.32	.28	.27	.17
South						
Mfg.	49	.53	.36	.36	.34	.28
Trade[a]	335	.59	.33	.30	.23	.23
Services	63	.61	.41	.40	.39	.34
Total[b]	565	.58	.35	.33	.32	.27
West						
Mfg.	41	.53	.39	.36	.31	.16[c]
Trade[a]	182	.60	.38	.34	.29	.33
Services	35	.62	.41	.40	.42	.36
Total[b]	318	.59	.38	.35	.32	.23

SOURCE: Birch, *Job Generation Process*, appendix D.
[a]Includes wholesale and retail trade.
[b]Measures all private sector employment recorded by Dun and Bradstreet: manufacturing, trade, and services, plus other industries not shown here (farming, mining, transportation, utilities, and finance).
[c]Includes only eighty-six establishments.

TABLE A.3

Start-Ups (or Reorganizations) and Closings of Private Business Establishments in Ten Industries in New England: 1969–76

Industry and Form of Ownership[a]	Start-Ups or Reorganizations		Closings		Rates of Change		
					Ratios of Closings to Openings		Net Percentage Change in Employment Associated With Start-ups and Closings
	Establishments	Jobs	Establishments	Jobs	Establishments	Jobs	
	(%)	(%)	(%)	(%)			
Women's Apparel							
Total	100	100	100	100	1.9	2.0	−10.1
Independent	56	42	67	53	2.2	2.5	−10.5
Corporate	41	52	28	39	1.3	1.5	−7.8
Conglomerate[b]	3	6	5	8	3.4	2.9	−20.0
Paper Mills							
Total	100	100	100	100	1.0	1.3	−2.1
Independent	40	8	39	7	1.0	1.3	−1.8
Corporate	56	89	51	91	0.9	1.3	−2.4
Conglomerate[b]	4	3	10	2	2.0	0.5	+2.0
Commercial Printing							
Total	100	100	100	100	1.2	1.2	−1.9
Independent	79	35	89	53	1.4	1.8	−4.2
Corporate	16	33	7	32	0.6	1.1	−2.3
Conglomerate[b]	5	32	4	15	1.0	0.6	+9.9

TABLE A.3 (continued)

Industry and Form of Ownership[a]	Start-Ups or Reorganizations		Closings		Rates of Change		
	Establishments	Jobs	Establishments	Jobs	Ratios of Closings to Openings		Net Percentage Change in Employment Associated With Start-ups and Closings
	(%)	(%)	(%)	(%)	Establishments	Jobs	
Shoes							
Total	100	100	100	100	2.6	4.2	−18.4
Independent	40	17	49	33	3.1	8.1	−24.7
Corporate	54	76	37	51	1.8	2.9	−13.4
Conglomerate[b]	6	7	14	16	6.0	9.5	−28.4
Metalworking Machinery							
Total	100	100	100	100	1.6	1.6	−4.4
Independent	74	15	81	24	1.8	2.6	−4.4
Corporate	23	78	15	58	1.0	1.2	−2.3
Conglomerate[b]	3	7	4	18	2.2	4.6	−10.5
Computers							
Total	100	100	100	100	0.9	0.8	+3.3
Independent	43	8	56	10	1.2	1.1	−0.5
Corporate	51	91	36	89	0.6	0.8	+3.9
Conglomerate[b]	6	1	8	1	1.1	1.2	−1.4
Aircraft Engines							
Total	100	100	100	100	2.0	3.6	−3.3
Independent	57	7	57	10	2.1	5.3	−4.6
Corporate	37	91	28	55	1.6	2.2	−1.6
Conglomerate[b]	6	2	15	35	4.5	76.2	−22.8

| Industry and Form of Ownership[a] | Start-Ups or Reorganizations | | Closings | | Rates of Change | | |
| | Establishments | Jobs | Establishments | Jobs | Ratios of Closings to Openings | | Net Percentage Change in Employment Associated With Start-ups and Closings |
	(%)	(%)	(%)	(%)	Establishments	Jobs	
Department Stores							
Total	100	100	100	100	0.7	0.5	+11.3
Independent	9	4	14	8	1.1	1.0	0.0
Corporate	82	93	60	69	0.5	0.4	+17.4
Conglomerate[b]	9	3	26	23	2.1	4.0	−27.0
Grocery Stores- Supermarkets							
Total	100	100	100	100	2.3	1.0	+0.3
Independent	75	38	93	64	2.8	1.7	−6.4
Corporate	24	61	6	27	0.6	0.4	+18.4
Conglomerate[b]	1	1	1	9	3.0	12.5	−24.6
Hotels-Motels							
Total	100	100	100	100	1.2	0.8	+3.4
Independent	72	39	87	70	1.5	1.5	−5.8
Corporate	26	59	10	20	0.4	0.3	+4.6
Conglomerate[b]	2	2	3	10	1.7	3.9	−21.5

SOURCE: Authors' calculations from an extract from Dun's Identifiers File, prepared for the authors by David L. Birch.

NOTE: "Closings" include outmigrations; "openings" include immigrations, as in table A.1.

[a] "Ownership form" refers to the relationship of the establishment (factory, office, division, store, hotel) to its parent firm, if any. *Independent* establishments operate at only one location, and have no "parent." A *corporate* headquarters or branch facility is an establishment that is part of a multifacility enterprise, and that carries the identification number of the parent corporation. A *conglomerate* headquarters or subsidiary is an establishment that is part of a family of usually quite heterogeneous businesses, all owned by a single parent but each carrying its own i.d. number. These definitions represent our interpretations of file descriptions distributed by Birch in *The Job Generation Process*.

[b] The conglomerate openings in the table represent either literally new establishments or, quite commonly, pre-existing businesses that have been acquired and then reorganized to prompt Dun and Bradstreet to assign a new i.d. number to them (acquired companies that retain their original identities and i.d. numbers are not counted as new openings and do not appear in this table). Analogously, conglomerate divestitures may sometimes appear here as apparent closings, even though they have been bought and continued in operation under the new owner.

TABLE A.4

Investment, Disinvestment, and Transfers of Ownership of About 17,000 Manufacturing Plants Belonging to 410 Large U. S. Corporations During the 1970s

| Region | Plants in Operation at the Beginning of the Decade | | | | | | | | | | | | Physically Expanded at Some Time During the Decade[e] | | New Plants Added During the 1970s | | | | | | Openings or Acquisitions Subsequently Closed or Divested | |
| | Total | | Stayed put[a] | | Relocated[b] | | Shut Down[c] | | Divested[d] | | | | | | Total | | Openings[f] | | Acquisitions[g] | | | |
	No.	(%)	No.	(%)	No.	(%)	No.	(%)	No.	(%)			No.	(%)	No.	(%)	No.	(%)	No.	(%)	No.	(%)
New England	772	100.0	577	74.7	35	4.5	87	11.3	73	9.4			101	13.1	279	100.0	77	27.6	202	72.4	48	17.2
Mid Atlantic	1723	100.0	1343	77.9	46	2.7	137	8.0	197	11.4			188	10.9	595	100.0	137	23.0	458	77.0	107	18.0
E.N. Central	2803	100.0	2231	80.0	83	3.0	250	8.8	239	8.3			394	14.1	1022	100.0	252	24.7	770	75.3	154	15.1
W.N. Central	934	100.0	754	80.7	37	4.0	70	7.5	73	7.8			143	15.3	398	100.0	125	31.4	273	68.6	50	12.6
South Atlantic	1914	100.0	1539	80.4	77	4.0	129	6.7	169	8.8			259	13.5	765	100.0	311	40.7	454	59.3	105	13.7
E.S. Central	853	100.0	698	81.8	24	2.8	59	6.9	72	8.4			122	14.3	476	100.0	198	41.6	278	58.4	55	11.6
W.S. Central	1094	100.0	893	81.6	47	4.3	73	6.7	81	7.4			241	22.0	573	100.0	262	45.7	311	54.3	54	9.4
Mountain	386	100.0	307	79.5	19	4.9	23	6.0	37	9.6			74	19.2	207	100.0	83	40.1	124	59.9	16	7.7
Pacific	1556	100.0	1157	74.4	83	5.3	152	9.8	164	10.5			184	11.8	654	100.0	165	25.2	489	74.8	113	17.3
United States	12063	100.0	9499	78.7	446	3.7	1016	8.4	1102	9.1			1706	14.1	4978	100.0	1615	32.4	3363	67.6	703	14.1

SOURCE: Roger W. Schmenner, "The Location Decisions of Large, Multiplant, Companies," manuscript (Cambridge, Mass.: MIT-Harvard Joint Center for Urban Studies, September 1980), final report to the Office of Policy Development and Research, U. S. Department of Housing and Urban Development, through research grant no. H-2981-RG. Based on our calculations from tables 1-2, p. 30, and 1-5, pp. 36–39 in Schmenner. The time period varies for different companies; in general, the base year is 1970–72, while the most common terminal year is 1978. The definitions are from Schmenner, pp. 11–12.

[a]"A plant which has been in existence since about 1970 or before and which has remained at the same site during the past decade."

[b]"A plant closing since about 1970, followed by the simultaneous or near-simultaneous opening of a new plant which performs essentially the same tasks, and which often employs some of the same people and equipment." Nearly all "relocations" were to other sites within the same region (predominantly into rural areas, even in the crowded Mid-Atlantic states).

[c]"The shut-down of a facility of the corporation since about 1970. The building itself may subsequently have been sold to another company, but the former operation is *not* continued as it was under new management."

[d]"The sale of a plant of an existing business of the corporation to another company. The plant can be expected to continue operations, much as before, but under new management."

[e]"An expansion of 'bricks and mortar' [or significant purchases of equipment] at the plant site since about 1970." Employment may or may not have expanded as well.

[f]"A new plant built [by the corporation itself, purchased, or leased since about 1970, usually hiring new personnel and using new equipment."

[g]"An on-going business facility which merged with or was purchased by the corporation since about 1970."

TABLE A.5
Textron, Inc.:
Acquisitions and Known Divestitures 1943–80

INDUSTRIAL

Adcock-Shipley Ltd.
A- 1971
(milling machines)

American Crossarm & Conduit Co.
A- 1967
D- 1970
(electronic transmission equipment)

A. P. DeSanno & Son, Inc.
A- 1967
D- 1973
(abrasive products)

Bridgeport Machines
A- 1968
(metal working machinery)

California Technical Industries
A- 1957
(electronic equipment)

Cam Cast, Inc.
A- 1976

Cleveland Metal Abrasive Co.
A- 1966
D- 1973
(abrasive products)

Dalmo Victor Co.
A- 1954
(electronic equipment)

Fafnir Bearing Co.
A- 1968
D- (Fafnir-INA Needle Roller
Bearing Co.) 1969
(bearings)

G. C. Electronics
A- 1959
D- 1966

General Cement Manufacturing Co.
A- 1956

Globe Electronics
A- 1959
(electronic equipment)

Jones & Lamson Machine Co.
A- 1964
(machine tools)

Le Progres Industriel
A- 1965
(machine tools)

Ledeen Inc.
A- 1964
(fittings and pressure valves)

M. B. Skinner Co.
A- 1961
(fittings and pressure valves)

Nuclear Metals Inc.
A- 1959
D- (Nuclear Metals Division) 1964
(research)

Ryan Industries, Inc.
A- 1955
(electronic equipment)

Schafer Custom Engineering
A- 1959
(electronic equipment)

Spencer Kellog & Sons, Inc.
A- 1961
(agrochemicals)

Sprague Meter Co., Inc.
A- 1961
(measuring instruments)

Townsend Co.
A- 1959
(industrial fasteners)

Trebel-Werk
A- 1964
(balancing machines)

Appendices

Vita Var Corp.
A- 1962
(paints)

Walker-Brothers (underfloor division)
A- 1964
(electrical transmission equipment)

Waterbury Farrel Foundry & Machine Co.
A- 1958
(machine tools)

Zapata Hayhie
A- 1974
(resin plant)

TEXTILES

(note—In 1963 Textron divested itself of all textile
holdings with the sale of its Amerotron Co. Division.)

American Woolen Co.
A- 1955

Carolina Bagging Co.
A- 1956
(industrial batting)

Chadwick-Hoskins Co.
(a subsidiary of Gorham Corp.)
A- 1946

F. Burkhart Manufacturing Co.
(inventories and miscellaneous assets of)
A—1953
(industrial batting)

Gossett Mills
A- 1946

Lonsdale Co.
A- 1945

Manville Jenckes Corp.
A- 1945

Robbins Mills, Inc.
A- 1955

Suncock Mills
A- 1943

Ware Cotton Batting Co., Inc.
(a subsidiary of F. Burkhart
Manufacturing Co.)
A- 1953

AEROSPACE

Accessory Products Corp.
A- 1957
(aircraft and parts)

Bell Aircraft Corp.
A- 1960
(aircraft and parts)

M B Manufacturing Co., Inc.
A- 1954
(aircraft and parts)

METALS

Aero Zipp Ltd.
A- 1970
(slide fasteners)

American Screw Co.
A- 1962
(industrial fasteners)

Amsler Morton Corp.
A- 1959
D- 1970
(foundry supplies)

Benanda Aluminum Products Co.
A- 1956

Bostitch, Inc.
A- 1966
(industrial fasteners)

Camcar Screw & Manufacturing Corp.
(and certain affiliates)
A- 1955
(industrial fasteners)

Campbell Wyant & Cannon Foundry Co.
A- 1956
(iron and steel castings)

Erie Toolworks and Lakeview Forge Co.
A- 1965
(metal pipe and tubing)

Fanner Mfg. Co.
A- 1958
(foundry supplies)

Parkersburg Aetna Corp.
A- 1963
(bearings)

Peat Manufacturing Corp.
A- 1956
(die casting)

Pittsburgh Steel Foundry Co.
A- 1959
(iron and steel castings)

Precision Methods & Machines, Inc.
A- 1958
(metal working machinery)

Randall Co.
A- 1959
(metal stampings)

Richline Co.
A- 1975

Thompson Grinder Co.
A- 1967
(machine tools)

Wagner Mfg. Co.
(a subsidiary of Randall Co.)
A- 1959
(metal stampings)

Zenite Metals Corp.
A- 1963
(metal stampings)

CONSUMER

Albert H. Weinbrenner Co.
A- 1960
(shoes)

Calan Co.
A- 1970

Continental Optical Co.
A- 1963
(optical instruments)

Durham Manufacturing Corp.
A- 1964
(furniture)

E-Z-Go Car Corp.
A- 1960
(golf carts)

E-Z-Go, Nassau
A- 1972

Gorham Corp.
A- 1967
(silverware)

Hall-Mack Co.
A- 1956
D- (Hall Mack division) 1975
(bathroom fixtures)

H. K. porter Co.
(Patterson-Sargent paint business of)
A- 1965
(paints)

Homelite Corp.
A- 1955
(chain saws)

John Sands Holding Ltd.
A- 1978

Appendices

Mikin Co.
A- 1970

Modern Optics, Inc.
A- 1961
(optical instruments)

Norman J. Field & Co.
A- 1980

Sheaffer Pen Co.
A- 1966

Shuron Optical Co.
A- 1958
(optical instruments)

MISCELLANEOUS

American Modular Systems Design, Inc.
A- 1979

Auto-Soler Co.
A- 1971

Bandon Veneer & Plywood Assoc.
A- 1956
(plywood)

Bayard V. Carmean, Inc.
(the business of)
A- 1963

Caroline Poultry Farms, Inc.
(certain assets of)
A- 1963

Component Parts Co.
A- 1959

Coquille Plywood Co.
A- 1955
D- 1958
(plywood)

Donahue Sales Corp.
A- 1969

Dorset Plastic Corp.
A- 1960
(boatbuilding and marine hardware)

Ellingsworth Mfg. Co.
(and related companies)
A- 1969

Speidel Corp.
A- 1964
(watch bracelets)

Talon, Inc.
A- 1968
(zippers)

Valentine Holdings Australia
A- 1972
(greeting cards and business forms)

Wernicke Co.
A- 1972
(optical equipment)

Ellingsworth Realty Co.
A- 1969

Federal Leather Co.
A- 1956
(plastic products)

Industrial Stapling Sales, Pty.,
Ltd.
A- 1968

Jacobsen Manufacturing Co.
A- 1978

Kordite Corp.
A- 1955
D- 1958
(plastic products)

LPG (division of Weatherhead Co.)
A- 1966
D- 1976

Mich. Fastener Co.
A- 1969

Myrtle Point Veneer Co.
A- 1956
(plywood)

Newmarket Manufacturing Co.
A- 1954

O. Ames Co.
(kitchen and juvenile furniture line of)
A- 1963
(furniture)

Old King Cole, Inc.
A- 1965
(plastic products)

Paw-Paw Box Co.
A- 1969

Polaris Industries, Inc.
A- 1968

Reizart, Inc.
A- 1969

Security Corp.
A- 1973

Sofrembal
A- 1973

South Coast Marine Co.
A- 1965
(boatbuilding and marine hardware)

S. S. LaGuardia
A- 1956
(passenger liner)

Telautograph Corp.
(certain assets of)
A- 1956

Terry Industries Ltd.
(including Terry Machinery Co. Ltd. and
Terry Machinery Acceptance Corp. Ltd.)
A- 1960

Tilden Co.
A- 1960
(pharmaceuticals)

True Trace Corp.
(a subsidiary of Bridgeport Machines)
A- 1968

Tubular Rivet & Stud Co.
A- 1961

Welsh Manufacturing Co.
A- 1970
D- 1976

SOURCE: Compiled from *Moody's Industrial Manual*, 1961 1968, and 1980 volumes.
NOTE: A = date of acquisition; D = date of divestiture, if known.

Notes

Chapter 1

1. "The Reindustrialization of America," *Business Week* (Special Issue), 30 June 1980, p. 58.

2. Organization for Economic Cooperation and Development, as reported in Leonard Silk, "The Ailing Economy: Diagnoses and Prescriptions," *New York Times*, 4 April 1982, p. 4E.

3. In 1980, the inflation rate averaged about 12.5 percent while the unemployment rate averaged 7.0. During the 1960s, the average annual inflation rate was a mere 2.3 percent and unemployment averaged 4.8 percent of the labor force. Council of Economic Advisors, *Economic Report of the President 1981* (Washington, D. C.: U. S. Government Printing Office, 1981), table B-29.

4. Godfrey Hodgson, "State of the Nation," *Boston Globe Magazine*, 18 January 1981, p. 16.

5. Council of Economic Advisors, *Economic Report*, p. 71.

6. "Reindustrialization of America," p. 74.

7. Council of Economic Advisors, *Economic Report*, table 9, p. 71. Increases in the capital-employment ratio were roughly constant at 2.9 percent per year from 1949 until 1974. Since 1974 the capital-labor ratio has actually declined at an annual rate of −.1 percent.

8. Frederick C. Klein, "Some Firms Fight Ills of Bigness by Keeping Employee Units Small," *Wall Street Journal*, 5 February 1982, p. 1.

9. Winston Williams, "Why Business Won't Invest," *New York Times*, 31 January 1982, p. 1F.

10. See, for example, Richard B. McKenzie, *Restrictions on Business Mobility* (Washington, D. C.: American Enterprise Institute, 1979).

11. David L. Birch, *The Job Generation Process* (Cambridge, Mass.: MIT Program on Neighborhood and Regional Change, 1979).

12. Lester Thurow, *The Zero-Sum Society* (New York: Basic Books, 1980), p. 77.

13. Joseph Schumpeter, *Capitalism, Socialism, and Democracy* (New York: Harper & Row, 1942).

14. Louis S. Jacobson, "Earnings Losses of Workers Displaced from Manufacturing Industries," in William G. Dewald, ed., U. S. Department of Labor, *The Impact of International Trade and Investment on Employment* (Washington, D. C.: U. S. Government Printing Office, 1978).

15. Frank de Leeuw, et al., "The High-Employment Budget: New Estimates, 1955–80," *Survey of Current Business*, 60, no. 11 (November 1980). The dollar figure is derived from the difference between potential GNP at 5.1 percent unemployment and actual GNP at 6.1 percent unemployment in the first quarter of 1980.

16. See, for example, George Gilder, *Wealth and Poverty* (New York: Basic Books, 1981); Amitai Etzioni, "America's Most Critical Choice," The Smith-Kline Forum for a Healthier American Society, advertisement in *Newsweek*, 15 September 1980; and Walter Goodman, "Irving Kristol: Patron Saint of the New Right," *New York Times Magazine*, 6 December 1981, p. 90.

17. Gilder, *Wealth and Poverty*, p. 28.

18. Etzioni, "Critical Choice."

19. A good statement of supply-side economics can be found in Jude Wanniski, *The Way the World Works* (New York: Basic Books, 1979). For the official Reagan administration position, see Executive Office of the President, *America's New Beginning: A Program for Economic Recovery* (Washington, D. C.: U. S. Government Printing Office, 1981).

20. Japan Automobile Manufacturers Association, *Motor Vehicle Statistics of Japan* (Tokyo: J.A.M.A., 1981), p. 17.

21. Cited in the *Wall Street Journal*, 6 January 1981, p. 1.

22. F. Thomas Juster, "Savings, Economic Growth, and Economic Policy," *Economic Outlook USA* (Summer 1981): 55.

23. United Nations, *Yearbook of National Account Statistics, 1977*, vol. 1 (New York: United Nations, 1978), p. 348.

24. Daniel M. Holland and Steward C. Myers, "Profitability and Capital Costs for Manufacturing Corporations," *American Economic Review* 70, no. 2 (May 1980): 321.

25. "The Second War Between the States," *Business Week*, 17 May 1976, pp. 92–114.

26. *Business Week*, 12 October 1974.

27. John Friedmann, "Life Space and Economic Space: Contradictions in Regional Development," manuscript (Los Angeles: University of California at Los Angeles, 1981).

28. Paul Samuelson, "Aspects of Public Expenditure Theory," *Review of Economics and Statistics* (November 1958): 337.

29. Schumpeter, *Capitalism*, p. 61. The full thesis that capitalism creates a web of social relationships that become increasingly obstructive to entrepreneurship is set out in chs. 5–14.

Chapter 2

1. William Glenn Cunningham, "Postwar Developments and the Location of the Aircraft Industry in 1950," in G. R. Simonson, ed., *The History of the American Aircraft Industry* (Cambridge, Mass.: MIT Press, 1968), p. 190; and R. C. Estall, *New England: A Study in Industrial Adjustment* (New York: Praeger Publishers, 1966), p. 163.

2. David L. Birch, *The Job Generation Process* (Cambridge, Mass.: MIT Program on Neighborhood and Regional Change, 1979).

3. For an overview of the New England project findings, see Bennett Harrison, "The Economic Transformation of New England Since World War II" (*Working Paper* no. 72 of MIT-Harvard Joint Center for Urban Studies, Cambridge, Mass., February 1982).

4. All users of these data agree that D & B undoubtedly misses some short-term relocations, and instead, mistakenly codes them as closings (what Birch calls "deaths") in the origin area and openings in the destination area. Birch himself has acknowledged this, in an interview with David Moberg in *In These Times*, 27 June 1979, p. 13. The upshot is that D & B outmigration data provide only a *minimum* estimate of actual physical capital flight.

It should be noted that D & B never intended these data—designed originally to keep track of credit ratings on private *firms*—to be used for the purpose of measuring the relocation of those firms' individual plants or *establishments*; thus, users of it must take full responsibility for our applications of this information.

5. While these figures provide, we believe, the best estimates available of job creation and destruction due to new establishment births and establishment deaths, the precise numbers must be used with caution. These estimates are based on a sample of establishments in the United States employing 44–85 percent of all private sector workers, depending on the state. Our population estimates are based on the assumption that the rates of job creation and destruction in the non-surveyed plants were equal to those in the plants covered in the D & B file. To the extent that those establishments not surveyed were part of smaller enterprises that have a higher death rate, our figures for jobs lost are *underestimates*.

On the other hand, the method used by D & B to register "births" and "deaths" treats changes in ownership as though an actual plant closing and an actual new plant opening had simultaneously occurred, when in fact, in such a case, employment may have remained unchanged—only the ownership has been altered. While we do not know the precise magnitude of the upward bias this might impart to our estimates, we do know from Birch's own research that such acquisitions of existing plants accounted for only 2 to 3 percent of all southern employment growth connected with the births of allegedly "new" enterprises. If this 2 to 3 percent figure holds for the United States as a whole, a true estimate of 1969–76 birth-related job growth would be only slightly lower than that reported in table 2.1—24.5 million as compared with 25.3 million. Similarly the number of jobs destroyed by actual closings would be more like 21.6 million instead of 22.3 million. The differences are clearly small.

Notes

Overall we suspect the upward biases in table 2.1 due to the possible misrepresentation of buy-outs by D & B are probably swamped by the downward bias due to the sampling characteristics of the D & B file. But this cannot be proven.

6. "Can Congress Control Runaways?," *Dollars and Sense*, No. 51 (November 1979): 9.

7. These are the tendencies indicated by modern industrial organization theory. Much more detailed information would be needed, on a case-by-case basis, to be more definite. We present these D & B data on ownership with some trepidation. Part of the categorizing of an establishment in the files has been done by D & B, and part by Birch, which creates some real ambiguity. For example, as we noted a moment ago, when a business is acquired, its ownership status is always relabeled, but D & B also sometimes records this as a closing and a new opening. It is also not clear whether large conglomerate-owned corporations such as Pratt & Whitney are listed as "corporations" or under their parent "conglomerate" category (in this case, United Technologies Inc.). Finally, what D & B calls a conglomerate "closing" may in fact be a divestiture or re-sale of the subsidiary, in which case the question becomes: Does that enterprise continue to operate under the new owners? Birch believes that these ambiguities are relatively minor—note his remarks on p. 4 and again on p. 13 of *Job Generation Process*—but he really does not know, and we are apprehensive about it. Thus, these numbers on openings, closings, and relocations by ownership should be treated with special caution. Or, as one of our research assistants, Glynnis Trainer, has suggested, the data on corporations and conglomerates should perhaps be aggregated into a single category of "non-independent ownership."

For what it is worth, the criterion we used to distinguish a multi-establishment "corporation" from a multi-establishment "conglomerate" was as follows: If the various establishments belonging to a central firm share the same i.d. number (and therefore the same credit rating), and if they do not have legal standing to be sued individually in court, then Birch assigns them to a category he calls "headquarters or branch." We refer to this as the "corporate" sector. Otherwise, all of the establishments that make up the multi-establishment firm—each with its own individual i.d. number and court standing—are assigned by Birch to what he calls the "parent-subsidiary" category, which we label "conglomerate." This procedure *unquestionably* understates the degree of conglomeratelike behavior in the sample. For example, a corporation with a famous name may acquire a totally unrelated product or service line, yet treat it as a division rather than as a separate entity, perhaps in order to exploit its own famous name. Birch's and our procedure would classify these as corporate establishments, even though this would be a clear case of conglomerate behavior in the eyes of, for example, the Federal Trade Commission. Future researchers will need to develop a more market-structure-oriented definition of "conglomeration" than the essentially legalistic definition used here. Such a definition should explicitly recognize conglomeration as a *process* of corporate expansion that involves both product (and service) diversity and acquisition of existing facilities as distinct from the construction of new ones.

8. Carol MacLennan and John O'Donnell, "The Effects of the Automotive Transition on Employment: A Plant and Community Study," Transportation Systems Center, U. S. Department of Transportation, December 1980. As we know now, the epidemic of auto closures has become a tidal wave in the 1980s.

9. U. S. Department of Transportation, *The U. S. Automobile Industry, 1980: Report to the President from the Secretary of Transportation* (Washington, D. C.: U. S. Government Printing Office, 1981), p. 88.

10. "America's Restructured Economy," *Business Week*, 1 June 1981, p. 87.

11. Ron Shinn, "Through the Wringer at Goodyear," *New York Times*, 24 May 1981, p. F1.

12. Reginald Stuart, "Boom in Sunbelt Bypasses Older Industrial Towns in the South," *New York Times*, 4 June 1981, p. 18.

13. California Association for Local Economic Development, *Economic Adjustment Report* 1, no. 1 (August–September 1981): 1–2.

14. United States Steel Corporation, *Annual Corporate Reports* and *10 K Reports to the Securities and Exchange Commission* for the years 1976–1979. Between 1970 and 1975, the steel industry as a whole paid out 43 percent of after-tax profits in dividends (a rate above the average for all industry), at a time when industry spokespersons were loudly complaining that pollution control expenditures required by law were preventing them from upgrading their old plant and equipment. Some Wall Street analysts saw this as a strategy for buying time—holding investors' confidence—while management developed a plan for diversifying into new fields. In the late 1970s the entire industry, of course, did just that, shifting capital into cement, petrochemicals,

coal, natural gas, nuclear power plant components, containers and packaging, and real estate. Perhaps symbolically, in the middle of 1978, Armco Steel Corporation legally dropped "Steel" as its middle name. Helen Shapiro and Steven Volk, "Steelyard Blues," *North American Congress on Latin America Report* (January–February 1979): 14–15.

15. "The Reindustrialization of America," *Business Week*, 30 June 1980, p. 78.

16. Roger Schmenner, "The Location Decisions of Large, Multiplant Companies," manuscript (Cambridge, Mass.: MIT-Harvard Joint Center for Urban Studies, 1980). Starting with the Dun and Bradstreet Corporate Family Tree file, Schmenner and his staff studied hundreds of corporate reports, conducted sixty interviews with corporate executives, and implemented a mail survey of the investment and employment activities of a sample of 410 of the largest U. S. manufacturing corporations, nearly all of them members of the *Fortune* 500. During the course of the 1970s, these 410 firms retained, built, scrapped, acquired, or divested over 17,000 individual manufacturing plants located somewhere in the United States. Together, the sample plants (which include corporate giants such as Allied Chemical, A T & T, Boeing, Cannon Mills, Coca-Cola, Dupont, GE, GM, Honeywell, Kraft Foods, Mobil Oil, Procter and Gamble, Texas Instruments, Textron, U. S. Steel, and Xerox) accounted for two fifths of all the manufacturing employment in the country reported in the 1977 Census of Manufacturers.

17. Council of Economic Advisors, *Economic Report of the President 1981* (Washington, D. C.: U. S. Government Printing Office, 1981), tables B–1, B–103.

18. John M. Volpe, "The Effect of the Multinational Corporation on American Labor" (Ph. D. diss., New York University, 1972), tables 2–1, 2–4.

19. William M. Bulkeley, "As U. S. Economy Falters, Multinationals Put Increased Stress on Overseas Business," *Wall Street Journal*, 11 December 1979, p. 48; Robert D. Hershey, Jr., "Banking's International Face," *New York Times*, 5 February 1978, pp. 38–39.

20. See Robert B. Stobaugh et al., *U. S. Multinational Enterprises and the American Economy* in U. S. Office of International Investment, Bureau of International Commerce, U.S. Department of Commerce, *The Multinational Corporation: Studies on U. S. Foreign Investment* (Washington, D. C.: U. S. Government Printing Office, 1972), vol. 1.

21. Richard Barnet and Ronald Müller, *Global Reach* (New York: Simon and Schuster, 1973), p. 301.

22. In 1976, sales of "majority-owned foreign affiliates of U. S. companies" equaled $515 billion. Seven percent of this output, or about $36 billion was imported directly into the United States. (This does not count the sales of inputs to other overseas producers for the manufacture of other commodities that are *then* imported into the United States.) Total 1976 U. S. merchandise imports amounted to about $124 billion. Dividing $36 billion by $124 billion yields 29 percent. See William K. Chung, "Sales by Majority-Owned Foreign Affiliates of U.S. Companies, 1976," *Survey of Current Business* 58, no. 3 (March 1978).

23. Robert H. Frank and Richard T. Freeman, "The Distributional Consequences of Direct Foreign Investment," in William G. Dewald, ed., *The Impact of International Trade and Investment on Employment, A Conference of the U. S. Department of Labor* (Washington, D. C.: U. S. Government Printing Office, 1978), p. 153.

24. Ibid., p. 156.

25. Raymond Vernon, *Sovereignty at Bay* (New York: Basic Books, 1971).

26. Barnet and Müller, *Global Reach*, p. 302.

27. "Current U. S. tax law allows a full credit for foreign taxes paid; under present foreign and domestic tax rates, the result is that over 90 percent of taxes paid on foreign subsidiaries' earnings go to foreign treasuries. . . . This exercise provides some additional support to the argument that higher total taxes on overseas earnings could raise aggregate U. S. welfare." Frank and Freeman, "Distributional Consequences," p. 164.

28. Using independent data and methods, Professor Peggy Musgrave of Northeastern University estimates that labor income in 1968 would have been about 4 percent higher, and capital income (profits, rents, dividends, and royalties) 17 percent smaller, in the absence of direct foreign investment. Peggy B. Musgrave, "Direct Investment Abroad and the Multinationals: Effects on the U.S. Economy," paper prepared for the Subcommittee on Multinational Corporations, Committee on Foreign Relations, U. S. Senate, Washington, D. C., August 1975.

29. Birch, *Job Generation Process;* and David L. Birch, "Who Creates Jobs?" *The Public Interest* 65 (Fall 1981): 71. This has not stopped advocates for business from continually *threatening* to move out of town if they do not get their way. For example, in an interview with a trade magazine, Associated Industries of Massachusetts lobbyist Jim Sledd asserted that the state's

high-technology firms are "very mobile" and that "they can be on the back of a flatbed truck tomorrow and be in North Carolina if things do not go the way they want them to." *New England Business*, 1 October 1979, p. 14.

Chapter 3

1. Linda Snyder Hayes, "Youngstown Bounces Back," *Fortune*, 17 December 1979, pp. 102–106.

2. Carl Sandburg, "The People, Yes," *The Complete Poems of Carl Sandburg*, rev. ed. (New York: Harcourt Brace Jovanovich, Inc., 1969), p. 507.

3. C & R Associates, "Community Costs of Plant Closings: Bibliography and Survey of the Literature" (Report prepared for the Federal Trade Commission under Contract No. L0362, July 1978).

4. J. W. Dorsey, "The Mack Truck Case: A Study in Unemployment," in Otto Eckstein, ed., *Studies in the Economics of Income Maintenance* (Washington, D. C.: The Brookings Institution, 1967).

5. Michael Aiken, Louis A. Ferman, and Harold L. Sheppard, *Economic Failure, Alienation, and Extremism* (Ann Arbor: University of Michigan Press, 1968).

6. Robert L. Aronson and Robert B. McKersie, *Economic Consequences of Plant Shutdowns in New York State* (Ithaca, N. Y.: New York State School of Industrial and Labor Relations, Cornell University, May 1980), pp. 11–12, 36.

7. Ibid., p. 61.

8. Edwin Young, "The Armour Experience: A Case Study in Plant Shutdown," in G. Somers, E. Cushman, and N. Weinberg, eds., *Adjusting to Technological Change* (New York: Harper & Row, 1963).

9. Thomas A. Barocci, "Disinvestment in Massachusetts: A Case Study of Personal and Economic Impacts" (Sloan School of Management *Working Paper* no. 1080–79, Massachusetts Institute of Technology, October 1979), p. 5.

10. Terry Buss and F. Stevens Redburn, "Shutdown: Public Policy for Mass Unemployment," (Draft Report, Center for Urban Studies, Youngstown University, September 1980), p. 7.4.

11. Herbert S. Parnes and Randy King, "Middle-Aged Job Losers," *Industrial Gerontology* 4, no. 2 (Spring 1977): 77–95.

12. Ibid., p. 86.

13. Ibid., p. 87.

14. Ibid., p. 82.

15. Aronson and McKersie, *Plant Shutdowns*, p. 39.

16. Gregory D. Squires, "Runaway Factories are a Civil Rights Issue," *In These Times*, 14–20 May 1980, p. 10.

17. U. S. Bureau of the Census, "The Social and Economic Status of the Black Population in the United States: An Historical View, 1970–1978," *Current Population Reports* (Special Studies P-23, No. 80) (Washington, D. C., U. S. Government Printing Office, 1979).

18. Ohio Public Interest Campaign, "Industrial Exodus Hits Minority Workers the Hardest" (n.d.; reprinted in *Shutdown: Economic Dislocation and Equal Opportunity* report prepared by the Illinois Committee to the United States Commission on Civil Rights, June 1981), p. 7.

19. Martin Anderson, George Byron, and John O'Donnell, "Regional Employment and Economic Effects of a Chrysler Shutdown—Preliminary Data and Analysis," Transportation Systems Center, U. S. Department of Transportation, Cambridge, Mass., October 1979, exhibit 10, p. 23.

20. James A. Hefner, "The Economics of the Black Family from Four Perspectives," in Charles Vert Willie, ed., *Class & Caste Controversy* (Bayside, N. Y.: General Hall, Inc., 1979), p. 83, as reported in the Illinois Committee, *Shutdown*, p. 13.

21. Squires, "Runaway Factories," p. 10.

22. These figures come from only a handful of specific enterprise case studies. Large surveys indicate the same phenomenon. An Illinois survey involving 2,380 firms that shut down between 1975 and 1978 showed that 20 percent of the affected workers were minorities, compared to a statewide minority work force of just 14.1 percent. See the Illinois Committee, *Shutdown*, p. 32.

23. Parnes and King, "Job Losers," p. 88.

24. Ibid., pp. 90–91.

25. See Louis S. Jacobson, "Earnings Losses of Workers Displaced from Manufacturing Industries," in William G. Dewald, ed., *The Impact of International Trade and Investment on Employment,* (Washington, D. C.: U. S. Government Printing Office, 1978); Louis S. Jacobson, "Earnings Loss Due to Displacement" (Working Paper CRC-385 of The Public Research Institute of the Center for Naval Analyses, McLain, Va., April 1979); and Arlene Holen, "Losses to Workers Displaced by Plant Closure or Layoff: A Survey of the Literature" (Paper of The Public Research Institute of the Center for Naval Analyses, McLain, Va., November 1976).

26. The Social Security data used in these studies are found in the Longitudinal Employer-Employee Data (LEED) file available from the Social Security Administration (SSA). This extraordinary information source contains complete nineteen-year (1957–75) work histories on 1 percent of all workers covered by Social Security. This large sample of workers' records is drawn from the quarterly reports submitted to SSA by employers. The work history for each person among the 1.5 million workers on the file includes data on sex, race, and age, and for each year, the state, county, industry, and quarterly earnings for each social security covered job. Each firm is identified by a unique employer identification code and in most cases each separate unit of a multiunit employer is identified as well. The data therefore permit a comprehensive analysis of job mobility at the county, region, firm, and industry level. The data on quarterly earnings permit an analysis of wage mobility within a single employer, single industry, or across any of the job mobility patterns described above.

The most important shortcoming of the LEED file is that, in years when a worker is not in covered employment, it is not possible to directly ascertain whether he or she has taken a noncovered public or private sector job, is unemployed, or is out of the labor force. This tends to lead to slight overstatements of earnings loss in studies like those of Jacobson, but the bias is likely to be small.

27. Although the LEED file does not distinguish between normal attrition and displacement for each worker in the sample, Jacobson was able to distinguish between groups with a high probability of being displaced and groups with higher rates of attrition. This was done by dividing workers in each industry on the basis of whether employment in the industry in the worker's Standard Metropolitan Statistical Area (SMSA) was rising or falling in the year of separation. He found, based on an ingenious statistical technique, that the measured loss in earnings for separated workers in SMSAs with falling employment proved to be a "reasonably accurate estimate of the loss due to displacement alone." However, since even the elaborate technique still leaves some voluntary separations in the "displaced group," the earnings loss estimates he generated are *minimum* estimates. Therefore the percentage loss figures in table 3.1 may seriously *underestimate* real losses of displaced workers and especially plant closing victims. See Jacobson, "Earnings Losses," pp. 3–4.

28. Ellen I. Rosen, "Job Mobility and Job Loss: A Study of the Effects of Unemployment and Underemployment Among Blue-Collar Working Women in New England," Social Welfare Research Institute, Boston College, 1981.

29. Aronson and McKersie, *Plant Shutdowns,* p. 51.

30. The results of this Mathematica Policy Research Center survey are reported in Harry J. Gilman, "The Economic Costs of Worker Dislocation: An Overview," in a paper prepared for the National Commission for Employment Policy, July 1979.

31. James E. McCarthy, *Trade Adjustment Assistance: A Case Study of the Shoe Industry in Massachusetts* (Boston: Federal Reserve Bank of Boston, June 1975).

32. Labor-Management Services Administration, U. S. Department of Labor, "What You Should Know About the Pension and Welfare Law: A Guide to the Employment Retirement Income Security Act of 1974," (Washington, D. C.: U. S. Government Printing Office, 1978).

33. Melvin A. Glasser, "Diamond-Reo Pension Plan Termination," Inter-office communication to the International Executive Board, United Automobile Workers (UAW), April 9, 1976.

34. A similar taxonomy of industries is found in Barry Bluestone, "Low-Wage Industries and the Working Poor," *Poverty and Human Resources* 3, no. 2 (April 1968) and in Bennett Harrison and Edward Hill, "The Changing Structure of Jobs in Older and Younger Cities," in Benjamin Chinitz, ed., *Central City Economic Development* (Cambridge, Mass.: Abt Books, 1979).

35. Katherine Dupre Lumpkin, "Shutdowns in the Connecticut Valley," *Smith College Studies in History* 19 (1934), as reported in C & R Associates, "Community Costs," p. 33.

36. J. W. Dorsey, "Mack Truck Case," pp. 214–17.

37. Paula Rayman and Barry Bluestone, "The Private and Social Costs of Job Loss: A Metro-study," Social Welfare Research Institute, Boston College, 1982.

38. Aronson and McKersie, *Plant Shutdowns*, p. 57.

39. Felician Foltman, *White and Blue Collars in a Mill Shutdown* (Ithaca, N. Y.: Cornell University Press, 1968).

40. Thomas A. Barocci, "Disinvestment," p. 10.

41. Peter B. Meyer and Mark A. Phillips, "Worker Adaptation to Internationally Induced Job Loss: Final Report on a Pilot Study," Bureau of International Labor Affairs, U. S. Department of Labor, April 27, 1978.

42. Stanislaw Kasl and Sidney Cobb, "Blood Pressure Changes in Men Undergoing Job Loss," *Psychometric Medicine* 32 (January-February 1970). pp. 106–122. See also Stanislaw Kasl, Sidney Cobb, and George Brooks, "Changes in Serum Uric Acid and Cholesterol Levels in Men Undergoing Job Loss," *Journal of the American Medical Association* 206 (November 1968) pp. 1500–07; and Stanislaw Kasl, Susan Gore, and Sidney Cobb, "The Experience of Losing a Job: Reported Changes in Health, Symptoms, and Illness Behavior," *Psychosomatic Medicine* 37, no. 2 (March–April 1975), pp. 106–22.

43. Sidney Cobb and Stanislaw Kasl, "Termination: The Consequences of Job Loss," Public Health Service, Center for Disease Control, National Institute for Occupational Safety and Health, U. S. Department of Health, Education, and Welfare, Washington, D. C., June 1977, p. 179.

44. Aronson and McKersie, *Plant Shutdowns*, p. 57.

45. Don Stillman, "The Devastating Impact of Plant Relocations," *Working Papers*, 5, no. 4 (July–August 1978): 49.

46. Harvey Brenner, "Estimating the Social Costs of National Economic Policy: Implications for Mental and Physical Health and Clinical Aggression," a report prepared for the Joint Economic Committee, U. S. Congress (Washington, D. C.: U. S. Government Printing Office, 1976).

47. Brenner has developed estimates of the total foregone income plus direct prison and mental hospital outlays for the years 1970 to 1975 attributable to the 1.4 percent rise in national unemployment since 1970. The cost for these was nearly $7 billion. Adding estimated unemployment and welfare payments of $2.8 billion annually, the Joint Economic Committee staff of the U. S. Congress calculated a total economic loss of $21 billion from 1970 to 1975 as a result of the increased unemployment.

48. Stillman, "Devastating Impact," p. 43.

49. Cobb and Kasl, *Termination*, p. 134.

50. Richard Wilcock and W. H. Franke, *Unwanted Workers: Permanent Layoffs and Long-Term Unemployment* (New York: Glencoe Free Press, 1963), pp. 166, 185.

51. Walter Strange, "Job Loss: A Psychosocial Study of Worker Reactions to a Plant Closing in a Company Town in Southern Appalachia," National Technical Information Service (NTIS), 1977 as quoted in C & R Associates, "Community Costs," p. 39.

52. C & R Associates, "Community Costs," p. 39.

53. Strange, "Job Loss," p. 39.

54. Alfred Slote, *Termination: The Closing of Baker Plant* (Indianapolis, Ind.: Bobbs-Merrill, 1969), p. xix.

55. Memorandum from Richard A. Lynch, former executive vice-president, New Jersey State AFL-CIO, n.d.

56. Jack Metzgar, "Plant Shutdowns and Worker Response: The Case of Johnstown, Pa.," *Socialist Review* 10, no. 5 (September–October 1980): 18–19.

57. The U. S. Chamber of Commerce estimate is reported in "Erie Shares Grant to Fight Closings," the *Daily Times* (Erie, Pennsylvania), 13 November 1980.

58. Metzgar, "Plant Shutdowns," p. 22.

59. Ibid.

60. David Moberg, "Shuttered Factories—Shattered Communities," *In These Times*, 27 June 1979, p. 11.

61. This excellent case study, written by Bill Curry, appeared in the *Los Angeles Times*, 11 January 1981 and continued on 22 February 1981 and 5 April 1981.

62. Bill Curry, "Smelter Closing Gives Cash Registers a Hollow Ring," *Los Angeles Times*, 11 January 1981, p. 11.

63. Ibid.

64. Bill Curry, "Town Loses Its Payroll but It Finds a Will to Survive," *Los Angeles Times*, 5 April 1981, p. 11.

65. Cited in Carol MacLennan and John O'Donnell, "The Effects of the Automotive Transition on Employment: A Plant and Community Study," (Draft for the Transportation Systems Center, U. S. Department of Transportation, December 1980).

66. Ibid.

67. These estimates are generated using the 1963 Multiregional Input-Output Model (MRIO) developed by Dr. Karen R. Polenske of M.I.T. See Karen R. Polenske, *The U. S. Multiregional Input-Output Accounts and Model* (Lexington, Mass.: D. C. Heath, 1980). While the data refer to 1963, the relationships between industries still provide a reasonably good approximation to the actual pattern of interaction between industries. The major changes would likely be in the amount of steel and plastics used in the production of automobiles. Today less steel and more plastic goes into production. There has also been an increase in the amount of electronics used in the modern vehicle. As a result the estimates presented here may overestimate the number of jobs lost in the steel industry as a result of the Michigan plant shutdown, but underestimate the loss in other sectors.

68. These regional impact statistics are probably different today than in 1963. With the greater dispersion of the automobile industry, particularly in the South, the regional distribution depicted is only broadly illustrative of the nature of interregional industry linkages now prevailing. Research that will eventually update the MRIO linkages to 1977 is currently underway at the Social Welfare Research Institute, Boston College.

69. U. S. House of Representatives, Committee on Small Business, *Conglomerate Mergers—Their Effects on Small Business and Local Communities*, 96th Cong., 2d sess., Report No. 96–1447, October 2, 1980, p. 10.

70. Arthur Strang, Executive Office of Economic Affairs, Commonwealth of Massachusetts, in an internal memo on the "home-based life insurance companies" in the state, February 1977.

71. "Uniroyal Closing: A $500,000 Tax Loss," *Bay State Employee*, AFSCME Council 93, AFL-CIO, Commonwealth of Massachusetts, March 1980, pp. 7–8.

72. Cited in Moberg, "Shuttered Factories," p. 12.

73. "Plant Closings in Campbell Force Higher Taxes," *Ohio AFL-CIO News and Views*, 29 February 1980.

74. Anderson, Byron, and O'Donnell, "Chrysler Shutdown," exhibit 3, p. 8.

75. Transportation Systems Center, U. S. Department of Transportation, "If Chrysler Shuts Down," *Challenge*, November-December 1979, p. 51–52. Even smaller, more limited plant closings take an enormous toll on tax revenues. The decision of General Motors to pack up its St. Louis assembly plant and, in effect, move it to Wentzville, Missouri, thirty-five miles from the city will cost St. Louis $10 million a year in revenue over the next ten years. [See MacLennan and O'Donnell, "Automotive Transition."] GM currently pays $7.5 million of the city's $23 million merchants' and manufacturers' tax. During the last quarter of 1978 and the first three quarters of 1979, GM employees paid over $2.1 million in earnings taxes. The company paid over $400,000 in other taxes during that same period.

76. Policy and Management Associates, Inc., "Socioeconomic Costs and Benefits of the Community-Worker Ownership Plan to the Youngstown-Warren SMSA," 1978, as reported in Moberg, "Shuttered Factories," p. 12.

77. U. S. Department of Transportation, *The U. S. Automobile Industry, 1980: Report to the President from the Secretary of Transportation* (Washington, D. C.: U. S. Government Printing Office, 1981) p. 98.

78. Aronson and McKersie, *Plant Shutdowns*, pp. 85–86.

79. U. S. Department of Health and Human Services, Social Security Administration, *Social Security Bulletin: Annual Statistical Supplement, 1977–1979*, (Washington, D. C.: U. S. Government Printing Office, September 1980), table 27, p. 79.

80. Barry Bluestone and James Sumrall, "An Overview of Recent State AFDC Benefits and Caseload Dynamics" (Publication no. 25 of the Social Welfare Research Institute, Boston College, February 1977), pp. 10–14.

81. Kathleen Sestak, "AFDC Caseload and Benefits Dynamics—Washington," Social Welfare Research Institute, Boston College, July 1976, p. 257.

82. These figures are based on Frank de Leeuw et al., "The High-Employment Budget: New

Notes

Estimates, 1955–80," *Survey of Current Business* 60, no. 11 (November 1980) table 5, p. 29 and table 19, p. 43.

83. Staughton Lynd, "Reindustrialization: Brownfield or Greenfield?" *Democracy* 1, no. 3 (July 1981) p. 31.

84. William M. Bulkeley, "Government Workers Find that Job Security can Suddenly Vanish," *Wall Street Journal*, 29 July 1981, p. 14.

85. Rich Ratliff, "Schools — Taxes = ?" *Detroit Free Press*, 24 August 1980, p. G1.

86. Walter Guzzardi, Jr., "A Determined Detroit Struggles to Find a New Economic Life," *Fortune*, 21 April 1980, p. 84.

87. Aronson and McKersie, *Plant Shutdowns*, p. 91.

88. Ibid., p. 69.

89. Ibid.: p. 71.

90. Ibid., p. 91.

Chapter 4

1. Paul Recer, "The Texas City That's Bursting Out All Over," *U.S. News and World Report*, 27 November 1978, p. 47.

2. "Houston: The International City," *Fortune* (Advertisement Section), 14 July 1980, pp. 38–58.

3. "The Texas City," p. 47.

4. "Houston: Supercity," *Newsweek*, 12 December 1977, p. 41.

5. "Houston: The International City," p. 42.

6. Ibid., p. 49.

7. U. S. Department of Commerce, Bureau of the Census, "Money Income of Families and Persons in the United States: 1978," *Current Population Reports, Consumer Income*, Washington, D. C.: U. S. Government Printing Office, Series P-60, no. 123, June 1980, table 12, pp. 58–61.

8. "Autumn 1979 Urban Family Budgets and Comparative Indexes in Selected Urban Areas," U. S. Department of Labor, Bureau of Labor Statistics, Washington, D. C., April 30, 1980, table D.

9. Michael A. Verespej, "Where Will Industry Find Its New Frontiers?" *Industry Week*, 22 January 1979, p. 57.

10. Bruce A. Jacobs, "Growth for the Sunbelt's Smaller Cities," *Industry Week*, 4 February 1980, p. 47.

11. "The Texas City," p. 47.

12. Melinda Beck and Ronald Henkoff, "A City's Growing Pains," *Newsweek*, 14 January 1980, p. 45.

13. Steven Frazier, "Driving Costs Endanger Growth in Sun Belt Cities like Houston," *Wall Street Journal*, 11 July 1980, p. 17.

14. David Nyhan, "Albuquerque: Isolated, Aware," *Boston Globe*, 8 September 1981, p. 14.

15. "Houston: Supercity," p. 41.

16. Based on data available in International City Management Association, *The Municipal Year Book, 1981* (Washington, D. C.: I.C.M.A., 1981), pp. 94–96.

17. "Houston: Supercity," p. 26.

18. The top 5 percent of the population in the remaining regions of the country enjoyed 15.2 percent of family income while the poorest 20 percent of the population received 5.5 percent. Calculated from Bureau of the Census, "Money Income of Families," pp. 167–68.

19. Quoted in Jim Montgomery, "Deep Poverty Persists in the South Despite New Wealth of Area," *Wall Street Journal*, 29 December 1978, p. 1.

20. Gurney Brechenfeld, "Business Loves the Sunbelt (and Vice Versa)," *Fortune*, June 1977, p. 124. One reason for the lack of black advancement, *Fortune* notes, "is that industry has tended to locate new factories in places where it can find surplus underemployed white labor, and has generally avoided counties with a high proportion of unskilled, impoverished Blacks."

21. U. S. Department of Commerce, Bureau of the Census, "Money Income of Families and Persons in the United States: 1980" (Advance Data), *Current Population Reports, Consumer*

Income, Wash. D. C.: U. S. Government Printing Office, Series P-60, no. 127, August 1981, table 20, p. 33.

22. "The Texas City," p. 47.

23. U. S. Bureau of the Census, Department of Commerce, *Statistical Abstract of the United States 1980* (Wash. D. C.: U. S. Government Printing Office, 1980), p. 184.

24. Sam Allis, "Commission on South's Future Grapples with Conflicting Goals," *Wall Street Journal*, 23 December 1980, p. 23.

25. Beck and Henkoff, "Growing Pains," p. 45.

26. Ibid.

27. Atlanta's overbuilding of its downtown area during the 1960s boom has left the city struggling with a glut of new hotel space, vacant offices, condominiums, and apartments. Gurney Brechenfeld, "Business Loves the Sunbelt," p. 146.

28. David Nyhan, "Sunny Florida Struggling with Rapid Growth, Success," *Boston Globe*, 23 August 1981, p. 7.

29. Ibid.

30. Robert Howard, "Second Class in Silicon Valley," *Working Papers* 8, no. 5 (September–October 1981): 22.

31. Anna Lee Saxenian, "Outgrowing the Valley," *Working Papers* 8, no. 5 (September–October 1981): 25.

32. Ibid.

33. Ann R. Markusen, "Class, Rent, and Sectoral Conflict: Uneven Development in Western U. S. Boomtowns," *Review of Radical Political Economics* 10, no. 3 (1978): 117–29.

34. Ibid.

35. Gene F. Summers, et al., *Industrial Invasion of Non-metropolitan America: A Quarter Century of Experience* (New York: Praeger Publishers, 1976), p. 49.

36. Ibid., pp. 33–34.

37. Ibid., p. 60.

38. El Dean V. Kohrs, "Social Consequences of Boom Growth in Wyoming" (Paper presented at the Rocky Mountain Association for the Advancement of Science Meeting, Laramie, Wyoming, July 24–26, 1974), as reported in V. Edward Bates, "The Impact of Energy Boom-Town Growth on Rural Areas," *Social Casework*, February 1978, p. 74.

39. Boomtowns can apply for federal aid under 130 different programs such as HUD planning grants and EDA sewer and water development grants. Spokespersons for states with boomtown problems are currently arguing for generic programs addressed directly to the rapid growth phenomenon. In 1976 Congress passed a revised Coastal Zone Management Act that included a $1.6 billion program of domestic aid for small communities and states affected by offshore oil and natural gas development. Also in 1976 Congress increased to 50 percent from 37½ percent the share of federal mineral-leasing revenues returned to state and local governments where such land is mined. See Ann R. Markusen, "Federal Budget Simplification: Preventive Programs vs. Palliatives for Local Governments with Booming, Stable, and Declining Economics," *National Tax Journal* 30, no. 3 (September 1977).

40. Michael A. Verespej, "Industry," p. 56.

41. For an historical overview of the "revitalization" of New England and who has and has not been sharing in the benefits, see Bennett Harrison, "The Economic Transformation of New England Since World War II" (*Working Paper* no. 72 of the MIT-Harvard Joint Center for Urban Studies, Cambridge, Mass., February 1982).

42. These figures, based on data from the U. S. Department of Commerce's *County Business Patterns* series, were calculated by Lynn B. Ware, Denise D. Pasquale, and Barry Bluestone at the Social Welfare Research Institute, Boston College, 1978.

43. Federal Reserve Bank of Boston, *New England Economic Indicators*, various issues.

44. Sarah Kuhn, *The Computer Industry of New England* (Cambridge, Mass.: MIT-Harvard Joint Center for Urban Studies, 1982).

45. Robert Vinson and Paul Harrington, "Defining 'High Technology' Industries in Massachusetts," Policy and Evaluation Division, Department of Manpower Development, Commonwealth of Massachusetts, September 1979, p. 12.

46. Ibid.

47. These calculations were made by Alan Matthews at the Social Welfare Research Institute, Boston College.

48. Again, as in chapter 3, these two LEED "transition probabilities" stand for everyone who leaves his original "state"—in this case, mill employment in 1958. We cannot distinguish those who voluntarily left from those who were involuntarily displaced. But it is virtually certain that if we could, the "upward" mobility of the former would be greater than that of the latter. In other words, the average behavior of the entire cohort—which is all we have to work with—almost surely *overstates* the upward mobility of those who in fact lost their mill jobs in the process of deindustrialization.

49. U. S. Department of Commerce, Bureau of the Census, "Geographical Mobility: March 1975 to March 1979," *Current Population Reports, Population Characteristics*, Washington, D. C.: U. S. Government Printing Office, Series P-20, no. 353, August 1980, p. 1.

50. Ibid., table 18, pp. 38–39.

51. U. S. Department of Commerce, *Statistical Abstract of the United States 1980* (Washington, D. C.: U. S. Government Printing Office, 1980), table 131, p. 91.

52. Julie DaVanzo, *Why Families Move: A Model of the Geographic Mobility of Married Couples* (R & D Monograph 48, U. S. Department of Labor, Employment and Training Administration, 1977), p. 8.

53. In a particularly interesting synthesis of the "push" and "pull" theories, Michael Piore of MIT has published an argument that recent nonwhite immigrants to American cities were *recruited* by low-wage employers finding it increasingly difficult to get Americans (especially second-generation black northerners) to work under such conditions. Michael J. Piore, *Birds of Passage* (New York: Cambridge University Press, 1980).

54. DaVanzo, *Why Families Move;* J. B. Lansing and E. Mueller, eds., *The Geographic Mobility of Labor* (Ann Arbor: Survey Research Center, Institute For Social Research, University of Michigan, 1977); and Michael J. Greenwood, "Research on Internal Migration in the United States: A Survey," *Journal of Economic Literature* 3, no. 2 (June 1975): 397–433.

55. Lansing and Mueller, *Geographic Mobility*, p. 136.

56. See R. A. Fabricant, "Regional Labor Markets and Migration: An Analysis of Gross Migration in the United States, 1955–1960" (Ph.D. diss., University of California at Berkeley, 1967); and Philip Nelson, "Migration, Real Income, and Information," *Journal of Regional Science*, 1, no. 2 (Spring 1959): 43–74.

57. For an elucidation of this argument, see Gunnar Myrdal, *Rich Lands and Poor* (New York: Harper & Row, 1957).

58. One economist who has made this argument is the late Harry G. Johnson, until his untimely death a leader of the "Chicago" school of economics along with Milton Friedman. Harry G. Johnson, "The Economics of the 'Brain Drain': The Canadian Case," *Minerva* (Spring 1965).

59. See, for example, Albert O. Hirschman, *The Strategy of Economic Development* (New Haven: Yale University Press, 1965); Gunnar Myrdal, *Economic Theory and Underdeveloped Regions* (London: Duckworth, 1957); and Stuart Holland, *Capital vs. the Regions* (London: St. Martin's, 1976).

Chapter 5

1. George Gilder, *Wealth and Poverty* (New York: Basic Books, 1981); Jude Wanniski, *The Way the World Works* (New York: Basic Books, 1979); Amitai Etzioni, "America's Most Critical Choice" (the Smith-Kline Forum for a Healthier American Society, vol. 2, no. 5, published as a paid advertisement) in *Newsweek*, 15 September 1980; and Lester Thurow, *The Zero-Sum Society* (New York: Basic Books, 1980). Arthur Laffer's unpublished ideas are reported in Wanniski. The political philosophies of David Stockman and Jack Kemp are embodied in Executive Office of The President, *America's New Beginning: A Program for Economic Recovery* (Washington, D. C.: U. S. Government Printing Office, 18 February 1981).

2. This section draws substantially on "The Decline of U. S. Power," *Business Week*, 12 March 1979.

3. Daniel R. Fusfeld, "Fascist Democracy in the United States," *Conference Papers of the Union for Radical Political Economics*, reprint no. 2 (New York: U.R.P.E., 1968).

4. Steve Babson, "The Multinational Corporation and Labor," *Review of Radical Political Economics* 5, no. 1 (Spring 1973): 19.

5. Peggy Musgrave, "Direct Investments Abroad and the Multinationals: Effects on the U.S. Economy" (Paper prepared for the Subcommittee on Multinational Corporations, Committee on Foreign Relations, U. S. Senate, Washington, D.C., August 1975), p. 14.

6. Ronald E. Müller, "National Economic Growth and Stabilization Policy in the Age of Multinational Corporations: The Challenge of Our Postmarket Economy," in Joint Economic Committee, Congress of the United States, *U. S. Economic Growth, 1976, to 1986: Prospects, Problems, and Patterns* 12 vols. (Washington, D. C.: U. S. Government Printing Office, 1977), vol. 12: 49.

7. Quoted in Richard Barnet and Ronald Müller, *Global Reach* (New York: Simon and Schuster, 1974) p. 305.

8. "Decline of U. S. Power," p. 41.

9. Motor Vehicle Manufacturers' Association, *Motor Vehicle Facts and Figures 1981*, (Detroit Mich.: Motor Vehicle Manufacturers' Association, 1981).

10. U. S. Department of Commerce, *Survey of Current Business* 49, no. 7 (July 1969).

11. Ronald E. Shaw, *Erie Water West: A History of the Erie Canal, 1779–1854.* (Lexington, Ky.: University of Kentucky Press, 1966), p. 214.

12. Ernest Mandel considers these recent developments in the forces of production to constitute a "third technological revolution," based upon electronic (and, perhaps, nuclear) power. The first two technical "revolutions" of capitalist development were based on steam, and then on electrical powering of the process of combustion. Ernest Mandel, *Late Capitalism* (London: New Left Books, 1975), ch. 4.

13. Robert E. Jacobson, "Satellite Business Systems and the Concept of the Dispersed Enterprise: An End to National Sovereignty?" *Media, Culture and Society* 1 (1979): 237.

14. The tendency toward the progressive deskilling of workers during capitalist development —that is, toward the continued polarization of skills as the "middle" of the job structure is selectively automated—is the central theme of Harry Braverman, *Labor and Monopoly Capital* (New York: Monthly Review Press, 1974). See also Andrew Friedman, *Industry and Labor* (London: Macmillan, 1977); and Andrew Zimbalist, ed., *Case Studies in the Labor Process*, (New York: Monthly Review Press, 1979).

15. See Louis T. Wells, Jr., "International Trade: The Product Life Cycle Approach," in Louis T. Wells, Jr., ed., *The Product Life Cycle and International Trade* (Boston: Harvard Business School, 1972); Raymond Vernon, "International Investment and International Trade in the Product Cycle," *Quarterly Journal of Economics* 80, no. 2 (May 1966); R. D. Norton and John Rees, "The Product Cycle and the Spatial Decentralization of American Manufacturing," *Regional Studies* 13 no. 2 (1979): 141–51; John Hekman, "The Product Cycle and New England Textiles," *Quarterly Journal of Economics* 94, no. 4 (June 1980): 697–717; and John Hekman, "The Future of High Technology Industry in New England: A Case Study of Computers," *New England Economic Review*, January-February 1980: 5–17.

16. Edward S. Herman, *Corporate Control, Corporate Power* (New York: Cambridge University Press, 1981).

17. The U. S. government does not construct concentration ratios for non-manufacturing industries. However, a reasonably comparable figure, the "market power factor," can be constructed for all industries using the Internal Revenue Service *Statistics of Corporate Income* data. A discussion of the construction of this indicator can be found in Barry Bluestone, "The Personal Earnings Distribution: Individual and Institutional Determinants" (Ph.D. diss., University of Michigan, 1974), pp. 328–29.

18. Fred J. Weston, "Do Multinational Corporations Have Market Power to Overprice?" in Carl H. Madden, ed., *The Case for Multinational Corporations* (New York: Praeger Publishers and the National Chamber Foundation, 1977).

19. Müller, "National Economic Growth," p. 43.

20. John M. Blair, *Economic Concentration* (New York: Harcourt Brace, 1972), p. 260. See Blair's entire book, but especially chs. 11–12, for the definitive empirical study of corporate and conglomerate centralization and concentration in the United States. The two essays that most ingeniously attempt to *explain* numbers like Blair's (from completely different theoretical perspectives) are Alfred D. Chandler, Jr., *Strategy and Structure: Chapters in the History of Industrial Enterprise* (Cambridge, Mass.: MIT Press, 1962); and Mandel, *Late Capitalism*, especially ch. 10.

21. United States Federal Trade Commission, Bureau of Economics, *Statistical Report on Mergers and Acquisitions*, Washington, D. C. July 1981, pp. 104 and 115.

Notes

22. *Forbes Magazine*, 15 October 1968, p. 30.

23. Alan Feld, "Tax Policy and Competition" (Paper prepared for the Bureau of Competition and the Office of Policy Planning and Evaluation, Federal Trade Commission, 1979), p. J-5.

24. Committee on Small Business, U. S. House of Representatives, *Conglomerate Mergers: Their Effects on Small Business and Local Communities—Report* (Washington D. C.: U. S. Government Printing Office, 1980), p. 46.

25. Margaret Dewar, "The Usefulness of Industrial Revenue Bond Programs for State Economic Development: Some Evidence from Massachusetts," *New England Journal of Business and Economics* 7, no. 2 (Spring 1981): 23–34.

26. Feld, "Tax Policy," p. J-11.

27. Müller, "National Economic Growth," p. 59.

28. Mark Nadel, *Corporations and Public Accountability* (Lexington, Mass.: D. C. Heath, 1976), p. 125.

29. Barnet and Müller, *Global Reach*, pp. 230–31.

30. On transfer pricing, see Ibid.; and Sidney M. Robbins and Robert B. Stobaugh, *Money in the Multinational Enterprise* (New York: Basic Books, 1973).

31. David Rutenberg, "Maneuvering Liquid Assets in a Multinational Corporation," *Management Science* 16, no. 10 (June 1970): B–671.

32. S. M. Miller, "The Recapitalization of Capitalism," *Social Policy* 9, no. 3 (November–December 1978): 13.

33. John M. Volpe, "The Effect of the Multinational Corporation on American Labor," (Ph.D. diss., New York University, 1972).

34. George Kohl, "U.S. Tax Dollars and Runaway Shops," *The Washington Spectator*, 15 February 1979; and Kohl, "Campaign to Stop Runaway Shops," mimeograph of the Center for Development Policy, November 16, 1978.

35. Two good introductions to this history are: Sidney Lens, *The Labor Wars* (New York: Doubleday Anchor, 1974); and Melvyn Dubovsky, *Industrialism and the American Worker, 1865–1920* (Arlington Heights, Ill.: AHM Publishing Co., 1975).

36. This paragraph draws on the following sources: Daniel Nelson, *Unemployment Insurance: The American Experience, 1915–1935* (Madison, Wisc.: University of Wisconsin Press, 1969); Herman Miles Somers and Anne Ramsey Sullivan, *Workman's Compensation* (New York: John Wiley and Sons, 1954); and Bruno Stein, *Work and Welfare in Britain and the U.S.A.* (New York: John Wiley and Sons, 1976).

37. Staughton Lynd, *Labor Law for the Rank and Filer* (San Pedro, Calif.: Singlejack Books, 1978), pp. 15–21.

38. James Kuhn, "Electrical Products," in Gerald Somers, ed., *Collective Bargaining: Contemporary American Experience* (Madison, Wisc.: Industrial Relations Research Association, 1980), p. 225.

39. The following discussion of the Taft-Hartley Act draws on Lynd, *Labor Law*, pp. 21–23.

40. Solomon Barkin, *The Decline of the Labor Movement* (Santa Barbara, Calif.: Center for the Study of Democratic Institutions, 1961), pp. 68 ff. See also Ronald Schatz, "American Electrical Workers" (Ph.D. diss., University of Pittsburgh, 1977).

41. U. S. Bureau of the Census, *Statistical Abstract of the United States: 1980* (Washington, D. C.: U. S. Government Printing Office, 1980), p. 429.

42. Bruce Nissen, "U. S. Workers and the U. S. Labor Movement", *Monthly Review* 33, no. 1 (May 1981): 25.

43. Jack Metzgar, "Plant Shutdowns and Worker Response: The Case of Johnstown, Pa.," *Socialist Review* 53 (September-October 1980): 38.

Chapter 6

1. John Judis, "How Reagan is Speeding the American Empire's Decline," *In These Times*, 4–10 November 1981, p. 15.

2. A prodigious and exciting literature on economic crisis and the "new international division of labor" has emerged since the mid-1970s. A basic bibliography in the field should include at least the following: Samir Amin, *Accumulation on a World Scale* (New York: Monthly Review,

1976); Samir Amin, *Unequal Development* (New York: Monthly Review, 1976); Samir Amin, "The World Crisis of the 1980's," *Monthly Review* 33, no. 2 (May–June 1981); Richard Barnet and Ronald Müller, *Global Reach* (New York: Simon and Schuster, 1974); Fred Block, *The Origins of International Economic Disorder* (Berkeley: University of California Press, 1977); Manuel Castells, *The Economic Crisis and American Society* (Princeton: Princeton University Press, 1980); Folker Fröbel et al., *The New International Division of Labor* (Cambridge, England: Cambridge University Press, 1980); Katherine Gibson, Julie Graham, Don Shakow, and Robert Ross, "A Theoretical Approach to Capital and Labor Restructuring" (Worcester, Mass.: CENTED, Clark University, 1980, mss.); Stephan Hymer, "The Multinational Corporation and the Law of Uneven Development," in Jagdish Bhagwati, ed., *Economics and World Order* (New York: Macmillan, 1970); Ernest Mandel, *Late Capitalism* (London: New Left Books, 1975); Doreen Massey and Richard Meegan, *The Anatomy of Job Loss* (London: Methuen, 1982); Alejandro Portes and John Walton, *Labor, Class, and the International System* (New York: Academic Press, 1981); A. Sivanandan, "Imperialism in the Silicon Age," *Monthly Review* 32, no. 3 (July-August 1980): 24–42; Union for Radical Political Economics (URPE), "Special Issue on Uneven Regional Development," *Review of Radical Political Economics* 10, no. 3 (Fall 1978); URPE, *U. S. Capitalism in Crisis* (New York: URPE, 1978); and Richard Walker and Michael Storper, "Capital and Industrial Location," *Progress in Human Geography* 5, no. 4 (1981): 473–509.

3. Organization for Economic Cooperation and Development, Committee on International Investment and Multinational Enterprises, "Recent International Direct Investment Trends," mimeographed (Paris, February 13, 1980), p. 58.

4. Ibid., p. 34.

5. Lawrence F. Franko, "Multinationals: The End of U. S. Dominance," *Harvard Business Review* 56, no. 6 (November-December 1978). By the mid-1970s, the annual rate of direct foreign investment by the other capitalist countries had also slowed, as the recession deepened. Among the thirteen OECD countries (including the United States) keeping such records, average annual growth of direct foreign investment during 1974–78 fell to 9.4 percent, compared with a rate of 15.6 percent per year between 1960 and 1973. Organization for Economic Cooperation and Development, "Investment Trends," p. 11.

6. Jack Baranson, "Technology Transfer: Effects on U. S. Competitiveness and Employment," in William G. Dewald, ed., *The Impact of International Trade and Investment on Employment: A Conference of the U. S. Department of Labor* (Washington, D. C.: U. S. Government Printing Office, 1978).

7. American firms also build plants for their foreign competitors directly. In the steel industry, for example, "Armco has built steel mills in Argentina; U. S. Steel has built mills in Brazil and Colombia and has been supervising the construction of Taiwan's integrated steelworks at Kaohsiung." Export-Import Bank, *Active Authorizations by Supplier as of February 28, 1978; Metal Bulletin*, October 26, 1975; and *New York Times*, 7 December 1978; all cited in Helen Shapiro and Steven Volk, "Steelyard Blues," *NACLA Report* 13, no. 1 (January–February 1979).

8. Steve Babson, "The Multinational Corporation and Labor," *Review of Radical Political Economics* 5, no. 1 (Spring 1973): 23–24.

9. James Kuhn, "Electrical Products," in Gerald Somers, ed., *Collective Bargaining: Contemporary American Experience* (Madison, Wisc: Industrial Relations Research Association, 1980), p. 218.

10. "U. S. Lifts Ban on Jet Engine Venture with France's SNECMA," *New York Times*, 23 June 1973, p. 37.

11. David Boulton, *F-16: Sale of the Century*, (Boston: WGBH Educational Foundation, 1979), p. 8.

12. The following is drawn from Jemadari Kamara, "Plant Closings and Apartheid: The Steel Connection," *Journal of Southern Africa Affairs*, forthcoming.

13. Daniel M. Holland and Stewart C. Myers, "Profitability and Capital Costs for Manufacturing Corporations," *American Economic Review* 70, no. 2 (May 1980): 321. While there is some dispute as to whether the drop in profitability is a permanent or cyclical feature of the economy, other studies support the basic point of Holland and Myers. Martin Feldstein and Lawrence Summers note, for example, that "the year 1970 appears to mark the beginning of this new 'low return' period." See Martin Feldstein and Lawrence Summers, "Is the Rate of Profit Falling?" *Brookings Papers on Economic Activity* 1 (1977): 221.

Notes

14. Quoted in Eleanore Carruth, "K-Mart has to Open Some New Doors on the Future," *Fortune*, July 1977, p. 144.

15. "A Note on the Boston Consulting Group Concept of Competitive Analysis and Corporate Strategy," Harvard Business School, Intercollegiate Case Clearing House, Case no. 9–175, revised June 1976.

16. William Foote Whyte, Statement in Support of the Voluntary Employee Ownership and Community Stabilization Act, H.R. 11222, before the U. S. House of Representatives, March 20, 1978, p. 19. Interestingly, in the first year after the discarded plant was bought by its workers through an Employee Stock Ownership Plan, it earned a 17 percent after-tax profit, "a level community residents say they are more than happy to tolerate." Daniel Zwerdling, *Democracy at Work* (New York: Harper & Row, 1980).

17. "In all cases, the ultimate consideration was: 'Does this operation have the potential to produce a 25 percent pretax return on assets employed?'" Genesco, Inc., *1977 Annual Report*, Nashville, Tenn., p. 2. By contrast, the average rate of return on total assets of a very successful apparel conglomerate, the VF Corporation (formerly Vanity Fair), was only 8.6 percent in 1976. And that average includes what the firm's managers call their "very profitable" overseas operation. *Annual 10-K Report to the Securities and Exchange Commission, VF Corp.*, December 31, 1977. Obviously, some managements are greedier—or simply have lower tolerances for deferred gratification—than others.

18. "There's More than Ships and Steel in the Lykes Family Vault," *Fortune*, 17 July 1978, p. 56.

19. "Give it a Shot," *The New Englander* (now *New England Business*), 25, no. 7 (November 1978): 57.

20. Belden H. Daniels et al., *An Investigation of the Impact of Acquisition on the Acquired Firm* (Cambridge, Mass.: Counsel for Community Development Inc., 1981), p. 156.

21. Whyte, Statement, pp. 19–20.

22. Daniels et al., *Investigation*, p. 155.

23. "Big Oil's Move into Retailing," *Chain Store Age Executive*, September 1976, p. 30.

24. Shapiro and Volk, "Steelyard Blues," pp. 14–15.

25. United States Steel Corp., *Annual Reports and 10-K Reports to the Securities and Exchange Commission*, Pittsburgh, Pennsylvania, 1976–1979.

26. David Moberg, "Crazy Logic Dictates Pullman Closing," *In These Times*, 5–11 November 1980, p. 6.

27. "Foreign Investment Invades New England," *New England Business*, 1, no. 16 (1 October 1979): 10.

28. John Blair, *Economic Concentration* (New York: Harcourt, Brace, 1972), p. 225.

29. Quoted in Janet Novack, "Merger Mania: Some Say Philadelphia Has Lost," Philadelphia *Bulletin*, 10 March 1980, pp. B13–15.

30. "Big Steel Jumps In," *New York Times*, 22 November 1981, p. F20.

31. Berkeley Bedell, "Merger Fever: Feeding Inflation and Starving Productivity," *Des Moines Register*, 6 August 1981, p. 14–A. Bedell is the former Chairperson of the Subcommittee on Antitrust of the U. S. House Small Business Committee and a Representative from the 6th District of Iowa.

32. Quoted in "The New Urge to Merge," *Newsweek*, 27 July 1981, p. 57.

33. Bureau of Labor Statistics, U. S. Department of Labor, *Employment and Earnings for the United States: 1909–1980* (Washington, D. C.: U. S. Government Printing Office, 1981).

34. David M. Gordon, "Capital-Labor Conflict and the Productivity Slowdown," *American Economic Review, Papers and Proceedings* 71, no. 2 (May 1981), pp. 30–35.

35. The earliest study we have been able to identify that explicitly examines this question is: C. Wright Mills and Melville Ulmer, *Small Business and Civic Welfare*, Report of the Small War Plants Corporation to the special Committee to Study Problems of American Small Business, U. S. Senate, 79th Cong., 2d sess., document no. 135, serial no. 11036, Washington, D. C., 1946.

36. Neal R. Pierce, *The New England States* (New York: W. W. Norton, 1976), p. 37.

37. Along with Los Angeles, Houston, and Dallas, these were the top ten locations of the home offices of the *Fortune* 500 in the late 1970s. Novack, "Merger Mania," p. B–15.

38. David L. Birch, *The Job Generation Process* (Cambridge, Mass.: MIT. Program on Neighborhood and Regional Change, 1979), pp. 45–46.

39. Peter Dicken, "The Multiplant Business Enterprise and Geographical Space: Some Issues in the Study of External Control and Regional Development," *Regional Studies* 10 (1976): 403.

40. Allen Pred, "The Interurban Transmission of Growth in Advanced Economics: Empirical Findings Versus Regional Planning Assumptions," *Regional Studies* 10 (1976): tables 1, 2, and 4. Pred interprets his own findings as casting strong doubt on those urban and regional development policies that presume the spatial propinquity of industries still implies the likely presence of so-called agglomeration economies: interindustry linkages that will transmit growth impulses from one local industry to another. As Stuart Holland does in *Capital vs. the Regions*, (New York: St. Martin's, 1975), Pred insists that the growth of sprawling networks of multiplant, multiregion, multinational corporations profoundly vitiates the theorems of orthodox regional economics. Spatial proximity by no means implies the presence of economic exchange between two business establishments when one or both are controlled from somewhere else.

41. Arthur Hochner and Daniel Zibman, "Plant Closings and Job Loss in Philadelphia—The Role of Multinationals and Absentee Control," manuscript (Philadelphia: Temple University, 1981).

42. Statements of David L. Birch, in Subcommittee on Antitrusts and Restraint of Trade Activities Affecting Small Business, Committee on Small Business, U. S. House of Representatives, *Hearings*, 96th Cong., 2d sess., 1980, pp. 231–35; and Alfred Dougherty, Jr., director, Bureau of Competition, Federal Trade Commission, Ibid.

43. Birch, Statements, p. 234.

44. Michael Booth, "Ownership of Industry: The Maine Case," Center for Community Economic Development, Cambridge, Mass., 1972; Jon G. Udell, "Social and Economic Consequences of the Merger Movement in Wisconsin," Graduate School of Business, University of Wisconsin, Wisconsin Economy Series No. 3., May 1969; Stanley Brue, "Local Employment and Payroll Impacts of Corporate Mergers," *Growth and Change* 6, no. 4 (October 1975): 8–13; and David Barkley, "Plant Ownership Characteristics and the Locational Stability of Rural Iowa Manufacturers," *Land Economics* 54, no. 1 (February 1978): 92–99. Barkley's main finding is "the tendency of independent concerns to be more locationally stable than [corporate] branch plants," p. 597.

45. Robert N. Stern and Howard Aldrich, "The Effect of Absentee Firm Control on Local Community Welfare: A Survey," in Subcommittee on Antitrust and Restraint of Trade Activities Affecting Small Business, *Hearings*, pp. 598–627.

46. Quoted in Richard B. McKenzie, *Restrictions on Business Mobility* (Washington, D. C.: American Enterprise Institute, 1979), p. 42.

47. Roger Schmenner, "The Location Decisions of Large, Multiplant Companies." Manuscript of the MIT-Harvard Joint Center for Urban Studies, Cambridge, 1980. The quotation is from a summary of findings distributed by Professor Schmenner through the Graduate School of Business Administration, Duke University, Durham, N. C., 1980, pp. 13, 15, 18.

48. Paul Luebke, Bob McMahon, and Jeff Risberg, "Selective Recruitment in North Carolina," *Working Papers* 6, no. 2 (March–April 1979): 17.

49. Transportation Systems Center, Report to the president from the secretary of transportation, *The U. S. Automobile Industry, 1980* (Washington D. C.: U. S. Department of Transportation, January 1981), figure E.7.

50. "G.E.'s Engine Group Will Set Up Airfoils Forge, Cast Plant in Kentucky," *American Metal Market*, 3 December 1979, p. 20.

51. Robert Porterfield, "As Costs Climb, Lumber Producers Close Down," *Boston Globe*, 2 December 1980, p. 36.

52. On September 17, 1980 Teague testified on the Brown and Williamson shutdown procedure before the U. S. Senate Committee on Labor and Human Resources; see Bureau of National Affairs, *Daily Labor Report*, 2 October 1980, pp. A1–A3 and D1–D3. However, this public testimony omitted a number of important points made earlier by Teague in a press release issued on April 18, 1980 in Louisville, the site of the closed plant. The quotation here is from the latter document, p. 4. In contrast to many of the companies whose practices we have studied, Brown and Williamson provided its workers and their unions advance notification, severance pay, six-month continuance of life and medical insurance, transfer rights to the Macon plant for 325 of the 3,000 Louisville workers, moving expense assistance for this group, and counseling, job placement assistance, and company-financed retraining for the rest. Brown and Williamson even used its considerable influence with the governor of Kentucky to obtain a waiver of state law that

would have prevented those laid off from drawing both severance pay and unemployment insurance simultaneously. These unusually equitable arrangements were designed to buy the company an orderly three-year transition to the Macon consolidation.

53. Kuhn, "Electrical Products," pp. 212, 216.

54. The following is drawn from United Auto Workers of Detroit, "Workers Rope a Runaway —But the Tug-of-War Continues," *Solidarity*, 10 December 1979, pp. 4–5.

55. *Boston Globe*, 21 October 1979, p. 40.

56. "Why the Wayward Plants?" *Dollars and Sense*, April 1979, pp. 6–7.

57. Babson, "Multinational Corporation," p. 27.

58. Peter Baird and Ed McCaughnan, "Hit and Run: U. S. Runaway Shops on the Mexican Border," *North American Committee on Latin America, Report* 9, no. 5 (July-August 1975): 7.

59. " 'Little Detroits' Boom in Mexico," *New York Times*, 3 March 1980, p. D1.

60. *Boston Globe*, 1 September 1979, p. C1.

61. Quoted in a memo of the Massachusetts Coalition to Save Jobs, "General Instrument's Responsibility for Plant Closings in Western Massachusetts," December 1980, p. 1.

62. A. Sivanandan, "Imperialism," p. 27. This article is *mandatory* reading for anyone who still believes the romantic notion that the trade zones are rapidly raising the level of living of the people who work in them. In chapter 7, we will present a detailed critique of the urban enterprise-zone proposal, which has its roots in the trade-zone experience overseas.

63. Memo from George Kohl, "Foreign Trade Zones," The Center for Development Policy, Washington D. C., February 1979.

64. The following is based on Charles Craypo, "Collective Bargaining in the Conglomerate, Multinational Firm: Litton's Shutdown of Royal Typewriter," *Industrial and Labor Relations Review* 29, no. 1 (October 1975): 3–25.

65. Craypo, "Collective Bargaining," p. 17.

66. Ibid., p. 19.

67. Rich Kronish, "Crisis in the West European Automobile Industry," *Monthly Review* 31, no. 4 (September 1979): 35–36.

68. Quoted in Marg Hainer and Joanne Koslofsky, "The World Car: Shifting Into Overdrive," *North American Committee on Latin America, Report* 13, no. 4 (July-August 1979): 5.

69. Ibid., p. 25, based upon a report by Maryann Keller of the research department of Kidder, Peabody and Co., Inc., "Ford of Europe," July 19, 1978, p. 15.

70. Brazil has become an especially important source area for the European auto makers. VW now ships engines and gearboxes from Brazil to West Germany. FIAT-Brazil sends engine blocks to Argentina, cylinder heads to Belgium, rings and plates to the Philippines, and other parts to Australia. Hainer and Koslofsky, "The World Car," p. 27. Similarly, Ford's Canadian assembly plants now make "U. S.-produced" Mustangs with French transmissions and Brazilian engines. Kronish, "Crisis," p. 43. Such intensified international competition among the several giant makers of world cars (with their respective networks of branch plants and sources) is already leading to a crisis of overcapacity, which previously occurred in steel, with the railroads, and in commercial aviation. A British government research institute already forecasts "35 percent overcapacity in western Europe for the next seven years, which implies intense competition [and] low profits." It may also lead to a greater degree of international labor cooperation, as workers experience a growing sense of urgency at the extent of dislocation resulting from company rationalization schemes. To some extent, this is already occurring. For example, the Organization for Economic Cooperation and Development (OECD) recently called for the prohibition of the multinationals' practice of moving certain key employees around from one country to another, as a way of breaking strikes. International labor unions have been seeking to halt such corporate tactics for years. OECD finally spoke out officially when the Hertz Corporation attempted to bring foreign employees into its operations in Denmark to maintain services during a local strike.

71. Ron Chernow, "Grey Flannel Goons: The Latest in Union-Busting," *Working Papers* 8, no. 1 (January–February 1981).

72. *Boston Globe*, 21 October 1979, p. 40.

73. Robert Goodman, *The Last Entrepreneurs*, (New York: Simon and Schuster, 1979); Bennett Harrison and Sandra Kanter, "The Political Economy of State Job-Creation Business Incentives," *Journal of the American Institute of Planners* 44, no. 4 (October 1978): 424–35; Jerry Jacobs, *Bidding for Business: Corporate Auctions and the Fifty Disunited States* (Washington, D. C.: Public Interest Research Group, 1979); Michael Kieschnick, *Taxes and Growth* (Washing-

ton, D. C.: Council of State Planning Agencies, 1981); Michael Luger, "The Regional Employ-ment Effects of Business Tax Incentives" (Ph.D. diss., University of California at Berkeley, 1981); and Roger Vaughn, *State Taxation and Economic Development* (Washington, D. C.: Council of State Planning Agencies, 1979).

74. Jim Strang, "Mississippi's Sun Shines for Business," *Cleveland Plain Dealer*, 20 September 1979, p. 12-A.

75. Jim Strang, "Eyes of Texas are Upon Us," *Cleveland Plain Dealer*, 22 September 1979, p. 11-A.

76. U. S. Senate, Subcommittee of the Committee on Interstate and Foreign Commerce, *Investigation of Closing of Nashua, New Hampshire Mills and Operations of Textron, Inc.*, 80th Cong., 2d sess. (Washington, D. C.: U. S. Government Printing Office, 1948).

77. Testimony by Belden Daniels in "The Effects of Tax and Spending Limitations on the Formation of Business Tax Policy," *American University Law Review* 29 (1980): 264–67.

78. Gary Blonston, "Poletown: The Profits, the Loss," *Detroit* (the Sunday Magazine of the Detroit Free Press) 22 November 1981.

79. To compute the tax rates appearing in table 6.4, we summed the value of manufacturing shipments, the value of retail and wholesale trade receipts, and the receipts from service industries to arrive at a figure for the "total value of business receipts." Total state and local corporate income tax revenue and business property tax revenue by state is derived from statistics appearing in Vaughn, *State Taxation*, table 14, pp. 74–75. These estimates probably overstate the true tax rate because the tax data refer to 1977 and 1975, while the business receipt data are for 1972. For data on the latter, see U. S. Department of Commerce, Bureau of the Census, *Statistical Abstract of the United States, 1975* (Washington, D. C.: U. S. Government Printing Office, 1975), tables 1267, 1317, 1323, and 1331.

80. Most experts now believe that *federal* tax incentives to business do not cause relocation of capital either, inasmuch as they reward companies that are relocating. According to Urban Institute economist George Peterson, "Federal Tax Policy and the Shaping of Urban Develop-ment," in Arthur P. Solomon, ed., *The Prospective City* (Cambridge, Mass.: MIT Press, 1980), until recently, six provisions of the U. S. Tax Code promoted (or rewarded) capital shift—from older urban centers to the suburbs, and from metropolitan areas in the Frostbelt generally into rural areas, especially in the Sunbelt. The six are: (1) the unwillingness of the Internal Revenue Service before 1978 to consider land as a depreciable asset; (2) the favorable treatment of new building construction versus rehabilitation of older structures, in terms of eligibility for accelerated depreciation; (3) the bias in the Investment Tax Credit in favor of the purchase of new vintages of equipment (which favors new construction again, because of the complementarity between vintages of plant and vintages of tools); (4) the ability to write off the costs of scrapping old plants (and land), and any moving expenses, against profits earned elsewhere in the company; (5) the federal income-tax deductibility of interest earned on investment in state or local Industrial Development Bonds, which nearly all jurisdictions now float on behalf of companies they are trying to attract into or retain within their borders; and (6) the IRS' encouragement of single-family, low-density home ownership through the deductibility of mortgage interest, a provision that promotes suburbanization and facilitates long-distance interregional population migration, thereby helping relocating firms to re-form labor pools at their new locations. In fiscal year 1978, this group of so-called tax expenditures cost the U. S. Treasury $11 billion in foregone revenue, with 80 percent of the subsidy going to recipients in the upper one fifth of the income distribution. U. S. Department of Housing and Urban Development and U. S. Economic Development Administration, *Local Economic Development Tools and Techniques* (Washington, D. C., U. S. Government Printing Office, 1979), p. 34.

Michael Luger in "Regional Employment" has shown that the kinds of corporations that tend to benefit the most from tax credits, accelerated depreciation allowances, and other business incentives are those whose products serve growing markets; whose plants operate at a high rate of capacity utilization, at a large scale, using equipment-intensive production processes; and are earning high profits so that there is something to shelter. Tax incentives do not *cause* or geographically redirect investment so much as they ratify it. For example, over the period 1963–76, after accounting for differences in their industry mix and scales of operations, Los Angeles's manufacturing plants qualified for about 15 percent more in tax credits per production hour than Philadelphia's plants. Luger's interpretation is that the government used the tax code to reward corporations already investing in Southern California with a bonus.

Notes

In terms of this analysis, the allegedly revolutionary "supply-side" Tax Recovery Act of 1981 was really only more of the same (at least with regard to its treatment of *business* taxation). This most recent of the six post-1953 tax "reforms" greatly accelerates industry's ability to write off older capital. Also, while it has been true for some time that a business could shut down a plant and write it off as an operating loss to be charged against profits earned from other operations, with the new tax program a company can now carry that loss "forward" on its books for up to fifteen years *after* the date of the shutdown. Similarly, unused investment tax (and certain other) credits can be carried forward. Or companies may take tax credits for which they are currently eligible but cannot profitably use at the moment, and *sell them on the open market*—like hogs and wheat futures on the Chicago Commodity Exchange—to other companies which are eligible but which have exhausted their own credits: the so-called tax leasing arrangement.

The whole program increases corporate profits directly, by reducing business tax liability, thereby continuing the process by which federal tax policy has been used since the 1950s to shelter American industry from having to experience the full brunt of global competition. Luger has shown that each of these tax break "fixes" followed a period of shrinking corporate profits. This is a far different picture of the true effects of tax "reform" than is usually presented. Whether these tax policies have stimulated or redirected private investment now seems quite doubtful; that they have made the rich richer seems absolutely certain.

81. Office of Research and Statistics, Social Security Administration, *Public Assistance Statistics*, June 1979, tables 4 and 8.

82. This is the main theme of the path-breaking book by Frances Fox Piven and Richard Cloward, *Regulating the Poor* (New York: Random House, 1971).

83. *AFL-CIO News* 26, no. 34 (August 22, 1981): 1. What *is* certain about the Tax Recovery Act of 1981 (which, it should be noted, was supported overwhelmingly by Democrats as well as Republicans) is that, with this most recent set of changes in the laws by which capital is taxed, a process underway for three decades is finally approaching its logical conclusion. For all practical purposes, the corporate income tax in the United States has been repealed. Thirty years ago, one dollar out of every four collected by the U. S. Treasury came from taxing business profits. In 1981 that figure had fallen to one in ten. The *New York Times* says of this history:

> Though the course was at times erratic, the overall direction has been unmistakable: American business has had to bear a smaller and smaller share of the Federal tax burden, while the burden on the individual taxpayer, in income taxes as well as payroll levies [for social security], has risen steeply. (2 August 1981, p. 1F)

As one law professor told the *Times*, "We now seem to be moving to a zero or even negative tax on capital." The catch is that, while the official (statutory) maximum rate on corporate income remains high, the *effective* tax—the rate that companies *really* pay, after taking all of their various credits and allowances—has fallen precipitously.

84. Neal Pierce, "Corporate Mergers That Ruin Cities," *Washington Post*, 27 December 1981, p. D2.

85. Powerful business organizations seem fully aware of these contradictions. For example, in the words of the prestigious Committee for Economic Development, a private nonprofit business research group, "The power of public employees to cause irritation or inconvenience to the public need not be totally curbed. To do so would be excessively costly, even if it were possible. Such action might also unnecessarily deprive employees of a measure of power that it may be desirable for them to have in order to protect their own interests and dissuade them from seeking power through other routes." Committee for Economic Development, *Improving Management of the Public Work Force*, New York: Committee for Economic Development, November 1978, p. 89. In a similar vein, *Business Week* warns that the president's budget meat-axe is beginning to cut deeply into the public infrastructure—highways, airports, bridges, hospitals, and sewer and water systems. Apart from the public furor this is creating, such public sector "deindustrialization" is undermining the capacity of private industry to maintain its own levels of productivity. "State and Local Government in Trouble," *Business Week*, 26 October 1981, p. 89. Because its staunchest advocates (notably the president) are choosing to ignore such advice, "Reaganomics" is far more of a gamble than even its most self-critical supporters imagine.

Chapter 7

1. Godfrey Hodgson, "State of the Nation," *Boston Globe Magazine*, 16 January 1981, p. 16.

2. Clinton Rossiter, *Conservatism in America* (New York: Random House, 1962), p. 21.

3. Lester Thurow, *The Zero-Sum Society* (New York: Basic Books, 1980), p. 210; "The Reindustrialization of America," *Business Week*, 30 June 1980.

4. Quoted in Walter Goodman, "Irving Kristol: Patron Saint of the New Right," *New York Times Magazine*, 6 December 1981, p. 202.

5. This notion finds its basis in the now famous "Laffer Curve" developed by the University of Southern California economist Arthur Laffer and publicized by Jude Wanniski in *The Way the World Works* (New York: Basic Books, 1979).

6. See, for example, F. Thomas Juster, "Saving, Economic Growth, and Economic Policy," *Economic Outlook USA*, Summer 1981, p. 54.

7. Council of Economic Advisors, *Economic Report of the President 1981* (Washington, D. C.: U. S. Government Printing Office, 1981), table B–23, p. 260.

8. Paul Sweezy, "Are Low Savings Ruining the U. S. Economy," *Monthly Review* 32, no. 7 (December 1980): 4.

9. "Money is There for the Capital Spending," *Business Week*, 18 September 1978, pp. 97–126.

10. Martin Holmer, "Urban, Regional, and Labor Supply Effects of a Reduction in Federal Individual Income Tax Rates," in Norman J. Glickman, ed., *The Impacts of Federal Policies* (Baltimore: Johns Hopkins University Press, 1980), p. 505.

11. Edith Stokey and Richard Zeckhauser, *A Primer for Policy Analysis* (New York: W. W. Norton, 1978), pp. 299–300.

12. Garrett Hardin, "The Tragedy of the Commons," *Science* 162, no. 3859 (December 13, 1968) as paraphrased in Stokey and Zeckhauser, *Policy Analysis*, p. 305.

13. E. J. Mishan, *Economics for Social Decisions* (New York: Praeger Publishers, 1973), p. 89.

14. Stokey and Zeckhauser, *Policy Analysis*, p. 308.

15. Douglas F. Dowd, *The Twisted Dream*, 2d ed., (Cambridge, Mass.: Winthrop Publishers, 1977) p. 92.

16. Ibid, p. 90.

17. For more detail on this account of uneven development in the American economy, see Barry Bluestone, "Economic Crisis and the Law of Uneven Development," *Politics and Society* 2, no. 4 (Fall 1972).

18. This point is made quite persuasively in Charles Lindblom, *Politics and Markets* (New York: Basic Books, 1977), pp. 173–74.

19. The classic book on the subject of the tension between "economy" and "society"—and of the historical impossibility of a pure market economy "disembedded" from other social relations—is Karl Polanyi, *The Great Transformation* (New York: Rinehart, 1944).

20. Arthur Okun, *The Political Economy of Prosperity* (New York: W. W. Norton, 1970), p. 31.

21. Barry Bluestone, "The Tripartite Economy: Labor Markets and the Working Poor," *Poverty and Human Resources* 5, no. 4 (July–August 1970): 15–17.

22. Bureau of the Census, U. S. Department of Commerce, *Current Population Reports*, (Washington, D. C.: U. S. Government Printing Office), series P–23, no. 28 and P–60, nos. 81, 115, 119, 123, and 124.

23. Bureau of the Census, U. S. Department of Commerce, *Statistical Abstract of the United States 1980*, (Washington D. C.: U. S. Government Printing Office, 1980), p. 761.

24. Ibid., table 372, p. 217.

25. Raford Boddy and James Crotty, "Class Conflict and Macro-Policy: The Political Business Cycle," *Review of Radical Political Economics* 7, no. 1 (Spring 1975).

26. Ronald Alsop, "Property Tax Abatements Proliferate, but Need is Disputed," *Wall Street Journal*, 30 June 1978, p. 1.

27. Steven R. Weisman, "The Swap: Reagan's New Federalism-Bold Strike or Smokescreen," *New York Times*, 31 January 1982, p. 1E.

28. From the *New York Times* as quoted by Alfred J. Watkins, "Felix Rohatyn's Biggest Deal,"

29. Felix Rohatyn, "Reconstructing America," *New York Review of Books*, 5 February 1981.

30. Felix Rohatyn, "The Disaster Facing the North," *New York Review of Books*, 22 January 1981, p. 16.

31. For a fascinating history of the RFC, see Edward Robb Ellis, *A Nation in Torment: The Great American Depression 1929–1939* (New York: Capricorn Books, 1971).

32. Felix Rohatyn, "A New RFC is Proposed for Business," *New York Times*, 1 December 1974, Sect. 3, p. 1.

33. Watkins, "Biggest Deal," pp. 50–51. Although he has been uncharacteristically silent during the current debate, Harvard labor economist John Dunlop is generally considered to be the most thoughtful long-standing academic advocate for greater corporatist planning of the American economy.

34. Lester Thurow, "Reindustrialization and Jobs," *Working Papers* 7, no. 6 (November–December 1980): 49.

35. Ellis, *Nation in Torment*, pp. 191–92.

36. Quoted in Ibid., p. 194.

37. This discussion of MITI is heavily influenced by the work of Ezra Vogel, *Japan as Number 1* (New York: Harper & Row, 1979); and M. Y. Yoshino, *Japan's Managerial System: Tradition and Innovation* (Cambridge, Mass.: MIT Press, 1968).

38. On the textile situation, see Philip H. Trezise, "Industrial Policy in Japan" (Paper prepared for the Conference on Industrial Revitalization: Toward a National Industrial Policy, Hubert H. Humphrey Institute, University of Minnesota, April 26–28, 1981), p. 5.

39. "Japan Inc. Goes International with High Technology," *Business Week*, 14 December 1981, pp. 40–41.

40. "How Japan will Finance its Technology Strategy," *Business Week*, 14 December 1981, p. 51.

41. Quoted in Ibid., p. 54.

42. In a high-wage, high-skill industry like the aircraft industry, the average annual employee turnover rate approached 17 percent between 1957 and 1975. In a more volatile industry like retail trade, turnover rates of 45 to 50 percent are not uncommon. See Barry Bluestone, Peter Jordan, and Mark Sullivan, *Aircraft Industry Dynamics* (Boston: Auburn House, 1981), p. 139; and Barry Bluestone, Patricia Hanna, Sarah Kuhn, and Laura Moore, *The Retail Revolution: Market Transformation, Investment, and Labor in the Modern Department Store* (Boston: Auburn House, 1981), pp. 85–86.

43. Vogel, *Japan*, p. 137.

44. Robert E. Cole, *Work, Mobility, and Participation: A Comparative Study of American and Japanese Industry* (Berkeley, Calif.: University of California Press, 1979), p. 67.

45. This criticism of American management is being leveled by an increasing number of business experts and business managers themselves. "Managers Who Are No Longer Entrepreneurs," *Business Week* 30 June 1980, pp. 74–82, provided a blistering attack on managers who seem to be interested only in good quarterly profit figures. Robert Hayes and William Abernathy, "Managing Our Way to Economic Deadline," *Harvard Business Review* 58, no. 4, (July–August 1980): 68, have put the issue thus:

> Our experience suggests that, to an unprecedented degree, success in most industries today requires an organizational commitment to compete in the marketplace on technological grounds—that is, to compete over the *long run* by offering superior products. Yet guided by what they took to be the newest and best principles of management, American managers have increasingly directed their attention elsewhere. These new principles, despite their sophistication and widespread usefulness, encourage a preference for (1) analytic detachment rather than the insight that comes from "hands on" experience and (2) short-term cost reduction rather than long-term development of technological competitiveness. *It is this new managerial gospel, we feel, that has played a major role in undermining the vigor of American industry.* [Emphasis added]

The Hayes-Abernathy critique focuses on the incentive structures used by the modern American corporation to motivate their managerial corps. These, they argue, have led to a form of competitive myopia about the types of investments made and to the short-term low-risk planning horizon that has come to dominate many corporate board rooms.

46. Bluestone et al., *Aircraft Industry Dynamics*, p. 134.

47. Vogel, *Japan*, p. 46.

48. John Junkerman, "Japan Worship," *Working Papers* 9, no. 1 (January–February 1982): 65.

49. Vogel, *Japan*, p. 151.

50. Norman S. Fielche, "Productivity and Labor Mobility in Japan, the United Kingdom, and the United States," *New England Economic Review*, November–December 1981, pp. 35–36.

51. Yoshino, *Japan's Managerial System*, pp. 73–75.

52. Shuichi Kato, "The Japan Myth Reconsidered," *Democracy* 1, no. 3 (July 1981).

53. This estimate is based on a recalculation by Robert F. Cole of data found in Ronald Dore, *British Factory–Japanese Factory* (Berkeley, Calif.: University of California Press, 1973), pp. 304–05; cited in Cole, *Work*, p. 61.

54. Vogel, *Japan*, pp. 137–39. The 80 percent subcontracting ratio is reported in William J. Abernathy, Kim B. Clark, and Alan M. Kantrow, "The New Industrial Competition," *Harvard Business Review* 59, no. 5 (September–October 1981): 73.

55. Vogel, *Japan*, p. 149.

56. Cole and Junkerman quotes from Junkerman, "Japan," p. 65.

57. David L. Birch, "Who Creates Jobs?" *The Public Interest* 65 (Fall 1981): 71.

58. David M. Gordon, *The Working Poor: Toward a State Agenda* (Washington, D. C.: Council of State Planning Agencies, 1979), pp. 54–59; and Harvey A. Garn and Larry C. Ledebur, *The Estimation of Development Impacts* (Washington, D. C.: The Urban Institute, March 1981).

59. David L. Birch, "Generating New Jobs: Are Government Incentives Effective?" *Commentary* (magazine of the National Council for Urban Economic Development), July 1979, p. 4.

60. Roger Schmenner, "The Manufacturing Location Decision" Manuscript of the Harvard Business School and MIT-Harvard Joint Center for Urban Studies, March 1978, pp. 4–108. See also "Some Firms Fight Ills of Bigness by Keeping Employee Units Small," *Wall Street Journal*, 5 February 1982, p. 1.

61. Schmenner provides some research support for the hypothesis that the need to improve managerial control over the work force is indeed a significant (partial) motivation for the shift to smaller branch plants at new sites—a "downsized greenfield location strategy." Roger Schmenner, "Choosing New Industrial Capacity: On-Site Expansion, Branching and Relocation," *Quarterly Journal of Economics* 95, no. 2 (August 1980): 105.

62. Roger Schmenner, "Look Beyond the Obvious in Plant Location," *Harvard Business Review* 57, no. 1, (January–February 1979): 126–32.

63. Peter Hall, "Enterprise Zones: A Justification," *International Journal of Urban and Regional Research*, forthcoming.

64. Ibid.

65. Stuart M. Butler, *Enterprise Zones: Pioneering in the Inner City* (Washington, D. C.: The Heritage Foundation, 1980); reprinted in Robert Friedman and William Schweke, eds., *Expanding the Opportunity to Produce: Revitalizing the American Economy through New Enterprise Development* (Washington, D. C.: The Corporation for Enterprise Development, 1981), p. 288.

66. William W. Goldsmith, "Bringing the Third World Home," *Working Papers* 9, no. 2, (March–April 1982), p. 27.

67. See Arthur Blaustein and Geoffrey Faux, *The Star-Spangled Hustle: Black Capitalism and White Power* (New York: Doubleday, 1972); Bennett Harrison, *Urban Economic Development: Suburbanization, Minority Opportunity, and the Condition of the Central City* (Washington, D. C.: The Urban Institute, 1974), pp. 147–64; William K. Tabb, *The Political Economy of the Black Ghetto* (New York: W. W. Norton, 1970) ch. 4; and Barry Bluestone, "Black Capitalism: The Path to Black Liberation?" *Review of Radical Political Economics* 1, no. 1 (May 1969).

68. Harrison, *Urban Economic Development*, p. 163 and the references therein.

69. Bennett Harrison, "Rationalization, Restructuring, and Corporate Reorganization: The Economic Transformation of New England since World War II" (*Working Paper* no. 72, of the MIT-Harvard Joint Center for Urban Studies, Cambridge, Mass., February 1982).

70. On the nature of the labor process in the semiconductor industry, especially as regards the role of women workers, see Rachel Grossman, "Women's Place in the Integrated Circuit," *Southeast Asia Chronicle* 66 (January–February 1979): 2–17; and Robert Howard, "Second Class in Silicon Valley," *Working Papers* 8, no. 5 (September–October 1981): 20–31.

71. Another possibility—not really inconsistent with the sweatshop forecast—is that the zones located near harbors and major airports might attract multinational corporations seeking new sites for transshipping operations: warehousing, light assembly, or final processing. In such cases, however, it would be the nullification of the customs duties—the freeport aspect—that provided

however, it would be the nullification of the customs duties—the freeport aspect—that provided the attraction, and this is in fact *not* a major element in the American version of the plan. Andrew Brimmer, "Can Enterprise Zones Work?" *Black Enterprise* 11, no. 3 (March 1981): 71.

72. Jack F. Kemp, "Greenlining Urban America: Enterprise Zones for Economic Growth," *Commentary* (National Council for Urban Economic Development) 4, no. 3 (July 1980): 5.

73. Panels of small business owners are on record as explicitly rejecting the need for tax breaks. Instead, in addition to venture capital, they most often express a need for accessible, low-interest operating capital and—most of all—*strong demand for their products.* Edward Humberger, "The Enterprise Zone Fallacy," *Journal of Community Action,* September–October 1981, p. 24.

74. cf. "State and Local Government in Trouble: Special Report," *Business Week,* 26 October 1981, pp. 135–55; and Pat Choate and Susan Walter, *America in Ruins* (Washington, D. C.: Council of State Planning Agencies, 1981).

75. A. Sivanandan, "Imperialism in the Silicon Age," *Monthly Review* 32, no. 3, (July–August 1980).

76. Goldsmith, "Third World," p. 30.

Chapter 8

1. For example, Otis L. Graham, Jr., *Toward a Planned Society: From Roosevelt to Nixon* (New York: Oxford University Press, 1976), chs. 1, 2.

2. David Rogers and Thomas Oliphant, "The Reagan Shift: Arms First," *Boston Globe,* 18 January 1982, p. 1.

3. Fred Barbash, "States Can Tax Companies' Outside Earnings," *Washington Post,* 20 March 1980, p. 1. Also *United States Law Week,* 48 LW, March 18, 1980, pp. 4306–16.

4. For a more detailed discussion of tax reform, see Barry Bluestone and Bennett Harrison, "Economic Development, The Public Sector, and Full Employment," in Marcus G. Raskin, ed., *The Federal Budget and Social Reconstruction* (New Brunswick, N.J.: Transaction, 1978), pp. 439–51. Also see Joseph A. Pechman, *Federal Tax Policy,* 3d ed. (Washington, D. C.: The Brookings Institution, 1977), pp. 169–79.

5. Bob Baugh, Department of Research, Education and Collective Bargaining Coordination, International Woodworkers of America, "Shutdown. Mill Closures and Woodworkers," International Woodworkers of America, Portland, Oregon, December 3, 1979. On the standard rights of employees in what are legally referred to as "work-removal situations," as guaranteed by the National Labor Relations Act—and on the limits of strictly collective bargaining solutions—see National Lawyers Guild, *Plant Closings and Runaway Industries: Strategies for Labor* (Washington, D. C.: National Labor Law Center, 1981).

6. Baugh, "Shutdown," p. 32.

7. Labor Union Study Tour Participants, *Economic Dislocation: Plant Closings, Plant Relocations, and Plant Conversion,* United Automobile Workers, United Steelworkers of America, and the Int'l Assoc. of Machinists, Washington, D. C., May 1, 1979, pp. 7–8. See also C & R Associates, *Plant Location Legislation and Regulation in the United States and Western Europe: A Survey,* Federal Trade Commission, Washington, D. C., January, 1979.

8. For a legal history and analysis of proposed plant-closing bills in the United States and Canada, see Joseph Cipparone, "Advance Notice of Plant Closings: Toward National Legislation," *University of Michigan Journal of Law Reform* 14, no. 2 (Winter 1981).

9. There is a long legal history to this case, and more generally to the question of a company's duty to engage in "shutdown bargaining." See John D. Feerick, "Partial Closures and Duty to Bargain," *New York Law Review,* March 6, 1981.

10. Quoted by Liz Bass, "Runaway Plants Leave Workers Out in Cold," *The Citizen Advocate* (Boston), March 1979, p. 3.

11. Richard McKenzie, *Restrictions on Business Mobility* (Washington, D. C.: American Enterprise Institute, 1979) pp. 57, 60. See also Richard McKenzie, "Frustrating Business Mobility," *Regulation,* May–June, 1980.

12. *Providence Evening Bulletin,* December 28, 1979, p. A-6.

13. Daniel D. Cook, "Laws to Curb Plant Closures," *Industry Week,* 4 February 1980, p. 41. For other critiques of the proposed legislation, from an explicit or implicit business perspective,

Industrial Development, November–December 1979, p. 4; Audrey Freedman, "Plant Closed—No Jobs," *Across the Board* (Magazine of the Conference Board), August 1980; and John S. Hekman and John S. Strong, "Is There a Case for Plant Closings?" *New England Economic Review,* July/August, 1980.

14. California is developing a set of guidelines for managing the consequences of plant shutdowns that includes the assembly of similar information. See a manuscript draft of the Office of Planning and Policy Development, Employment Development Department, State of California, "Plant Closure Planning Guidebook," Sacramento, October 1981. Moreover, a statewide network of California labor union locals and plant-closing coalitions is developing its own standardized (and computerized) shop-level information system for anticipating shutdowns.

15. Edward Altman and Thomas McGough, "Evaluation of a Company as a Going Concern," *Journal of Accountancy* 138, no. 6 (December 1974): 50–57. Altman was recently hired by the state of Illinois to develop an early warning system for predicting shutdowns there.

16. Martin Carnoy and Derek Shearer, *Economic Democracy* (White Plains, N.Y.: M. E. Sharpe, 1980).

17. Ira Magaziner and Robert Reich, *Minding America's Business* (New York: Harcourt Brace Jovanovich, 1982); and Lester C. Thurow, *The Zero-Sum Society* (New York: Basic Books, 1980).

18. Douglas F. Lamont, *Foreign State Enterprises: A Threat to American Business* (New York: Basic Books, 1979).

19. Stuart Holland, ed., *Beyond Capitalist Planning,* (New York: St. Martin's, 1978), p. 3.

20. All schools of economic policy now teach this to their students as conventional wisdom, and it is actually rather remarkable that the conservatives presently running the government have chosen to ignore it. A good standard text is Walter Nicholson, *Intermediate Microeconomics and its Applications,* 2d ed. (Hinsdale, Ill.: Dryden, 1979), chs. 19–20.

21. Raskin, ed., *Federal Budget.* A fifth sector, education, was identified as in need of radical organizational restructuring to promote student and parent participation and experimentation in teaching methods, more than new capital investment *per se.*

22. On the history of this conflict of interest, see Bradford Snell, "The Right to Travel," in Raskin, *Federal Budget.*

23. The Kennedy proposal is reported in Gar Alperovitz and Geoffrey Faux, "An Economic Program for the Coming Decade," *Democratic Review,* November 1975.

24. For one such study of the possibilities for converting old automobile plants to new uses, conducted by researchers with the Detroit City Council and the United Auto Workers, respectively, see Jack Russell and Dan Luria, *Rational Reindustrialization* (Detroit, Mich.: Widgetripper Press, 1981).

25. Carnoy and Shearer, *Economic Democracy,* pp. 221–30.

26. Quoted in John P. Beck, "Unions, the Economy, and the Right to Useful Work," Program in Social Economy and Social Policy, Boston College, *The Social Report* 2, no. 2 (December 1981): 5.

27. Carnoy and Shearer, *Economic Democracy,* pp. 229–30.

28. Jack Metzgar, "Plant Shutdowns and Worker Response," *Socialist Review* 10, no. 5 (September–October 1980): 11–14. For a wonderfully detailed history of the politics of organizing such a coalition at the local level, see Thomas Fuectman, "The Ecumenical Coalition of the Mahoning Valley" (Manuscript at Lake Forest College, Lake Forest, Ohio, 1981).

29. Quoted in Staughton Lynd, "What Happened to Youngstown," *Radical America* 15, no. 4 (July–August 1981): 43–44.

30. Harley Shaiken's criticism of the auto companies' demands for wage givebacks in "UAW Concessions Won't Save Jobs," *Dollars and Sense* 73 (January 1982).

31. Bruce M. Stave, ed., *Socialism and the Cities* (Port Washington, N.Y.: Kennikat, 1975); and Carnoy and Shearer, *Economic Democracy,* ch. 4.

32. Joseph Rayback, *A History of American Labor* (New York: The Free Press, 1966), p. 160.

33. Select Committee on Small Business, U. S. Senate, *The Role of the Federal Government in Employee Ownership of Business* (Washington, D. C.: U. S. Government Printing Office, January 1979).

34. Paul Bernstein, "Run Your Own Business," *Working Papers* 2, no. 2 (Summer 1974): 441–51.

35. Carnoy and Shearer, *Economic Democracy,* pp. 149–52; and Anna Gutierrez-Johnson and William F. Whyte, "The Mondragon System of Worker Production Cooperatives," *Industrial and Labor Relations Review* 31, no. 1 (October 1977): 18–30.

Notes

36. This discussion is based on Daniel Zwerdling, "The Double-Edge of Employee Stock Ownership Plans," *Working Papers* 7, no. 1 (May–June, 1979): 23.

37. Select Committee on Small Business, *Employee Ownership*.

38. Carnoy and Shearer, *Economic Democracy*, pp. 152–57.

39. Raybeck, *American Labor*, p. 174.

40. David Moberg, "Owners on Strike," *In These Times*, 8–14 October 1980, p. 24.

41. James Smith, assistant to the president, United Steelworkers of America, "The Labor Movement and Worker Ownership," *The Social Report* 2, no. 2 (December 1981): 2.

42. Robert Howard, "Solidarity Begins at Home," *Working Papers* 9, no. 1 (January–February 1982), pp. 19–27.

43. Ibid., p. 25.

Index

accelerated depreciation allowance, 127
acquisitions, 6, 11, 40–41, 123, fig. 5.1 (p. 125), 198; federal tax law promotes, 128, 129
Action Resources West (Salt Lake City), 259
advertising, 127
aerospace industry, 56, 77, 138
Aetna Life Insurance Company, 117
affirmative action, 185, 247
Africa, 172
age: and mobility, 100, 104
agglomeration economies, 298n40
Aid to Families with Dependent Children (AFDC), 76–77, 134, 187, 209; UP, 77; see also welfare
air pollution, 86, 89
aircraft industry, 9, 11, 34, 62, 117, 132, 166; co-production in, 153–54; income loss through termination, 59–61
Albuquerque, N. Mex., 87, 100
Alcoa, 132
Allen brothers, 83
Allied Corporation, 121
Alperovitz, Gar, 253
Amalgamated Clothing and Textile Workers Union of America, 235
American Federation of Labor-Congress of Industrial Organizations (AFL-CIO), 68, 212, 227; Research Department, 42
American Motors Corporation, 119
American Tobacco Company, 123
Anaconda, Mont., 79, 81; plant closings in, 68, 69–71
Anaconda Copper & Mining Co., 69
anticommunist movement, 135–36
anti-trust laws, 143, 158, 200
anti-union animus, 80, 135–36, 138–39, 164–70
apparel industry, 8, 33, 34, 56, 93, 94, 132, 166; concentration in, 121; income loss through termination, 58
Argentina, 130
Armco Steel Corporation, 132, 296n7; name changed to Armco Corporation, 156, 286 n14

Armour and Company, 52
Aronson, Robert, 52, 58, 62, 64, 76, 80
Asian Development Bank, 215
Associated Catholic Charities (Newark, N. J.), 68
Associated Industries of Massachusetts (AIM), 240–41
Atlanta, Ga., 85, 88, 162
Atlantic Richfield Co. (ARCO), 69–71
Australia, 142
automobile, private: impact on U. S. economy, 114–15
automobile industry, 3, 10, 18, 56, 117, 138, 140; capital investment in, 6–7; employment created by, 115; European, 299n70; foreign investment in, 113; Japanese invasion of, 14, 37; parallel production in, 166–67; ripple effects of closings in, 71–72; shutdowns in, 36, 54; world car, 175–78, 299n70

balance of payments, 5, 113, 144; see also exports/imports
Bank of America, 213
bankruptcies, 10, 201
banks, banking, 84, 145, 147
Barkin, Solomon, 136–38
Barnet, Richard, 42; and Ronald Müller, Global Reach, 43–44, 45
Baxter, William, 190
Belgium, 5, 144–45
Bell, Alexander Graham, 116
Bell, Griffin, 253
Bethlehem Steel, 40; Johnstown, Pa., plant, 68–69
Birch, David, 8, 9, 29, 31, 34, 47, 161, 163–64, 221, 222, 223–24, 228, 285n7
black ghetto: investment in, 227
blacklisting, 80, 135
blacks, 87, 101–02, 291n20; effect of plant closings on, 54–55
Blair, John, 123, 157
"blaming the victim," 66, 111
Bluestone, Barry, 62

309

Index

311

Index

Index

International Harvester Company, 123
International Ladies' Garment Workers Union, 132
International Union of Electrical Workers, 168
interstate highway system, 116
investment, 6, 27–34, 42, 195, 198, 203; in corporatist strategy, 213–14; data re, 26–27; decline of, 147; incentives to, 126, 127; multinational policies re, 141; need for, 248; relation to disinvestment, 106; see also capital mobility; corporate investment and disinvestment decisions; disinvestment
investment portfolio, 150–51
investment tax credits, 127, 301n80
"invisible hand," 107, 197
Iowa, 164
Ireland: Shannon Airport free-trade zone, 173
Italy, 14
ITE Circuit Breaker Company, 169
ITE Imperial Corporation, 169

Jacobson, Louis, 56, 59
Jamestown Metal Products, 254
Japan, 5, 13–14, 141, 142, 143, 148, 213; Agency of Industrial Science & Technology, 215; auto industry, 176–78; Development Bank, 215; Export-Import Bank, 215; full employment, 106; Housing Loan Corporation, 215; industrial planning, 214–20, 228, 230; invasion of U. S. auto market, 37; Medical Care Facilities Finance Corporation, 215–16; Ministry of International Trade and Industry (MITI), 214–15; multinationals, 176–78; People's Finance Corporation, 215; steel industry, 145, 147
"Japan, Inc.": as model for U. S. economy, 195, 214–20
Jerrold Electronics, 172
jet aircraft, cargo, 18, 116, 117, 118
job creation, 27; through foreign investment, 43–46; in high-technology fields, 89–90; in Houston, 83; large corporation and conglomerate capability, 162–64; openings, closings, relocations, table A.1 (pp. 266–71); reindustrialization (New England), 94, 95, 98; through small business subsidies, 220–24
job loss, 94, 95–98, 193, 256; due to absentee ownership, 162; through foreign investment, 42–46; openings, closings, relocations, table A.1 (pp. 266–71); overseas, 42–46, 143, 174, 175; in plant closings, 9–10, 25–48, 51–55; protection from, 235–36
job replacement, 238

job satisfaction: in worker-owned production, 260
job security, 27, 94, 216–17; in Japan, 220; see also economic security
Johnson, Harry G., 293n58
Johnstown, Pa., 79; Bureau of Employment Security, 69; plant closings, 68–69
joint production, 142; see also co-production; production
Jones and Laughlin Company, 253
Junkerman, John, 220

K-Mart, 121
Kaiser Incorporated, 132–33
Kalecki, Michael, 207
Kasl, Stanislav, 63–64, 65
Kayser-Roth Company, 172
Kellogg Incorporated, 119
Kemp, Jack, 111, 226–27, 228
Kemp-Garcia Urban Jobs and Enterprise Zone Act, 226–27, 228
Kemp-Roth proposal (tax cuts), 199
Kennecott Copper, 123
Kennedy, Edward M., 249
Kennett, Mo., 39
Keynes, John Maynard, 196
Keynesianism, 133, 141
King, Randy, 53, 55, 56
Knights of Labor, 257, 260
Kohrs, El Dean V., 91
Kopkind, Andrew, 257
Kristol, Irving, 12, 13, 196

labor contracts, 16, 136, 235–36
labor cooperation, international, 299n70
labor costs, 43, 165, 179, 180, 252; foreign, 44, 117, 171; in urban enterprise zones, 228
labor discipline, 16, 188, 207, 218, 224, 252; in Japan, 220; in small business, 222
labor displacement, 18, 51, 55–56; vulnerability to, 53–54; see also job loss; workers, displaced
labor force participation, 14
labor-intensive industries, 33
labor legislation, 135, 136, 139, 180
labor/management relations, 18, 112, 185, 216; capital mobility and, 178; effect of plant closings on, 79–80; in Japan, 216–18; parallel production and, 166–67; see also Collective bargaining; social contract; unions
labor market, 135–39; effect of economic growth on, 207; primary and secondary sectors, 59n, 222, 228

Index

Index

identified corporations, 155–56; Textron, 182–83
Miller Brewing Company, 121
mine safety rules, 207
mineral resource depletion allowances, 127
mining industry, 27, 45
Minnesota iron range, 72
minorities, 54–55, 81; in poverty, 87–88; *see also* blacks
"misery index," 5
Mishan, E. J., 200
Mississippi, 182, 187
Mitsubishi Company, 143
Mobil Oil: acquisitions, mergers, 41, 156, 157, 158
Mobil Oil Corp. v. *Commissioner of Taxes of Vermont*, 234
mobility: downward, 55–56, 97–98; upward, 94, 227, 228; *see also* population mobility
Mondale, Walter, 237–38
Mondragon system (Spain), 258
monetary policy, 206–08
Monsanto Chemical Company, 39
Montana, 134
Montgomery Ward, 157; acquired by Mobil Oil, 41, 156
mortgage rate, 5
Motorola Corporation, 171
Mueller, Eva, 102, 103
Müller, Ronald, 42; Richard Barnet and, *Global Reach*, 43–44, 45
multinational corporations, 113–14, 136, 142, 298n40; foreign, 140, 142; global communications system, 117; help/harm to U.S. workers, 42–46; parallel production, 178; search for unionfree environment, 170–78; subsidiaries, 15; taxes paid by, 131–32; unions in, 263; *see also* conglomerates
multiple sourcing, 166, 167, 170, 176, 178
multiplier effect, 67–72, 74–75; employment, 71–72, 80, 90–91; income, 80
Multistate Tax Commission, 234
Muscle Shoals, Ala., 39
Musgrave, Peggy, 286n28
Myers, Stewart, 147
Myrdal, Gunnar, 104

NATO, 144–45
Nashua Manufacturing Company, 182
"Nashua Plan," 183
National Association of Manufacturers, 136, 185
National Center for Economic Alternatives (NCEA), 253
National Center for Employee Ownership (Washington, D.C.), 259

National Employment Priorities Act (NEPA) (1979), 238, 239
National Institutes of Health, 233
nationalization, selective, 248
National Labor Relations Act, 305n5
National Labor Relations Board, 135, 179, 236
Nebraska, 164
Nelson, Philip, 103
Netherlands, the, 5
Newark, N.J.: plant closings, 68
New Deal, 232
New England: jobs created by new establishments in, 223; plant closings, 9, 34; reindustrialization, 92–98; start–ups and closings, table A.3 (pp. 273–75)
New Federalism, 92, 209
New Hampshire, 33
New Jersey, 41
New York (city), 92–93, 162; bankruptcy threat, 195; cost of living, 85; per capita tax, 84; welfare, 76
New York (state), 41; Love Canal, 200; plant closings, 52, 76, 79, 80; welfare benefits, 187
New York Times, 37, 158, 301n83
Nixon, Richard, 135, 142
non-manufacturing industries: concentration in, 121
Norris-LaGuardia Act (1932), 135
North, the: costs of reindustrialization, 92–98; ownership and control of production in, 161–62; *see also* Frostbelt
North American Rockwell Company, 172
North Carolina, 31
North Central states, 85; migration from, 100
Northeast: employment change in, 31; migration from, 100; real income in, 85
Northeastern University, 93
Norton Simon Company, 26
no-strike clause, 136
numerically-controlled machines, 117

occupational status: decline of, due to layoffs, 55–56; and vulnerability to layoff, 53; *see also* job loss; mobility
"offset" agreements, 144–45
Ohio, 263; plant-closing legislation, 238
Ohio Public Interest Campaign (OPIC), 238
oil companies, 56, 84, 123, 131, 149; mergers, 157–59
Oklahoma City, 33, 52
Okun, Arthur, 206, 207
oligopolies: pricing behavior of, 141
Olin Corporation: Winchester rifle factory, New Haven, 170
Organization for Economic Cooperation and Development (OECD), 142, 299n70

Index

9–10, 36, 37; real incomes in, 84–85; uneven economic development in, 33; unions in, 165–66

"sunrise" industries, 212, 245–47, 262; creative destruction and, 11–12

"sunset" industries, 8, 249–55, 262

supermarkets, 34

supplemental unemployment benefits (SUB), 57, 58, 236

supply-side economics, 12–14, 188–89, 190, 196–97, 198, 199, 204, 205, 208, 230, 231, 232, 301n80

Survey Research Center (University of Michigan), 260

sweatshops, 228

Sweden, 5, 14, 105, 237

Sweezy, Paul, 198

Switzerland, 5

Taft-Hartley Act, 136, 139, 236

Taiwan, 130; free-trade zone, 173

tax and tariff laws and regulations; and international expansion of capital, 129–33; Kemp-Garcia Act, 227, 228; promotion of centralization and concentration by, 126–29; reform of, 230, 233–34; and spread of American business abroad, 130, 132

tax credits, 46

taxes, taxation, 13, 14, 196; breaks in, for business, 4, 18, 19, 91, 159, 195, 221, 300n80; cuts in, 199, 208–09; local, 181, 182; paid by business, 185–87, 301n83; per capita, 84; in Reaganomics, 188–89; in Sunbelt, 92; in Texas, 84

Tax Recovery Act of 1981, 234, 301n80, 83

Teague, Carroll H., 168

technology, 44, 217–18, 227–28, 294n12; and capital mobility, 18, 209, 210; control of, 224; and need for public goods, 201; permissive, 115–18, 178; transfer of, abroad, 142, 143–44, 145

Texas: business tax rates, 182, 185

Texas Gulf Coast, 84

textile industry, 8, 33, 93, 94, 132, 140; Japan, 215

Textile Workers Union, 183

Textron Incorporated, 124, 182–83; acquisitions and divestitures, table A.5 (pp. 278–82); "Nashua Plan," 183

Thatcher, Margaret, 226

Thatcher administration, 173

third party movements, 134

Third World: free-trade zones, 173, 229

"throwaway" culture, 12

Thurow, Lester, 8, 9, 31, 47, 111, 195, 198, 232; planned economic investment, 212–13, 214; *The Zero-Sum Society*, 205

Thyssen Incorporated, 156

timber industry, 38; parallel production in, 167–68

tire industry, 37, 146

Torres, Juan de, 92

Toshiba Electronics Systems Co., Ltd., 143, 216

toy industry, 57, 166, 171

Toyota Company: production strategy, 176

trade-marks, 123

Trade Readjustment Assistance (TRA), 57, 75, 76, 81

"Tragedy of the Commons" (Hardin), 200

Trainer, Glynnis, 285n7

training (employee), 14, 105–06, 217, 226

Transitron Incorporated, 171

transportation industry, 42, 72, 149

transportation system, 248–49; technology of, 115–16, 117, 118; and transfer of production, 17–18

Triumph-Adler Corporation, 174

Truman, Harry S, 136

Tupelo, Miss., 39

turnover, 94, 172, 216

underemployment, 55–61

unemployed, 10–12, 76–78

unemployment: costs of, 76–78, 289n47; effect of boomtown syndrome on, 90–91; "frictional," 51; long–term, 51–53, 55, 62; in South, 39; see also job loss

unemployment insurance (UI), 45, 61, 134, 185, 187, 190, 236; benefits, (UIB), 11, 17, 57, 58, 70, 77, 81, 182, 239

unemployment rate, 5, 6, 11, 64, 206, 207, 283n3; effect of deindustrialization on, 77–78; Houston, 83; in North, 92–94; and social trauma, 65

unfair labor practices, 135, 136, 179, 236

Union Carbide Incorporated, 133

unionization, 167, 257–58

union leaders: and worker ownership, 261

unions, 16, 133–39, 143, 144, 179; blamed in plant closings, 80; challenge to companies in plant relocation, 169–70; collective bargaining with conglomerates, 173–75; corporate attack on, 178–80; decertification, 136, 179; defense against worker dislocation, 235–36; must "go multinational," 263; percent of workers belonging to, 138, 180, 236; plant relocations to avoid, 164–70, 170–78; power of, 170–72; and worker buy-outs, 257–58, 261; see also cooperation, as strategy for economic revitalization

Uniroyal Corporation, 37, 40, 73

United Aircraft, Chance–Vought Division, 25